TEACHING
READING AND WRITING PreK-3

A Practical Approach

Susan Lenski
Portland State University, Emerita

Jerry L. Johns
Northern Illinois University, Emeritus

Laurie Elish-Piper
Northern Illinois University

Roya Q. Scales
Western Carolina University

Kendall Hunt
publishing company

Book Team

Chairman and Chief Executive Officer   Mark C. Falb
President and Chief Operating Officer   Chad M. Chandlee
Vice President, Higher Education   David L. Tart
Director of Publishing Partnerships   Paul B. Carty
Vice President, Operations   Timothy J. Beitzel
Senior Development Editor   Angela Willenbring
Permissions Editor   Tammy Hunt
Cover Designer   Heather Richman

Author Information for Correspondence, Professional Development, and Workshops

Susan Lenski, Ph.D
Portland State University
Professor Emerita
sjlenski@pdx.edu

Laurie Elish-Piper, Ph.D.
Dean, College of Education
Northern Illinois University
laurieep@niu.edu

Jerry L. Johns, Ph.D.
Consultant in Reading
Email: jjohns@niu.edu

Roya Q. Scales, Ph.D.
Professor of Literacy Education
Western Carolina University
rqscales@wcu.edu

Ordering Information

Address: Kendall Hunt Publishing Company
4050 Westmark Drive
Dubuque, IA 52002
Telephone: 800-247-3458, ext. 6
Web site: www.kendallhunt.com
Fax: 800-772-9165

A password-protected website that contains reproducibles and resources accompanies this text. The URL and access code for the website is found on the inside front cover. The access code is unique and non-transferable. If you purchased a used book, the code will not work.

Web addresses and margin notes in this book were correct as of the publication date but may have become inactive or otherwise modified since that time. If you notice a deactivated or changed Web address or margin note, please email Angela Willenbring (awillenbring@kendallhunt.com) with the words "Website update" or "Margin Note update" in the subject line. In your message, specify the Web link or margin note, the book title, and the page number on which the link appears.

ISBN 978-1-7924-2149-5

Published in the United States of America

Brief Contents

Contents

Section II: How to Teach Reading and Writing 96

Chapter 5: How Do I Teach Print Concepts and the Alphabet? 98

Chapter 6: How Do I Teach Phonemic Awareness? 126

Chapter 7: How Do I Teach Students to Recognize and Spell Unknown Words? 153

Companion Website Contents

About the Authors

SUSAN LENSKI is a Professor Emerita at Portland State University. Before becoming a professor, Susan taught school for 20 years working with children from kindergarten through high school. During her years as a teacher, Susan was awarded the Nila Banton Smith Award from the International Reading Association (IRA) for integrating reading in content area classes, and she was on the IRA Board of Directors from 2004–2007. Susan's research interests focus on strategic reading and writing. She also conducts research on preparing teacher candidates. Susan has published more than 60 articles and 20 books.

LAURIE ELISH-PIPER is Dean of the College of Education as well as a Distinguished Teaching Professor and Distinguished Engagement Professor at Northern Illinois University. She directed the Jerry L. Johns Literacy Clinic at NIU for fifteen years where she expanded programming and built partnerships with schools, families, and community agencies. Laurie has provided leadership to professional organizations, including her service as the president of the Association of Literacy Educators and Researchers (2010) and as a member of the International Literacy Association Board of Directors (2013–2016). She has co-authored ten books and more than 80 articles and chapters. Prior to her work in higher education, Laurie worked as an elementary and middle school teacher and an educational therapist in an acute care psychiatric hospital working with patients in grades 4–8.

JERRY L. JOHNS has been recognized as a distinguished teacher, writer, outstanding teacher educator, and professional development speaker for schools, school districts, and conferences. He has taught students from kindergarten through graduate school and also served as a reading teacher. Jerry spent his career at Northern Illinois University. He served in leadership positions at the local, state, national, and international levels. He has been president of the International Reading (now Literacy) Association, the Illinois Reading Council, the Association of Literacy Educators and Researchers, and the Northern Illinois Reading Council. He also served on the board of directors for each of these organizations, as well as the American Reading Forum. Dr. Johns has authored or co-authored nearly 300 articles, monographs, and research studies as well as numerous professional books. His *Basic Reading Inventory*, now in the 12th edition, is widely used in undergraduate and graduate classes as well as by practicing teachers.

ROYA Q. SCALES is a Professor of Literacy Education at Western Carolina University in Cullowhee, NC. An educator for more than 20 years (11 as a classroom teacher), she is noted for her research on thoughtfully adaptive teaching, enactment of teachers' visions, literacy teacher education, and effective teaching of literacy. Roya served as the Program Coordinator of the Elementary Education and Middle Grades Education Programs for 5 years. She teaches reading, language arts, and children's literature courses at the undergraduate and graduate levels.

Acknowledgments

This book would never have been written without the support of family, colleagues, teachers, and students. First, we would like to thank our families for giving us the time, space, and encouragement each step of the way—even when we felt discouraged. We also are grateful the reviewers, Dr. Melissa E. Adams-Budde from West Chester University, Dr. Kristin Webber from Edinboro University, Dr. Dana Biddy from University of Houston—Clear Lake, and Dr. Timothy Rasinski from Kent State University, whose feedback from an initial draft helped us reconceptualize the scope of the book.

The following educators also gave us valuable feedback on drafts of book chapters: Roberta Berglund, School/District Consultant in Reading, Lou Ferroli, Professor Emeritus, Rockford University, Mary Gardner, Director, Jerry L. Johns Literacy Clinic, Northern Illinois University, Kristy Ricker, Teacher, North Grove Elementary School, Sycamore CUSD 427, Peet Smith, Assistant Professor in Reading, Northern Illinois University, Melanie Walski, Assistant Professor in Reading, Northern Illinois University, Jolene Ward, Reading Teacher, Sycamore CUSD 427, and Kristine Wilke, Instructor, Northern Illinois University.

We extend a heartfelt thank you to Roya's 2019 reading methods students who previewed several chapters and offered ideas from their perspective as teacher candidates. We also would like to thank the children, parents, and teachers who provided the writing samples in the book.

Writing the book was only one step of the process of publishing a book. We have had a long-standing relationship with Kendall Hunt Publishing Company and have been continually impressed with the attention they devote to their authors. We would like to acknowledge the responsiveness of Angela M. Willenbring, as she shepherded us through the writing and editing processes. We are also so grateful to Heidi Grauel and Gail Barker who copyedited and Trimensions who formatted the book.

Finally, we want to acknowledge the many scholars, mentors, students, and colleagues we've had over our careers who have shaped our thinking about what it means to teach reading and writing.

Preface

*B*ecoming a teacher is complicated. You will need to know theory and content, and you also need to be able to put your knowledge into practice with a group of children who are growing into literacy. You need a practical approach. We acknowledge that learning to become a teacher is multi-layered. One layer is for you to understand the underpinnings of literacy learning and another layer is to learn the strategies that you can use to teach readers and writers to comprehend and compose text.

To help you learn the foundational ideas of PreK–3 literacy instruction, we've written a book for you to determine how to design and implement effective reading and writing lessons and programs that are accessible, engaging, and practical. The book is written directly to you in an approachable and inclusive style. As a way to make this book inclusive, we've used gender-neutral pronouns, including singular *they*. Singular *they* was accepted by linguists in 2015, and we believe this language change demonstrates how English is a living language while acknowledging through language that gender is not binary.

As we wrote this book, we kept several big ideas in mind that we wanted you to think about as you read this book. These ideas are the recurring themes of the book that are important as you learn how to teach reading and writing to PreK–3 students.

Recurring Themes

CONNECTING RESEARCH AND THEORY TO CLINICAL PLACEMENTS. Teacher candidates often struggle to connect what they are learning in their courses to what they are experiencing in their clinical placements. We provide specific discussions about how you can make meaningful connections and how you can handle situations when there is conflict between what you are learning in these two different contexts.

STUDENT DIVERSITY. New teachers will teach in a diverse society; therefore, it's imperative that we provide you with information about language and literacy as it applies to students who are English Learners, newcomers to North America, and from culturally diverse backgrounds.

TEACHING FROM AN EQUITY PERSPECTIVE. We address culturally relevant pedagogy throughout the text and provide many examples of how to embrace students' funds of knowledge and leverage them for effective teaching and learning.

STRATEGIES FOR DIFFERENTIATING INSTRUCTION. Because you will have students with a range of abilities, skills, and backgrounds in your classrooms, you must think of ways to meet the needs of all your students. Throughout this book, we emphasize how students grow into literacy in unique ways and how you can prepare lessons that are both developmentally appropriate and are based on standards.

INSTRUCTION-ASSESSMENT CYCLE. We provide an introductory chapter on assessment and discuss how assessment is tied to instruction. We also embed assessment information and strategies along with instruction throughout most chapters. We show you how assessments inform instruction and how instruction informs assessment.

PREPARING LEARNER-READY TEACHERS. This book is focused on preparing you to be a learner-ready teacher who can effectively teach students on Day 1 in the classroom. We also provide a wide range of resources so you can continue learning after you have finished reading this book.

DEVELOPING A TEACHING IDENTITY. Throughout this book, we promote the idea that you are unique and that you are forming a teaching identity with opinions and viewpoints that will guide your decision making. Through the book we will guide you in identifying what you believe, and then we show you how to use these beliefs to develop your own identity as a teacher.

Pedagogical Features

In order to help you connect the ideas in your teaching lives, we have developed several pedagogical features. These features acknowledge that you need to be able to apply the ideas in practical ways and also that you use digital resources to extend your learning.

REAL-LIFE EXAMPLES. Each chapter opens with a vignette designed to introduce issues and topics that will be addressed in the chapter. The vignettes focus on teacher candidates as they work in classroom settings.

MARGIN NOTES. Throughout each chapter, we present brief notes with resources or activities to help you clarify and deepen your understanding of the content and strategies addressed in the chapters.

CONNECTION TO THE FIELD. Since we want you to use the ideas in each chapter in your clinical placement, we suggest specific activities for you to put into practice right away.

ENGAGING WITH FAMILIES. In each chapter, we present specific ideas for you to implement with families of students from your clinical placement related to the topic of the chapter. These ideas focus on ways to work effectively with PreK–3 families. We would like to stress that any family activity needs to be done with the consent of your mentor teacher.

LESSON PLANNING. Lesson plan outlines are provided for each chapter in Section II to show you how to plan effective reading lessons that link standards to objectives about topics presented in the chapter.

EMBEDDED TEACHING STRATEGIES AND ASSESSMENTS. Specific instructional strategies and assessments that are connected to the content of the chapters are embedded in each of the chapters in Section II.

WHAT DO YOU BELIEVE. Throughout the book we will invite you to consider what you learned and to reflect on how it influences your beliefs and plans for teaching. We provide a template in each chapter so you can record your ideas and reflections, and, in the final chapter, we invite you to synthesize your thoughts into your very own literacy learning philosophy.

TAKEAWAYS. Each chapter concludes with bullet points about the big ideas from the chapter to help you summarize your learning about the content of the chapter.

To LEARN MORE . . . Since we believe in ongoing learning, we offer books, websites, articles, and other resources for you to expand your knowledge about the chapter topic. These suggestions could also be the basis for independent or group projects.

Organization of Book

This book is organized into three sections that we believe will help you learn how to become an effective PreK–3 teacher. We begin the book with foundational ideas that will help you understand how to teach. Even though we know you want to jump right in and learn teaching strategies, we urge patience. Chapters 1–4 will set the stage for learning the practical strategies we promised you. Chapters 5–11 are the heart of the book. These chapters give you information about teaching components of reading and writing and present both instructional and assessment strategies. The final section of the book, Chapters 12–14, help you connect the dots. In this section we show you how you can use your beliefs to articulate a teaching identity and use that information to make decisions about literacy programs. We also help you think about yourself as a professional who engages with families and the community. We end the book with a chapter that summarizes what you need to do to be that learner-ready teacher who is ready to teach on Day 1 of your career as a teacher.

Companion Website

We have developed a comprehensive companion website to provide you with easy access to the margin notes and resources from each chapter. In addition, we provide useful templates, graphic organizers, and record sheets that you can use to implement teaching and assessment strategies from the chapters in Section II of the book. We have also included the resources from the To Learn More section from each chapter. Finally, we provide a What Do You Believe template for Chapters 2–13 so you can record what you have learned and what that new learning means for your beliefs about teaching and learning.

How to Use This Book

Dear Teacher Candidates,

Welcome to *Teaching Reading and Writing PreK–3: A Practical Approach*. We've designed a user-friendly and engaging approach to learning to teach reading that contains much more than just the text between the covers. You will find numerous features that will help you learn by viewing videos and using many of the resources described in the paragraphs below.

As you read this book, you will notice the interactive features: Margin Notes and Website resources. Margin Notes appear in every chapter. If you have the e-book, the Margin Notes are hotlinks. If you have the physical book, the Margin Notes are QR codes. Regardless of the format, the Margin Notes take you to online materials that enhance the text. Consider the Margin Notes as portals that quickly provide you with videos and other helpful online resources that add to information presented in the text. We included QR codes and hotlinks because they are easy to access. You should be able to open QR codes using your camera app if you have an iPhone, iPad, or a Windows laptop. Open your camera app, hold your smart phone so the QR code appears in the screen, and you will be prompted to open the link. Other devices, such as Mac laptops and Android phones, may require that you install a QR code reader app. If you are not familiar with QR codes, you may want to do a quick Internet search for directions on how to open QR codes for your specific device.

Website resources are mentioned throughout the book. These items supplement the teaching and assessment strategies provided, so don't miss them! Website resources are additional items from the chapters that appear on the book's website in an easy-to-print format. We wanted you to have these resources in a format that you can (and will) use in this course and beyond. We recommend that you explore the Website resources as you encounter them in the text. The website is easy to navigate and organized by chapter.

Boxes in the chapters feature Engaging with Families and Connections to the Field. As a teacher, it is important to engage with families to support your students' learning. We want you to consider families as your partners in teaching and learning because families want to help their children learn. Throughout your career, you will seek opportunities to reach out to families and our ideas will help get you started. Always secure your mentor teacher's permission before you reach out to families. Connections to the Field provide you with ideas for how you can connect your learning from the chapter with your placement. Talk with your mentor teacher about ways you can be actively involved and how you might use or adapt the suggested ideas for the classroom.

We present a practical, research-based approach to teaching reading, and we offer numerous lesson planning ideas, teaching strategies, and assessment strategies for you to consider, use, or adapt in your placement and beyond. We think these resources will enhance your ability to provide responsive instruction now and in the future.

The end of each chapter prompts you to review the major points, consider your own beliefs about teaching based on the chapter content, and extend your learning through the To Learn More section. As chapters prompt you to reflect on your beliefs, be sure to add to the What Do You Believe template. Your beliefs about teaching reading and writing are important because they ultimately inform how you teach. Use the To Learn More resources to gain further understanding of the content as well as to collect additional teaching resources to help you continue to grow as a teacher. If you have a course that offers options where you can pursue an additional project, then consider our ideas in the To Learn More sections as a possibility. Items listed in the To Learn More section vary by chapter, but they typically include professional books, scholarly articles, and websites featuring lesson ideas and hands-on learning center resources. We provide ideas for how you can use each resource to dig deeper into how to teach reading and writing. If there's a chapter where you're unsure of whether you really understand the content, then it's especially important for you to explore the To Learn More resources because we want you to have a solid understanding of how to teach reading and writing. Sometimes these supplemental materials can result in greater competence because the content is presented in different ways. After exploring the resources, be sure to return to the chapter to see if you grasped the concepts. Learning to teach reading and writing is essential to your success as a PreK–3 teacher. Throughout this book we invite you to be an active learner in your own professional development. We hope you will make this book work for you and, more importantly, your students!

Happy reading!
Sue, Laurie, Jerry, and Roya

Dear Instructors,

We are delighted that you chose *Teaching Reading and Writing PreK–3* as your course resource. We've designed this book as a practical approach to teaching reading that contains much more than just the text between the covers. You will find numerous features that will help you consider your class sessions and assignments by using many of the resources described in the paragraphs below.

As you read this book, you will notice two interactive features: Margin Notes and Website resources. We can't be sure if your teacher candidates will attend to these or skip them, so you will want to be sure to emphasize how they will help enhance their preparation to teach reading and writing. You may want to reinforce the benefit of these features by using them to supplement your lectures and spark group discussions. We put a lot of time and effort in selecting resources that will extend chapter content and be helpful to you.

Margin Notes appear in every chapter. If you have the e-book, the Margin Notes are hotlinks. If you have the physical book, the Margin Notes are QR codes. Regardless of the format, the Margin Notes take you to online materials that enhance the text. Consider the Margin Notes as portals that quickly provide you with videos and other helpful online sources that add to information presented in the text. We included QR codes and hotlinks because they are easy to access. You should be able to open QR codes using your camera app if you have an iPhone, iPad, or a Windows laptop. Open your camera app, hold your smart phone so the QR code appears in the screen, and you will be prompted to open the link. Other devices, such as Mac laptops and Android phones, may require that you install a QR code reader app. If you are not familiar with QR codes, you may want to do a quick Internet search for directions on how to open QR codes for your specific device.

Website resources are additional items in the chapters that appear on the book's website. The website is easy to navigate, organized by chapter, and the materials are in easy to print format. These items supplement the teaching and assessment strategies provided, and you may want to use them during demonstration lessons. If your candidates have field placements, consider asking them to adapt and teach lessons from the chapters to appropriate small groups of students or in a tutoring situation. They can use the assessment strategies to help monitor their students' learning. If your candidates do not have placements, consider how they can practice the teaching strategies and lesson planning ideas during your class sessions.

We present a practical, research-based approach to teaching reading, and we offer numerous lesson planning ideas, teaching strategies, and assessment strategies for your candidates to consider, use, or adapt in their placements and beyond. We think these resources will enhance their ability to provide responsive instruction now and in the future.

Boxes in the chapters feature Engaging with Families and Connections to the Field. Candidates we've worked with over the years have expressed uncertainty about how to engage with families to support students' learning. We want candidates to consider families as their partners in teaching and learning, and we hope you will use the ideas in these boxes to stimulate discussions about ways to connect with families. While our ideas should help get candidates started, you have experiences that can also be used to help candidates consider exactly how they will connect with families. Connections to the Field boxes provide candidates with ideas for how they can connect their learning from the chapter with their placements. Consider using these boxes to generate additional ways candidates can be actively involved and how they might use the ideas in their placement classrooms.

The end of each chapter prompts candidates to review the major ideas, consider their own beliefs about teaching based on the chapter content, and extend their learning through the To Learn More resources. We suggest highlighting the importance of candidates writing their belief statements using the What Do You Know template available on the website. What they write will help them highlight and refine their literacy beliefs.

You may want to use the To Learn More resource ideas as required explorations for an assignment. Perhaps candidates could choose two resources to explore from each chapter. Items listed in the To Learn More section vary by chapter, but typically include professional books, scholarly articles, and websites featuring lesson ideas and hands-on learning center resources. We provide ideas for how candidates can use each resource to dig deeper into how to teach reading and writing. Use or adapt our suggestions to create assignments that deepen candidates' understanding. Learning to teach reading and writing is essential to candidates' success as PreK–3 teachers. Throughout this book we invite candidates to be active learners in their own professional development, and we hope you will reinforce that this is a journey that spans their career. We hope you will make this book work for your teacher candidates!

Happy reading!

Sue, Laurie, Jerry, and Roya

Section I

Knowing how children learn will help you make decisions about what and how to teach.

*W*elcome to the teaching of PreK to grade 3 (PreK–3) reading and writing! You are embarking on a rich adventure that we hope you find as fascinating as we do.

In Section I, we present the foundational ideas about teaching reading and writing. We're sure you've been in other classes where you've heard these words before and perhaps you've wondered why you have to learn general things before getting to the nitty gritty of how to teach. We understand. Just as you have to pour the foundation for a skyscraper before building additional stories, you have to understand some of the foundational components for teaching reading and writing.

We want you to be prepared to be a good teacher on Day 1 of your career. You may not realize it now, but once you have your own classroom, you will have to make dozens of decisions every day that will rely on your knowledge and skills and also your beliefs. There will be lots of latitude. We want you to be prepared to make those decisions by understanding the ideas and theories that underpin the teaching decisions you will make.

Backing up a step, you're probably in a clinical placement right now or you will be soon. You'll have to make decisions in that situation as well, even though some decisions will be made by your mentor teacher. Your mentor teacher will expect you to have a framework on which to draw as you prepare lesson plans. In addition, you'll likely find some areas of disagreement with your mentor teacher. As long as you're respectful to the work your mentor teacher is doing, disagreements are healthy. Those disagreements will help you form your own beliefs about how to teach reading and writing.

Developing the Building Blocks
for Teaching Reading and Writing

You'll see that all of the chapter titles in this book are posed as questions. We've done this in order to get you thinking about the focus of the chapter and to encourage you to incorporate the ideas we present into your own belief system and teaching situation.

Section I has four chapters. In Chapter 1, Why Focus on Teaching Reading and Writing?, we ask you to think about why you want to become a PreK–3 teacher and also present some of the basic ideas related to teaching young children. Chapter 2, What Are the Foundations of Literacy Instruction?, continues the description of foundational theories of learning and reading. In Chapter 3, What Is the Role of Assessment in Teaching?, we describe the teaching/learning/assessment cycle that will be critical for lesson planning and teaching. We also provide you with the necessary framework for understanding assessment in education. Chapter 4, How Do I Promote Engaged Learning?, takes you in a new direction providing you with the research and foundational elements of why and how to get students engaged in their own learning.

We think these four chapters will give you the necessary foundation and background that you need before we present chapters focused on teaching and assessment strategies. We are excited to share this information with you and look forward to assisting you in your journey to becoming a PreK–3 teacher.

© Monkey Business Images/Shutterstock.com

This teacher shares how literacy is a tool for learning.

Why Focus on Teaching Reading and Writing?

REAL-LIFE EXAMPLE

On the first day of classes, Dena and Kofi walked into their literacy methods course together. Dena was dreading this course because she didn't get why reading and writing were such a big deal. She would rather be in the STEM lab, researching and experimenting with various materials and designs to make homemade catapults with the four-year-old twins that she babysits regularly. While waiting for class to begin, Dena posted her latest design update on social media while scrolling through websites related to this STEM lab project to gather more ideas that she could try after class.

Kofi couldn't wait to take this literacy methods course because he loved to read and write in his spare time. He had the latest mystery novel from his favorite author in his backpack so he could read it during breaks between classes. Before class began, Kofi checked his blog to interact with his followers' comments about his latest fanfiction posting. He jotted ideas in his notebook about a follow-up blog posting and quickly searched the online library catalog for resources to support his ideas.

The real-life examples of Dena and Kofi illustrate two teacher candidates with different perspectives on reading and writing. Perhaps you identify with Dena, Kofi, or a combination of the two. No matter what your experiences with literacy have been, you can be an effective PreK–3 teacher.

In this chapter, we explore why we read and write, discuss why reading and writing are so important, consider emergent literacy theories, and help you begin your journey of becoming an effective teacher of reading and writing.

Why Did You Choose Teaching as a Career?

It's important for you, as a future teacher, to know why you chose to teach. Perhaps you were inspired to teach because of positive school experiences. Maybe you want to be just like your favorite teacher(s) because they cared about you and helped you in some way. Some of you may not remember many positive experiences in school, and you might want to become a teacher who is different than what you encountered. Knowing why you want to teach can give you a sense of purpose that will help you overcome the challenges you face once you become a teacher (Fairbanks et al., 2010).

Take a few minutes to jot down why you want to be a teacher. Also, consider what you want your students to remember about you when they see you in the grocery store several years from now. What do you hope they will remember? This reflects why you want to teach—your **purpose** for teaching. The blog featured in Margin Note 1.1 reveals what practicing teachers say about why they teach. Compare your reasons to teach with the teachers' reasons from Margin Note 1.1.

Margin Note 1.1: Blog: Why Do You Teach?

https://blog.edgenuity.com/why-do-you-teach/

YOUR SCHOOL EXPERIENCES. It's likely that some of your reasons for becoming a teacher have to do with your own experiences with school. Whether you went to public, private, or home school, you all have had experiences with schooling. These experiences are a valuable foundation for your teaching career. You may have learned to read at home before you came to school, or you may have learned to read at school. Reading may have come easily for you, or reading may have been an area of struggle for you. Perhaps you received extra help with reading or writing, such as help from a resource teacher or tutor. You successfully learned to read and write, despite your struggles, and you understand what it's like to struggle and the nature of that struggle. Each of you has had different experiences with school, but you all have spent years experiencing some sort of schooling. Therefore, you have a good idea about what it means to be a teacher. Right?

Teaching Is Complicated

As you reflect on your own schooling, keep in mind that being a teacher is different from your memories of being a student. You will be on the other side of the desk. Lortie (1975) used the term the "apprenticeship of observation" (p. 61) to explain how some people believe they are experts on teaching simply because they watched teachers while they were students. Although your memories from your student days may be vivid, we need to take you behind the "employees-only" door so you will understand the complexity of teaching from the teacher's side of the desk.

If you've ever worked in retail or in a restaurant, you have seen the difference between the customer area and what's behind the employees-only door. A clothing store may be brightly lit, orderly, and enticing in the customer area. Behind the employees-only door, you may find dust bunnies, piles of hangers, boxes, and disarray.

Teaching is similar because, as a student, you saw the polished instruction with well-planned learning activities. You didn't see your teachers in the behind-the-scenes aspects, such as gathering ideas, collecting materials, configuring and reconfiguring groups, deciding how to pace instruction, analyzing data, planning, and so forth. Teaching is complex because it is a human endeavor, which means there is no one right way to do it.

Teaching reading and writing is complicated, because you make countless in-the-moment decisions while you teach, based on students' cues (Duffy & Hoffman, 1999; Griffith & Lacina, 2018). For example, let's say that Jasmine struggles with sounding out (decoding) the word "cat" as she reads. How you will respond will look and sound different from the way you respond to and help Ian as he struggles with fluently reading a page from the book *Thank You, Omu!* (Mora, 2018). To help your students, you will need to know a variety of methods and strategies, and you can't rely on only what you experienced as a student. Knowing how to teach reading and writing is essential, because reading and writing are the bedrock of teaching in PreK to grade 3.

The Importance of Reading and Writing

As we consider the importance of reading and writing, let's think about how **critical** these skills are to our lives. Take 2 minutes to make a list of everything you read in the past 24 hours. Then make a list of everything you wrote in the past 24 hours. You may be wondering what counts as reading and what counts as writing. Let's say reading is looking at print of any kind and making sense of it. Let's consider that writing is any kind of communication in print, including typing and handwriting. See if your lists are similar to the ones from Roya in Figure 1.1.

What did you include on your lists that didn't appear on Roya's lists? Perhaps you included reading directions for games or writing explanations (such as cheat codes) for how to "level up" in

Figure 1.1. Roya's Lists of Reading and Writing in the Past 24 Hours

Reading in the past 24 hours	Writing in the past 24 hours
Emails	Emails
Texts	Texts
Social media	Posting on social media
Memes	Feedback to students
Textbook chapters	Lesson plans for classes
Journal articles	Assignment directions
Novel	Reports
Magazine article	Manuscript drafts
Local newspaper	Conference proposals
Prescription dosage information	To-do lists
Recipes	Grocery list
Nutrition labels	Calendar items
Street signs	Note replying to my child's teacher
Notes from my child's teacher	Jottings in margins of articles
Calendar	Signing various forms for work
Grocery list	
Bills	
Directions	

various online game situations. You may have other items on your lists, or perhaps you forgot about something and you want to add it to your list now.

What surprised you as you thought about reading and writing? Perhaps you didn't realize how much you read and how much you wrote. Return to your lists and consider the consequences, imagining what might happen if you hadn't read anything and you hadn't written anything in the past 24 hours. Although it may sound blissful to not respond to emails and texts, perhaps you would have negative consequences for not doing so because we rely so heavily on those forms of communication. For instance, a professor may have emailed the class to say there would be a quiz tomorrow. By not reading your email, you would not know to prepare for the quiz which could impact your grade for the course. Or, maybe a friend or loved one sent you a text about something important, and they are now worried because you did not respond to them. Although those situations may seem minor, consider how you would navigate the world if you could not read or write.

Let's look back at the example with Dena and Kofi at the start of this chapter and their **recreational** and **personal purposes** for reading and writing. Dena may not recognize that what she is doing for specific real-world purposes is *actually* considered reading and writing. Apparently, the twins Dena babysits are interested in making homemade catapults, and the research involves literacy that may not resemble the kinds of reading and writing that she remembers from school when she was a young student. By contrast, Kofi identifies as an avid reader and writer. He engages with writing for real purposes through a blog, which connects him with an extended literate community sharing his interests. Kofi's interest in fanfiction began with reading, participating as a follower of others' fanfiction blogs, and then extended into his own writings about his favorite characters. Dena and Kofi are examples of users of reading and writing that illustrate how important reading and writing are to our lives.

The examples provided indicate functional purposes for reading and writing. Take time to consider your thoughts about why students should be able to read and write in and beyond school and how that fits with the idea of literacy as a tool for learning beyond the school walls. These are among many reasons why you need to learn how to teach reading and writing. It's not just to have students be able to pass a test. Providing students with the ability to read and write will help enrich their lives which takes us to the goal we have for you: to become a **learner-ready teacher** on Day 1.

Becoming a Learner-ready Teacher

As you are learning to become a teacher, you might feel overwhelmed. How can you learn so much before you have your own classroom? You're not expected to become an exemplary teacher all at once. Instead, your goal should be to become a "learner-ready" teacher (Council of Chief State School Officers [CCSSO], 2018). This term might be new to you, but we think that you'll find that it fits perfectly with what you should be able to learn and be able to do by the time you have your own classroom.

Read the definition of a learner-ready teacher as described by the CCSSO (2012) and look for the descriptors that will be your goals as you learn to become a teacher.

A learner-ready teacher is one who is ready on Day 1 of his or her career to model and develop in students the knowledge and skills they need to succeed today, including the ability to think critically and creatively, to apply content to solving real-world problems, to be literate across the curriculum, to collaborate and work in teams, and to take ownership of their own continuous learning. More specifically, learner-ready teachers have deep knowledge of their content and how to teach it; they understand the differing needs of their students, hold them to high expectations, and personalize learning to ensure each learner is challenged; they care about, motivate, and actively engage students in learning; they collect, interpret, and use student assessment data to monitor progress and adjust instruction; they systematically reflect, continuously improve, and collaboratively problem solve; and they demonstrate leadership and shared responsibility for the learning of all students. (pp. iii–iv)

Does that sound like something you'll be able to do? We think so. It's a tall order, but we've organized some of these thoughts for you to consider. As a beginning teacher, you'll need to focus your learning on the following:

- Knowing what it means to read and write.
- Understanding how young children learn.
- Knowing what to teach.
- Understanding ways in which students are diverse and what that means for teaching them.
- Being prepared to be a lifelong learner.

These are the goals that we focus on in this book. We present **content knowledge** about reading and writing so you have a deep understanding of what it means to read and write. We also help you pin this knowledge to the theories of how children learn. Knowing how children learn will help you make decisions about what to teach. After you understand these principles, we introduce many ideas about how to teach reading and writing. This is the core of the book, and we help you find ways to incorporate how to teach in your clinical placement. As you teach, you'll also need to remember that every child is different, and you'll need to consider how each child's background and current skills should inform what you teach them. Finally, we don't expect you to know everything before you begin to teach. Teaching is a continual learning process so we provide you with resources that will help you continue to learn after you've finished reading this book.

WHAT IF I'M WORRIED THAT I'LL DO IT WRONG? Becoming a learner-ready teacher may sound daunting, and some of you might be worried that you'll do something wrong. Teaching reading and writing is not a right or wrong endeavor. As you teach some of the strategies in this book, some of your lessons will go great, and others will not. This happens to all teachers. When you have a lesson that doesn't go well, it's important to reflect on your planning and delivery to try to remedy what didn't work.

Rest assured that you will never know all there is to know about how to teach reading and writing because it is a career-long endeavor. Plus, students' needs are vastly different and ever-changing. What works for one student may not work for another. Although you have at least one course devoted to literacy methods, it is up to you to continue your own professional development once your coursework ends. You can empower yourself as a literacy teacher by reading professional books, such as this one, and professional journals that focus on the teaching of reading and writing.

Connections to the Field: Observing Teaching and Learning

Once you have a clinical placement, you'll have a chance to observe how your mentor teacher orchestrates teaching and learning. The first time you observe, there might be too much happening to make sense of it all. Our suggestion is to focus on different things each time you observe. For example, you might begin by observing and writing down what the teacher does. Another time you might focus on the students' responses to the teacher's directions. You will probably spend several visits observing before you begin to take an active role in the classroom.

What Are Reading and Writing?

Let's begin with some foundational aspects of reading and writing that you'll need to learn. You might be thinking that you already know what reading and writing are. You definitely know how to read and write, but there's more to learn. You have to understand the **cognitive processes** that occur during reading and writing so you understand what you are doing.

DEFINING READING. Reading is most often defined as **constructing meaning from print**. To construct meaning, readers need to interact with print using a variety of thought processes. As people read, they can carry away different levels of meaning: **literal**, **inferential**, and **evaluative**. This is something you do automatically because you are a proficient reader. Think about what these different levels mean for your young students who are learning how to read or who are learning to be better readers.

LITERAL READING. Readers use words to construct meaning. That sounds simple, but there are different levels of meaning. Let us explain. When you read a difficult history chapter, you might just read for the basic facts. When that is the case, you read for the literal meaning. **Literal reading** means that you are reading for just the facts. You might have heard the use of literal in a different context. Let's say you are talking with your roommate and say, "I didn't study at all for the history final," and your roommate responds, "I thought I saw you studying yesterday." You were exaggerating, but your roommate took you literally.

Let's think about this in terms of how it relates to students. Amelia Bedelia books feature a lady who follows directions literally, exactly as they are stated. For example, when she is asked to dust the furniture in *Amelia Bedelia* (Parish & Siebel, 2013), she scatters more dust all over the furniture instead of removing the dust. Students as young as PreK will appreciate the humor from these situations because most students can consider the literal versus intended messages through talking about the word play. Students who are learning English may not understand these situations, so we need to talk about what's going on with Amelia Bedelia and with other books that feature idioms and word play. It is important that we build students' awareness of taking things literally so they can also think about meaning beyond the words on the page. If a student is reading for the literal meaning, they are pronouncing the words to construct a literal meaning. Questions such as, "What color was Little Red Riding Hood's cap? Where did she go? What did she find?" get at the literal level because the answers are directly in the text. When answering literal questions, we typically point at the answers provided in the print in front of us and say, "The text says . . ." Literal reading is reading the surface of meaning.

Watch the video from Margin Note 1.2 and think about the difference between the literal and inferential meanings.

Margin Note 1.2: Literal Reading Example: How to Teach Literal vs. Inferential Questions

https://www.youtube.com/watch?v=n_g7Nq-sTIA

INFERENTIAL READING. The next level of meaning is **inferential**. For example, let's say you were reading that history chapter about the American Revolutionary War. If you were reading literally, you would just read for the dates, places, and people. However, if you were asked, "What were the causes of the American Revolutionary War?" then you would have to take those facts and use your own knowledge to answer the question, which requires thinking beyond the text to make inferences.

The meaning that readers construct may not be exactly the same when developing inferences. Think for a moment about a time when you and a friend read the same text. Did you construct the very same meaning from the text? You may have retrieved the same details (literal meaning), but how you organized them and constructed them was different (inferential meaning). For inferential reading, we often say, "I think . . ." and our inferences are drawn from our knowledge of the text, the content, and our prior experiences.

Another way of thinking about drawing inferences is to consider the text as **clues** that the reader puts together to determine meaning. Books by Chris Van Allsburg are perfect for teaching students how to make inferences because he never tells you the answer to the situations presented in his books. For example, we are never told the identity of the man in *The Stranger* (Van Allsburg, 1986), and we don't know what the stone really is in *The Wretched Stone* (Van Allsburg, 1991). Instead, we must think about information presented on each page and fit it with our own **background knowledge** from our **prior experiences** to determine the answers.

Margin Note 1.3: Introduction to Reading Skills: Making Inferences

https://www.youtube.com/watch?v=acZzllplYz4

As you watch the video in Margin Note 1.3, think about how the actor is drawing inferences and notice how he explains his reasoning.

EVALUATIVE READING. There is a third level of meaning and that is **evaluative**. For evaluative reading, you are not only adding your own background to make meaning, but you are also offering an opinion or evaluating. For example, you are not just looking for details or saying what it means; you are answering the question, "Was it a good movie?" To answer that question, you might use the literal details and some of your inferences, but you are taking the next step and forming an opinion. Can you think of a time when you saw a movie with a friend, and you enjoyed it but your friend thought it was terrible? You shared your opinions while using specific scenes from the movie to support why that part was awesome.

Margin Note 1.4: Opinion Writing Flocabulary

https://www.youtube.com/watch?v=fOCNsAn-hws

Watch the short video clip in Margin Note 1.4 about opinion writing. Although the boy makes a case for pancakes and orange juice as being the best breakfast food options, you may prefer something else. What do you think is the perfect breakfast? Why? Those questions require you to state and justify your opinions. As you do that, you are evaluating the options.

WHAT IS WRITING? Writing is **composing text** rather than constructing meaning from text. When people write, they compose a message and write it, either manually or digitally. Writing is **communication in print**. There are many skills associated with writing, including knowing how to write or type, using words, sentences, and paragraphs. Writing is a complex skill that encompasses both forming thoughts and expressing them through words.

Connection to the Field: Observing Reading and Writing

When you are at your clinical placement, you can observe the kinds of reading and writing that your mentor teacher demonstrates and what students do. If you are at a preschool, you'll most likely observe the teacher doing most of the reading and writing. Notice the kinds of questions the teacher asks and try to determine whether the questions are literal, inferential, or evaluative. When the teacher demonstrates writing, observe how the teacher shows students how messages are composed.

How Children Learn to Read and Write

In addition to knowing how students construct meaning and compose messages, it's important to remember that children don't learn to read or write all at once or when they reach school. Although a few students may enter kindergarten already reading, it will take others much longer (maybe years!) to become readers and writers. Learning to read and write is not a competition and it does not happen for all students by a certain age. Instead, students develop as readers in their own time with your **developmentally appropriate instruction**. Let's explore what this means, by exploring **emergent literacy theories**.

READINESS THEORY. Have you ever heard someone say something like, "Oh, that child just wasn't ready to read yet"? The concept of a child being ready to read is one that has permeated American culture for decades. The idea is based on the premise that students need to have a certain set of skills, characteristics, and abilities before they can read. This idea evolved after a flawed research study suggested this idea and developed into what is commonly called **readiness theory** (Teale, Hoffman, Whittingham, & Paciga, 2018). Those who believed in readiness theory supported the ideas that reading is a separate subject unto itself and that a period of preparation must come before formal reading instruction. Some teachers believed that students should be able to cut on a line with scissors, skip across a gymnasium, or be able to write their names before reading instruction could begin. Until students could do those things, they reasoned, they were not ready to read.

EMERGENT LITERACY THEORY. While readiness theory was becoming widely popular in the United States, Marie Clay, a researcher from New Zealand, began observing young children and posited the idea that literacy is a dynamic, ongoing process that begins long before children start formalized school, perhaps even shortly after birth. Clay (1966) suggested that literacy emerges as children are exposed to oral language, books, and reading. This way of thinking eventually became known as **emergent literacy theory** (Teale & Sulzby, 1986).

Although remnants from readiness theory remain today, most teachers of young children embrace emergent literacy theory, which relies on a developmental perspective of how children learn to read. A developmental perspective encompasses the biological, cognitive, and socioemotional processes that are interwoven as a child grows and changes. Armed with basic knowledge about some of the developmental characteristics of young children, you can begin to understand how literacy emerges and begin to think about implications for teaching. There are many ways that young children develop the foundations of literacy before they come to you. Once children enter preschool or kindergarten, you'll be an important facilitator of each of your student's literacy development. Among the ways you will help foster literacy are honoring each student as an individual, supporting oral language, teaching grammatical structures and unique features of English, helping students learn concepts of print, and teaching the alphabet.

Watch the two short video clips in Margin Note 1.5 and consider how reading was promoted in your early years. Perhaps you had loved ones who talked with you, shared stories with you, and made reading an enjoyable experience. It is possible that your experience may have been very different.

Although we cannot control students' early literacy experiences before they enter our classrooms, we can absolutely provide them with rich reading and writing experiences starting as early as the PreK years. Regardless of the

Margin Notes 1.5:
The 4 E's for Excellent Reading
https://youtu.be/0382z K1DsYA

The ABC's of Reading to Your Child
https://youtu.be/JxyvQna B2NI

grade level you teach, you will notice that your students are reading and writing at different levels. Researchers Chall (1983) and Juel (1994) described how children develop as readers and writers in stages and how teachers can set the foundation for literacy learning while building on the skills that students bring with them to the classroom. Every student moves through the continuum of reading and writing development at their own pace because every child is a unique being with individual learning needs. Figure 1.2 describes the **developmental continuum** that most children follow as they learn how to read and write and the kinds of activities that promote their development. Read the continuum carefully to get a sense of the experiences students need as they develop literacy.

Figure 1.2. Continuum of Children's Development in Early Reading and Writing

Note: This list is intended to be illustrative, not exhaustive. Children at any grade level will function at a variety of phases along the reading/writing continuum.

Phase 1: Awareness and exploration
(goals for preschool)
Children explore their environment and build the foundations for learning to read and write.

Children can
- enjoy listening to and discussing storybooks
- understand that print carries a message
- engage in reading and writing attempts
- identify labels and signs in their environment
- participate in rhyming games
- identify some letters and make some letter-sound matches
- use known letters or approximations of letters to represent written language (especially meaningful words like their name and phrases such as "I love you")

What teachers do
- share books with children, including Big Books, and model reading behaviors
- talk about letters by name and sounds
- establish a literacy-rich environment
- reread favorite stories
- engage children in language games
- promote literacy-related play activities
- encourage children to experiment with writing

What parents and family members can do
- talk with children, engage them in conversation, give names of things, show interest in what a child says
- read and reread stories with predictable texts to children
- encourage children to recount experiences and describe ideas and events that are important to them
- visit the library regularly
- provide opportunities for children to draw and print, using markers, crayons, and pencils

Phase 2: Experimental reading and writing
(goals for kindergarten)
Children develop basic concepts of print and begin to engage in and experiment with reading and writing.

Kindergartners can
- enjoy being read to and themselves retell simple narrative stories or informational texts
- use descriptive language to explain and explore
- recognize letters and letter-sound matches
- show familiarity with rhyming and beginning sounds
- understand left-to-right and top-to-bottom orientation and familiar concepts of print

- match spoken words with written ones
- begin to write letters of the alphabet and some high-frequency words

What teachers do
- encourage children to talk about reading and writing experiences
- provide many opportunities for children to explore and identify sound–symbol relationships in meaningful contexts
- help children to segment spoken words into individual sounds and blend the sounds into whole words (for example, by slowly writing a word and saying its sound)
- frequently read interesting and conceptually rich stories to children
- provide daily opportunities for children to write
- help children build a sight vocabulary
- create a literacy-rich environment for children to engage independently in reading and writing

What parents and family members can do
- daily read and reread narrative and informational stories to children
- encourage children's attempts at reading and writing
- allow children to participate in activities that involve writing and reading (for example, cooking, making grocery lists)
- play games that involve specific directions (such as "Simon Says")
- have conversations with children during mealtimes and throughout the day

Phase 3: Early reading and writing
(goals for first grade)
Children begin to read simple stories and can write about a topic that is meaningful to them.

First graders can
- read and retell familiar stories
- use strategies (rereading, predicting, questioning, contextualizing) when comprehension breaks down
- use reading and writing for various purposes on their own initiative
- orally read with reasonable fluency
- use letter-sound associations, word parts, and context to identify new words
- identify an increasing number of words by sight
- sound out and represent all substantial sounds in spelling a word
- write about topics that are personally meaningful
- attempt to use some punctuation and capitalization

Figure 1.2. *(continued)*

What teachers do

- support the development of vocabulary by reading daily to the children, transcribing their language, and selecting materials that expand children's knowledge and language development
- model strategies and provide practice for identifying unknown words
- give children opportunities for independent reading and writing practice
- read, write, and discuss a range of different text types (poems, informational books)
- introduce new words and teach strategies for learning to spell new words
- demonstrate and model strategies to use when comprehension breaks down
- help children build lists of commonly used words from their writing

What parents and family members can do

- talk about favorite storybooks
- read to children and encourage them to read to you
- suggest that children write to friends and relatives
- bring to a parent-teacher conference evidence of what your child can do in writing and reading
- encourage children to share what they have learned about their writing and reading

Phase 4: Transitional reading and writing (goals for second grade)

Children begin to read more fluently and write various text forms using simple and more complex sentences.

Second graders can

- read with greater fluency
- use strategies more efficiently (rereading, questioning, and so on) when comprehension breaks down
- use word identification strategies with greater facility to unlock unknown words
- identify an increasing number of words by sight
- write about a range of topics to suit different audiences
- use common letter patterns and critical features to spell words
- punctuate simple sentences correctly and proofread their own work
- spend time reading daily and use reading to research topics

What teachers do

- create a climate that fosters analytic, evaluative, and reflective thinking
- teach children to write in multiple forms (stories, information, poems)
- ensure that children read a range of texts for a variety of purposes
- teach revising, editing, and proofreading skills
- teach strategies for spelling new and difficult words
- model enjoyment of reading

What parents and family members can do

- continue to read to children and encourage them to read to you
- engage children in activities that require reading and writing
- become involved in school activities
- show children your interest in their learning by displaying their written work
- visit the library regularly
- support your child's specific hobby or interest with reading materials and references

Phase 5: Independent and productive reading and writing (goals for third grade)

Children continue to extend and refine their reading and writing to suit varying purposes and audiences.

Third graders can

- read fluently and enjoy reading
- use a range of strategies when drawing meaning from the text
- use word identification strategies appropriately and automatically when encountering unknown words
- recognize and discuss elements of different text structures
- make critical connections between texts
- write expressively in many different forms (stories, poems, reports)
- use a rich variety of vocabulary and sentences appropriate to text forms
- revise and edit their own writing during and after composing
- spell words correctly in final writing drafts

What teachers do

- provide opportunities daily for children to read, examine, and critically evaluate narrative and expository texts
- continue to create a climate that fosters critical reading and personal response
- teach children to examine ideas in texts
- encourage children to use writing as a tool for thinking and learning
- extend children's knowledge of the correct use of writing conventions
- emphasize the importance of correct spelling in finished written products
- create a climate that engages all children as a community of literacy learners

What parents and family members can do

- continue to support children's learning and interest by visiting the library and bookstores with them
- find ways to highlight children's progress in reading and writing
- stay in regular contact with your child's teachers about activities and progress in reading and writing
- encourage children to use and enjoy print for many purposes (such as recipes, directions, games, and sports)
- build a love of language in all its forms and engage children in conversation

From International Reading Association. (1998). Learning to read and write: Developmentally appropriate practices for young children, *The Reading Teacher, 52*, 193–216. This is a joint position statement of the International Reading Association and the National Association for the Education of Young Children.

Engaging with Families: Learning about a Child's Reading Background

Throughout this book, we ask you to engage with families in ways that connect with your learning about reading and writing. Since you are not the primary teacher of your students, you'll need to ask your mentor teacher for permission for every activity. Some activities might not be appropriate for your placement, so you can skip or adapt our suggestions.

For this first suggestion, see if you can talk with a parent or guardian about a student's background with books. Simply ask, "Can you tell me about the times your child has attempted to read or write?" (You can adapt the question to fit your style.) Then just listen to learn about your student's background experiences to get a better understanding of how children's literacy emerges through experiences.

How Will I Know What to Teach?

As you think about the enormity of learning how to teach reading and writing, you may be wondering what exactly you are supposed to teach at each grade level. Many states have **standards** that they have adopted that guide what you will teach. Some states have adopted the Common Core State Standards (CCSS) for grades K–12 (National Governors Association for Best Practice & CCSSO, 2010). Other states have their own English Language Arts (ELA) standards. PreK has a different set of standards, which tend to be guided by the National Association for the Education of Young Children (NAEYC) position statement on developmentally appropriate practice and the Head Start Early Learning Outcomes Framework. Follow the link in Margin Note 1.6 to read the NAEYC Developmentally Appropriate Practice Position Statement. Each state is different, and most use their own state-developed early childhood standards. Often, the PreK curriculum considers what should be accomplished to prepare young students for the kindergarten curriculum.

Margin Note 1.6: NAEYC Developmentally Appropriate Practice Position Statement

https://www.naeyc.org/resources/position-statements/dap

Margin Note 1.7: ELA Common Core State Standards

http://www.corestandards.org/ELA-Literacy/

Regardless of the version your state uses, all ELA standards describe *what* should be taught at each grade level. The standards, however, do not provide information about *how* to teach. As the teacher, you will want to gather curriculum resources that you can adapt for use in your classroom to address your required standards while keeping students' learning needs and interests in mind. Your district may provide curriculum materials but remember that the teacher is the decision maker. Decisions about how to teach reading and writing must connect directly to students' needs.

There is no one-size-fits-all approach to teaching reading and writing. In Section II of this book, we provide lots of teaching strategies and sample lesson plans to address each of the major areas of reading and writing. Although they are based on ELA CCSS, you can easily connect our sample lesson plans and teaching strategies with your state's standards. Follow the link in Margin Note 1.7 to learn more about the ELA CCSS. Click on the Anchor Standards to explore expectations by grade level.

As you explore the ELA CCSS, you will notice the anchor standard for **reading foundational skills**. This provides you with expectations for the individual reading skills—the nuts and bolts of reading. Each of the foundational skills represented in the ELA CCSS are addressed in Section II of this book. The ELA CCSS anchor standard for reading literature, for example, provides expectations for what you should accomplish using fiction in your classroom.

Notice the ELA CCSS anchor standard focused on **reading informational text**, an anchor standard for **writing**, and another for **speaking and listening**. These standards fit well with teaching science and social studies. You can weave science and social studies texts into your designated ELA time (the literacy block) to ensure students are getting content area instruction along with literacy instruction.

Literacy instruction doesn't happen in a vacuum—you must have a **context** and **purpose** for reading. Indeed, literacy should be viewed as tools for learning beyond the school walls. Consider reading and writing as the hub of the school curriculum. In math, we prompt students to read the problems (numeric and word problems) and write answers with explanations of their thinking. Science requires observations with journals; lab work involves reading directions and writing hypotheses, steps, findings, and so forth. Social studies instruction involves reading about certain topics, navigating timelines and maps, and creating written products that demonstrate understanding.

HOW DO STANDARDS FIT WITH EMERGENT LITERACY THEORY? We've presented two concepts that may seem contradictory. First, students develop literacy uniquely as they experience reading and writing through their lives. As a teacher, you'll be helping your students develop literacy by giving them developmentally appropriate experiences. Therefore, you'll need to learn where students are in their literacy experiences and provide activities to promote learning.

Standards are something different. Standards were developed to determine whether students have learned what is expected at each grade level. Whether students have learned what is expected by the end of that grade level or not is something you should know. Say for example, that you have provided Daniel, a first-grade student, with many literacy activities. You know what Daniel knows and can do. However, that information doesn't tell you how Daniel compares with other first-grade students. Standards are a measure that let you know whether Daniel's literacy skills are below expectations, meet expectations, or are above expectations. Standards are a measuring stick, but you should still organize your teaching according to your students' developmental needs. As you will learn, students are diverse, and you need to tailor instruction so that each student can succeed.

The Diversity of Students in Your Classroom

Have you ever been compared to your sibling, cousin, or other family member? Maybe you had a teacher who remembered them, and they expected you to be the same, or family members point out how different you are from your sibling or cousin. For instance, your brother or sister may have been a star athlete, and you may be clumsy. Consider how unfortunate and unfair it is to have these kinds of comparisons because we are unique individuals and should be appreciated for our different talents. The same is true for our students.

As advocates for developmentally appropriate practices, we understand that students have wide-ranging abilities. Our goal is to design our instruction to meet students where they are and move them all forward, so they become proficient readers and writers who also choose to read and write. This kind of instruction requires teachers to know about and make decisions to use a variety of methods for teaching reading and writing and to be equipped with teaching strategies to help every student learn to read and write (Afflerbach, 2016; Copple & Bredekamp, 2009; Malloy, Marinak, & Gambrell, 2019).

Differences in reading abilities mean that some students will be considered to be reading below grade level, some will be considered on grade level, and others will be considered above grade level in their literacy development, regardless of the age range or grade level. Some students will not be ready for the materials provided by your school, such as reading books (e.g., basal readers, reading anthologies, leveled readers) or other subject area resources (e.g., math, science, social studies), because they are too difficult. Some students will find those same materials too easy, whereas others may find them to be just right for their reading levels. This book will help guide your thinking about how you can plan and implement reading instruction that is appropriate for each student in your classroom using various **grouping practices** and specific **teaching strategies**.

FUNDS OF KNOWLEDGE. Consider the many differences that children have (e.g., linguistic, socioeconomic status, background) and how that matters in teaching them to read and write. Instead of seeing these differences as what students are lacking, let's recognize them as strengths. Every child knows something about the world around them, but their knowledge may not be academically oriented. Moll et al. (2005) introduced us to the term **funds of knowledge**, which means every student has riches of knowledge that we can tap into as we teach. Students are not deficient if their knowledge is different from ours. Students are naturally curious beings who want to learn; moreover, they can learn, if we provide them with **student-centered** classrooms. In the short video in Margin Note 1.8, Professor Luis Moll describes the concept of funds of knowledge. Watch the video and think about what it means to you as a teacher candidate in a placement as well as the implications for your future teaching.

Margin Note 1.8: Funds of Knowledge Video

https://www.youtube.com/watch?v=aWS0YBpGkkE

KNOWING STUDENTS AS INDIVIDUALS. As a teacher, you need to know students as individuals so you can plan instruction that meets their unique learning needs. Getting to know your students as people who have interests and areas of strength will help build the classroom community while allowing you to consider ways to support individual students and their families (Copple & Bredekamp, 2009). For example, knowing that Bobby is fascinated by rocks, Nakia is a walking encyclopedia about dinosaurs, Samer loves anything related to space, and Sarah brought a bag of cicada casings to share with the class provides you with important information about the topics, materials, and texts you promote in your classroom. By vocally recognizing students as experts in their topics of interest, you boost their sense of belonging and demonstrate that you value their contributions in the learning community. More importantly, you have this opportunity to turn a reluctant reader into an avid reader because tapping into students' interests motivates them to want to read more, especially when they can choose what they want to read (Springer, Harris, & Dole, 2017).

Providing students with opportunities to share their expertise on their topics through creating their choice in written products (e.g., brochures, posters, picture dictionaries) and sharing with others, such as with peers or special visitors, promotes reading and writing for authentic purposes (Copple & Bredekamp, 2009; Guthrie & Barber, 2019; Kissel, 2017). For instance, you could ask another teacher if your class can visit on a specified date so students can share their written products, and you could invite family members to the classroom to celebrate your students as young authors. These experiences are powerful ways to build and embrace students' identities and differences as individuals who want to read and write.

Connection to the Field: Learning Students' Interests

Work with your mentor teacher to learn about your students' interests outside of school. For example, you might spend a few minutes with each child asking them about the kinds of things they like to do when they leave school for the day. After you meet with each child, write down notes so you remember each child's interests.

LINGUISTIC DIFFERENCES. In addition to discovering students' interests, you also need to learn about their linguistic differences. Understanding that some students are learning English provides you with essential information because you will need to use additional strategies to support them and their families. For example, Jovi, Chunbo, and Erik are three students in the same classroom, and they speak three different languages. Do their family members speak and/or read English? Sending a newsletter or other communications home with them translated into Spanish won't help them or their families because their native languages are Russian, Chinese (Cantonese), and Swedish. Tapping into students' interests while promoting their use of native languages to demonstrate what they already know will help them gain confidence with being part of the learning community while building knowledge of how English works (Domínguez & Gutiérrez, 2019; Helman, Rogers, Frederick, & Struck, 2016).

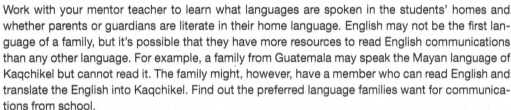

Engaging with Families: Language Spoken at Home

Work with your mentor teacher to learn what languages are spoken in the students' homes and whether parents or guardians are literate in their home language. English may not be the first language of a family, but it's possible that they have more resources to read English communications than any other language. For example, a family from Guatemala may speak the Mayan language of Kaqchikel but cannot read it. The family might, however, have a member who can read English and translate the English into Kaqchikel. Find out the preferred language families want for communications from school.

Teaching for Equity

A major component of becoming a learner-ready teacher is being able to effectively teach students from all backgrounds. There are many terms for this kind of teaching, but we use **culturally relevant teaching (CRT)** in this book. As educators learn more about how to teach students from diverse backgrounds, ideas and terms change, and you'll find that some terms you learn this year will change during your career. That's the case with CRT. Some educators call it culturally responsive pedagogy (Sleeter, 2012), and others call it culturally sustaining pedagogy (Paris, 2012), depending on their focus. Regardless of the term used, effective teachers recognize potential in every student and strive to provide experiences that build on students' individual strengths while connecting to their lives beyond school. In this way, effective teachers tailor their instruction to meet students' learning needs while respecting students as individuals who bring a wealth of knowledge and experiences to school with them.

When teachers use CRT—making connections between cultural knowledge, beliefs, and practices that students bring from home and the content they are teaching—diverse students' academic performance and school experiences improve (Gay, 2000). However, CRT is not merely a set of teaching practices, but instead is a central belief—a mindset—about teaching, learning, students, families, and communities and an "unyielding commitment to see student success become less rhetoric and more of a reality" (Howard, 2010, p. 67).

According to Gay (2013), assumptions about ethnic, racial, and cultural differences are often embedded in instructional practices. That means we need to learn to recognize and appreciate different experiences that students bring to school so every student in our classroom has opportunities to flourish as a learner, especially in reading and writing.

EXAMINING YOUR OWN CULTURE. Pause for a minute and make a list about who you are as a **cultural being**. You might consider these categories: ethnicity, marital status, gender identity, religion, family, nationality (perhaps including region), and other memberships (e.g., academic or social clubs, hobbies, sports). Also include messages you heard while growing up, such as the importance of family, the role of respect and responsibility, and the balance of work and play.

Now that you have your list, think about your classmates. Every person's background is unique. Your classmates look, dress, talk, eat, worship, and think differently than you. They have heard different messages growing up. You may have similarities, but you also have differences.

STUDENTS ARE DIFFERENT FROM EACH OTHER. Now turn to the students you see in your clinical placement. Each child is different, and they may have very different cultural experiences from the ones you had. Perhaps your students live in houses, apartments, trailers, tents, shelters, or cars. Maybe they are being raised by two parents, a single parent, a family member, friends of the family, foster parents, or perhaps they live in a group home. Don't assume anything by glancing at the class and by reading statistics posted on the school's website. Instead, get to know your students and understand who they are as individuals because they all need your careful guidance and attention.

If you enter the classroom with the attitude that everyone will be treated exactly the same way, that's malpractice. Think of it this way: Two men walk into the Emergency Room. One has a knife wound and the other is having symptoms of a heart attack. Do you give them both stitches? Or do you give them both an aspirin? That would be treating them the same. Although that is a medical scenario, it also applies to teaching, because each student comes to you with different learning needs. If you give them all the same instruction, then some will do well whereas others will not progress as rapidly as possible. Instead of thinking along the lines of equality, let's adopt a stance for equity. Treating students the same is not equity. **Equity** is when you know your students as individuals, you respect who they are as people, and you provide them with **differentiated instruction** that meets their learning needs.

This Is Just the Beginning

In this book you'll learn how to be a learner-ready teacher—a teacher who is ready to effectively teach on Day 1. However, this won't be the end of your learning. As you progress through your career, you'll refine the strategies that are successful for your students, and you'll learn new ways of teaching reading and writing. In addition, researchers will learn new ways of teaching that you'll want to add to your teaching repertoire. This book and your corresponding coursework will help you be prepared to be a good beginning teacher. However, you'll need to continue learning new things as you progress through your career to become even more effective.

Teaching students how to read and write is not the same as following a recipe. When you carefully follow a recipe, you get the same result each time you make the dish. Teaching reading and writing should never be like following a recipe because your students have vastly different needs. Instead of following curriculum materials rigidly, consider them as guides that you supplement based on your students' learning needs. By adopting a flexible approach to teaching reading, you will be using your own **professional judgment** to make instructional decisions for your students.

You'll learn many great ideas in this book about how to teach reading and writing as well as the foundational theories that underpin the teaching strategies. How you organize the ideas presented will vary depending on the school in which you teach and the curriculum or literacy program they use. You'll learn that there is no one right way to teach reading and writing. Instead, you'll be asked to use the school's materials and programs, the ideas from this book, and apply them to the individual students you teach. The danger of simply following program materials with the whole class is that not every student is developmentally ready for those materials, and those materials are too easy for some students. You must know who your students are as individual learners so you can tailor instruction to meet all your students' learning needs.

This book promotes **effective literacy teaching** by providing you with knowledge and strategies to equip you for success. You could simply read this book to complete assignments and activities for your literacy methods course. However, your students need you to internalize the concepts and consider your impact as a teacher of literacy and as a lifelong learner. In that way you'll become a **learner-ready teacher**.

Closing Thoughts

At the beginning of this chapter, we introduced you to Dena and Kofi at the start of their literacy methods course, and we learned about how they are readers and writers for different purposes. Just like Dena and Kofi, you and your classmates have different views on purposes for reading and writing. Regardless of those differing views, you have the potential and promise to be an effective teacher of reading and writing, a learner-ready teacher. Consider what you already know and open your mind to learning as much as possible about how to teach reading and writing in and beyond your literacy methods course.

Takeaways from Chapter 1

- We have different views on the purposes of reading and writing.
- Reading is constructing meaning from text.
- Students develop as readers and as writers at their own pace.
- Students have different strengths and learning needs.
- There is no one right way to teach reading.
- Reading and writing are the hub of the curriculum.
- The ELA standards are a framework you can use to know what to teach.
- Apply what you know about your students' cultural backgrounds to your lessons.
- You goal is to become a learner-ready teacher.

To Learn More about the Focus of Reading and Writing

Books about Culturally Relevant Pedagogy and Equity in Education

Delpit, L. D. (2012). *"Multiplication is for white people": Raising expectations for other people's children.* New York, NY: The New Press.

https://thenewpress.com/books/multiplication-for-white-people

This book is a frank view on the need for culturally relevant teaching (CRT) and equity in education. As you read this book, consider your experiences as a student and as a teacher candidate in a placement classroom, and what this means for you as a future teacher.

Ladson-Billings, G. (2009). *The dreamkeepers: Successful teachers of African-American children* (2nd ed.). San Francisco, CA: Jossey-Bass, Inc.

https://www.wiley.com/en-us/The+Dreamkeepers%3A+Successful+Teachers+of+African+American+Children%2C+2nd+Edition-p-9781118622988

This book provides examples from real classrooms and exemplary teachers who use CRT. As you read this book, consider the implications for your future teaching and your future classroom. Also, consider how the concepts from this book relate to your placement and to your experiences as a student.

Books about Emergent Literacy

Clay, M. M. (2015). *Becoming literate: The construction of inner control*. Portsmouth, NH: Heinemann.

https://www.heinemann.com/products/e07442.aspx

This updated classic explains how literacy develops in young children before they enter school. This book corresponds with the concept of every child developing at their own pace. Read this book while thinking critically about diversity in students' literacy learning experiences before they enter school. How can you build on those prior experiences? As a teacher, how can you ensure that every student in your classroom gets the instruction they need to become readers and writers?

Clay, M. M. (2014). *By different paths to common outcomes*. Portsmouth, NH: Heinemann.

https://www.heinemann.com/products/e05955.aspx

This book affirms that all children are different, and they develop as readers and writers at their own pace. Differences are not deficiencies. Instead, differences are opportunities to build on students' strengths. Read this book to supplement your understanding of emergent literacy theory from Chapter 1. Prepare a brief presentation that will help you explain Marie Clay's ideas to a classmate.

Literacy Leadership Brief: What Effective Pre-K Literacy Instruction Looks Like

https://www.literacyworldwide.org/docs/default-source/where-we-stand/ila-what-effective-pre-k-literacy-instruction-looks-like.pdf

This short literacy leadership brief from the International Literacy Association (ILA) explains what the research says about effective literacy instruction in PreK and what that looks like in a PreK classroom. Consider how the main points about effective PreK literacy instruction from this literacy leadership brief correspond with concepts from this chapter. Think deeply about the implications for your future teaching.

Literacy Leadership Brief: Characteristics of Culturally Sustaining and Academically Rigorous Classrooms

https://www.literacyworldwide.org/docs/default-source/where-we-stand/ila-culturally-sustaining-classrooms-brief.pdf?sfvrsn=7b80a68e_10

This short literacy leadership brief from the International Literacy Association (ILA) explains what the research says about how teachers can use CRT in their classrooms. As you read this brief, reflect on what you learned from this chapter about CRT. Make a plan for how you will use CRT in your clinical placement and in your future classroom.

Professional Journals

Search at least one of the following journals for a concept presented in this chapter to dig deeper and to enhance your understanding of teaching reading and writing while familiarizing yourself with a scholarly professional resource.

The Reading Teacher

Check with your university library for free access to *The Reading Teacher*. This is a professional journal for elementary classroom teachers who want to learn more about teaching reading and other aspects of literacy effectively. *The Reading Teacher* is published by the International Literacy Association (ILA).

https://ila.onlinelibrary.wiley.com/journal/19362714

Language Arts

Check with your university library for free access to *Language Arts*. This is a professional journal for elementary classroom teachers who want to learn more about teaching writing. *Language Arts* is published by the National Council of Teachers of English (NCTE).

https://www2.ncte.org/resources/journals/language-arts/

Young Children

Check with your university library for free access to *Young Children*. This is a professional journal for teachers of children from birth through third grade and the focus is on meeting the needs of all children. *Young Children* is published by the National Association for the Education of Young Children (NAEYC).

https://www.naeyc.org/resources/pubs/yc

Websites

Top 10 Things You Should Know about Reading

http://www.readingrockets.org/article/top-10-things-you-should-know-about-reading

This top 10 list is from the Reading Rockets website. The list is a brief overview of what is needed to learn how to read, how to teach it, components of early literacy development, and other facts. The Reading Rockets website is a professional resource with evidence-based research about reading. It provides information for teachers and parents, including videos, articles, and teaching strategies. Compare this list to the information presented in this chapter. Keep the list handy so you can compare it to future chapters.

Literacy Daily: Teaching Tips

https://www.literacyworldwide.org/blog/the-engaging-classroom/teaching-tips

This daily blog is published on the International Literacy Association's (ILA) website and features practical ideas that you can use to promote literacy learning in your classroom. Blog contributors include teachers, literacy coaches, and professors. Skim through this blog and find a post that relates to concepts presented in this chapter. How was the information presented? Who authored the blog? What are the implications for your future teaching?

Three Principles for Culturally Relevant Teaching

https://blogs.edweek.org/edweek/urban_education_reform/2018/09/three_principles_for_culturally_relevant_teaching.html

This blog from Education Week briefly explains research findings about CRT. Make a visual representation to demonstrate your understanding of CRT from this blog. How does your learning from the blog enhance your learning from this chapter?

Videos

Introduction to Culturally Relevant Pedagogy

https://www.youtube.com/watch?v=nGTVjJuRaZ8

Experts in the field explain culturally relevant pedagogy and how teachers can use it in their classrooms. The experts also explain the difference between race and culture. Think about ways culture is different from race. How does this video extend your knowledge from the chapter?

Teacher of the Year Discusses Culturally Responsive Teaching

https://www.youtube.com/watch?v=_xxSZe0Sfrs

In this short video, Teacher of the Year Wendy Nelson-Kauffman discusses how important it is to make personal connections with students and tap into their cultures and background experiences to make learning more meaningful. What are the top five points from this video? How do those points connect with this chapter? What are the implications for your future teaching?

© mangopor2004/Shutterstock.com

Your beliefs about teaching guide your literacy instruction.

What Are the Foundations of Literacy Instruction?

REAL-LIFE EXAMPLE

Ashley was just beginning her teacher preparation program and was scheduled to student teach in first grade. Both of Ashley's parents were primary-grade teachers, so she had heard talk about teaching her entire life. Her parents disagreed for years about how to teach reading, and Ashley had listened to them discuss whether to teach the alphabet one letter a week or to teach the alphabet in the context of reading books. As Ashley listened to the debate, she wavered back and forth about her preference.

Ashley was armed with extensive background knowledge about the different ways to teach the alphabet, but she didn't know the background or theories for these different viewpoints. She wanted to make up her own mind and develop her own theoretical base to make decisions. Therefore, Ashely was excited to connect what she knew about reading, what she had learned about learning theories, and what she would learn about reading to make her own decisions about what she believed. Ashley knew that she had to form her own preliminary theory before she could make decisions about how to teach reading and writing.

Even if you don't have the background knowledge of teaching reading that Ashley has, you have some experience with learning to read and write. As mentioned in Chapter 1, these experiences will form the basis for your beliefs about teaching. Think about how you learned to read and whether those experiences fit your learning needs. Your teachers had beliefs about how to teach reading and writing, and now it's your turn. You need to refresh your memory about learning theories and add to your knowledge base with more information about how children learn to read and write. As you do, you'll be able to make decisions about what you believe and begin developing your own **literacy learning theory**. You'll find as you go through your career that your literacy learning theory will develop and change as new research is published and new ideas about reading are generated. However, you need to begin your teaching career with some ideas about how your students learn how to read and write.

This chapter focuses on literacy theories and also encourages you to develop your own theory of literacy learning. We begin this chapter with the focus on you: what do you believe about literacy? Then we turn to some of the foundational learning theories, such as behaviorism, social constructivism, and sociocultural theories. Then we get specific by describing literacy theories: bottom-up, top-down, and transactional theories. Finally, we turn to what happens when people read. They first look at print and make sense of words using the visual, meaning, and structural cueing systems. And, most importantly, readers use strategies to make meaning from text. This chapter is dense and heavy, but it is important for you as you learn how to teach reading and writing.

Developing Your Own Theory of Literacy Learning

It is important for you as a new teacher to develop and articulate what you believe about teaching and learning. By putting what you believe into words, you can begin to understand how those beliefs underpin your philosophy of literacy learning and how that philosophy directs what you do in the classroom. Regie Routman (2000) wrote, "Our beliefs about teaching and learning directly affect how and why we teach the way we do, even when we do not or cannot verbalize these beliefs. Therefore, it is important to articulate our beliefs and match them with practice: If this is what I believe, how does that influence what I do in the classroom?" (p. 17). Further, understanding your views about how children learn and the literacy research that supports your views will determine not only your teaching practices, but also your teaching effectiveness. Your philosophy will evolve from your own experiences as a learner, the knowledge you gain through study, from learning to be a responsive teacher, from your understanding of the role of assessment, and from policy.

You may have already crafted a **theory of teaching and learning** in other classes. You can use some of your previous thoughts as you develop a personal theory of literacy learning. To begin thinking about what you believe, write a **literacy autobiography** that details your experiences learning to read and write. An example of a literacy autobiography can be found in Figure 2.1.

After you document your history of learning to read and write, begin to take notes on the processes you used as you learned. For example, if your family members read to you, you were hearing language and you were learning how stories are structured. Then write what you believe. We've developed a partial chart for you to see as an example in Figure 2.2. A template for your Experiences and Beliefs about Reading and Writing can be found in the Chapter 2 Resources on the website. As you read this chapter and the rest of the book, we'd like to you think about what you believe. At the end of the chapter we'll ask you to identify what you believe in response to what you've learned.

Figure 2.1. Literacy Autobiography

My earliest memory of reading is having my mother read bedtime stories to me and my two brothers. We had a large basket of books that we had all checked out from the library, and each night my mother read two books to us. I loved that time. It was relaxing to be cuddled in my bed hearing stories about Frog and Toad or Winnie the Pooh. I frequently took the books from the basket and pretended to read them using the illustrations as a guide. I got pretty good at telling the stories, but I doubt if the story I told was exactly like the one written in the book.

As I got older and went to school, I was excited to learn how to read by myself. I went to kindergarten expecting to read, but I found out I first needed to learn the alphabet in order. Luckily, the teacher sang us an alphabet song that helped me learn the letters quickly. As each kindergartener recited the alphabet correctly, the teacher gave us a picture she drew with stars on it.

During my primary grade years, I vaguely remember reading class. We were divided into groups and every group had a core reading text at their level. I remember reading in a circle, with each student taking a turn reading a page. I remember being bored as I listened to my classmates read and self-conscious when it was my turn. In addition to reading from a text, we also had sight word lessons and spelling lessons. We didn't learn much about phonics, and I always had trouble sounding out words. When I came to a word I didn't know, I just skipped it and tried to make sense of the sentence without the unfamiliar word. This worked pretty well for me until I got to middle school. Then the teacher showed us how to divide words into syllables and figure out word parts.

As I progressed through the grades, I continued my love of reading books. Each week my mother would take us to the library to get books, and each class I was in had a classroom library where I could check out books. I remember in sixth grade, the class library had 20 biographies. I read every one. I read every chance I got, including in bed, under the covers, with a flashlight; and in school when the teacher was talking. Books and reading have always been important to me.

Figure 2.2. Experiences and Beliefs about Reading and Writing

Experiences	What this Means	What I Believe
Mother read to me at night.	I was immersed in stories as a child.	Children need to hear language and stories.
We went to the library each week to get books.	I was surrounded by books.	It's important for children to have access to books.

Foundational Theories of Learning

As you reflect on your literacy autobiography and develop a chart of literacy processes and beliefs, think beyond your experiences to what you know about how people learn. As you reflect on learning also consider what you need to know when you begin teaching. As a teacher, you'll be making many lightning-quick decisions throughout your day. You'll be making decisions about what to teach, how to teach, and how to respond to students. Each of these decisions will be based on your beliefs about teaching, your instincts and experiences as a teacher, what you know about your students, and the theories that you have generated about teaching and learning.

You may be thinking, "Why should I care about theories? Just show me what to do." Well, you'll be making hundreds of instructional decisions as a teacher. Theories will be your ground zero. What you do in your future classroom will be directly influenced by what you believe about how children learn to read and write, which is why we're going to review both learning theories and reading theories.

You probably know quite a bit about learning theories in general from your background and from other college courses. For decades, researchers and theorists have been investigating learning processes. You can use the knowledge they have gleaned to help you form a personal theory of literacy learning that you can apply to your future teaching situations. As you read the theories, think about the extent to which you agree with their ideas. We're going to start with a theory that's over 100 years old.

THORNDIKE AND CONNECTIONISM. Learning theories are relatively new in human history. One of the first learning theories was developed by Thorndike in the early 20th century. Perhaps you have read or learned about him in psychology class. Thorndike conducted experiments with chicks, dogs, fish, cats, and monkeys and drew conclusions about both animal and human behavior. In his experiments, Thorndike placed animals in cages that had a latched door and food just outside the door. He observed the animals as they attempted to open the door and get the food and measured the time it took for the animals to escape. From these experiments, Thorndike (1913) developed the **theory of connectionism**, which stated that responses are associated with stimuli during repeated learning attempts.

PAVLOV AND CLASSICAL CONDITIONING. While Thorndike was conducting experiments in the United States, another psychologist in Russia was thinking along the same lines. Pavlov also conducted experiments with animals to determine how they behaved. You're probably familiar with Pavlov's famous salivating dogs. Pavlov sounded a tuning fork immediately before giving meat powder to a dog. After repeating the experiment several times, the dog salivated at the sound of the tuning fork without the meat. Pavlov concluded that responses automatically occur after certain stimuli (Pavlov, 1928). His theory is known as **classical conditioning**.

BEHAVIORISM AND EDUCATION. You may be wondering at this point about the relevancy of the theories of Thorndike and Pavlov to literacy learning. The work of Thorndike and Pavlov forms the basis for **behaviorism**, a theory made popular by Skinner (1953). Behaviorism was extremely popular in the early and middle parts of the 20th century, and many teaching practices in schools today are still rooted in behaviorist theories.

According to behaviorist thinking, reading should be taught primarily through a series of skills: drill, practice, and repetition. The curriculum would be divided into discrete bits of knowledge and organized into a hierarchy of skills. Student learning would be assessed through multiple-choice tests. This kind of teaching was very popular in the 1960s through the 1970s, and there are many ideas from behaviorist theories that are present in schools today. Think of the terms behavioral management, measurable behavioral objectives, behavioral modification, positive reinforcement, guided practice, mastery, and many more. These concepts and terms stem from behaviorism. Now think about what you believe. Do you believe that children learn primarily through stimulus–response? For example, have you seen teachers who clap their hands to get students to listen? Clapping their hands is the stimulus, and teachers want students to stop talking and listen as the response. Perhaps you could add to the chart that you're developing with experiences you've had with behaviorist teaching and what you believe about behaviorism. Look at the video in Margin Note 2.1 to get another description about behaviorism in education. Talk with your classmates to see if your understanding of behaviorism is similar to theirs.

Margin Note 2.1: Using a Learning Theory: Behaviorism

https://www.youtube.com/watch?v=KYDYzR-ZWRQ

SOCIAL CONSTRUCTIVISM. The **social constructivist theory** is a combination of three theories that were developed in the last half of the 20th century: cognitive, constructivist, and sociocultural

Connection to the Field: Behaviorism in the Classroom

There are many vestiges of behaviorism in classrooms that are now part of our educational culture, such as ringing a bell for students to quiet down. Look for terms and examples that are the products of behaviorism. What do you think? What examples of behavioristic activities do you agree with? Why? Which ones do you disagree with? Why?

theories (Shepard, 2000). The seeds for these three learning theories were planted while behaviorist practices were at their height in schools.

COGNITIVE THEORIES. Beginning in the 1960s, theorists began to hypothesize that learners do not passively receive knowledge but that they actively participate in and process learning in unique ways. **Behaviorists** believed that the mind passively reacts to new information. **Cognitive theorists**, however, suggested that the mind actively tries to make sense of new information by applying it to existing knowledge. These new thoughts led to what has been called the cognitive revolution. One of the theories developed during the cognitive revolution was schema theory.

Schema theory was developed by Rumelhart (1980) who stated that knowledge is organized in the mind in structures called schemata. Schemata are the background knowledge that learners use to make sense of new learning. You can think about the role of schemata by comparing the mind to a computer. When you turn on your computer, you boot up a specific application, such as a word processing program. This application allows you to access any number of files. Let's say that you open a file that contains a paper you've been writing for a history class. As you open the file, you find you have notes, references, and the first two pages of your paper. You use this partially completed work to continue writing your paper. Opening the computer files is analogous to accessing schemata during learning.

Schema theory is a key component of **cognitive theory**. Cognitive theory suggests that the mind actively accesses knowledge and applies that knowledge to make sense of new information. Think how different this theory is from behaviorist theory. Learners actively use their minds to construct meaning, which leads us to the second theory embedded in social constructivism: constructivist theories. Take a look at the video in Margin Note 2.2 to get a better understanding of how cognitivism could be used in education. Add any information you learn to your learning theory chart.

Margin Note 2.2: Using a Learning Theory: Cognitivism

https://www.youtube.com/watch?v=gugvpoU2Ewo

CONSTRUCTIVIST THEORIES. **Constructivism** is a metatheory that has been developing for the past several decades (Spivey, 1997). Constructivists contend that learners do not merely respond to stimulus as stated by behaviorists, but that knowledge is actively acquired, socially constructed, and created or re-created. Constructivists believe that leaners actively use their minds to construct their own individual meaning (Fosnot, 1996). This meaning is constructed using their background knowledge, and because every learner's background knowledge is different, every person's construction of meaning is unique. Learners also construct meaning in concert with other people. Knowledge, therefore, is socially constructed which is why classroom discussions are such valuable learning tools.

Let's think about what this means to you. Think about a movie that you saw recently, one that was more complex than an action film. As you were watching the movie, you were constructing your perception of the movie in your mind. You may have been recalling other similar films, thinking about the main character's motivations, predicting what would happen next in the plot, and wondering how the movie would end. After the movie, you may have asked a friend a question about the movie to ascertain your friend's perceptions, which most likely were different from yours. The thinking process that you experienced is an active construction of meaning. You didn't just watch the movie and accept the visual and auditory input, your mind worked to make sense of the movie as you were watching. You didn't just accept your construction of meaning, you talked with others about their perception as well. If the movie was based on a book that you've read, then you're also including the author's perspectives because you are comparing events in the book to what's happening on the screen. Even while watching movies, you construct meaning in social ways, which illustrates constructivism.

Influence of Piaget. Some of the beliefs of constructivism stem from Dewey's belief in experience as the foundation of learning (Dewey, 1938). More recently, however, constructivist perspectives have been developed from the theories of Piaget and Vygotsky. Piaget's work has been extremely influential in several areas of education, but his writings during the 1970s have served as the foundation for constructivism (Fosnot, 1996). According to Piaget (1977), learners assimilate new information within existing knowledge structures, accommodate the knowledge structures to new situations, and move between assimilation and accommodation as necessary. These cognitive activities are quite different from behaviorist thinking. Piaget suggested that leaners' minds are actively engaged in mental activities as they are exposed to new information.

Influence of Vygotsky. Vygotsky added a new dimension to Piagetian constructivism. Vygotsky (1978) suggested that learners not only use their minds actively to develop new knowledge, but that they also use language and personal interactions to develop learning, as in the previous example of discussing a movie. Vygotsky's theories suggested that learning begins on the social level through language and then is internalized. The language events that most effectively facilitate learning are social, but they also involve learners and more knowledgeable others in these social interactions. As people learn, they have a sphere of actual and potential learning.

This area of most effective learning is called the **zone of proximal development** (ZPD) which Vygotsky (1978) described as "[t]he distance between the actual developmental level as determined through problem solving and the level of potential development as determined through problem solving under adult guidance or in collaboration with more capable peers" (p. 84). Just think that learning can be too easy, just right, or too difficult.

The ZPD is a useful concept for you to understand. As you think about ZPD, think about how you learned different skills, such as learning to read. Some of you may have learned to read outside of school, but most of you probably learned to read in school. Think about the social aspects of your experience. As a young child, you very likely had an adult who read to you and with you. Then when you went to school, your teachers modeled reading by reading aloud, taught you letters and sounds, and organized literacy experiences for you. During these literacy experiences, you had opportunities to read with the teachers, with classmates, and alone. Much of your learning was social.

Margin Note 2.3: Zone of Proximal Development

https://www.youtube.com/watch?v=Zu-rr2PRNkE

Early in this process, you could read, but you couldn't read everything. When you were in first grade, you couldn't read a biology textbook, even with help. That difficulty of learning would have been way outside your ZPD. In the same respect, when you were in high school, a first grade story would have been too easy. As you learned to read, you had to have materials that were in the range of your expertise. You could read more difficult material with help, but only if those materials were within your ZPD. Look at the explanation of ZPD in the video in Margin Note 2.3. Think of ways your literacy learning was scaffolded by more experienced mentors. You might add more to your chart to detail these experiences.

SOCIOCULTURAL THEORIES. Cognitive theory and constructivism suggest that learning is an active process, occurring in the mind but influenced by social interactions. Learning is also influenced by social and cultural relationships.

Individuals can learn alone but that learning is based on **social mediation.** Think about yourself learning something new. For example, let's say that your friend, Jeni, has a new computer game that you would like to try. Jeni tells you about the game, and you watch her play it while she discusses the aspects of the game. She then encourages you to learn it while she's at work. You boot up the computer and attempt the new game. Are you learning alone? In many respects you are; however, you also bring hours of socially mediated learning to the situation. While you are trying the new game, you're probably remembering past attempts at learning new computer games, strategies you've learned from others who you've played games with, and even conversations with Jeni about the new game. You are recalling socially mediated learning even while you're learning alone. Learning can be mediated socially in one-on-one instruction, in small groups, or in large groups.

Learning is also socially mediated because much of your prior learning has been conducted in social situations or groups. Therefore, learning is socially mediated even when it occurs individually. Here's another example: Think of one of your college classes in which the teacher taught by way of lecture. You were expected to listen to the teacher, take notes, read the textbook, and study for a test. Think about the times you turned to another student and asked for clarification and the times you formed study groups in preparation for a test. In those situations, you combined individual learning with learning in social situations.

As a classroom teacher, you will need to keep in mind that your students are social learners. Students learn best when they have opportunities to collaborate with others and learn from their peers as well as from you. In a classroom where the teacher applies sociocultural theories, the teacher will also acknowledge the wealth of background knowledge each student brings to the class. The teacher will understand that students work alone and in groups and that all learning is valued. You can learn more about social learning theory by watching the video in Margin Note 2.4.

Margin Note 2.4: Social Learning Theory

https://www.youtube.com/watch?v=lqScOlrHx2A

YOUR BELIEFS ABOUT LEARNING THEORIES. You can see from the overview of learning theories in this chapter that we have learned quite a lot about how people learn as theorists have developed new learning theories. As we illustrated with behaviorism, just because a new theory is popularized doesn't mean older theories disappear. Instead, many teachers develop an eclectic view of learning that focuses on different aspects of each of the learning theories. As you gain more experiences in classrooms, you'll see how this can work. In the meantime, add to your Experiences and Beliefs about Reading and Writing template with what you have learned about theories and what you believe right now. Your beliefs may change, but it's useful to be able to reflect on your beliefs as they evolve. The Experiences and Beliefs about Reading and Writing template can be found in the Chapter 2 Resources on the website.

Reading Theories

We have described general learning theories. These theories were probably somewhat familiar to you. Now we're going to take a look at reading theories which may not be so familiar but will be really important as you think about teaching reading and writing. They are the bottom-up theory of reading, the top-down theory of reading, and the transactional theory of reading.

BOTTOM-UP THEORY OF READING. The **bottom-up theory of reading** stems from behaviorism and was popular in schools during the second half of the 20th century. Bottom-up means that when reading, readers first notice letters, then words, then sentences, and finally the meaning of the entire text, almost like climbing steps from the bottom up. This theory was made popular by LaBerge and Samuels (1974) who, at that time, believed that reading was an information processing activity and that decoding (figuring out) words and comprehending them (understanding meaning) were separate mental processes. Another name for the bottom-up theory of reading is the skills approach.

Bottom-up is like learning to play the piano using notes and scales rather than music. For example, imagine learning to play the piano as a young adult. The teacher gives you a sheet of music that has the notes of the scale. During lessons, you learn which note on the printed scale corresponds to the key on the piano. At successive lessons, you learn more notes and more keys, but you don't play any songs. You continue learning the notes and the keys until you know them well. After you have mastered the notes, you begin to play simple songs.

Not every teacher who teaches letters and sounds is using the bottom-up approach. All kindergarten and first grade teachers teach letters and sounds—the difference is in the way teachers approach them. If a teacher reads a story aloud to the class and discusses the words that begin with the letter *s*, that teacher is not using a bottom-up approach because they began with the whole text. A teacher using a bottom-up approach has students complete a worksheet in which they identify pictures and circle the pictures that begin with the letter *s*. An emphasis on letters and sounds rather than whole text is the determining factor of the bottom-up approach.

TOP-DOWN THEORY OF READING. Psycholinguists, who combine knowledge from psychology and linguistics, reason that reading is primarily an active, meaning-making endeavor. In order to make sense of the print on a page, the reader must begin with the whole text, not the parts. Psycholinguistic theory is sometimes referred to as a **top-down model** in contrast to the bottom-up theory you just learned. Kenneth Goodman (1965) observed that readers access cueing systems, which are informational sources that allow them to make sense of print. Goodman asserted that all readers make mistakes, which he called miscues, and that those very miscues can provide evidence to teachers of what is happening in a reader's mind.

Psycholinguistics is like learning to play baseball. You see the players warming up before the game. Watching the batters face the pitchers while the umpire calls balls and strikes shows you that a batter gets only so many tries before they have to sit down. You witness a batter hit a ground ball and start running down a base path toward an opposing team member who is standing near first base. A player in the field catches the ball and throws it to the waiting player near first base, who catches the ball in their mitt with their feet planted on first base. The batter is out. You might have to watch all nine innings before you begin

© kedrov/Shutterstock.com

Students use strategies to construct meaning as they read.

to understand the concepts of the game, but gradually you get the idea. Consider learning about baseball by watching the game versus learning all of the rules before seeing a game.

You can observe excellent teachers in the early grades who believe in the top-down model of reading. In their classrooms, they read aloud daily to children, using expressive voices and pointing out brightly drawn illustrations in books. They ask children to predict what might happen next in the story and read on to see if those predictions come true. They purposefully demonstrate, in shared reading experiences using Big Books, that books have letters, words, and sentences. These teachers explain that when you look at the pictures, you can find information to help you figure out the words. They know that young children enjoy looking at whole books and reading some of the words before they even know all the names of the letters of the alphabet or all the sounds the letters make, especially after the teacher has read those books aloud to the children. To get a better understanding of top-down and bottom-up theories of reading, look at the video in Margin Note 2.5. Develop a Venn diagram with two of your classmates to see how the theories are alike and different.

Margin Note 2.5: Explanation of Top-down and Bottom-up Information Processing: Using Top-down Reading Strategies in Your Lesson

https://www.youtube.com/watch?v=GmIbfbYMfUE

TRANSACTIONAL THEORY OF READING. The **transactional theory of reading**, developed by Louise Rosenblatt (1978), states that reading is a transaction between the reader, the text, and the social context. By transaction, Rosenblatt meant that when readers read, they bring their prior knowledge to the reading event and then that knowledge combines with the information from the text. The meaning that results from the combination of the readers' prior knowledge and the text is influenced by the social and cultural background of each reader. Therefore, meaning from reading transactions is a combination of a reader's knowledge, the text, and the social context.

The transactional theory of reading is like buying a car. When you buy a car, you're bringing your likes and dislikes, your transportation needs, and your money to a car dealer or to a company on the internet. The dealer offers cars that have certain characteristics, style, color, mileage, and report histories. When you decide to buy a car, you enter an agreement. Influencing the transactions are the social mores of your age group. For example, young adults tend to buy certain types and colors of cars, and the social information also is part of the transaction. When you buy a car, therefore, you bring your own preferences and needs to a situation where the dealer offers their cars, and your final decision is influenced by social knowledge.

Something similar happens during reading. The reader enters a situation in which they decide to learn about a specific topic or wants to enter into the lives of others through the story. The reader has a purpose for reading, and that purpose guides the selection of reading materials, which results in the reader choosing a text. The text is an author's views on a subject or, in the case of fictional texts, an author's story. The author has written the text at an earlier time, so the text is the representative of the author. The reader enters the reading situation, bringing their purposes, background knowledge, and linguistic ability. The reading event is situated in a social context, such as reading for school. During reading a transaction occurs: The reader changes as a result of the reading, and the text changes in the reader's mind. The text in the reader's mind is no longer the same text that was published by the author—it is now a construction of meaning within the reader. In other words, the words did not stay on the page containing universally agreed upon meaning. Rather, the meaning is unique to each reader because of each person's background experiences and prior knowledge.

When you think about meaning being unique, you might think about the meaning you would construct from a poem versus how an 8-year-old would interpret the poem. You would most likely have vastly different ideas about the text because of your different life experiences. If we ask readers to explain what they think the text means to them, then we can't deem them as being wrong because

Margin Note 2.6: Transactive Model of Reading

https://www.youtube.com/watch?v=qHBYjM-SZ9k

they're interpreting the text through their lenses (filters), determined by their prior experiences and knowledge—which are different from yours. You can get an additional description of the transactional theory in the video in Margin Note 2.6. Write down any questions about this theory that you might have.

The transactional theory suggests that reading is a transaction between the reader, the text, and the context. This theory was developed in contrast to behaviorist thinking, which viewed the reader and the text as separate entities, with meaning residing in words, and being the same for all readers. Instead, Rosenblatt theorized that reader, texts, and contexts are linked during the reading process. Each of the components of reading contributes to the meaning that readers construct during reading events.

THE READER. Readers come to reading situations with unique knowledge and abilities. When you teach reading, consider the metaphor of a party to understand what each reader brings to any reading situation. Imagine yourself planning a party for several good friends. You invite your friends to the party, and they bring food or drinks, individual personalities, different agendas, and a variety of expectations—based on past experiences. You don't know beforehand how successful the party will be for each of your friends; you bring people together, and they take away different experiences. Teaching reading is like that. You'll be bringing a group of students together to read, but they'll all be very different. What they bring to the reading situation will, in many respects, determine the outcomes of their reading experiences. Some of the ingredients that readers bring to reading events are background knowledge, interests, linguistic abilities, and abilities to apply reading strategies. You'll learn a lot more about students' motivations and interests in Chapter 4 and a whole host of reading strategies in Chapters 5 to 11.

THE TEXT. When students read, they use a text. Any reading material is considered to be a text, and even though early readers also read texts, the texts of older readers are much more demanding—chapter books are longer, core reading stories are more complex, and informational text has fewer illustrations. Some readers enter second or third grade feeling successful, only to find that the required grade-level texts are much more difficult. Texts are also organized into different structures. Narrative texts are organized into what Stein and Glenn (1979) call story grammar. Story grammar is a way to characterize the organization of narrative texts using terms that describe the plot such as initiating event, internal response, attempt, and resolution. Teachers use different terms to describe the organization of narrative text. Many elementary teachers use these terms: setting, characters, the problem events, solving the problem, and conclusion. The kinds of texts that young students will read or have read aloud to them are typically stories, poetry, and informational texts. Each of these kinds of texts are organized differently.

THE CONTEXT. Reading does not occur in isolation, even when you are reading alone. Reading consists of a transaction between readers, texts, and context. The context of reading is where reading occurs, but not just the physical space. Context includes the cultural and social backgrounds each of the readers brings to the reading situation.

Patterns of socialization. Each of us has been socialized into different attitudes about print, reading, and the content of text. Print exists in social contexts, and all of us have been socialized in many ways about print. For example, some children grow up in homes that are filled with books and others do not have many books in their lives. Perhaps when you think of picture books, you get a warm feeling because your grandmother read to you as a child. Perhaps you become anxious when you read math books because you had trouble with math in high school. These examples illus-

trate the social contexts that readers bring to reading. We discuss this issue much more in the coming chapters.

What Happens When You Read?

Think about what happens when you look at print and try to make meaning. First, you see the words, right? As a mature reader, you probably know almost all of the words that you encounter on a page, and you can probably figure out words that you don't know. As you say the words in your mind, you construct meaning of the text. In Chapter 1 you learned that there are three ways to construct meaning: you can understand the literal meaning of the text; you can make inferences about the text; and you can draw evaluative conclusions. Each of these processes is part of meaning making, which is the goal of reading. Before you can make meaning, however, you need to be able to read most of the words on the page.

READING THE WORDS ON THE PAGE. When you look at any text and attempt to read that text, you draw from or search through sources of information that help you read the words. These sources of information have been referred to as cueing systems—systems that you, as an experienced reader, access with such speed, ease, and flexibility that you don't even recognize what you are doing. Goodman (1967) stated that reading is an interaction between thought and language that results from skill in selecting the cues necessary to produce predictions for words. It's important to know about the different cueing systems because effective teachers can diagnose reading difficulties through listening to students read, thinking about what the students are doing as they read (e.g., which cueing systems students are using), and then teach strategies to help students navigate cueing systems they may not be using. The three cueing systems that are most often taught are the visual, meaning, and structure cueing systems.

VISUAL CUEING SYSTEM. The **visual cueing system**, also called the graphophonic cueing system, refers to the written alphabet and the sounds associated with the letters. When you think of visual cueing system, think "the letters on the page." When children are attending to the visual cueing system, they are using their knowledge of letter and sound relationships to make an attempt that "looks right," or matches the printed word on the page. It is what parents and teachers mean when they say, "Sound it out." What they are saying to the child is this, "Look at the letters, think about the sound that each letter or group of letters make, and blend the sounds together to make a word."

We all use visual cues. Here's an example. Have you ever been on an interstate highway trying to see the big green signs way down the road? Say you're looking for the turnoff to Chicago. You squint at the green sign up ahead and can see that the word on the sign starts with *C*. However, as you drive a little closer, you notice that the word is too long to be *Chicago*. As you get even closer, you can see that the word has a chunk of short letters in the center. Soon you are able to read the sign. It says *Cincinnati*. You just used visual clues to keep you from turning in the wrong direction.

It's the same thing with reading. Here is an example of a child attending to the visual cueing system. This sentence is printed on the page: Red Riding Hood came upon a wolf in the forest. Instead she reads, "Red Riding Hood came upon a fox in the forest." Then she says, "Oops, that can't be fox. The word starts with a *w*. It must be w-w-wolf." The child in this example is using visual or graphophonic (letter/sound) cues.

Visual cues are extremely important because graphic symbols represent the message in the text. All readers must attend to the letters. You may notice, however, that early readers who struggle with learning to read typically are overly dependent on trying to sound out new words (Allington & Mc-Gill-Franzen, 2017). Parents and teachers often keep prompting them to sound it out. Such children become intent on saying the sounds of each letter to figure out a new word. While they are spending so much energy figuring out words, they can lose the thread of the meaning. We will help you discover ways to help children who rely too heavily on the visual cueing system by teaching them to also use the meaning and structure cueing systems.

MEANING CUEING SYSTEM. The **meaning cueing system**, also called the semantic cueing system, has to do with making meaning from the text. Semantics refers to the study of the meaning of language. Just as we noted earlier in this section, the primary purpose of reading is the construction of meaning; therefore, one of your primary goals will be to help your students to continually ask themselves, "Does this make sense?" You can observe students stopping themselves and self-monitoring when trying a new word. Suppose a child comes upon the word *house*. They might say the word *horse* because both words start with *h*. However, they might pause at this point and say, "Wait. That didn't make sense because you don't live in a *horse*." If the child does this, they are trying to make sure that their reading makes sense, which is what we always want students to do. Some factors that help readers decide whether something makes sense are their prior knowledge and story illustrations.

Role of prior knowledge. The **prior knowledge** that readers bring to a text is a composite of all experiences in their lives, all beliefs and biases, and all their knowledge about reading and that particular kind of text (Malloy, Marinak, & Gambrell, 2019). Imagine that a friend says to you, "You have to read this book! It is the best romantic novel I have ever read. You'll love it." You may already be thinking of your reaction. Perhaps you don't like romantic novels. However, you take the novel gracefully from your friend so that you don't hurt their feelings. Your initial resistance to this book is a problem at first, but then something happens. You find out that the story takes place in a time in history about which you have a lot of knowledge. This connection starts to lure you into the story, and you begin to enjoy the book, especially the parts that deal with the historical knowledge you have. You are able to picture what is happening and why, make predictions about what will happen next, and you are even able to read difficult words such as names of cities and castles. Because of your prior knowledge, you are better able to construct meaning (Almasi & Hart, 2019).

Some children's prior knowledge does not match the kinds of texts that we present to them. Such a situation makes reading more difficult because they cannot link their prior experiences to what is happening in the story. That's why it is so important for you to tap into students' prior knowledge and experiences to find books that help them make essential meaning connections (Madda, Griffo, Pearson, & Raphael, 2019). Matching books to children's prior knowledge will ease your students' ability to monitor their reading comprehension as they continually ask themselves, "Does this make sense?"

Illustrations. Another component of the meaning cueing system is the text illustrations. You should provide your young students with texts that contain abundant, rich illustrations. You will also teach your students that illustrations can provide readers with valuable clues for figuring out words. To extend the example above about *house* instead of *horse*, a teacher could say, "Look at the picture.

Read up to the hard word and then look at the picture. It will give you a clue about the word." Helping students attend to the pictures and teaching them how to access information from the illustrations can help them connect meaning to their reading.

STRUCTURE CUEING SYSTEM. The **structure cueing system** is sometimes called the syntactic cueing system, because syntax refers to the study of how sentences are formed as well as the rules of grammar of that language. As a teacher, you will be supporting students' understanding of how sentences are put together in English and the rules of grammar in formal writing, such as textbooks, children's books, and other classroom reading materials. Some teachers like to pose the question, "Does it sound right?" to help students evaluate their understanding.

Role of oral language. Much of children's knowledge of English comes from their experiences out of school as users and hearers of language. At times, all of us speak in ways that are not conventional English—in other words, in ways that are not "book talk." For example, around your friends you might say things like, "She don't (rather than *she doesn't*) know him." However, in formal usage, chances are the written sentence would read, "She doesn't know him." Helping readers think about the structure cueing system means helping them ask themselves, "Does it sound right?" In other words, can I say it that way in conventional, Standard English? The structure cueing system is supported by children's natural language, their knowledge of English, and correct grammatical patterns and language structures that we would expect to see in books. We'll discuss the role of oral reading in more detail in Chapter 5.

ORCHESTRATING ALL THREE CUEING SYSTEMS. Readers need to access all three cueing systems—meaning, structure, and visual—when they read. When readers access all cueing systems, we say they are orchestrating the cueing systems. In other words, just like a symphony conductor signals different instruments when they are needed to play the musical pieces, a reader uses different sources of information to read the words on the page.

Each student has unique linguistic abilities. Some students will be able to make accurate predictions about words through the use of contextual clues (the meaning cueing system), whereas other students will rely more heavily on visual clues. Later in this book we'll bring you specific ideas about how to teach students to use the cueing systems to figure out words through a variety of reading and writing strategies. The purpose of figuring out words, however, is for students to be able to construct meaning from text.

We know that understanding the cueing systems takes time and practice. We've provided brief descriptions in this text, but it also helps for you to see what it looks like. The video in Margin Note 2.7 has you try to name the cueing system, and the video in Margin Note 2.8 gives you additional information about how the cueing systems works. Try it out for yourself by pairing up and role playing a first grader and a teacher helping the "student" read using the prompts for the different reading cues.

CONSTRUCTING MEANING. When you read, you not only read the words on the page, but you construct meaning. Going back to the transactional theory of reading that was described earlier in the chapter, remember that readers use their background knowledge and experiences to make meaning from the words. How does that happen?

Margin Note 2.7: Name the Cueing System

https://www.youtube.com/watch?v=pJdzllaq6sE

Margin Note 2.8: Prompting for Purpose: Reading for Meaning, Structure, and Visual Cues

https://www.youtube.com/watch?v=pfM58VnaoD4&t=33s

USE OF STRATEGIES. When you read, you use a variety of strategies to construct meaning (Pressley, 2000). You might be thinking, "I don't think I use strategies when I read." You do, but you may not realize it. Experienced readers use a variety of strategies automatically and have incorporated them into their reading routines. For young students using strategies is relatively new. Most students in the primary grades have had enough experiences with texts to be comfortable applying cueing systems so that when they reach second or third grades, they are able to develop their ability to apply strategies that help them control the processes of reading.

When students read, they use a wide variety of strategies to make meaning from the print. You'll learn more about these strategies in Chapters 5 to 11, but for now, know that when students read, they use strategies before they read, while they read, and after they read. Before reading, readers might preview the text, set purposes for reading, and choose appropriate reading strategies for the demands of the text. While reading, readers might check their understanding, reread difficult sections, make inferences, and get the gist of the selection. After reading, readers might summarize and synthesize what they read and respond in some way. Each reader applies these reading strategies in different ways.

What Do You Believe about the Foundations of Literacy Instruction?

In this chapter you learned about learning and reading theories and about the cueing systems readers use to figure out unknown words. Much of this information may be new to you, but we imagine that you hold some beliefs about each of the theories we presented. For example, when we discussed the bottom-up theory of reading, what did you think? Did you think, "That really didn't make sense about how children learn"? Or did you think, "Wow, that really describes what I believe about learning"? Or maybe you thought, "I need to learn more about how these theories are used before I can decide which one makes sense to me." All of these thoughts are important. As you read this book you are forming a system of beliefs. Even though your beliefs may change as you learn more and experience classroom teaching, we would like you to begin identifying what you believe as you read the chapters in this book.

Your beliefs are the bedrock of who you will be as a teacher. In Chapter 12, we'll have you put all of your beliefs together to articulate your teaching identity. In the meantime, however, we want you to begin identifying and articulating what you believe as you encounter new ideas in each chapter.

Think about the important takeaways from this chapter and write the ones that are personally important to you on the What Do You Believe template that can be found in the Resources for Chapter 2 on the website. Then write a brief paragraph of what you believe about the foundations of literacy learning as a result of what you learned.

Closing Thoughts

At the beginning of the chapter, we introduced you to Ashley, who wanted to learn the theories of reading. Ashley was surprised to learn that the learning theories she studied in freshman psychology applied so directly to education. The reading theories were new to her, and she took careful notes on the different ways reading can be approached so she could develop her own theory of literacy learning. We hope you also have learned from this chapter that "there's nothing so practical as theory" as you begin your journey learning about how to teach reading and writing to PreK–3 students.

Takeaways from Chapter 2

- ▪ You should continue to develop and refine a theory of literacy learning throughout your career.
- ▪ Learning theories that have contributed to understanding learning are connectionism, classical conditioning, behaviorism, and social constructivism.
- ▪ Piaget and Vygotsky contributed to constructivism.
- ▪ Vygotsky's zone of proximal development is especially useful for teaching PreK–3, because it emphasizes teaching skills and strategies students can learn with support.
- ▪ The reading theories that are most common are the bottom-up, top-down, and transactional theories.
- ▪ Reading includes the reader, the text, and the context.
- ▪ You read the words on the page by figuring out new words using the visual, meaning, and structure cueing systems.
- ▪ You construct meaning from print using a variety of strategies.

To Learn More about the Foundations of Literacy Instruction

Websites

Comparison of Different Learning Theories

https://davidwees.com/content/comparison-different-learning-theories/

If you want to see how learning theories are connected and different from each other, check out this visual that compares the major learning theories.

Overview of Learning Theories

https://gsi.berkeley.edu/gsi-guide-contents/learning-theory-research/learning-overview/

Examine the charts of learning theories in these links. These charts have additional theories to the ones presented in this chapter. Look at how the theories interact. You might also do a search for other images that compare learning theories to help you understand how they fit together to help explain learning. You might also consider developing your own chart of theories, especially if you are in a program that requires you to take edTPA.

What Is the Zone of Proximal Development?

https://www.simplypsychology.org/Zone-of-Proximal-Development.html

Read this article to learn more about the zone of proximal development and scaffolding. Scaffolding will be a really important concept to consider as you learn how to teach reading and writing.

Reading Models SlideShare

https://www.slideshare.net/jhayko/reading-model

Look at this short slideshare that describes the three basic reading models. Develop a presentation that describes the three reading models in a succinct way to use as you think about how the reading theories could be used to teach reading and writing.

Videos

Behaviorism: Pavlov, Watson, and Skinner

https://www.youtube.com/watch?v=xvVaTy8mQrg

Look at this video description of behaviorism to solidify your understanding of the basic principles of this theory.

Teaching and Learning Approaches: Behaviorism, Cognitivism, and Social Constructivism

https://www.youtube.com/watch?v=gkzLAz25KPI

Watch this video to see how behaviorism, cognitivism, and social constructivism are explained.

Top-down and Bottom-up Information Processing

https://www.youtube.com/watch?v=Xl3CoDy0wb0

We discussed the top-down and bottom-up theories of reading in this chapter. You might be able to understand the differences better by viewing this video on top-down and bottom-up information processing.

Prompting for Purpose: Reading for Meaning, Structure, and Visual Cues

https://www.youtube.com/watch?v=pfM58VnaoD4

You may already feel like you understand the cueing systems and how readers use them to read words. This video shows a teacher explaining how students read for meaning using the cueing systems. Her explanation might help you deepen your understanding of how readers approach words.

TED Talk: How Language Shapes the Way We Think

https://www.youtube.com/watch?v=RKK7wGAYP6k

This TED Talk strays a bit from the content on theories but is a powerful reminder of the importance of language.

© Herndorff/Shutterstock.com

Assessments help teachers determine what students know and what they need.

What Is the Role of Assessment in Teaching?

REAL-LIFE EXAMPLE

Dylan looked at his watch to figure out how many steps he'd taken so far that day. He was trying to increase his physical fitness by taking 10,000 steps each day. His watch kept track of his steps, his heart rate, and the number of calories he expended. It also told time. Since Dylan had been sitting in class most of the day, he had only walked 5,329 steps. He knew he needed to go for a walk to reach his daily goal. Dylan's watch also compiled his daily exercise into a weekly plan. Each week he used the summary of his week's exercise to plan for the next week. Dylan's goal was to increase the number of hours he exercised each week until he reached 10 hours. After that, Dylan planned on beginning a training program to prepare to run a marathon.

Dylan's classmate, Josie, noticed him looking at his watch frequently, and she asked him, "Do you like that smart watch?" Dylan, responded, "I do because it tells me how I'm doing with taking 10,000 steps each day. I set goals, check in periodically, get reminders when I've not been walking at least 250 steps in an hour, and see how I'm doing from one day to the next. If I meet my goal for a few days, I can then increase my goal to make sure I'm making as much progress with my fitness as I can."

What do you measure in your life? Do you measure steps as Dylan does, count calories, or record how many hours you practice violin? You'll notice that Dylan used information to make decisions. Just as Dylan assessed the number of steps he took through the day and made decisions about how much exercise he needed, teachers use assessment to make instructional decisions.

In this chapter we add to the information you learned in Chapters 1 and 2 by describing the role assessment plays in teaching. We present the teaching/learning/assessment cycle that you'll continually use as you develop lesson plans and teach your students. In addition, this chapter provides you with general information about assessment so you can decide which kind of measure fits each instructional situation.

Teaching/Learning/Assessment Cycle

This teaching/learning/assessment cycle is the process teachers use on a continual basis. The goal of teaching is for students to learn, which requires the teacher to assess students in order to determine what to teach, and then to assess how students are progressing, and so on. Each child in a Pre-K or elementary classroom has different strengths and needs as well as different ways of approaching literacy tasks. Therefore, assessment plays a central role in every instructional decision that teachers make.

You can see our rendition of the teaching/learning/assessment cycle in Figure 3.1. Look at the top of the figure, where it says Plan from standards. In Chapter 1, we described the kinds of reading and writing standards that you'll use to develop lesson plans. This is most likely where you'll begin as you prepare a teaching lesson. Then you'll move clockwise around the cycle to teaching. In most lessons, you'll need to have some kind of assessment so you can determine whether students have learned what you taught. This is the next step in the cycle, to assess. After you assess, you'll analyze the assessment data to adapt your teaching or lessons. Finally, you'll reflect on the lesson and make future decisions about what to teach. Then you begin the cycle again, using the information you learned to combine with standards to plan your next lesson.

Figure 3.1. **Teaching/Learning/Assessment Cycle**

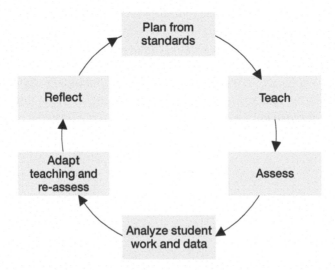

Teachers use this process on a continual basis. Although the teaching/learning/assessment cycle that your mentor teacher uses may be slightly different from the one we presented, teachers are always engaged in planning, teaching, assessing, analyzing, adapting, reflecting, planning, and so on. We are devoting Section II of this book to teaching, but before we get to the details of how to teach, we want you to know how to think about assessment. So right now, let's dig more deeply into what assessment is and how you will use it in all facets of your work as a teacher.

What Is Assessment?

Educational assessment is an intentional attempt to determine a student's performance on different measures and tasks. According to Wolsey, Lenski, and Grisham (2020), assessment tells a story. The story should paint a clear picture of a student's interests, achievement, and abilities. It can tell the story of a student's progress and the effectiveness of the instructional program. Assessment can inform instruction and provide students with the kinds of information they need to set their own instructional goals.

Sometimes teachers and students think that assessment means giving tests and that the primary purpose of assessment is to give grades. Although tests and grades are often associated with assessment, we believe that the primary purpose of assessment is to gather data to inform teaching. This is similar to police or mystery television shows you might watch. Detectives gather clues and then develop "theories" of the case to test out and see what happens. As detectives get more data, they analyze it for patterns, draw conclusions, and determine next steps to take. This is a similar process to what teachers go through as they use assessment to inform their instruction. In short, by using assessment, you will develop knowledge of your students and their literacy development which will guide you in what you need to teach.

If we look at the word *assess*, we see that its Latin root is *assessus* which means "a sitting by," and the past participle form, *assidere,* means "to sit beside." In meaningful assessment, teacher and student frequently sit side-by-side working together so that the teacher can observe closely, understand the student as both a person and a learner, and use that information to guide the student's learning. Assessment connects to social constructivism because learning is a process of actively constructing knowledge with other people in social settings. Students then construct their own understandings using their background knowledge as they interact with other people. Perspectives that place assessment in an inquiry model align with social constructivist theory (Fosnot, 1996). An inquiry approach to assessment acknowledges that each child's knowledge is unique because of differing prior knowledge, focuses on process as well as product, and advocates the ongoing nature of assessment. You can learn more about the purposes of assessment by watching the video in Margin Note 3.1.

Margin Note 3.1: Purposes of Assessment

https://thelearning
exchange.ca/videos/
purposes-of-assessment/

Assessments in Lesson Planning

You've probably already starting writing lesson plans in some of your classes. If so, there will most likely be a place for you to put the English Language Arts (ELA) state standard and your teaching objective (or learning target). Teaching objectives often begin with the term, "The student will be able to . . .". Another way to describe what students will be learning is through a learning target (Stiggins, 2005). A learning target indicates what students should know at the end of the lessons and typically begins with the term, "I will . . .".

Standards and objectives are guides for your lesson activities, and assessment is how you measure the students' learning of the objectives or learning targets. For example, let's say you are developing a lesson on how to teach first grade students what the setting is in a story. You base this lesson on your state standard. Your objective might be, "Students will be able to identify the setting (place and time) of a story they hear read aloud." Your lesson activities will focus on ways students can learn to listen for the time and place of a story. However, this objective and lesson are incomplete. According to Wiggins and McTighe (2005), you should also think about how you will assess your objective. They called this *backward design planning* which means that, as you teach, you also think about how you will know what students have learned. Therefore, a complete objective should look like this: "Students will be able to identify the setting (place and time) of a story they hear read aloud by drawing a *picture of the setting*." Now the objective has an assessment.

Now that you have an assessment, you have one more step. How will you evaluate your assessment data? If you are developing a classroom assessment, you will need scoring criteria. In this case, you may consider a picture that illustrates both the time and place as exemplary, one that only has the place as satisfactory, and one that has neither as needing improvement. If you are planning a lesson using the backward design model, you should think about your assessment and the scoring criteria before you determine your instructional activities. Your instructional activities should be based on the objectives and how they will be assessed. There will be more to think about as you design lesson plans, including "checking in," or formative assessment, and giving feedback to students, but we'll get to that later. For now, we wanted you to think about the role assessment plays in your lesson planning and the part assessment plays in the teaching/learning/assessment cycle.

Types of Assessments

There are basically four types of assessments: diagnostic, formative, summative, and benchmark (sometimes called progress monitoring). We're also going to include self-assessment as another important type of assessment. These categories overlap, and specific assessments can be used in different ways. Let us explain.

Think about going for a 4-hour hike up Dog Mountain in Washington. Before you begin, you might think about your background related to hiking and whether your legs are strong enough to hike for that long or if you should try a shorter hike. That's diagnostic assessment because you are assessing your current state. As you hike, you check in on yourself. How am I doing? Do I need to drink some water? Do I need to eat something? As you check in on yourself, you're using formative assessment because you are checking your progress while engaged in the task. You're assessing different aspects of the hike and making decisions based on the results so that you can achieve your goal. As you hike, you might monitor your progress. Since the hike is rather steep, you know it will take you about 2½ hours to reach the top. You measure your progress when you get to the fork in the trail by looking at the time it took to reach that point. You get to the Puppy Point overlook. How long did it take to reach that point? Now you are assessing using progress monitoring. If you had benchmarks, such as it takes 1½ hours to get to Puppy Point, you try to reach the overlook in that time. Finally, you reach the top. You look at the time. It took you 2 hours and 15 minutes, better than you expected. This is a summative assessment because you do it after the task is completed so you can determine if you met your objective. If the standard is 2½ hours, then you can be considered to have exceeded the standard.

Diagnostic assessment examines the current state of a student's knowledge or ability. Before you teach the alphabet, you might give a diagnostic assessment to students to determine which letters the students know before you teach. **Formative assessment** happens while you are teaching, and it's used to make decisions as you teach (and your students learn). If you are teaching the letter *B*, you can use "kid watching" to observe closely to see how well students are learning during your lesson. **Progress monitoring** is an assessment that uses data to see how well a student performs on a skill by identifying a goal that students are working toward. For example, you might expect your students to know the names of the alphabet by the end of the year. Throughout the year, you may measure what students know about the letters of the alphabet to see the extent they are meeting benchmarks, such as knowing 14 letters by December. **Summative assessment** is the assessment at the end of the lesson or unit. In the example of learning the alphabet, you might want to give students an assessment at the end of the year to see how many letters they know. Summative assessments can include high-stakes tests such as unit tests and standardized tests. Now we're going to re-frame assessments in a way that might be easy for you to remember.

Assessment *for* Learning: Formative Assessments

The primary purpose of **formative assessments** is to identify the learning needs of your students so you can improve your instruction. Black and Wiliam (2009) found that formative assessment can make a big difference in student achievement. Formative assessments are the kinds you use when you "check in" with students, maybe asking for a thumbs-up or thumbs-down on whether they understand something. You are assessing whether students are learning what you are teaching.

As you use formative assessments, you might adapt your teaching as a result. Let's say that you're teaching the letter *d* and its sound. You write *d* on the board and ask students to say the sound. As students respond, you pay attention to whether students are able to pronounce *d* correctly. You write the words *dog, dot,* and *duck* on the board and ask students to read each one aloud with you. You then ask the students to brainstorm other words that begin with *d*. You write them down and ask the students to give a thumbs-up if the word begins with *d*. You then guide the students to identify the letter that makes the *d* sound in each word, and you underline or circle that letter to draw the students' attention to how we spell the /d/ sound. As you are teaching this lesson, you are observing carefully and making notes about student performance and understanding so you know if you can continue, if you need to slow the lesson down or speed it up, or if you need to work individually or in

a very small group with any students who are struggling with the concept of the letter *d*. By using formative assessment, you are able to adjust your teaching to meet the needs of your students. Some teacher teams even develop common formative assessments to guide their instruction (Ainsworth, 2015). By having some common "look fors" (or specific literacy behaviors that teachers expect students to develop), teachers at a certain grade level can ensure that they have the same understanding of literacy development and expectations so they can discuss how their students are progressing and determine appropriate instructional steps to enhance student understanding.

© Monkey Business Images/Shutterstock.com

Providing specific feedback to students helps them grow as readers and writers.

PROVIDING FEEDBACK. According to Hattie and Timperley (2007), the feedback you give on formative assessment can go a long way to improving student achievement. By providing students with feedback, you are helping them understand what they have learned and what they still need to learn. Hattie and Timperley (2007) offer three questions that should be addressed by the feedback you provide to your students to guide their learning. These questions are from the learner's perspective and ask:

- How am I going? (defines the goal the student is working toward)
- Where am I going? (what the student is currently doing)
- What next? (guidance for the student about the next step toward attaining their goal)

Hattie and Timperley also caution against providing general feedback such as "good work" or "nice job" because that type of feedback does not provide specific information for the student to enhance their learning. For example, a student may not know why the teacher considered something as "good work," so they may focus on the wrong aspect of their learning process or consider that their learning is done and no more work is needed. A more effective way to approach feedback in that situation is to say something like, "You are working hard to monitor your reading by asking if it makes sense." (Feedback on what the goal is and how the student is engaged with the goal.) Or, "You are using re-reading to make sense of what you are reading." (Feedback on what the student is currently doing to put the focus on a strategy that will help them move toward the learning goal.) And, "When you read this book to yourself, be sure to focus on your understanding and use your fix up strategies to help you." (Feedback on what the student should work on next as they work toward attaining the goal of monitoring their reading.) Check out the video in Margin Note 3.2 to see a short video about this approach to providing effective feedback to support student learning.

Margin Note 3.2: Providing Feedback to Students: The Power of Feedback

https://www.youtube.com/watch?v=S770g-LULFY

Assessment *of* Learning: Summative Assessments

When you are finished teaching a lesson or unit, you might give students a **summative** assessment. This is the kind of assessment that measures student learning at the end of a unit or lesson by comparing it to an ELA standard or benchmark. In other words, you are evaluating whether students have met the standard or benchmark or if they need additional instruction. So, to recap, you teach a lesson, checking in with formative assessment during the lesson, and at the end you give an assessment to see how well students have learned. The primary purpose of a summative assessment is to determine a student's achievement. Summative assessments are generally given at the end of a lesson or unit. The results can help you decide what to teach next, to understand your students' achievement, and to consider grouping or re-teaching for students who have not reached the standard or benchmark. A summative assessment can be as simple as having students answer questions about the content of the lesson or it might be a quiz, project, or presentation at the end of a unit. The bottom line is that summative assessments happen at the conclusion of the lesson or unit, and the purpose is to evaluate what students learned from the lesson or unit. Sometimes teachers must assign grades, prepare progress reports, or fill out report cards, and summative assessments can be very useful in those situations.

Benchmark Assessments

If you were to put formative assessments on one end of a continuum and summative assessments on the opposite end, **benchmark** assessments would go somewhere between the two. As you recall from earlier in this section, formative assessments (i.e., assessments *for* learning) are embedded in ongoing classroom instruction and inform teaching and learning goals in real time. Summative assessments (i.e., assessments *of* learning) provide indication of how students are performing in comparison to specific ELA standards or performance targets. Benchmark assessments are administered on a set schedule—say, once a month or every 6 weeks and the assessment results can be aggregated, or combined, at the classroom, grade, school, or district level to inform decision makers, parents, and teachers how well students are learning and to determine ways to accelerate progress toward standards or annual goals. Sometimes the terms *interim assessment* and *progress monitoring* are used interchangeably with benchmark assessment.

Benchmark assessments have four interrelated but distinct purposes: communicating expectations for learning, planning curriculum and instruction, monitoring and evaluating instructional effectiveness, and predicting future performance (Herman, Osmundson, & Dietel, 2010). Some examples of literacy assessments that are used to monitor progress are oral reading fluency assessments such as the Dynamic Indicators of Basic Early Literacy Skills (DIBELS), AIMSWeb, 1-minute oral reading fluency probes, running records, and informal reading inventories. Although these types of benchmark assessments are frequently used, it's important to keep the results in perspective and not overgeneralize them. For example, DIBELS, AIMSWeb, and 1-minute oral reading fluency probes provide useful information about oral reading fluency, specifically accuracy and rate, but they do not provide a complete picture of all aspects of a student's reading. Therefore, it's important to understand the purpose of benchmark assessments and to use the results accordingly.

Assessment *as* Learning: Self-assessment

Students can assess themselves through **self-assessment**. An example that you're probably familiar with would be for students to evaluate their own writing with a checklist. By having children engage in self-evaluation, they can understand the goals they are working toward, consider their own learning performance and progress, and take ownership for their own learning. **Self-assessment** is also sometimes called self-evaluation or self-reflection, and although the names are different, the bottom line is the same: having students assess themselves promotes metacognition (a student's ability to think about their own thinking and thinking processes), which is the center of effective and independent reading (Veenman, 2016). Check out Margin Note 3.3 for an example of how a teacher and student work together to promote the student's self-assessment.

Margin Note 3.3:
Precision Teaching:
Student Self-assessment

https://www.youtube.com/
watch?v=4wTrpErRiKA

---

*C*onnection to the Field: Self-Assessment

Talk to your mentor teacher to see if they use self-assessment with their students. If so, ask if you can observe how self-assessment is used in the classroom. If not, ask your mentor teacher if you can work together to create a simple self-assessment to implement with the students in your classroom.

Assessment Tools

Throughout this book, we provide you with a variety of assessments as they apply to each of the topics we present. For example, in Chapter 8 about fluency, we present the One-minute Fluency Probe in Assessment Strategy 8.2. This strategy can be used as either a formative or summative assessment. In other words, it depends on why you are using the assessment. If you used this assessment to get a sense of your students' fluency so you can decide how to form instructional groups and which aspects of fluency to target in instruction, you would be using it as a formative assessment. On the other hand, if you used this assessment after instruction to determine your students' oral reading fluency so that you can make judgments about which students meet expectations and which ones will need further instruction, that would be summative assessment. Do you remember how to keep those terms straight—formative assessment and summative assessment? Formative assessment is assessment *for* learning and summative assessment is assessment *of* learning.

You have experienced many kinds of assessments during your life as a student. Here is a list of possible assessment tools that you may have experienced and that you may be using as a teacher candidate.

- *Rubrics:* A set of criteria for rating students with descriptors that tell the teacher what characteristics to look for in a student's performance or work.
- *Checklists:* Lists of information, data, attributes, or elements that should be present.
- *Observation:* Observing students closely and intentionally can be used in a variety of ways, including "kid watching" (Goodman, 1985).
- *Anecdotal records:* Brief written notes based on observations.
- *Continua:* Visual representations of progression of achievement.
- *Anchor papers or exemplars:* Samples of student work that serve as concrete standards against which other samples are evaluated.

There are commercial assessments that your school may provide through textbooks and other curricular materials, and many literacy assessments are available for free on the internet. But because of the specific needs of your classroom, you will likely need to adapt or create some of your own assessments. To help you in that process, we have provided templates in the Resources for Chapter 3 on the website for creating an assessment checklist and taking anecdotal records. In the To Learn More about Assessment section at the end of this chapter, we have also provided several useful resources to help you locate and develop literacy assessments and scoring criteria for use in your classroom.

Connection to the Field: Types and Purposes of Assessments

Ask your mentor teacher to show you some of the assessments they use in their classroom and school. Discuss the purpose for each assessment and how your mentor teacher uses the results.

The various tools we use for assessment can be used for different purposes. You might have noticed in your education courses that rubrics are currently used as an assessment in many situations. Wilson (2017) reminds us that rubrics are valuable assessment tools for summative assessment, but teachers need to use other more descriptive types of assessments as well.

We often categorize assessment tools based on what we want to do. For example, we might want to observe the process of literacy; we might want to observe the product of literacy; or we might want to observe students working in context; or we might want to assess students outside of the context of instruction. Figure 3.2 shows how some assessment tools can be categorized by the way they are used. Although there is no magic formula for the best approach to assessment, we think it's important to use multiple assessments over time to get a more accurate picture of students' learning, to evaluate students' learning processes and products, and to use more contextualized than decontextualized assessments.

Figure 3.2. **Assessment Options for Literacy**

Observation of Learning Process	Observation of Learning Product
Running records	Response journals
Miscue analysis	Writing samples
Retelling	Student self-evaluations
Informal observations	Portfolios
Anecdotal records	Reading logs
Conversations	Assignments
Conferences	
Discussions	
Listening to readers	
Contextualized Measures	**Decontextualized Measures**
Interest surveys	Standardized achievement tests
Attitudes about reading surveys	School, district, and state tests
Checklists	Norm- and criterion-referenced tests
Teacher-made tests	Spelling tests
Book tests	Worksheets
Dictations	

Scoring Criteria

Although you may use some commercially available assessments, you will likely need to develop assessments for use in your classroom. Many teachers do this as grade level teams so that they are all looking for the same things in their students' literacy development and performance. Many of the assessments you will want and need to use in your classroom focus on performance—such as reading orally, writing in a specific genre, or demonstrating comprehension through discussion or writing. What each of these examples has in common is that students are performing a specific literacy task. In order to develop appropriate **scoring criteria** for a literacy performance task, you need to analyze the task carefully to determine exactly what students must do to perform the task. You will also need to consider if what you are assessing is truly important to understand the students' literacy performance. A good way to do this is to align the task with your state learning standards or district learning outcomes. Oftentimes, you will want to expand the scoring criteria to allow you to determine not only if a student meets expectations, but also if a student exceeds expectations or does not meet expectations. A rubric or scoring guide will allow you to do this and will help you ensure that you are being consistent in how you are evaluating student performance on the task.

CREATING RUBRICS. Let's consider how to create a **rubric** first. Popham (1997) provides three key criteria for a good rubric: it must provide the criteria used to evaluate student performance, it must specify the differential quality of student performance, and it must help you consistently and accurately score student performance. Let's walk through an example of how a first-grade teacher created a rubric to assess students' ability to retell narrative stories. Monique, a first grade teacher, has been teaching her students about stories—setting, characters, and plot—and how to retell them. She has been writing her observations down as anecdotal records, but she realized that she wanted to have a plan for exactly what to look for in her students' retellings so that she can document their performance in comparison to the expectations from her district's standard (which aligns with the state standards). For first grade, the standard states that students are expected to "Retell stories, including key details, and demonstrate understanding of the central message or lesson." Monique used this standard as the starting place for her rubric. She decided to break apart the pieces of the standard because she realized that students may be able to perform some parts of the retelling and not others and having that information would be very helpful to her for evaluation as well as for planning for instruction. You might wonder, how can that be? Is Monique creating a rubric that she will use for both formative and summative assessment? Yes, she is! She plans to use it as a formative assessment to help her plan for future instruction. She also will use it as a summative assessment at a certain point in time—say, after 2 weeks of instruction and practice on retelling—so that she can determine which students have met the standard and which ones have not yet met it. She can use this assessment data to help her with progress reports or even assigning grades on report cards, if that is done in her school.

Monique decided to break the learning target into two components: key details and central message or lesson. She decided to use the framework that she and her teaching teammates have used in the past: does not meet the standard, approaching the standard, meets the standard, and exceeds the standard. She realized that those levels were a good starting place, but she knew that she would need to provide specific criteria for each level of performance so she knows exactly what she is looking for and she can use the rubric consistently. Because this process can be a bit complicated, Monique decided to work with the other first-grade teachers in her school, Adam, Hilda, and Beth, to develop the criteria. They liked the idea of using the rubric with their own students, so they worked as a team to develop the rubric in Figure 3.3.

Figure 3.3. Rubric for Retelling Narrative Stories

The student can . . .	Does not meet the standard	Approaching the standard	Meets the standard	Exceeds the standard
Retell key details.	Does not include key details.	Includes some key details.	Includes all key details.	Includes and describes all key details.
Retell the central message or lesson.	Is not able to identify the central message or lesson.	Provides a general statement about the central message or lesson.	Retells the central message or lesson.	Describes the central message or lesson and connects it directly to the story.

You will also need to consider and develop scoring criteria for other types of assessments such as checklists, observations, or continua. Although each of those assessment tools has its own unique features, your approach to developing scoring criteria can be the same. You will always want to start with the standard or learning outcome. You will then want to put your expectations in terms of what the student will do so you know exactly what you are looking for in student performance. Next, you will need to identify levels of performance to determine how students are (or are not) progressing toward the standard. In the To Learn More about Assessment section at the end of the chapter, you will find several useful resources to help you develop scoring criteria for the teacher-made assessments you develop for your classroom.

ASSESSING FOR READING LEVELS. Another kind of scoring criterion is looking at a book's reading level. Have you even looked at the back of a book, seen something like Level 1.5 and wondered what that meant? We'll discuss the idea of a book's reading levels more later in the book, but, for now, we want you to think about using reading levels as scoring criteria.

Let's say you're placed in a first grade classroom listening to Jenna try to read a book that is considered to be for first grade readers. As you listen to Jenna, you notice that she is struggling to read the words and that she can't answer any questions about the book. To find out what book level Jenna could read successfully, you might have Jenna read a somewhat easier book orally and answer questions or retell what she just read. You may have heard your mentor teacher talk about running records (because teachers can do them "on the run") or doing an informal reading inventory to learn about students' ability to read fluently (i.e., accurately, at an appropriate rate, and with expression) and to comprehend

© Monkey Business Images/Shutterstock.com

Listening to students read helps teachers consider what each student needs.

what they read by answering questions or doing a retelling. This type of performance assessment focuses on students orally reading a passage—usually 100 words—while you record any **miscues** (mistakes) the student makes as well as other observations of reading performance such as pauses, repetitions, and whether they read with expression or not. You can also determine the student's reading rate by timing how long it takes the student to read the passage so you can calculate the words per minute (wpm). Here is the formula for determining wpm: divide the number of words read by the number of seconds. Then you multiply your answer by 60 to get your final words per minute (wpm).

Running records and informal reading inventories can provide you with rich information such as the types of miscues (mistakes) students make as well as the types of questions they can answer and those they can't. These assessments also provide an estimate of your students' reading levels that can help you match students with appropriate books for instruction and evaluate their reading performance against grade-level expectations.

The three reading levels you can determine with running records and informal reading inventories are independent, instructional, and frustration (Betts, 1946). The **independent level** means that the text is easy for the student because they have excellent comprehension, they have excellent word recognition, they have few or no repetitions, and they read very smoothly and easily. Texts at the independent level are perfect for students to read and enjoy on their own. The **instructional level** means that the text is appropriate for instruction such as guided reading. At the instructional level, students demonstrate good comprehension, have good word recognition, and read relatively smoothly and easily. At the **frustration level**, the text is too hard for the student to read—even with teacher support. When students read frustration level texts, they have weak comprehension and poor word recognition, they read slowly, and they sound labored when reading. Determining your students' independent, instructional, and frustration reading levels will help you select appropriate texts for instruction, plan instruction, and determine if your students are on track with their reading performance or if they need additional or more explicit instruction to help them make maximum progress in their reading development. In a typical classroom, you will have students at many different reading levels because every child develops at their own pace. Figure 3.4 provides a summary of the independent, instructional, and frustration reading levels. You will note that there are several gray areas; these represent borderline results that require your professional judgment to interpret. A general rule of thumb you can use for these gray areas is to place more emphasis on the comprehension score because the purpose of reading is to construct meaning.

Figure 3.4. Reading Levels

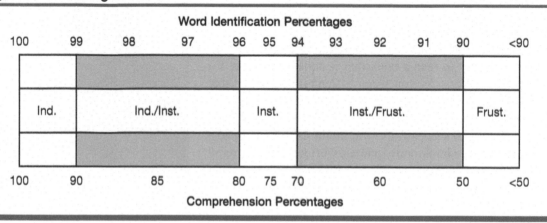

Source: Johns, Elish-Piper, & Johns (2017, p. 55).

Audiences for Assessment

As we've been describing assessments, we've mostly been writing about the kinds of information you can gather as a teacher that tells the story of their students' achievement. There are, however, other **audiences** for literacy assessment (Afflerbach, 2018) that you will need to consider as a teacher.

Remember when you were in elementary school? Who else, other than the teacher, wanted information about your achievement? Yes, your parents or guardians. Your parents wanted to know how well you were doing in school and that information was provided to them through grades and achievement scores. In the same respect, policy makers also want to know the results of assessment. They want to know how the students in a school are doing compared to other schools. See Figure 3.5 for the audiences and purposes for assessment.

Figure 3.5. Audiences and Purposes for Assessment

Assessment Audience	Assessment Purpose
Students	To guide learning To set goals To monitor progress To build ownership of learning
Teachers	To understand student learning To inform instruction To identify student strengths and areas for growth To evaluate student performance
Parents	To understand children's achievement To make connections between school and home
School Administrators	To determine the effectiveness of instruction and programs To address accountability To determine needs for teacher professional development
Policy Makers and Community Members	To demonstrate accountability To compare school or district performance

Adapted from: Afflerbach, P. (2018). *Understanding and using reading assessment K–12* (3rd ed.). Alexandria, VA: ASCD/International Literacy Association.

Tests Beyond the Classroom

We've focused mainly on classroom assessments in this chapter—formative and summative assessments that have the teacher as the primary audience. As noted in Figure 3.5, there are other important audiences for assessment: administrators and policy makers. Let's think about how public school systems are structured in the United States. Schools are governed by state law, although there are a few federal regulations that public schools must follow. Within states, schools are governed by local control. Each school district has a Board of Education that makes decisions about school policy and curriculum. The members of state governing bodies and school boards need information about how well students are learning in schools so that they can set policy that works for teachers and students.

When you consider the kinds of information that is most useful for policy makers, it won't be your class exit cards or thumbs-up/thumbs-down formative assessments. Policy makers need different kinds of information to evaluate how well students are learning in schools. Classroom assessments don't fill the bill for this purpose and audience. That's why states give norm-referenced and criterion-referenced tests, which fall under the umbrella of the term **standardized tests**.

STANDARDIZED TESTS. Do you cringe when you hear the words *standardized tests*? Standardized tests are given for a variety of purposes in schools and outside schools. For example, driving tests are standardized. Standardized tests are any form of a test that requires all test takers to answer the same questions in the same way and are administered and scored in a consistent manner. As you can imagine, classroom tests are not standardized. You don't read a script of directions for students to follow. All standardized tests, however, have a standardized procedure.

The results of standardized tests can be compared across groups of students, even in different schools, districts, and states. The scores are typically combined to provide an overall picture of how students are performing so that policy makers and administrators can evaluate programs. Standardized tests are subject to extensive reliability and validity testing.

RELIABILITY. **Reliability** in assessment has to do with consistency of evaluation of one assessment score to another. Determining test reliability is not an exact science. Reliability can only be estimated. Think of the root word, "reliable" to help you understand reliability in assessment. If an assessment has good reliability you can assume that over multiple times of giving the assessment you will get the same (or very similar) results. Afflerbach (2018) describes an assessment as reliable when it is considered accurate and consistent.

VALIDITY. Assessment **validity** is concerned with how well the test actually measures what it is supposed to measure. Is the assessment designed to determine the extent of a student's skills in spelling, grammatical usage, vocabulary, organization of ideas, content knowledge, or other skill areas? Do the assessment activities or prompts effectively elicit the kinds of vocabulary, grammatical points, content concepts, etc. that the teacher wants to assess? Does the measurement of the students'

Margin Note 3.4:
Not on the Test

https://www.youtube.
com/watch?v=8d
AujuqCo7s

writing skills on one assessment correlate with assessments of those skills on other assessment instruments?

Standardized tests should not be used to make instructional decisions for individual students. Classroom assessments are better measures to do this. Standardized tests should also not be the only measure of student growth. Some students do not score well on standardized tests because of test anxiety or because the tests are timed. Standardized tests have their place to tell the story of groups of students' literacy growth or the overall performance of a school or grade level, but they also have limitations. You can listen to a song about the abuses of standardized tests in Margin Note 3.4. As you watch this satirical video, jot down several concerns about standardized testing to discuss with your classmates and mentor teacher.

NORM-REFERENCED AND CRITERION-REFERENCED TESTS. As we noted earlier, there are two kinds of standardized tests: norm-referenced and criterion-referenced. You may be in a classroom where students are taking these tests and, as a teacher, you'll administer these kinds of tests. Remember, these tests are primarily for policy makers rather than for you to use to make instructional decisions.

NORM-REFERENCED TESTS. **Norm-referenced** tests are used to compare and rank students against a norming sample. A norming sample is a large group of students who have taken the test so that test makers can calculate statistics to show the range of scores expected on the test. Those scores are then used as a point of comparison for other students who take the test. Normative scoring is based on a bell curve, which is shaped just like the outline of a bell. In the bell curve, only a small percentage of students can perform at the top level or at the bottom level. Most students score somewhere in the middle. Check out Figure 3.6 to see what the bell curve looks like. Norm-referenced tests measure a large body of knowledge, not what has been taught. Test items vary in difficulty so that the test can discriminate between test takers. That means that it won't be possible for all of your students to score at high levels. Instead, they will be spread out across the bell curve in a manner very similar to the distribution of scores shown in Figure 3.6.

Figure 3.6. Bell Curve

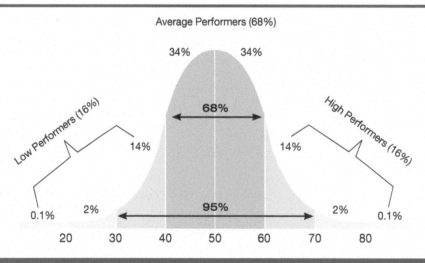

CRITERION-REFERENCED TESTS. **Criterion-referenced** tests determine whether students have achieved a specific set of skills. The score is not based on the bell curve but on a percentage of correct responses. Criterion-referenced tests measure what students have learned based on the curriculum and standards. Test items are similar in difficulty and measure what has been taught in the classroom. There is typically a preset benchmark to determine how many students have met the learning target. You can learn more about the differences between norm-referenced and criterion-referenced tests by watching the video in Margin Note 3.5.

State tests. Most state reading tests are criterion-referenced tests because they use standards as the criteria to develop the test. If you are teaching in a third-grade classroom, you'll find that teachers are often very concerned about how their students will score on the state test. Some schools create motivational music videos for their students before testing week. Look at Margin Note 3.6 for an example. Maybe your class could make a music video!

Margin Note 3.5: Criterion- vs. Norm-Referenced Assessment: Examples and Evaluation

https://www.youtube.com/watch?v=O5hJNpO0JPE

Margin Note 3.6: Test Me, Baby Video

https://www.youtube.com/watch?v=8gvVMW6NN38

Privacy and Confidentiality

A big part of being a teacher is keeping things you learn about students confidential. When it comes to assessment, there is federal legislation that specifically details what you can and cannot share. You might have heard about this; it's called **FERPA** (Family Educational Rights and Privacy Act, 1974). This legislation is similar to the one you know in the medical field where doctors can't tell anyone else about your health issues (i.e., Health Insurance Portability and Accountability Act, or HIPPA). FERPA is designed to protect the privacy of students' personally identifiable information and applies to all educational institutions that receive federal funding. The law details what information can be shared without violating confidentiality and what information can only be shared with the students and parents.

The purpose of FERPA is to protect the privacy of students and to safeguard the confidentiality of their educational records. That means that you must safeguard all of your students' assessment results and cannot share them with anyone, except your mentor teacher, school principal, other teachers such as a special education teacher or reading specialist who work with the students, and the students' parents. Here are some things that might surprise you. You cannot ask another student to pass out graded papers because then any student's scores are not confidential. The students handing out the papers would see the grades. You also cannot stack graded papers in a box for students to collect because they could see someone else's grades. To keep graded papers confidential, many teachers put graded papers in large envelopes with student's names on them. When they do that, teachers can have students pass out the envelopes or put them in a basket for students to collect.

You might be wondering whether you can have students grade each other's papers or use peer evaluation when students write. The law says that teachers can have students evaluate each other's work while they are learning, but once a paper is graded by the teacher, the paper can't be shared with anyone other than the student or parent.

There are a few exceptions to this privacy rule. Of course, you can share student results with your mentor teacher, and you can share the results with other teachers if those teachers have a legitimate reason to know. For example, sometimes teachers work across classrooms to group students

Margin Note 3.7: FERPA "Do's and Don'ts" Guide for Teachers

https://www.fordham.edu/download/downloads/id/1850/09_-_dos_and_donts_for_teachers.pdf

for instruction in reading or other areas of the curriculum. In that situation, you can share the students' assessment results with both your mentor teacher and the other teachers who work with your students. However, you can't tell the teachers at lunch the results of an assessment. Not all of those teachers have a legitimate interest in knowing the assessment information.

As you think about student assessment information, the best thing to do is to ask yourself whether you're revealing private information to someone who does not need it to benefit the student. If you are unsure, ask your mentor or instructor. You can find more detailed information about FERPA in Margin Note 3.7.

Assessing from an Equity Perspective

You learned in Chapters 1 and 2 about the importance of teaching for individual differences and viewing each student from a strengths or assets perspective. As a student teacher, you'll most likely be using mostly formative assessments with some teacher-designed summative assessments. However, as you think about having your own classroom, you'll also need to think about what assessment scores mean for different students.

THE ACHIEVEMENT GAP VS. AN OPPORTUNITY GAP. You might have heard about the achievement gap. Beginning with No Child Left Behind Act (2002), states had to report disaggregated data for their state tests. That means that states had to compare the scores using race/ethnicity categories which were White, Black, Hispanic, Asian/Pacific Islander, American Indian/Alaskan Native, and other or unclassified. Some states now also have a category for multiracial. Scores for each group were compared and the data showed higher achievement for White students than students of the other races/ethnicities. Since the data were reported by those categories, the gap has remained largely the same. This gap became known as the **achievement gap**.

The achievement gap has been defined as the discrepancy in educational outcomes between various student groups. According to Gay (2010), "achievement gaps in the quality of experiences and outcomes at all levels of U.S. public education is relentless and extensive" (p. xvii). The achievement gap was brought to the public's attention when No Child Left Behind legislation required states to disaggregate data based on subgroups. Once the achievement gap became publicized, scholars began to expand the conversation by asking for reasons for the differences in test scores (Ladson-Billings, 2006, 2014). Looking at achievement solely through the lens of test scores emphasized a symptom of a problem in education. Trying to identify the unequal opportunities that result in the achievement gap highlights the complex causes for the test scores (Milner, 2015; Welner & Carter, 2013) so some people began using the concept of **opportunity gap** rather than *achievement gap*.

According to Welner and Carter (2013), "the 'opportunity gap' frame, in contrast, shifts our attention from outcomes to inputs—to the deficiencies in the foundational components of societies, schools, and communities that produce significant differences in education—and ultimately socioeconomic—outcomes" (p. 3). In other words, some students have had different opportunities to learn. It's not so much that the achievement is different as that opportunities are different. Milner (2015) suggests that opportunity gaps can be present because teachers often bring the dominant culture's Eurocentric notions and ideologies to the classroom which can be in contrast with students' ways of knowing. He suggests that teachers need to take into account students' cultural backgrounds and assets as they teach to provide every student with equitable opportunities to learn. See

Chapter 4 for a more in-depth discussion of how to use students' cultural backgrounds and assets as a foundation for your teaching.

ASSESSMENT BIAS. I'm sure you won't be surprised to learn that assessments can be biased toward some groups and against others. To get a sense of what it's like to take a test that has been developed by a different culture, take the Original Australian Test of Intelligence provided in Margin Note 3.8. Check your scores; how did you do? You'll see what's it like to take a test outside what you instinctively know so you can gain insights into cultural bias in testing.

Margin Note 3.8: The Original Australian Test of Intelligence

https://studylib.net/doc/8810190/the-original-australian-test-of-intelligence

Assessment bias refers to how valid a test is for different groups of students based on their age, culture, race, and gender. If a test is biased, that means that different groups of students score above or below the other groups as a general rule. Even though test makers try to develop test items that are common to all students, they invariably ask questions for which some students have little background knowledge. For example, a state writing test asked third grade students to compare urban with rural life. That topic seems like it would be broad enough for all students in the state, right? Well, for students who lived in low-income suburbia, that topic was impossible. These students knew strip malls and crowded neighborhoods, but they had never been to an urban center. Additionally, the students had little or no knowledge of rural life. They may have seen a television show set in a farm or a ranch, but that didn't give them enough knowledge to write about rural living. This writing topic was biased against some students.

As a student teacher and even a new teacher, you won't have the influence over test makers to avoid testing bias. As you look at test scores, however, you should consider whether your students had cultural knowledge needed for the test and whether their scores were valid.

AVOIDING A DEFICIT PERSPECTIVE. Once you begin assigning scores to students, you'll find differences. It's important not to view students from a **deficit perspective**, where you are saying they "lack" something. Instead, think about what you learned in Chapter 1 about emergent literacy. Every student's literacy is emerging and that happens at different rates. Some students have lots of experiences with the kinds of literacies expected in schools. Remember Moll's funds of knowledge? Well, some students will have other kinds of experiences than those that are most valued in U.S. schools. It's critical that you acknowledge that students are learning and that their progress needs to be celebrated.

I'm sure you can understand what this would be like for students to always be thought of as lacking or deficient. Let us give you an example. Amber decided to learn the salsa so she could dance with her boyfriend, Carlos, at a Cinco de Mayo party. She recruited her roommate, Juanita, to go to a salsa lesson with her. Juanita was from a Mexican-American family who had danced salsa every Saturday evening. During the salsa lessons, Amber learned much more slowly than Juanita, who progressed to complex movements rapidly. Amber was learning at a different rate. It took Amber longer to become a competent salsa dancer than Juanita.

Once you impose a "standard," into the mix, however, looking at how long it takes each woman to progress from Salsa I to Salsa II, you might begin to look at things differently. You might begin to feel that Amber came to learning with deficits. This thinking is the conundrum of education. We have grade level standards, but we also believe that literacy develops individually. You'll have to hold both ideas in your mind as you teach: 1) every student progresses at their own rate; and 2) we teach toward standards that we want all students to reach. One of the consequences of a deficit perspective is that teachers do not look for instructional ideas that could benefit all students, and they ignore the cultural wealth that students bring with them to school (Yosso, 2005). In Chapter 14, we discuss how you can develop a literacy program that addresses both ideas and helps you avoid taking on a deficit perspective.

What Do You Believe about Assessment?

You've learned about the teaching/learning/assessment cycle and an overview of the kinds, tools, and audiences for assessment in this chapter. Think about the important takeaways from this chapter and write the ones that are personally important to you on the What Do You Believe template that can be found in the Resources for Chapter 3 on the website. Then write what you believe about teaching reading and writing to PreK–3 students as a result of what you learned.

Closing Thoughts

Remember Dylan from the beginning of the chapter? He was using his fitness tracker as a type of assessment to inform him about whether he was getting enough steps. He was also using assessment to guide him toward getting more exercise and determining when he would be ready to start training to run a marathon. His fitness tracker, as an assessment, became a part of his daily activities just like assessment is part of the daily operations of all classrooms.

You might have started this chapter thinking that assessment was just grading assignments or filling out report cards. We hope that you now understand that assessment is central to all teaching and learning and as a teacher you will be using assessment each and every day.

Takeaways from Chapter 3

- The teaching/learning/assessment cycle is an important foundation for education.
- There are five main types of assessment.
  - Diagnostic assessment determines the current state of a student's knowledge or ability.
  - Formative assessment or assessment *for* learning is embedded in your teaching and allows you to determine if students are learning what you are teaching.
  - Summative assessment or assessment *of* learning is done after instruction is completed and determines if students have met the objective for the lesson or unit.
  - Benchmark assessments are given at a specific time to determine student progress over time or to compare a student's performance to a preset benchmark or standard.
  - Self-assessment is when students analyze their own performance in order to engage them in their own learning process.
- Assessments have different purposes, and it's important to match them to meet your purpose.
- It's important to take an equity perspective when assessing students and interpreting assessment results.

To Learn More about Assessment

Resources for Your Professional Library

Bohart, H., & Procopio, R. (2018). *Spotlight on young children: Observation and assessment.* Washington, DC: NAEYC.

https://www.naeyc.org/resources/pubs/books/spotlight-observation-assessment

In this book, you will find practical tools and strategies to help you learn how to observe young children's learning and to implement useful assessments into your classroom. Skim through this book to find assessment ideas to use in your lesson plans. Since observation is a foundation to effective assessment, this book will be a helpful tool for you to practice and hone your observational skills for assessment purposes.

Gillanders, C., & Procopio, R. (2019). *Spotlight on young children: Equity and diversity.* Washington, DC: NAEYC.

https://www.naeyc.org/resources/pubs/books/spotlight-equity-diversity

Equity and diversity are essential elements of teaching, learning, and literacy. Read this book to help you understand how to focus your teaching on equity and how you can embrace diversity in your teaching and assessment processes.

Helman, L., Ittner, A. C., & McMaster, K. L. (2020). *Assessing language and literacy with bilingual students.* New York, NY: Guilford Press.

https://www.guilford.com/books/Assessing-Language-and-Literacy-with-Bilingual-Students/Helman-Ittner-McMaster/9781462540884

This book provides practical assessment tools for screening and monitoring English learners' reading and writing skills. Read this book to also gain information about establishing school supports for families and engaging with the community.

Popham, W. J. (2018). *Assessment literacy for educators in a hurry.* Alexandria, VA: ASCD.

http://www.ascd.org/Publications/Books/Overview/Assessment-Literacy-for-Educators-in-a-Hurry.aspx

The author provides clear, accessible information about six key aspects of assessment: validity, reliability, fairness, score reporting, formative assessment, and affective assessment. Read this book to deepen your knowledge about the assessment concepts we presented in this chapter. You can also find ideas to use in your lesson planning.

Assessment Resources

Burke, K. (2010). *Balanced assessment: From formative to summative.* Bloomington, IN: Solution Tree Press.

https://www.solutiontree.com/balanced-assessment.html

This practical text provides useful tools, templates, and step-by-step instructions to help you create your own rubrics, checklists, and scoring guides. It also provides access to a website with tools to help you build your own rubrics and checklists online. Skim through this book to find ideas to assess students and to develop scoring criteria.

Fisher, D., & Frey, N. (2014). *Checking for understanding: Formative assessment techniques for your classroom* (2nd ed.). Alexandria, VA: ASCD.

http://www.ascd.org/Publications/Books/Overview/Checking-for-Understanding-Formative-Assessment-Techniques-for-Your-Classroom-2nd-Edition.aspx

This book is a treasure trove of quick, easy-to-use formative assessments you can use while teaching to gauge student understanding. You can then use the results of these formative assessments to inform and plan your teaching. Skim through this book to find ideas to use as you plan lessons.

Johns, J. L., Elish-Piper, L., & Johns, B. (2017). *Basic reading inventory: Kindergarten through grade twelve and early literacy assessments* (12th ed). Dubuque, IA: Kendall Hunt Publishing Company.

https://he.kendallhunt.com/product/basic-reading-inventory-kindergarten-through-grade-twelve-and-early-literacy-assessments-0

The *Basic Reading Inventory* is an informal assessment that uses graded word lists and passages to assess students' word recognition, fluency, and comprehension. This resource also includes early literacy assessments and suggestions for how to use the assessment results for instruction to meet the needs of all students. Show this book to your mentor teacher and ask if you can try out some of the activities to assess your students.

Assessment Websites

MAP Suite of Assessments

https://www.nwea.org/

This suite of online assessments from NWEA is commonly used in many school districts. Three types of assessments are included in the MAP Suite. 1) MAP Growth is an interim assessment that can be used three times per year to see how students grow over time. 2) Reading Fluency is a 20-minute assessment that measures oral reading fluency, foundational reading skills, and comprehension. 3) MAP Skills can be used for progress monitoring and to learn more about specific skill gaps for students who struggle with reading.

Reading Rockets: Early Reading Assessment: A Guiding Tool for Instruction

http://www.readingrockets.org/article/early-reading-assessment-guiding-tool-instruction

This short article offers useful information about assessing students' reading in the areas of letter knowledge, phonemic awareness, decoding, fluency, and comprehension. It also provides links to several types of assessments that you can use in your classroom. Skim this article to find assessment ideas as you plan lessons.

Reading Rockets: Types of Informal Classroom-Based Assessment

http://www.readingrockets.org/article/types-informal-classroom-based-assessment

This website provides assessment tools for all areas of reading development in the early grades including phonemic awareness, phonics, fluency, and comprehension. It also provides instructions and tips for interpreting assessment results. Skim this article to find ideas that would be appropriate for your lesson plans.

Reading Rockets: Writing Assessment

http://www.readingrockets.org/article/writing-assessment

This web page provides a brief rationale for how to assess students' writing. It also offers links to a 6 + 1 Trait Writing scale, student writing self-assessment checklists, and a rubric-building tool. Read this article to find ideas for writing lesson plans.

Kathy Schrock's Guide to Everything: Assessment and Rubrics

https://www.schrockguide.net/assessment-and-rubrics.html

This website provides an enormous collection of assessment resources, tools, and rubrics for all grade levels and all areas of the curriculum. There is also a search feature to help you find exactly what you are looking for to use in your classroom. Skim the website to find topics of interest that you can delve into when you have questions.

Formative Assessments: 20 Simple Assessment Strategies You Can Use Every Day

https://www.teachthought.com/pedagogy/20-simple-assessment-strategies-can-use-every-day/

This website provides 20 formative assessment ideas you can use in your classroom today! The assessment strategies run the gamut from asking an open-ended question to promote discussion to a one-question quiz to partner sharing. Skim the website to find ideas for your lesson plans.

Learning at the Primary Pond

https://learningattheprimarypond.com/writing/writing-assessments-for-writing-workshop/

This website provides guidance and tools for assessing students' writing in a K–2 writing workshop model. The author even describes how you can use the writing rubrics to assign grades. Skim the website to find ideas for assessing writing.

© Monkey Business Images/Shutterstock.com

These students are engaged in the reading lesson.

Chapter
4

How Do I Promote Engaged Learning?

Samia had just finished the first day of her clinical placement in kindergarten. She had always wanted to teach kindergarten, so she was ready to soak up everything she could learn during her experience. When she arrived at the classroom, she saw her mentor teacher, Miss Pugh, waiting by the classroom door to greet each child as they arrived. Miss Pugh called each child by name, and she smiled warmly as they entered the classroom. She seemed to know each child so well that Samia wondered how she could know all 23 students.

Throughout the day, Samia observed Miss Pugh reading to and with her students and the students participating in hands-on learning activities, discussions, and partner work. Samia loved how involved the students were throughout the day. Samia had a million questions, and she planned to talk to Miss Pugh about how she got to know her students so well and how she got them excited about and involved in their learning. Samia was looking forward to learning from Miss Pugh how she built relationships with her students and created such a positive and inviting classroom environment.

Have you ever been in a situation that just exuded positive energy? Think about classes, workshops, events, groups, and even parties that left you feeling good about yourself. This is the kind of feeling we want in schools. Learning can be fun, and we want you to learn how to foster engaged learning, so you have the kind of classroom that Samia saw in Miss Pugh's room.

You are probably thinking a lot about the skills and strategies you will need to teach and the methods you should use to teach literacy in your classrooms, but the most important consideration is who you will be teaching—your students! In this chapter, we explore engaged learning and how you can get to know your students so well that you can use those insights to teach all of your students effectively.

What Is Engaged Learning?

Think of a time when you were really interested and involved in a class you were taking. Maybe you were excited to go to the class, found that the time passed quickly while you were there, and you looked forward to doing the reading and completing the assignments. You could say that you were engaged in the class. Why were you so interested and involved? What did your instructor do to foster your engagement? Chances are that you found the focus of the course interesting, you may have had some background knowledge about the topic, and you may have found the work challenging and interesting but not too hard. This is engaged learning.

The term **engaged learning** has become so common and overused that it is important for us to define it. Engagement is not just one thing. In fact, there are actually three dimensions of engagement: behavioral engagement, cognitive engagement, and emotional engagement (Fredericks, Blumenfeld, & Paris, 2004). Fisher, Frey, and Quaglia (2018) have taken the three-dimensional model of engagement and applied it in the classroom situations.

BEHAVIORAL ENGAGEMENT. **Behavioral engagement** focuses on the actual observable behaviors that are present when a learner is engaged. Think of the typical types of actions that students do such as sitting up, looking at the teacher, paying attention, and following directions—these are examples of what behavioral engagement may look like. Although these behaviors are easy for teachers to observe and although they can form the foundation of engagement, they alone are not sufficient for real engagement to occur. For example, some students who appear attentive are listening carefully and thinking deeply during a lesson. However, there may be other students who appear to be attentive but who are unable to tell what the lesson is about. Sometimes these students have become adept at "doing school" where it looks as if they are engaged but looks can be deceiving at times.

COGNITIVE ENGAGEMENT. An important goal for engaged learning is for students to demonstrate cognitive engagement. **Cognitive engagement** is a deeper level of engagement that requires students to put effort into their learning through planning, monitoring, and evaluating their own thinking and learning. Cognitive engagement requires students to welcome challenges that will help them enhance their learning and develop perseverance. When students are cognitively engaged, they are able to discuss what they are learning and they are interested in and in control of their learning. They also have the persistence to work through learning that requires effort and presents at least a modest challenge to them.

You may have heard the term *grit* (Duckworth, 2016). Grit is an important component of cognitive engagement. It's the tenacity and persistence to stick with challenging tasks to work toward long-term goals. For more information about grit, be sure to check out the video of Angela Duckworth in Margin Note 4.1.

Margin Note 4.1: Interview with Angela Duckworth about Grit

http://www.scholastic.com/browse/article.jsp?id=3758297

EMOTIONAL ENGAGEMENT. The third dimension of engagement is **emotional engagement**. Emotional engagement focuses on how students feel about their relationships with their teachers and peers as well as their general sense of belonging in the school and classroom community. Emotional engagement also encompasses students' interests, enjoyment, and enthusiasm for learning.

Students who are emotionally engaged are comfortable talking with the teacher and other students, working with partners and in groups, and asking questions. They generally enjoy and look forward to learning. In short, when students are emotionally engaged, they are comfortable, confident, and excited to learn in the school setting. When these three dimensions of engaged learning—behavioral, cognitive, and emotional engagement—are intentionally combined, teachers can create "engagement by design" to promote optimal student learning (Fisher, Frey, & Quaglia, 2018).

Connection to the Field: Observing Engaged Learning

Even though you can't always tell if students are engaged by their behavior, you can learn about engagement by observing students in the classroom. Select an activity, such as when the mentor teacher is giving directions or reading aloud. Sit in the back of the room and record the behaviors of the students. If needed, you can select part of the class to observe. When you are finished, share your observations with your mentor teacher and discuss what they observed while teaching.

Why Engagement Is Important

You probably know instinctively that engagement is important, but you may not know that engagement is one of the greatest predictors of student learning and achievement. It makes sense, right? If students are not engaged, it is very hard for them to learn. Fisher, Frey, and Quaglia (2018) explain that there are neuroscientific processes that account for how engagement leads to learning and achievement. Neuroscientific processes are the thinking and behaviors that are involved in learning.

Let's look at an example that shows what happens with engagement that promotes learning. First, the engaged learner uses selective attention to focus on specific things, rather than other things such as distracting information, to promote learning. Then, the student has to move to sustained attention to focus long enough to process information through working memory; making connections from prior knowledge to new information; and practicing, rehearsing, and applying the new knowledge.

When students are engaged, their learning tends to be effective which can lead to increased motivation to stay engaged or become even more engaged. For example, if Ian is engaged in learning about rhyming poetry, he will be more likely to read and think about the poems he is reading. Since Ian is thinking about poetry more, he can then acquire more knowledge about poetry, he is more likely to become even more interested in learning about other types of poetry, and he may even want to try his hand at writing original poems that incorporate what he has learned. In other words, engagement feeds the development of more engagement. Therefore, one of the greatest benefits of engagement is that it gets students on a positive cycle of learning that can spiral upward to promote even more engagement and learning.

When students are not engaged, on the other hand, the opposite effects can quickly take hold. For example, if Charlotte is disengaged when learning about informational text features such as the table of contents and headings, she will not learn much about these things which will then make those topics even less interesting to her. This will lead to decreased engagement when Charlotte's teacher expects her to use these features in her own informational writing. In short, engagement leads to learning and reinforces engagement to learn more and more.

What Research Tells Us about Engagement and Literacy Learning

You might be wondering whether there is research to back up these claims about engagement. Engagement has a robust research base. One of the most critical research studies for you to know is that students' engagement predicts their learning, grades, achievement test scores, retention, and even graduation (Parsons, Malloy, Parsons, & Burrowbridge, 2015). This is true not just in the United States, but in international studies like the Programme for International Student Assessment (PISA) which surveyed students in 63 countries. The researchers concluded that engagement is the most important factor in student reading achievement (Kirsch et al., 2003). Furthermore, research by Campbell, Voelkl, and Donahue (1997) concluded that reading engagement is such an important factor in learning that it can compensate for students' low socioeconomic status and low family education levels. And, most importantly, classroom instruction and teacher practices can promote and enhance student engagement. For example, researchers Pressley and Allington (2015) concluded that exemplary reading teachers had higher levels of student reading engagement in their classrooms as well as higher academic performance and outcomes. In other words, exemplary teachers are able to teach while supporting student engagement which leads to increased learning and reading achievement for the students in their classrooms.

In addition to those general research findings about the positive benefits of reading engagement on student learning and academic achievement, researchers have examined the types of learning tasks that contribute to increased reading engagement. Learning tasks that are associated with high levels of student engagement are characterized by "authenticity, collaboration, choice, appropriate challenge, and sustained learning" (Parsons et al., 2015, p. 224).

Authentic tasks match the types of real world activities that people do outside of school. Collaborative tasks are motivating to students because they can work and learn with their peers. Tasks that are challenging but not too difficult motivate students to work hard and cause them to feel proud of what they are doing. Finally, tasks that promote sustained learning allow students to dig in and commit to learning over time. When teachers consider how to incorporate literacy tasks that are authentic, collaborative, appropriately challenging, and promote sustained learning, they can help their students become and remain engaged in their literacy learning.

© Robert Kneschke/Shutterstock.com

Collaborating in reading and writing boosts this group's engagement.

What Is Motivation?

You have probably heard about motivation in your courses, but do you know what reading motivation is? **Motivation** is the "likelihood of engaging in reading or choosing to read" (Gambrell, 2011, p. 172). When students are motivated to read, they become engaged readers and learners, which can then lead to increased motivation, learning, and achievement.

Due to the many positive benefits of engaged learning, Gambrell identified several research-based principles for teachers to use to promote reading motivation and engagement in their classrooms. These principles overlap quite a bit with the literacy tasks described above that promote reading engagement, but they also provide a nice set of ideas for you to keep in mind as you create your classroom environments, plan lessons, and develop classroom routines and procedures. Students are more motivated to read when reading tasks, activities, and materials are relevant to their lives. When students have access to a wide range of reading materials, they will likely have increased motivation to read. Opportunities to participate in sustained reading so students can "get lost" in a book contributes to reading motivation. Choice must be a cornerstone of developing reading motivation in the classroom. Choice should include text selection and the types of tasks they complete to demonstrate learning and comprehension. Social interaction around texts can also contribute to students' reading motivation. Finally, appropriately challenging texts can reinforce students' reading motivation as they work hard and over time to read such texts.

As you think about your field experience classroom or your future classroom, the strong research base related to developing reading motivation and reading engagement confirm that authenticity, choice, social interaction, appropriate challenge, and opportunities for sustained reading and work must be key considerations. When you are designing your classroom environment and planning learning tasks, you will want to address these ideas intentionally so your students can develop and sustain reading motivation and engaged learning.

Creating a Classroom Environment that Promotes Engaged Learning

In the previous section, we discussed the types of tasks and principles you will want to consider to promote engaged learning in your classroom. Although those components are important, they are not sufficient. You will also need to consider your approach to teaching and your students as well as the type of classroom environment you create. The idea of invitational education is an interesting one that may be unfamiliar to you.

Over two decades ago, Purkey and Novak (1996) wrote about an invitational approach to education comprised of four elements: trust, respect, optimism, and intentionality. Let's consider each of these elements separately first and then collectively.

Trust is the bedrock of productive teaching and learning. In trusting relationships in the classroom, teachers and students work together and believe in each other. Students feel safe to take risks, try challenging tasks, ask for help, and resolve problems that arise. When **respect** is present in classrooms, students are valued and appreciated by the teacher and their peers for their unique attributes and identities. In respectful classrooms, teachers and students have shared responsibility for the well-being and success of others and the classroom as a whole. In such classrooms, **optimism** is the belief that each individual has untapped potential and that, as a member of the classroom, each person is expected to find ways to help others reach their potential. This means that cooperation and hope permeate the classroom, making it a positive and caring environment where every student can learn, grow, and succeed. The final element of invitational education is **intentionality**. This means that all practices, policies, and programs are designed to establish and support trust, respect, and optimism for all. It is not enough to assume that trust, respect, and optimism arise in the classroom or find their way into your teaching. This fourth element sits squarely on the shoulders of you—the teacher. By committing to creating a classroom where trust, respect, and optimism abound, you can ensure that your students have the right type of environment so they can become engaged (and successful) readers and learners. See Margin Note 4.2 for video examples of how teachers create intentionally inviting classrooms.

So, if you work hard to create a classroom that aligns with invitational education, what does that mean for you as a teacher and how you interact with your students? Fisher, Frey, and Quaglia (2018) describe intentionally inviting teachers as those who know their students well because they spend time and effort in building relationships. They are consistent and calm in their interactions with students. They notice when students are learning and when they are struggling. They respond regularly with useful feedback, and they seek to build, maintain, and repair relationships so the classroom can function well, and all members can feel valued, comfortable, and supported.

We bet that you aspire to be an intentionally inviting teacher. Therefore, the remainder of this chapter is organized around ways that you can get to know your students, promote engaged learning, and use what you know about your students to provide relevant and appropriate instruction. Let's begin by looking at an intentionally inviting classroom and teacher in first grade.

Margin Note 4.2:
Intentionally Inviting
Classrooms

https://players.brightcove.
net/268012963001/rJenIL
PQx_default/index.html?
videoId=5518274544001

Intentionally Inviting Teaching

Jasmine Ortiz is a kindergarten teacher with 4 years of teaching experience. From the time she decided to become a teacher, she knew that she wanted to be *that* teacher whom students love and other teachers want to be! She admits that things are not perfect every day, but she makes sure that each day she is focused on building relationships with her students, promoting cognitive engagement, and implementing engaging tasks with her 20 kindergarten students. Ms. Ortiz starts each day by warmly greeting her students at the classroom door. See Margin Note 4.3 for a video example of how a kindergarten teacher greets her students at the door each day.

Margin Note 4.3:
Kindergarten Teacher
Greeting Students

https://www.newsflare.com/
video/259487/health-
education/awesome-
teacher-lets-her-kids-pick-
a-morning-greeting

Ms. Ortiz greets her students at the door when they arrive in the morning, and while they hang up their backpacks and get organized for the day, she circulates around the room to visit with as many students as possible. She asks them how their morning has been, what they ate for breakfast, how they are feeling, and other questions so she can get a sense of who might need a little extra encouragement, support, or space. She asks each question respectfully, keeping in mind that some students may not want to answer every question. Then Ms. Ortiz reminds students to visit the classroom library to browse and choose books they want to read that day. As students select their books, Ms. Ortiz connects with students by saying things such as, "Olivia, you picked a book that Classie read and enjoyed last week. You two should talk about the book after you've read it." Or, "Jamal, is that the first Frog and Toad book for you? When I was your age, I *loved* Frog and Toad. After you read it, let me know what you think." As the day unfolds, Ms. Ortiz reads aloud to her students and teaches small guided reading groups while the other children work with partners in literacy play centers such as a pretend store or restaurant.

After doing a shared reading lesson about magnets, Ms. Ortiz has her students work in small groups to explore magnets and record their observations in small lab notebooks. As the day continues, Ms. Ortiz provides opportunities for students to use math manipulatives to understand and apply math concepts, and she encourages students to read independently for a minute longer than the day before to help them develop their reading stamina. At the end of the day Ms. Ortiz is tired, but her students appear to be even more tired which she considers a "win" because, in engaged classrooms, students should be busy doing most of the hard work of learning.

Engaging Students in Literacy Learning

It's generally pretty simple to learn your students' names (and how to pronounce them correctly), but that is just the beginning. To promote engaged learning, it is imperative that you know your students well, so you understand them as individuals. An easy-to-implement yet effective strategy is called two-by-ten. Although this strategy was originally designed to help teachers understand and get to know students with challenging behaviors, it works great with all students. In a research study, Wlodkowski (1983) found that when used with students with challenging classroom behaviors, the two-by-ten strategy resulted in behavior improvements 85% of the time. The strategy is easy to implement but requires planning so that you can interact with all of the students early in the year to begin building and understanding each student as well as establishing positive relationships. For 2 minutes at a time for 10 days, you will spend time talking to a specific student. The purpose of talking with the student is to get to know (not to judge or assess) the student. The conversation should focus on positive things and not address any behavior or academic problems. For example, you might ask a student what they enjoy doing, how they spend their free time, about their favorite food or activity, and so on.

If you use transition times, individual conference time, walking time to or from recess or the lunchroom, and other available moments throughout the day, you will be able to talk to 10 students per day for a total of 20 minutes per day. If you have a class of 20 students who you want to talk with over multiple days in the first week of school, you may want to modify the strategy so that you speak to each student for 2 minutes two times the first week. You can then create a rotation where you focus on 5 or 10 students (i.e., 10 or 20 minutes each day) for 10 days before shifting your focus to the next group of students. You may find it helpful to jot down a few notes for each student to help you remember what you are learning about each student, but be sure your focus is on having a conversation with your students rather than conducting a formal interview or making it feel like an assessment. If you are in your placement classroom one or two days a week, you may want to modify the approach or wait to use it until your full-time student teaching experience.

Regardless of whether you use the two-by-ten strategy this term or not, you will definitely want to learn the names of all of the children in your placement classroom as quickly as possible. An easy approach that many of our teacher candidates have used successfully is to take a photo of each child holding paper with their name on it and drawings of things they like to do. You can use these photos on your phone, tablet, or laptop like digital flashcards. You can review the photos prior to being in the classroom each week so you can learn and remember each child's name and a few things about them.

Connection to the Field: Learning Students' Names

On the first day of your placement, ask your mentor teacher for a seating chart or roster of students. Practice saying each student's name and ask either your mentor teacher or the child how to pronounce it correctly. Once you're able to pronounce each name, find a way to memorize the names that fits your learning style. Make sure you can identify students when they are outside at recess or at lunch as well as sitting in the classroom.

Learning Students' Interests

Knowing students' names is just the beginning. As you get to know your students, you should also get to know their interests. Once you know your students' interests, you can use those to make connections to the curriculum and to position children as experts and resources in the classroom. You can learn about children's interests simply by talking with them and listening carefully. You might find that it's helpful to jot down notes, so you remember this information and don't forget who loves to play soccer, who likes to bake, and who is a LEGO whiz. You can ask your mentor teacher if they already have this information that they can share with you. If not, you may want to ask permission to do an interest inventory to gather information about all of your students in an efficient and easy manner. There are lots of interest inventories available, and you can even create your own. A sample interest inventory called News about Me is provided in Assessment Strategy 4.1. You will also want to be sure to look at Margin Note 4.4 to check out the Interest-A-Lyzer which is a comprehensive interest inventory designed for use in kindergarten to third grade.

Margin Note 4.4:
Interest-A-Lyzer

http://www.prufrock.com/
Assets/ClientPages/pdfs/
SEM_Web_Resources/
Primary%20Interest-A-Lyzer.
pdf

© Michaeljung/Shutterstock.com

It's important to get to know your students as people and as learners.

Assessment Strategy 4.1: News about Me

Purpose: News about Me is a questionnaire that you can use to learn more about your students' backgrounds, interests, and lives. For younger students, you can use it as an interview template while you write the student's responses. Older students may prefer to respond in writing.

Procedures:

1. Print the News about Me sheets from the Chapter 4 Resources on the website.
2. Explain to the student that you want to learn more about them by using the News about Me questionnaire.
3. If you plan to give the assessment as an interview, you may wish to audio record the student's responses.
4. If the student will be responding in writing, explain that they can seek your help if the questions are unclear. Also, explain that in some sections they may not answer all of the questions. For example, if the student does not have any pets, they would leave that item blank.

Scoring and Interpretation:

Review the student's responses, noting any information that may help you suggest any appropriate books or texts for the student. Note any connections you can make from the student's interests and background to the curriculum.

© Tawan Jz/Shutterstock.com

This boy is working hard to fill out his News about Me survey.

A News Story About _____

(write your name here)

News About My Family

I have _____ brothers and sisters.

They are _____ years old.

I like to play with _____.

My family and I like to _____.

I (like/do not like) to play alone.

I help at home by _____.

The thing I like to do at home is _____

_____.

News About My Pets

I have a pet _____.

I (do/do not) take care of my pet.

I do not have a pet because _____

_____.

I would like to have a pet _____.

News About My Books and My Reading

I like to read about _____

_____.

The best book I ever read was _____

_____.

I (do get/do not get) books from the library.

I (have/do not have) a library card.

I have about _____ books of my own
at home.

I read aloud to _____.

My _____ reads to me.

News About My Friends

My best friend is _____.

I like (him/her) because _____

_____.

We play _____.

I would rather play (at my place/at my
friend's place) because _____

_____.

News About Things I Like and Dislike

I do not like _____.

I like _____.

I am afraid of _____.

I am not afraid of _____.

News About My Wishes

When I grow up, I might like to be _____

_____

_____.

If I could have three wishes, I would wish

(1) _____

_____.

(2) _____

_____.

(3) _____

_____

_____.

News About My Travels and Adventures

I have traveled by:

_____ bus   _____ car

_____ airplane   _____ truck

_____ boat   _____ train

_____ bicycle   _____ van

I have visited these places:

_____ circus   _____ zoo

_____ farm   _____ park

_____ hotel   _____ museum

_____ bakery   _____ library

_____ airport   _____ fire station

_____ factory, and _____.

The best adventure I ever had was _____

_____.

News About My School Subjects

My favorite subject is _____.

The subject I dislike most is _____.

I am best at _____.

I wish I was better in _____.

News About My Hobbies and Collections

One of my best hobbies is _____

_____.

My other hobbies are _____

_____.

I collect _____.

I want to collect _____.

Media Favorites

I (have/do not have) a computer at home.

I (use/do not use) a computer at home.

I watch _____ videos/DVDs each week.

I (have/do not have) my own cell phone.

I see _____ movies each week.

I like to listen to _____ on the radio.

I see _____ television programs a day.

My favorite programs are _____

_____

_____.

Write any other news about yourself below.

_____

_____

_____

_____

_____

_____

RESEARCH-BASED PRINCIPLES FOR FOSTERING STUDENT INTEREST IN READING. You can foster student interests in reading by using four research-based principles developed by Springer, Harris, and Dole (2017). When students are interested in reading, they comprehend the text better and enjoy the reading experience more (Renninger & Bachrach, 2015). They also read more strategically, remember what they read, and put more effort into their reading (Fulmer, D'Mello, Strain, & Graesser, 2015).

The first principle is to cultivate individual student's interests because young children come to school with well-developed interests that can help teachers recommend books and other texts and make connections from a student's interest to the curriculum using strategies such as allowing students to work on self-selected projects or to present information related to their interests to the class. Although cultivating a student's individual interests is important, it is not sufficient, because the curriculum is broad, and students will need to learn about new things that they may not have been interested in or even known about before.

That's where the second principle comes in—fostering situational interest. That simply means that you create a sense of excitement around a new topic the students will be studying. For example, you can create a table display with several plants, seedlings, seeds, magnifying glasses, dirt, pots, and a watering can. You may read a book about plants aloud to the class, focusing on the bright and interesting photographs in the book. You may then have the students walk around the school grounds looking at the plants and discussing what they notice about them. You can then tell the students that they are going to learn all about plants in their next science unit. As the unit unfolds, you can create a bulletin board about plants; involve the students in hands-on activities to observe plants closely, plant seeds, and care for seedlings; and read multiple texts about plants, their parts, how they grow, why they are important, and so on. Through these various activities, you can build the students' situational interest about the topic at hand—in this case, plants.

The third principle focuses on selecting interesting texts for the classroom library, for reading aloud, and for instruction. Researchers have even identified three main characteristics that make books interesting (Schraw, Flowerday, & Lehman, 2001). They found that for a text to be inherently interesting, it must have coherence, relevance, and vividness. Texts that have coherence are well organized and easy to understand. Relevance refers to how purposeful and important texts are as well as how likely students are to be able to make connections to the text. Vividness refers to how exciting and suspenseful a text is as well as how interesting the details are. For younger children, the vividness of illustrations, photos, and other visual elements are also of key importance when selecting interesting texts. A great source of interesting books for children is children; you can simply ask them what they want and like to read. Every year the International Literacy Association compiles a list of children's favorite books from those that have been published recently. This list is called *Children's Choices*, and you can access it by using the information provided in Margin Note 4.5.

Margin Note 4.5:
International Literacy
Association's Children's
Choices Reading List

https://literacyworldwide.
org/docs/default-source/
reading-lists/childrens-
choices/childrens-choices-
reading-list-2019.pdf

Although it is a great goal to teach only texts that all students find interesting, given the range of interests and the expectations of the school curriculum, it is almost certain that from time to time, students will be expected to read texts that they do not find particularly interesting. Therefore, the final principle focuses on teaching interest self-regulation strategies so students know how to approach and read texts that may not be of great interest to them. To address this principle, you can teach students to set a purpose for their reading, to re-read if they don't understand what they are reading, and to stop and ask themselves questions about what they are reading.

There are some easy-to-implement instructional strategies that you can use to learn, build, and leverage student interests to promote engaged literacy learning. Teaching Strategy 4.1 is a familiar idea—Student of the Week—but our version offers a few twists to put the spotlight on student interests. Teaching Strategy 4.2 will show you how to use inquiry projects to allow students to dig deeply into their interests as they apply and refine their literacy skills. Templates for inquiry projects for grades PreK and K and 1–3 are provided in the Chapter 4 Resources on the website.

© Monkey Business Images/Shutterstock.com

Read aloud from books that appeal to students' interests while fostering situational interest.

Teaching Strategy 4.1: Student of the Week

Purpose: The Student of the Week strategy is a popular activity in many classrooms. This adaptation of that common strategy focuses on learning, spotlighting, and leveraging students' interests, experiences, backgrounds, and expertise. The order of the days can be changed to meet the needs of the classroom or families.

Procedures:

1. Create a schedule so each student gets a chance to be the student of the week. Notify the student and their family several weeks prior to the scheduled week to allow for preparation.

2. Day 1 Sharing Sack: The student brings a sack filled with three to five objects that they will use to tell the class about themselves. Suggested objects can be favorite things, hobbies, family photos or memories, and special talents. Photos or drawings can be used if objects can't be obtained. Set aside 10–15 minutes for the Student of the Week to share their sack. Provide a few minutes for the student to practice with you if they are shy or anxious or want help with explaining the objects to the class.

3. Day 2 Favorite Book: The student shares a favorite book with the class and explains why it is their favorite book. The student decides if they want to read the book aloud to the class or if they want the teacher to do so. If the student plans to read the book to the class, set aside time to practice with them first.

4. Day 3 Teach the Class Something New: The student teaches the class something new that they know about or can do. This can be a skill, information about a topic, a demonstration of how to do something, or words or songs in the student's home language. You will need to coordinate with the student and family in advance to ensure that they are ready to teach the class something new and have any materials needed to do so.

5. Day 4 Lunch: The student invites family members or other important people to join them for lunch in the cafeteria or classroom. If family members are not able to come to school, the teacher eats lunch with the student and invites other school staff to join them such as the principal, librarian, and custodian.

6. Day 5 Star Student Poster: During the week, the teacher has a poster for the student of the week, and the other students are asked to write at least one thing they admire about the student. The student is presented with the poster, and each student reads or discusses what they admire about the student of the week. The class gives a round of applause or shakes hands with or gives high-fives to the student of the week.

Teaching Strategy 4.2: Student Inquiry Projects

Purpose: Student Inquiry Projects allow students to investigate topics that they are very interested in and to share their learning and knowledge with their classmates and others. Choice in topics and how to share their new knowledge are provided to students to foster self-directed learning.

Procedures:

1. As a culmination of a unit of study, invite students to complete inquiry projects on self-selected topics. For example, at the end of a unit of study on poetry or insects, students can choose the focus of their inquiry project. In this context, students may choose to learn more about haiku, poems from Mexico, or funny poems, or they may want to investigate ants, bees, or praying mantises.

2. Provide class time and access to relevant materials, the library, and appropriate websites for students to investigate their topics. If appropriate, invite parents, family members, community volunteers, and older students to be resources if they have expertise on the topics that students are investigating.

3. Teach basic inquiry skills such as using a table of contents and index in reference books, locating relevant books in the library, searching on the internet, and taking notes on what they are learning. Two sample learning logs for inquiry projects are provided in the Chapter 4 Resources on the website. If your school has a librarian or library clerk, they may be able to help the students on this important step.

4. Because the focus of student inquiry projects in the early grades is to promote learning, build interest, and foster a positive attitude toward learning, the process is more important than any final project. Therefore, depending on the amount of time available, which may range from a day to a week or more, you can invite students to choose how they will share their learning. Some options are:

   - Share what you have learned with a partner or in small groups.
   - Teach two new things you learned to the class.
   - Create a drawing or model, either online or in hard copy, to show what you learned.
   - Write a paragraph or list to show what you learned.
   - Create a book for the classroom library or website about what you learned through your inquiry project.
   - Invite students to develop their own way to demonstrate their learning.

© YAKOBCHUK VIACHESLAV/Shutterstock.com

Build engagement by providing time for small group work.

Attitudes and Academic Resilience

How students feel about reading, writing, and school affects their willingness and ability to engage in literacy learning. Attitude refers to the feelings a learner has toward a learning task or situation and can cause the learner to engage in or to avoid the task or situation (McKenna, Kear, & Ellsworth, 1995). For example, if Jaime has a positive attitude toward reading, he will be more likely to engage in reading tasks and to interact with texts which can support his literacy development and learning. On the other hand, if Hannah has a negative attitude toward writing, she will be more likely to avoid writing tasks which can impede further learning and development which can then reinforce her negative attitude. In short, attitudes can facilitate or impede student growth and progress in reading and writing; therefore, it's important for you to know what your students' attitudes are as well as ways to foster positive attitudes.

A widely used assessment to determine reading attitudes is the Elementary Reading Attitude Survey which is designed for use in grade one and up. See Assessment Strategy 4.2 for the survey as well as instructions on how to use it with your students.

Assessment Strategy 4.2: Elementary Reading Attitude Survey

Purpose: The Elementary Reading Attitude Survey gathers information about students' overall attitudes toward reading as well as in the specific areas of academic reading and recreational reading. This assessment can be administered to a group of students or individually, and norms are available to allow you to compare a student's attitude toward reading to a national sample of students who also took the assessment.

Procedures:

1. Print a copy of the Elementary Reading Attitude Survey from the Chapter 4 Resources on the website for each student you will be assessing.

2. Explain to the student(s) that you will be asking them to circle the Garfield that matches how they feel about each question you read aloud to them. Tell them that there are no right or wrong answers and encourage them to be honest with their responses.

3. Point out the happiest Garfield (on the left) and discuss how Garfield feels. Do the same for the somewhat happy Garfield, somewhat upset Garfield, and very upset Garfield.

4. Read each question aloud and ask the student(s) to circle the Garfield whose feelings most closely match how they feel about the question.

5. Continue until the entire survey has been completed.

Scoring and Interpretation:

1. To score the survey, give four points for each leftmost (happiest) Garfield, three for each slightly happy Garfield, two for each mildly upset Garfield, and one point for each very upset Garfield. Use the scoring sheet provided to record the scores.

2. You can determine three scores for each student: 1) a score for recreational reading (the first 10 items on the survey), 2) a score for academic reading (the last 10 items on the survey), and 3) a composite or total score.

3. You can interpret the scores in two ways. One is to note informally where the score falls in regard to the four points on the scale. A total score of 50, for example, would fall midway on the scale, between the slightly happy and the slightly upset Garfields, indicating an indifferent overall attitude toward reading. The other approach is more formal and involves converting raw scores into percentile ranks by using the Norms Table which can be found on page 84 and in the Chapter 4 Resources on the website. You can then interpret the percentile ranks as follows. A percentile rank of 99 indicates that the student has an attitude that is as good as or better than 99% of the students in the norming group. Likewise, a percentile rank of 15 indicates that the student's attitude is as good as or better than 15% of the students in the norming group. As a general rule of thumb, a percentile rank of 50 is considered average.

Elementary Reading Attitude Survey

Name _____ Date _____

1. How do you feel when you read a book on a rainy Saturday?

2. How do you feel when you read a book in a school during free time?

3. How do you feel about reading for fun at home?

4. How do you feel about getting a book for a present?

5. How do you feel about spending free time reading?

6. How do you feel about starting a new book?

7. How do you feel about reading during summer?

8. How do you feel about reading instead of playing?

9. How do you feel about going to a bookstore?

10. How do you feel about reading different kinds of books?

11. How do you feel when the teacher asks you questions about what you read?

12. How do you feel about doing reading workbook pages and worksheets?

13. How do you feel about reading in school?

14. How do you feel about reading your school books?

15. How do you feel about learning from a book?

16. How do you feel when it's time for reading in class?

17. How do you feel about the stories you read in reading class?

18. How do you feel when you read out loud in class?

19. How do you feel about using a dictionary?

20. How do you feel about taking a reading test?

Elementary Reading Attitude Survey

Michael C. McKenna and Dennis J. Kear

Scoring and Interpretation

1. To score the survey, count four points for each leftmost (happiest) Garfield circled, three for each slightly smiling Garfield, two for each mildly upset Garfield, and one point for each rightmost (very upset) Garfield. Three scores for each student can be obtained: the total for the first 10 items, the total for the second 10, and a composite total. The first half of the survey relates to attitude toward recreational reading; the second half relates to attitude toward academic aspects of reading.

2. You can interpret scores in two ways. One is to note informally where the score falls in regard to the four points on the scale. A total score of 50, for example, would fall about midway on the scale, between the slightly happy and slightly upset figures, indicating a relatively indifferent overall attitude toward reading. The other approach is more formal. It involves converting the raw scores into percentile ranks by means of Table 1.1 on page 27. Be sure to use the norms for the right grade level and to note the column headings (Rec = recreational reading, Aca = academic reading, Tot = total score). If you wish to determine the average percentile rank for your class, average the raw scores first; then use the table to locate the percentile rank corresponding to the raw score mean. Percentile ranks cannot be averaged directly.

Norms for the Elementary Reading Attitude Survey

To create norms for the interpretation of the Elementary Reading Attitude Survey scores, a large-scale study was conducted late in January 1989, at which time the survey was administered to 18,138 students in Grades 1–6. Several steps were taken to achieve a sample that was sufficiently stratified (that is, reflective of the American population) to allow confident generalizations. Children were drawn from 95 school districts in 38 states. The number of girls exceeded by only 5 the number of boys. Ethnic distribution of the sample was also close to that of the U.S. population in 1989. The proportion of Blacks (9.5%) was within 3% of the national proportion, whereas the proportion of Hispanics (6.2%) was within 2%. In 2013, estimates of the proportion of Blacks is slightly less than 13%; the proportion of Hispanics is approximately 15%.

Percentile ranks at each grade for both subscales and the full scale are presented in Table 1.1 on page 27. These data can be used to compare individual students' scores with the national sample, and they can be interpreted like achievement-test percentile ranks.

McKenna, M.C., & Kear, D.J. (1990). Measuring attitude toward reading: A new tool for teachers. *The Reading Teacher, 43,* 626–639. Reprinted with permission of Michael C. McKenna and the International Reading Association.

Elementary Reading Attitude Survey Scoring Sheet

Student's Name _____

Teacher _____

Grade _____ Administration Date _____

```
┌─────────────────────────────────────────┐
│             Scoring Guide                │
│   4 points    Happiest Garfield          │
│   3 points    Slightly smiling Garfield  │
│   2 points    Mildly upset Garfield      │
│   1 point     Very upset Garfield        │
└─────────────────────────────────────────┘
```

Recreational reading	Academic reading
1. _____	11. _____
2. _____	12. _____
3. _____	13. _____
4. _____	14. _____
5. _____	15. _____
6. _____	16. _____
7. _____	17. _____
8. _____	18. _____
9. _____	19. _____
10. _____	20. _____
Raw score: _____	**Raw score:** _____

Total raw score (Recreational + Academic): _____

Percentile Ranks

Recreational	
Academic	
Full scale	

Table 1.1. Mid-Year Percentile Ranks by Grade and Scale

Raw Score	Grade 1 Rec.	Aca.	Tot.	Grade 2 Rec.	Aca.	Tot.	Grade 3 Rec.	Aca.	Tot.	Grade 4 Rec.	Aca.	Tot.	Grade 5 Rec.	Aca.	Tot.	Grade 6 Rec.	Aca.	Tot.
80			99			99			99			99			99			99
79			95			96			98			99			99			99
78			93			95			97			98			99			99
77			92			94			97			98			99			99
76			90			93			96			97			98			99
75			88			92			95			96			98			99
74			86			90			94			95			97			99
73			84			88			92			94			97			98
72			82			86			91			93			96			98
71			80			84			89			91			95			97
70			78			82			86			89			94			96
69			75			79			84			88			92			95
68			72			77			81			86			91			93
67			69			74			79			83			89			92
66			66			71			76			80			87			90
65			62			69			73			78			84			88
64			59			66			70			75			82			86
63			55			63			67			72			79			84
62			52			60			64			69			76			82
61			49			57			61			66			73			79
60			46			54			58			62			70			76
59			43			51			55			59			67			73
58			40			47			51			56			64			69
57			37			45			48			53			61			68
56			34			41			44			48			57			62
55			31			38			41			45			53			58
54			28			35			38			41			50			55
53			25			32			34			38			46			52
52			22			29			31			35			42			48
51			20			26			28			32			39			44
50			18			23			25			28			36			40
49			15			20			23			26			33			37
48			13			18			20			23			29			33
47			12			15			17			20			26			30
46			10			13			15			18			23			27
45			8			11			13			16			20			25
44			7			9			11			13			17			22
43			6			8			9			12			15			20
42			5			7			9			10			13			17
41			5			6			7			9			12			15
40	99	99	4	99	99	5	99	99	6	99	99	7	99	99	10	99	99	13
39	92	91	3	94	94	4	96	97	5	97	98	6	98	99	9	99	99	12
38	89	88	3	92	92	2	94	95	4	95	97	5	96	98	8	97	99	10
37	86	85	2	88	89	2	90	93	3	92	95	4	94	98	7	95	99	8
36	81	79	2	84	85	2	87	91	2	88	93	3	91	96	6	92	98	7
35	77	75	1	79	81	1	81	88	2	84	90	3	87	95	4	88	97	6
34	72	69	1	74	78	1	75	83	2	78	87	2	82	93	4	83	95	5
33	65	63	1	68	73	1	69	79	1	72	83	2	77	90	3	79	93	4
32	58	58	1	62	67	1	63	74	1	66	79	1	71	86	3	74	91	3
31	52	53	1	56	62	1	57	69	0	60	75	1	65	82	2	69	87	2
30	44	49	1	50	57	0	51	63	0	54	70	1	59	77	1	63	82	2
29	38	44	0	44	51	0	45	58	0	47	64	1	53	71	1	58	78	1
28	32	39	0	37	46	0	38	52	0	41	58	1	48	66	1	51	73	1
27	26	34	0	31	41	0	33	47	0	35	52	1	42	60	1	46	67	1
26	21	30	0	25	37	0	26	41	0	29	46	0	36	54	0	39	60	1
25	17	25	0	20	32	0	21	36	0	23	40	0	30	49	0	34	54	0
24	12	21	0	15	27	0	17	31	0	19	35	0	25	42	0	29	49	0
23	9	18	0	11	23	0	13	26	0	14	29	0	20	37	0	24	42	0
22	7	14	0	8	18	0	9	22	0	11	25	0	16	31	0	19	36	0
21	5	11	0	6	15	0	6	18	0	9	20	0	13	26	0	15	30	0
20	4	9	0	4	11	0	5	14	0	6	16	0	10	21	0	12	24	0
19	2	7		2	8		3	11		5	13		7	17		10	20	
18	2	5		2	6		2	8		3	9		6	13		8	15	
17	1	4		1	5		1	5		2	7		4	9		6	11	
16	1	3		1	3		1	4		2	5		3	6		4	8	
15	0	2		0	2		0	3		1	3		2	4		3	6	
14	0	2		0	1		0	1		1	2		1	2		1	3	
13	0	1		0	1		0	1		0	1		1	2		1	2	
12	0	1		0	0		0	0		0	1		0	1		0	1	
11	0	0		0	0		0	0		0	0		0	0		0	0	
10	0	0		0	0		0	0		0	0		0	0		0	0	

Socioemotional skills closely connect with attitudes toward reading, and they predict academic resilience. McTigue, Washburn, and Liew (2009) describe socioemotional skills in two broad areas: temperament (innate behavioral style) and beliefs about self as learner. Students who are academically resilient can maintain positive attitudes even during challenging or frustrating learning experiences. They have self-efficacy (a belief that their actions can produce the desired outcome) and are likely to be persistent—to keep on trying—because they believe they can be successful.

What can you do in the classroom to foster and support your students' socioemotional skills? McTigue, Washburn, and Liew (2009) offer five ideas that can help you create a classroom that will encourage students to develop academic resilience. First, you will want to create a classroom environment that is warm and accepting so that students feel safe and comfortable to take risks in their learning. Second, you can address academic resilience when you assess and provide feedback to students. For example, as you monitor students' work and progress, you can consider students' engagement, effort, use of strategies, willingness to stick with challenging tasks, and requests for help or resources. Doing so communicates to students that learning is a process and academic resilience is valued. Third, you can also model academic resilience in guided reading instruction, shared reading and writing activities, and teacher think-alouds so that students understand how to work through challenging texts or tasks, how to recover from mistakes, how to use fix-up strategies, and how to maintain a positive attitude. By providing specific and accurate feedback and emphasizing effort, you can support students' development of academic resilience. For example, instead of saying, "good job," you might say something like, "I noticed that you caught and fixed your mistake by re-reading." Fourth, you can have your students set goals that are specific, proximal (immediate or in the near future), and have the appropriate level of difficulty (not too easy and not too hard). By having students set and work toward goals, they can take ownership for their learning, increase their motivation to learn, and see tangible progress in their own learning which will then enhance motivation and self-efficacy. Finally, you will want to promote self-evaluation so that students are able to reflect on their goals and to track their own progress.

You may notice that your mentor teacher sometimes offers feedback to students like, "good job" or "nice work." Since you are a guest in the classroom, it is important that you not judge what your mentor teacher is or is not doing, but that you learn from it. If you are observing your mentor teacher teaching, you can consider how you could offer specific and accurate feedback to students if you were the one teaching the lesson. You may also want to discuss with your mentor teacher what you are learning about giving specific and accurate feedback and ask for their opinion on when and why they might use it. You can also try to provide this approach to feedback for the lessons you are teaching, but you may find that you will need to wait until you are in the classroom on a daily basis during student teaching to fully implement this approach to feedback.

Fostering Motivation

We introduced the idea of motivation and its connection to engagement earlier in this chapter, but to understand motivation fully, we need to look at it more carefully. Guthrie and Barber (2019) explain that motivation is composed of interest (which we discussed in the previous section), confidence, and dedication. When students have confidence, they believe in themselves and their capacity to be successful. Dedication is an example of behavioral engagement that allows students to keep working, even when a task or text is difficult.

Margin Note 4.6: Growth vs. Fixed Mindsets: What Is Growth Mindset Really?

https://www.weare teachers.com/growth-mindset-in-education/

GROWTH MINDSET. Motivated students also have a growth mindset (Dweck, 2006), which means that they believe they can grow and improve as learners with effort and time. This perspective is compared to having a fixed mindset where learners believe that they are simply good or not good at something and no amount of effort or persistence will change the outcome. Clearly, we want our students to develop a growth mindset so they will be engaged and motivated to keep learning. Some effective ways you can help students develop a growth mindset are outlined in Figure 4.1. To learn more about a growth versus a fixed mindset, view the video provided in Margin Note 4.6.

Figure 4.1. **Promoting a Growth Mindset in the Classroom**

Strategy	Activities to Implement the Strategy
Make students aware of what a growth mindset is and why it is important.	Read and discuss books that have characters who experience challenges and work hard to overcome them.
Use language that promotes a growth mindset.	Replace comments such as "you are good at this" or "you are smart" with feedback that focuses on effort, perseverance, and the willingness to try additional strategies. For example, you can say things such as "Your hard work helped you improve your performance." "You are not there *yet*, but if you keep working, you will get there!" and "Mistakes are an important part of learning."
Display visible reminders of growth mindset.	Create and display anchor charts, bulletin boards, and inspirational posters that focus on growth mindset.
Provide attainable challenges.	Provide tasks that are challenging but that students will be able to complete if they work hard, try new strategies, and stick with it. Help students set goals to encourage them to work toward challenging outcomes.

Margin Note 4.7: Simple Practices to Nurture the Motivation to Read

https://www.readingrockets.org/article/simple-practices-nurture-motivation-read

EXTRINSIC VS. INTRINSIC MOTIVATION. When you hear the term *motivation*, you may think of things like stickers and prizes, which are examples of extrinsic motivators that some teachers use to try and convince students to complete learning tasks. Extrinsic motivation is external to the learner, short-term, and dependent on specific rewards or punishments to get a student do something. Intrinsic motivation, on the other hand, comes from within the individual who wants to do something because of personal reasons such as enjoyment, pride, or a sense of accomplishment. Because intrinsic motivation comes from within the individual, it is sustainable and should be the goal for our students. For some easy ideas you can implement in your classroom to build students' internal motivation to read, see the short article provided in Margin Note 4.7.

CONSIDERATIONS FOR ENGLISH LEARNERS' READING MOTIVATION IN ENGLISH. You will most likely have some English Learners (ELs) in your clinical classrooms as well as your own classroom in the future. In her research, Protacio (2012) found that ELs are motivated to read in English because a family member or friend in their immediate environment sets an example that they want to follow. Her study also found that ELs are motivated to use reading to form relationships with their English-speaking peers and to learn about their new culture and community. In addition, ELs tend to develop instrumental motivation to read—meaning that they are motivated to read in English because they believe it will contribute to their competence in English. Emergent bilinguals in the study also demonstrated perceived competence—their perceptions of their English language abilities were related to their motivation to read in English. In other words, those ELs who felt confident of their English language abilities were more motivated to read in English, and those who doubted their English language skills tended to avoid reading in English. Furthermore, Protacio (2012) found that access to interesting, relevant books that students could choose and teacher recommendations of books motivated students to read more. These findings offer helpful guidance for how you can create a classroom environment to support ELs' reading motivation.

One important way you can begin to address motivation in your classroom is to assess your students' current motivation to read. Assessment Strategy 4.3, the Young Reader Motivation Questionnaire (Coddington & Guthrie, 2009), provides useful information about your students' motivation in three broad areas: efficacy for reading, reading orientation, and perceptions of difficulty in reading. You can use the results of this assessment to plan instruction and to build a classroom literacy climate that will engage and motivate your students to read and learn.

© Christin Lola/Shutterstock.com

Choice in reading promotes motivation to read.

Assessment Strategy 4.3: Young Reader Motivation Questionnaire

Purpose: The Young Reader Motivation Questionnaire assesses students' efficacy for reading, reading orientation, and perceptions of difficulty in reading. The survey has two forms: one for the student to complete (as an interview) and one for the teacher to complete as a questionnaire.

Procedures:

1. To access the assessment forms for the Young Reader Motivation Questionnaire, consult this reference:

   > Coddington, C. S., & Guthrie, J. T. (2009). Teacher and student perceptions of boys' and girls' reading motivation. *Reading Psychology, 30*, 225–249.

   and visit this website: http://www.cori.umd.edu/measures/YRMQ.pdf.

2. Interview each student individually using the questions provided on the Student Form. Record each student response on the form.

3. The teacher will respond to each question on the Teacher Form.

Scoring and Interpretation:

1. Count up the number of "yes" and "no" responses for each of the sections on the Student Form. If the majority of the responses are "yes" in a section, you can consider it as a relative strength. If the majority of the responses are "no" in a section, consider that area as an area for improvement.

2. Count up the number of "yes" and "no" responses for each of the sections on the Teacher Form. If the majority of the responses are "yes" in a section, you can consider it as a relative strength. If the majority of the responses are "no" in a section, consider that area as one for improvement.

3. Compare the Student Form and the Teacher Form to see if there is agreement or not.

4. Use the findings to identify areas where you need to do additional work with students to build their motivation.

The Role Background Knowledge Plays in Engagement

Engagement can be fostered when you connect your classroom with students' personal lives. Classroom environments should support and encourage children to make personal connections with a wide range of printed materials (Gambrell & Dromsky, 2000). Children can learn more effectively when they can relate new learning to something they already know. For example, if you have knowledge about goats because you have seen them at a local farm or petting zoo, it will be easier for you to read and comprehend a book about goats. Even if your knowledge about goats is incomplete or based only on seeing pictures or videos of goats (without ever seeing them in person), it can still help you understand (and be motivated to read) a challenging text about goats. This type of prior knowledge or experience is often referred to as background knowledge or schema (Anderson, 1994). Children come to school with a wide variety of experiences and exposure to events, objects, and books. Yet another reason that you will need to get to know your students well!

The concept of building background knowledge focuses on providing new experiences to children. Building background knowledge can happen by providing children with concrete experiences and opportunities to use their senses to examine materials and objects. Because young children learn by doing, playing, and being actively involved, hands-on experiences are essential for building background knowledge.

Activating background knowledge refers to the process of helping children remember what they already know about a topic. You can help students activate their background knowledge by making connections between what they already know and what they will learn. Simple techniques such as making predictions, discussing or drawing what is already known about a topic, or brainstorming how two topics are alike are examples of strategies you can use to help children activate their background knowledge.

The IDEA strategy (ignite, discover, extend, affirm; Herrera, 2016) is a flexible strategy you can apply to activate background knowledge and to help students navigate through informational texts. It also demonstrates biography-driven instruction which is described in the next section. See Teaching Strategy 4.3 for step-by-step instructions for this strategy that was specifically designed for ELs but can be applied with any students who may need support to activate and apply their background knowledge.

UNDERSTANDING STUDENTS' CULTURAL BACKGROUNDS AND ASSETS. Children come to school with a wide variety of lived experiences, strengths, talents, and abilities. It's important that you view your students (and their families) from a strengths' perspective—view their backgrounds and diversity as assets rather than weaknesses. In Chapter 1, you learned about culturally relevant pedagogy. The term *culturally sustaining pedagogy* has also been introduced recently to show that we must move beyond just acknowledging or accepting students' cultures to explicitly supporting their cultures, languages, and literacies (Paris, 2012). What lies at the heart of these approaches to teaching culturally and linguistically diverse students is focusing on long-term academic achievement of students, developing cultural competence as teachers so we can support all students, and promoting a context for students to consider and critique social inequalities (CCSSO, 2018).

Teaching Strategy 4.3: Ignite, Discover, Extend, Affirm (IDEA)

Purpose: The IDEA strategy spans multiple lessons and is designed for ELs but is appropriate for all students who will benefit from conceptual vocabulary instruction (Herrera, 2016). The strategy focuses activating students' background knowledge and then using that as a foundation to navigate the content area curriculum.

Procedures:

1. Before teaching the lesson, prepare for the IGNITE stage of the strategy. Select five to seven words related to the unit of study. The words should all be related to the same concept.

2. **Ignite** the students' understanding of and interest in these words by activating their background knowledge. Show visuals or video clips or even pantomime the words to help activate what the students already know about the words or the concepts they represent.

3. Invite students to discuss what they know about each of the words with a partner or in a small group.

4. Explain that these words will be important in the upcoming lesson or unit of study.

5. During the lesson, guide students to **Discover** the meaning of the words as they encounter them in context. Guide this process by talking with students about the words in context, using aids (if they are provided in the text; e.g., glosses or callouts) that provide definitions or examples or the glossary.

6. Ask students to make connections back to their initial ideas about the words in the Ignite stage of the strategy. Were their initial ideas accurate, inaccurate, or somewhere in between? How has their understanding of the words developed through reading and discussing them in the context of the text and lesson?

7. Work together to generate "kid definitions" of each of the words. You can write these on the white board and ask the students to write them in their notebooks in a way that makes the most sense for them. Some students may use their home language and English, others may include drawings, and others may add an example to help them remember and understand the words.

8. After the lesson, focus on the **Extend** phase of the strategy by helping students create links between the individual words they are learning by creating a vocabulary chain using an index card for each word. The students organize the cards to form a chain by showing the links or connections from one word to the next. They will then explain their chain to a partner to ensure that it makes sense. An example is shown here and a template for making a vocabulary chain is provided in the Chapter 4 Resources on the website.

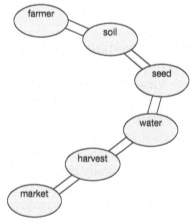

9. Now the students explain their vocabulary chains to you to **Affirm** their understanding of the words and the links between them. Help students clarify their understanding of the words and the connections between them as needed.

10. Reinforce the words in future lessons by discussing them, encouraging students to use them orally and in writing, and refining the "kid definitions" if additional information or nuances of the meanings are developed.

To get a better idea of what culturally relevant teaching looks like, let's look at the domains that comprise the approach. Figure 4.2 provides a summary of the five domains and offers suggestions for how teachers can address each of them in their teaching.

Figure 4.2. Culturally Responsive Teaching and Relevant Pedagogy

Domain	Examples of Teacher Practices
Identity and Achievement	Let students know that their voices are heard and valued. Encourage multiple perspectives. Embrace diversity as an asset that supports all students' learning.
Equity and Excellence	Provide instruction to help all students succeed. Include students' cultures in the curriculum. Maintain high expectations for all (and provide support needed for all students to succeed).
Developmental Appropriateness	Consider children's developmental needs. Build and activate prior knowledge that students bring to school.
Teaching the Whole Child	Learn about all students, especially those who are culturally different from you. Acknowledge and embrace the lived experiences and cultural knowledge that students bring to school. Understand cultural traditions but interact with each student as an individual.
Student–Teacher Relationships	Respect students and build warm relationships. Create an intentionally inviting classroom where students feel welcome, appreciated, and safe. Collaborate with families and the community.

Adapted from Brown-Jeffy & Cooper (2011).

BIOGRAPHY-DRIVEN INSTRUCTION (BDI). One specific approach to culturally relevant teaching is BDI (Herrera, 2016). In this approach, teachers consider each individual student's background knowledge, create a learning climate that fosters growth from the known to the unknown, and provide a range of opportunities for each student to demonstrate their learning. Because BDI emphasizes all four dimensions of each student's biography (i.e., sociocultural, linguistic, cognitive, and academic), it truly puts students at the center of your teaching and their own learning.

Let's look at some samples of instruction from classrooms where teachers use BDI. In Margin Note 4.8 you will see video clips of how first and second grade teachers use BDI in their classrooms.

After you view the video clips from Margin Note 4.8, did you notice how the teachers began the lesson by activating students' prior knowledge and experiences? During this phase, the teachers observed their students' prior knowledge, use of English and their native languages, and use of nonlinguistic representations such as drawings and gestures. Next, you probably noticed that the teachers helped students make connections from the content to the students' biographies—namely, in the areas of prior knowledge and experiences. This included making predictions that the teachers then had students confirm or reject based on their learning.

Margin Note 4.8: Biography-Driven Instruction

Grade 1 Linking Language Lesson Clips

https://coe.k-state.edu/cima/biographycrt/linking-language.html

Grade 2 Vocabulary Quilt Lesson Clips

https://coe.k-state.edu/cima/biographycrt/vocabulary-quilt.html

The teachers also served as learning facilitators to help the students deepen their understanding of vocabulary and content by using text, peers, the teacher, and other resources to enhance their learning. While helping students make connections, the teachers "revoiced" what the students said by repeating, expanding, rephrasing, or summarizing (Herrera, 2016). During this process, the teachers helped the students, especially those who were new to English, hear their ideas in English and make explicit connections from what they already know to the new content they are learning. Finally, the teachers shifted to the affirmation phase where they used authentic assessment to document student progress and to allow students to show (in varied ways) what they were learning.

In BDI teachers often use graphic organizers, visuals, partner or group discussion, and hands-on activities to immerse students in their own learning. But the real key to implementing BDI is getting to know your students' biographies and using that information to help them make connections and learn.

Engaging with Families: Learning about Students' Backgrounds

Talk with your mentor teacher about ways you can learn about your students' backgrounds by asking their families information. You need to be sensitive and respectful when you ask about families. Many are thrilled to share but others may not be. For example, you might ask families to develop a collage with internet images or pictures from magazines about things they like to do at home. This knowledge can help you as you learn how to teach in a culturally relevant way.

What Do You Believe about Promoting Engaged Learning?

In this chapter you've learned about the importance of engaged learning and how you can build a classroom and implement instruction that intentionally engages your students. Think about the takeaways from this chapter and write the ones that are most important to your understanding on the What Do You Believe template that can be found in the Resources for Chapter 4 on the website. Then write what you believe about engaged learning as a result of what you have learned.

Closing Thoughts

As you spend time in your placement or as you prepare for your own classroom in the future, a key to you being an effective teacher is your ability to get to know your students and to use what you know about them to engage them fully in their learning. If we were to fast-forward a few weeks for Samia and her mentor teacher, Miss Pugh, we would see them planning and differentiating instruction to address the varied needs, backgrounds, and experiences of their students. We might also hear Miss Pugh tell Samia, "It's a work in progress because there is always something new to learn about the students!" Although that idea might scare Samia a little, she knows that building relationships and getting to know her students well is central to what she will need to do to be an effective and learner-ready teacher!

Takeaways from Chapter 4

- Engaged learning has three components: behavioral engagement, cognitive engagement, and emotional engagement.
- Engagement is a strong predictor of student learning and achievement.
- Intentionally inviting teaching focuses on teachers getting to know their students well, being consistent and calm, noticing what their students are learning and struggling with, and providing useful feedback and support to help students succeed.
- Teachers need to know their students well so they can leverage that knowledge to provide instruction and support that will help students learn.
- Key areas where teachers need to know their students are interests, attitudes, academic resilience, motivation, background knowledge, and cultural and linguistic backgrounds and assets.

To Learn More about Promoting Engaged Learning

Resources for Your Professional Library

Duckworth, A. (2016). *Grit: The power of passion and perseverance.* New York, NY: Scribner.

https://www.goodreads.com/book/show/27213329-grit

If you want to learn about grit from the psychologist who developed and popularized the concept, this is the must-read book. Duckworth provides a concise and accessible description of grit, how it develops, and the value it has for various types of performance.

Erickson, J. D., & Wharton-McDonald, R. (2018). Fostering autonomous motivation and early literacy skills. *The Reading Teacher, 72,* 475–483.

https://doi.org/10.1002/trtr.1750

This article discusses how you can help children develop self-motivation for literacy and a love of reading. Read these sample activities and classroom-based examples to get ideas about how to implement engaged learning in your teaching.

Fisher, D., Frey, N., Quaglia, R. J., Smith, D., & Lande, L. L. (2018). *Engagement by design: Creating learning environments where students thrive.* Thousand Oaks, CA: Corwin.

http://us.corwin.com/en-us/nam/engagement-by-design/book256493

If you want to design a classroom environment and create classroom routines that promote engaged learning, this book is for you! The authors provide practical suggestions for how to create a classroom that is intentionally inviting and how to maximize your students' learning by becoming an intentionally inviting teacher.

Herrera, S. G. (2016). *Biography-driven culturally responsive teaching* (2nd ed.). New York, NY: Teachers College Press.

https://www.tcpress.com/biography-driven-culturally-responsive-teaching-9780807757505

This book provides a rationale, practical strategies, and sample lessons for biography-driven, culturally responsive teaching to support all students. This approach advocates using students' lived experiences and cultural and linguistic assets to build bridges to the school curriculum and to ensure that all students succeed. Learn about this approach to try in your placement.

Jacobs, G., & Crowley, K. (2014). *Supporting students, meeting standards: Best practices for engaged learning in first, second, and third grades*. Washington, DC: National Association for the Education of Young Children.

https://www.naeyc.org/resources/pubs/books/supporting-students-meeting-standards

This book provides a core set of best practices for promoting engaged learning. It includes many sample lessons and easy-to-implement assessments to help you promote engaged learning in first through third grade classrooms. Incorporate some of these ideas in your lesson plans.

Thomas, K. L. (2018). Building literacy environments to motivate African American boys to read. *The Reading Teacher, 72*, 761–765.

https://doi.org/10.1002/trtr.1784

Research shows that African American boys tend to be more likely to lag behind in literacy development than their peers. This article provides practical strategies you can use to create a classroom context that supports and motivates African American boys to read. Talk with your mentor teacher about implementing some of these ideas in your classroom.

Tough, P. (2013). *How children succeed: Grit, curiosity, and the power of character*. New York, NY: Houghton Mifflin Harcourt Publishing Company.

https://www.paultough.com/books/how-children-succeed/

The author examines why some children succeed and others fail, and he concludes that grit, curiosity, and character are the factors that matter! The book then provides ideas for how to foster the development of these factors for all students. Incorporate some of the ideas in your placement.

Tools and Strategies to Promote Engaged Learning

Cox, J. (n. d.). How to motivate students to love reading.

https://www.teachhub.com/how-motivate-students-love-reading

This short online article provides 10 practical tips you can use to build your students' motivation to read. The tips range from being a reading role model to using technology to providing for student choice in book selection. Add some of these ideas to your lesson plans.

Cullins, A. (2019, June 14). Nine activities to build grit and resilience in children.

https://biglifejournal.com/blogs/blog/activities-grit-resilience-children

This blog post provides nine activities you can use in the classroom to foster students' grit and resilience. The activities include finding purpose, studying "gritty" people, teaching about grit through nature and literature, and asking "what's the hard part?" Try to incorporate these ideas in your teaching.

Gambrell, L. B., & Marinak, B. (2009). Simple practices to nurture the motivation to read.

https://www.readingrockets.org/article/simple-practices-nurture-motivation-read

This online article offers simple practices you can implement easily in your teaching. The suggestions include self-selection, reading aloud, building your classroom library, and sharing your own passion for reading and books. The authors also discuss ways to promote the value of reading with your students. Talk with your classmates about which of these ideas would be appropriate for your community.

Gonzalez, J. (2016, July 10). A four-part system for getting to know your students.

https://www.cultofpedagogy.com/relationship-building/

This blog provides a practical framework for getting to know your students through breaking the ice, doing an inventory, storing your data, and doing regular checkups. The blog provides links to inventories and other tools you can use to implement the framework. Try some of these ideas in your placement.

Miller, A. (2014, January 7). Five steps to foster grit in the classroom.

https://www.edutopia.org/blog/foster-grit-in-classroom-andrew-miller

This short blog provides five simple steps you can use to help students build grit in the classroom. The steps the blog discusses are: 1) model grit, 2) don't grade formative assessments, 3) create authentic products, 4) provide for ongoing revision and reflection, and 5) celebrate success. Talk with your classmates about how you could incorporate these ideas in your teaching.

Section II

Point out concepts about print as you read with students.

*W*e've been looking at reading from a mile-high viewpoint and thinking about what reading is. But what does that mean to you? The principles you learned in Section I can help guide your decision making. Now we're going to look at reading and writing from an instructional viewpoint. In thinking about what it looks like to teach reading, the National Reading Panel (2000) has suggested that there are five pillars of reading: phonemic awareness, phonics, fluency, comprehension, and vocabulary. These five components of reading do not encompass all that you'll need to consider as a teacher, but they are helpful in your initial thinking about what to teach.

Another way to think about how to teach reading and writing is by using standards. The Common Core State Standards (NGA Center & CCSSO, 2010) were a state-led effort to develop consistent national standards so that all students would graduate prepared for college and career. Many states have adopted the CCSS whereas others have developed state standards that are very similar to the CCSS. Standards organize what students should know, but they don't describe how to teach. Standards are often one of the first things you decide on when planning a lesson. However, once you've decided what you want students to know or be able to do, you'll have to select teaching and assessment strategies along with the steps you'll take to teach the lesson. In this section, we'll discuss the content and teaching strategies you'll need to plan instruction and assessment.

In Section II we provide seven chapters that we believe will help you organize your thoughts when you teach literacy. Within these chapters we discuss the topic and supporting research, and we detail how to teach that specific literacy component. For example, you might be wondering what fluency is. We'll help you understand fluency and then give you specific teaching strategies and assessments you can use to develop and teach lesson plans.

How to Teach Reading and Writing

We are beginning this section with a chapter that is foundational to all PreK–3 teaching. Remember what you learned about emergent literacy in Chapter 1? Children grow in literacy as they experience language. Chapter 5, then, describes how you can leverage those experiences to help your students develop print concepts (e.g., directionality of print, front and back of a book) and the alphabet. If you are focusing on preschool or kindergarten, this chapter will be the bedrock of your work. Even if you want to teach second or third grade, you'll need to know how children develop literacy, especially if you have English Learners (ELs) in your classroom. Also, because of individual differences in children, don't be surprised if some students in second or third grade have trouble with print concepts.

After introducing you to how to teach print concepts, we go into chapters on how to teach phonemic awareness, word identification and phonics, fluency, vocabulary, comprehension, and writing. The important thing to remember, however, is that although it's helpful to learn about these topics separately, literacy can't be broken into discrete topics so easily. When reading or writing, children can access all of these avenues to make sense of print or to communicate in writing. So, when you teach, you might be focusing on fluency, but students will also be using what they know about print concepts, phonics, comprehension, and vocabulary. As you learn about the components that make up the teaching of reading and writing, keep in mind that they all work together in your students' literacy learning and in your teaching.

© Evgenly Kalinovskiy/Shutterstock.com

Young children are very active.

How Do I Teach Print Concepts and the Alphabet?

REAL-LIFE EXAMPLE

Cody was going to volunteer at a preschool during break to learn more about how young children develop literacy skills. He decided to volunteer at the class for 4- and 5-year-olds, many of whom would be entering kindergarten the next year. When Cody walked into the room the first day of his two-week experience, he was immediately struck with the activity in the class. The children seemed to be in perpetual motion as they moved between the bookshelf, the play area, and the tables. He also noticed the joy in the classroom. The children were laughing, talking, and singing!

The class had one teacher and two aides for 10 children. The teacher came over to Cody and asked him if he would listen to a child in the class, Yasin, tell a story and write it down exactly as he dictated it. Cody tried to write every word, but he was stumped by the sentence structure Yasin used. He seemed to forget to use articles before nouns, such as, "My brother went to baseball game."

After class Cody talked with the teacher, because he was concerned by Yasin's unusual sentences. The teacher informed Cody that Yasin's family had just come to their area from Iraq and, although Yasin could speak English, he wasn't familiar with certain aspects of how to put words together into a sentence. The teacher asked Cody to talk with Yasin every day and to emphasize adding articles before nouns so that Yasin could hear how we commonly express nouns in English.

Are you like Cody who hasn't been around young children for a while? If that's the case, you're in for a treat. Young children are learning at a rapid rate and are often excited about everything they're doing in school. Young children are emerging as literate beings and this transformation is exciting.

As a teacher of PreK–3 students, you'll want to know as much as possible about the students in this age group. This chapter will present the common developmental characteristics of young children, how to help children develop concepts about print, and how to teach the names of the letters of the alphabet.

Developmental Characteristics of Young Children

If literacy is based on a child's developmental progress, it's important that you know some of the basics of young children's development. You have probably heard the term **developmentally appropriate** in one of your education courses. In short, the term means that you need to make decisions that are consistent with the developmental nature of your students. In order to do this, you need to have a basic knowledge of what young children are like. If you have taken a human development course, you'll be very familiar with the development of young children. For the purposes of teaching PreK–3 literacy, however, we're going to review some of the basic characteristics of young children.

PHYSICAL CHARACTERISTICS. Think about the last time you saw a group of preschool children outside of a classroom. What did you notice? What were they doing? Most likely, they were moving, talking, and playing. As you prepare to be a PreK–3 teacher, it's important to remember that **young children are very active**. They cannot (and should not) sit for long periods of time, nor are they able to attend to one task for an extended duration. It is not unusual for young children to fidget while sitting, even if they are paying attention to what is happening. Neither is it unusual for a kindergartener to fall out of a chair sideways for no apparent reason. Some children just won't sit and find it helpful to stand at their tables while working. They may also complain that their hands "get tired" from writing, and they often squeeze their pencils hard. This physical restlessness and easy tiring do not mean that something is wrong with your students.

Margin Note 5.1: What Does "High-quality" Preschool Look Like?

https://www.youtube.com/watch?v=wbWRWeVe1XE

Children who move a lot are not necessarily hyperactive, nor do they have behavior problems. What it means is that you, as a teacher, should create engaging, attention-keeping activities, and change those activities often. And, since children need to move around, you will want to provide opportunities for your students to spend time out of their chairs or desks. Watch the video of a high-quality preschool in Margin Note 5.1 and notice how active the children are. Talk with your classmates about how this information could inform what you want your students to do in the classroom.

COGNITIVE DEVELOPMENT AND CHARACTERISTICS. Perhaps you remember learning about **Piaget's stages of development** (Piaget, 1977). We mentioned in Chapter 2 that Piaget's work influenced the theory of cognitivism. Piaget also conducted groundbreaking work on the **cognitive development** of children and young adults. Look at Figure 5.1 to refresh your memory on Piaget's stages of development. As you most likely learned, theories of development aren't always accurate for individual children, but they give a broad picture of how children learn at different ages. According to Piaget, children from the ages in PreK–3 are most likely in preoperational or concrete operational stages. Students in PreK–3, therefore, need to explore their environment by playing, being

Figure 5.1. Piaget's Stages of Development

- **Sensorimotor.** Birth through ages 18–24 months
  - ❑ Children interact with their environment by manipulating objects.

- **Preoperational.** Toddlerhood (18–24 months) through early childhood (age 7)
  - ❑ Children's thinking is dominated by perception but is more able to think symbolically.

- **Concrete operational.** Ages 7 to 12
  - ❑ Children can apply logical reasoning to objects that are real and can be seen.

- **Formal operational.** Adolescence through adulthood
  - ❑ Adolescents and adults can think logically about potential events or abstract ideas.

Margin Note 5.2: Piaget's Theory of Cognitive Development

https://www.youtube.com/watch?v=IhcgYgx7aAA

Margin Note 5.3: Social Emotional Learning: SEL

https://www.youtube.com/watch?v=tsRlfTsPukQ

active, and socializing. If you are unclear about how Piaget's stages of development, look at Margin Note 5.2 to get another explanation.

SOCIAL-EMOTIONAL CHARACTERISTICS. Children in PreK–3 will have a variety of different experiences with other children and how they listen to adults. They are **developing their personalities** and, as such, will be learning how to interact with other people. Some children will have had few experiences with other adults giving them directions, so they may have trouble knowing how to act when you tell them what to do in school. Typically, they want to be treated like a "big kid," but they will still need adult supervision since they frequently act impulsively. Many children will begin to develop friendships and even have a "best friend," but those friendships can change frequently which can cause hurt feelings. Young children are often tattletales looking for adults to intervene in social situations while they are learning to handle personal conflict. They also tend to need directions to be clear and concise because they can become confused easily. Children in PreK–3 need structure and routines to help them understand boundaries while they are learning social norms.

The **social-emotional characteristics** of children will vary, but, as you learn how to teach literacy, you need to be cognizant of how the children of your age group interact with others. Look at the video of one explanation of the competencies of social-emotional learning in Margin Note 5.3. Develop a chart with your classmates about how these competencies relate to young children. You might put the areas of competencies in rows down the page and write actions you can do as a teacher to foster these competencies.

The Importance of Oral Language

Have you ever been on an airplane and had a young child with an adult sitting near you? Most likely the child talked and the adult shushed. That's because not only do young children move a lot, they are often noisy. In fact, young children often talk out loud to themselves while they are working on a task. Vygotsky (1962) called this self-talk **private speech**—a kind of speech that serves a verbal memory to guide the child in the successful completion of a task. You might, for example, hear Lily, who is working on an art project say, "Now I'm going to cut out this teddy bear and glue it on the page." The child is using private speech to rehearse, plan, and finish a project. Language plays such an important role in helping children think, learn, and remember that you should not only allow talk in your classroom, you should encourage it. To require a silent, no talking, classroom is to stifle the very means of learning for young children. Additionally, repetition is important for young children. Just like when you are learning a new skill, such as learning to play the piano, you'll need to have directions and instructions repeated several times, and you'll need to practice. That's why you'll often hear children say, "Read it again!" Young children learn best through repetitive actions, so you should supply opportunities for them to hear and interact with stories, poems, and songs repeatedly.

Connection to the Field: Change Activities Frequently

Observe children in a preschool or kindergarten class. Notice how often the teacher changes activities to keep active children engaged. List the activities and record how long they last. As you develop lesson plans, remember to change activities frequently.

Supporting Oral Language Development

We've already mentioned that children use oral language to explore their worlds. **Oral language** is also the basis for learning to read. As children hear language, they begin to form generalizations about words and meanings. Children learn that talk carries meaning and that the words they use can cause reactions in others. As children experiment with oral language, they increase the number of words they know and become facile with grammatical structures. They also begin to develop literacy knowledge as they learn that oral language can be written and read.

Children will be exposed to years of oral language as babies and toddlers before they attend preschool or kindergarten. The language they hear may be English but may not be what is considered **Standard American English (SAE)**. SAE refers to a dialect of English that is generally used in professional communication in the United States and taught in American schools and is the dialect that is used by people in power.

SAE is not the language spoken in the homes of many students. Students may come from homes where they hear Spanish, Russian, or another language; or they may hear combinations of heritage languages and a dialect of English. Students from English-speaking homes may hear a dialect of SAE or **African American Language (AAL)**. According to Hollie (2001) more than 80% of African Americans speak AAL, which refers to a dialect used by many African Americans. Therefore, it is likely that children who come to your class will speak a dialect other than SAE. It will be your job to respectfully help students develop SAE in schools. You can learn more about the dialects in the United States by watching the series "Do You Speak American?" An overview for the series can be found in Margin Note 5.4. We will expand on issues of dialect in Chapter 9, but for now we'd like you to become more familiar with the different ways English speakers talk.

Margin Note 5.4: Do You Speak American?

https://www.pbs.org/speak/about/guide/

CODE-SWITCHING. Schools prioritize SAE because that is the language of power in the United States. It will be up to you to gently teach students SAE while also respecting the **student's home language** or dialect. You will need to teach in ways that do not denigrate a student's home language and yet teach students when and how to use SAE (Delpit, 1988). Some teachers explicitly tell students that we have a **school language** that may be different from the language they are speaking at home, and that both ways of speaking are valuable.

As you introduce SAE, children will need to learn when to use school language and when to use their home language. This is called **code-switching** (or dialect-shifting). Code-switching is not unusual. You probably code-switch yourself. Perhaps you speak a more formal dialect in class than you do when you're out with your friends. You might speak another dialect when you're at home with your family. Code-switching is a common way to tailor communications to your audiences.

Young children can learn how to code-switch when they are in school. In order for you to scaffold your students' learning of SAE, though, you will need to know something about the language or dialect that is spoken at home. One way you can do this is by listening to your students tell stories in their own words and writing them down using the Language Experience Approach strategy. Teaching Strategy 5.1 shows you how you can learn about a student's language as Cody did in the Real-life Example. An example of a story dictated by a student can be found in Figure 5.2.

Figure 5.2. Language Experience Story

The daddy polar bear didn't find the baby.

The sun was going down. The mommy polar bear taught her cub how to swim.

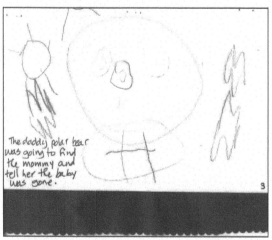

The daddy polar bear was going to find the mommy and tell her the baby was gone.

The mommy said the baby's here. They all went to sleep on the snow.

Teaching Strategy 5.1: Language Experience Approach

Purpose: The Language Experience Approach (LEA) helps children make connections between spoken and written language. The purpose of LEA is that children can talk about what they have experienced and their words can be written exactly as spoken providing a personal connection to learning.

Procedures:

1. Provide a hands-on experience for students, such as a field trip to a petting zoo or park.
2. After the experience, ask students to talk with a partner about what they remembered or what they liked about the experience.
3. Inform students that you will be recording their ideas in writing.
4. Select a student to tell about the experience. Ask the student to tell you what they remembered or liked.
5. Write the student's dictation on chart paper. Be sure to write exactly what the student says. Do not make corrections for grammar or usage unless you have been teaching a specific language convention. An example of a dictated experience follows:

   > This morning we went to the park and we went to the petting part of the park that was a zoo that had lots of animals. We saw a baby lamb with its mother and a turtle and a horse and another animal and a little animal that I don't know what it was and some ducks. I petted the horse and it neighed at me like this: NEIGH!

6. When the student has finished, read it aloud to them, identifying print concepts that you want to emphasize. You could say something like the following:

   > *I'm going to read the story back to you. Where should I start reading? Show me where to begin.* [Student points to first word.] *Yes, I need to start reading at the top of the page at the first word I see. Where does the sentence end?* [Student points to the period.] *Yes, at the period. I'm going to read the sentence for you.* [Read the sentence.] *How many words are there in this sentence? How do I tell where a word begins and ends? Yes, spaces between words show us where words begin and end. Let's count the number of words in the first sentence.*

7. Reread the story, inviting all students to participate in the reading. Reread the story several times.
8. Remind students that this story came from the words of one of the students. Discuss with students how their words can be spoken, written, and then read.
9. Have the students draw pictures of the story and bind the illustrations into a book. Place the book of illustrations next to the original story.

Supporting English Grammatical Structures and Features

Don't panic when you hear the word "grammar." You won't be teaching children parts of speech. However, as a PreK–3 teacher, it will be helpful to know a bit about how children learn the structures of language, so you can help support their learning.

We know that children learn their first language in stages. In 1975, Chomsky published a theory of universal grammar that illustrated how children learn languages. He suggested that universal grammar (UG) is a set of principles, conditions, and rules that are elements of all languages. UG helps us understand that children are able to learn their own grammatical systems quite easily because the rules of language are innate. Native English speakers are able to generalize the language systems they have heard since they were babies. That's why most native speakers are able to "hear" whether a sentence makes sense, but English Learners (ELs) might not "hear" what would be considered SAE.

LANGUAGE DIFFERENCES. Each language has its own grammatical system and other languages diverge from English in critical ways. According to Haussamen (2003), English is potentially different from other languages in a number of key ways, including the following:

- The nouns might take gender;
- Articles are used differently, or there are no articles at all;
- Plurals may be formed by adding words or syllables to the sentence, or by giving context clues in the sentence;
- Word order may not follow the familiar subject-verb-object pattern;
- Pronouns may not have to agree in gender or number with their antecedents; and
- There could be fewer prepositions or the preposition may precede its object.

When learning SAE, ELs sometimes generalize their native language grammatical rules in their speaking and writing. For example, a Spanish speaker might say, "I want that you help me," which follows a typical Spanish sentence structure, instead of "I want you to help me."

You don't need to know your students' languages to help support their learning of SAE. Instead, you just need to be aware that your students may need scaffolding in speaking SAE with the grammatical structures that seem natural for you. A list of common transfer errors for different languages can be found in Figure 5.3.

TEACHING CONTRACTIONS: A UNIQUE FEATURE OF ENGLISH. You probably never think about this, but the English language has a unique feature, and that is **contractions**. Maybe you've heard a nonnative English speaker who doesn't use contractions. It sounds strange, right? Well, contractions are a feature of English that confuses many ELs and some native English speakers as well. Contractions are two words put together, and unlike some languages in which two or three words are blended together in conversation but rarely in writing, contractions have a written form, and contractions need to be explicitly taught to ELs. Teachers can also help ELs understand that contractions are an informal way of speaking and writing. You can find many songs that teach contractions as well as other aspects of English. Watch the song that you can find in Margin Note 5.5 to see if you think that could help students learn about contractions. You can find other songs on YouTube as well. You might search for a variety of songs about contractions to see which one you think would fit best in your placement. You will also want to teach about contractions explicitly. Teaching Strategy 5.2 will give you an idea about how to teach contractions.

Margin Note 5.5: Contractions

https://www.youtube.com/watch?v=5xE-vw2ctqo

Figure 5.3. Sample Transfer Errors

Language Features	Language	Sample Transfer Error in English
Double negatives are routinely used	Spanish	He don't know nothing.
Definite articles omitted	Russian, Chinese, Japanese, Farsi, Urdu, Swahili	He is farmer. Father bought car.
Personal pronouns restate subject	Arabic, Spanish	My uncle he lives in California.
No -ing	Arabic, Chinese, Farsi, French, Spanish, Greek, Vietnamese, Portuguese	I enjoy to play tennis. She study now.
Be is omitted	Russian, Arabic, Haitian Creole, Chinese	He always busy. She working now.
No tense inflections	Chinese, Thai, Vietnamese	He have a good time yesterday. When I was little, I always walk to school.
Verb tense	Arabic, Farsi, Chinese, Haitian,Creole, French	I study here for a year. I need help yesterday.
No distinction between subject and object forms of pronouns	Chinese, Spanish, Thai, Korean	I gave the paper to he.
Verb precedes subject.	Hebrew, Russian, Spanish, Tagalog, classical Arabic	Good grades received every student in the class.
Verb last	Korean, Japanese, Turkish, German (in dependent clause), Bengali, Hindi	. . . (when) the teacher the books collected.
That clause rather than infinitive	Arabic, French, Haitian Creole, Spanish, Hindi, Russian	I want that he stay. I want that you try harder.
Subject can be omitted (especially pronoun)	Chinese, Spanish, Thai, Japanese	Is raining.
No equivalent of there is/there are	Russian, Korean, Japanese, Spanish, Portuguese, Thai	This book says four reasons to exercise. In the garden has many flowers.
No plural form after a number	Farsi, Chinese, Korean	Five new book.

From Lenski, S. D., & Verbruggen, F. (2010). *Writing instruction and assessment for English language learners K–8* (p. 117). New York, NY: Guilford Press.

Teaching Strategy 5.2: Teaching Contractions

Purpose: Contractions are a unique feature of English that will need to be taught to all students and reinforced and reviewed for ELs. This strategy can help you introduce contractions in general. You'll need to introduce new contractions every few weeks and review the ones you have taught until students become familiar with them.

Procedures:

1. Tell students that some words in our language, called contractions, are really two words joined together so that not all of the sounds are heard. Give students an example of a contraction, such as *isn't*. Explain that *isn't* is a contraction for *is not*.

2. Show students how to write the contraction *isn't* by writing both *is* and *not* on the board. Explain that when forming a contraction, the letters that are not written are replaced by an apostrophe. Have students say the word *apostrophe* out loud and write the apostrophe sign on the board in the word *isn't*.

3. Say a sentence with the word *isn't* in it and write it on the board such as the following:

   Her coat *isn't* in the closet.

4. Have students say or write a sentence with the words *is not*. Then ask them to replace *is not* with the contraction *isn't*.

5. Repeat these steps with other contractions that are found on the page Commonly Occurring Contractions that you can find in the Chapter 5 Resources on the website.

© Monkey Business Images/Shutterstock.com

These students are learning about contractions.

Supporting the Development of Concepts of Print

Concepts of print refers to the ability of a child to know and recognize the ways in which print works for the purposes of reading, particularly with regard to books. Under the umbrella of concepts about print are the following: words in English are written from left to right and top to bottom on the page; letters make up words and there are spaces between words; words have beginnings, middles, and ends; and the little marks on the page called punctuation help separate phrases and sentences and add emphasis.

As children grow, they learn about the world around them and gradually develop literacy skills. Knowledge about reading and writing begins early in children's lives. Very young children begin to notice that reading and writing are part of their world. For example, young children learn that their environment is full of print. They see print material such as newspapers and magazines in their homes; they see print on television; and they recognize signs and logos on products and in stores. As children begin to notice print, they are developing concepts of print (Clay, 1985).

Concepts of print refers to the basic knowledge about how books and print work in English. The components of concepts of print include the following:

- Reading from left to right,
- Reading from top to bottom,
- Pages turn from right to left,
- The "return sweep," to move from one line to the next,
- Books contain a front, back, and an author,
- Illustrations correspond to the print,
- Letters and words convey a message, and
- There is a space between words.

DIRECTIONALITY. Another of the concepts of print that children learn is the **directionality of writing**. Children who are exposed to books in English learn that reading moves from left to right horizontally and that pages are turned from right to left. Seems simple, right? Well, there are a few complications. First, students from other countries may have learned different directionality. Different writing systems can be written in different directions. Most of the modern languages are similar to English and are read from left to right horizontally. Some languages, however, are written from right to left horizontally; some are written left to right vertically; some are written right to left vertically; and still others can be written in more than one direction. If you have students who come from a home language other than English, check to see whether that language is written in the same direction as English. Remember that even if you teach preschool or kindergarten and children who come to you haven't learned to read yet, they still might not be familiar with the directionality of English because they have learned the concepts of print from a different writing system.

It can be helpful for teachers to learn how well young children and ELs understand print concepts. To assess and monitor student's concepts of print, you can give students a quick assessment found in the Concepts of Print Checklist in Assessment Strategy 5.1. You can teach concepts of print using a book or using Teaching Strategy 5.3, the morning message.

Assessment Strategy 5.1: Concepts of Print Checklist

Purpose: The Concepts of Print Checklist assessment measures how well a child knows the components of a book. Children need to have adequate book knowledge to read independently. This assessment can help you identify what Concepts of Print to teach.

Procedures:

1. Select a picture book that has words on most pages that are new for the student.

2. Show the book to the student. Say something like the following:

   I'd like you to show me some of the things you know about books and reading. You won't have to read.

3. Ask students the following questions.

   - **Front and back of book:** "Show me the front of the book." "Show me the back of the book."
   - **Print tells the story:** "Show me where I would start reading."
   - **Directionality:** "I want to point to the words as I read. Show me how my finger should move on the page as I read. Where do I go after that?"
   - **First and last:** "Show me the first part of the story and the last part of the story."
   - **Top/bottom of picture:** "Show me the top of the picture." "Show me the bottom."
   - **Punctuation:** Point to all available forms of punctuation. "What is this for? Do you know what it is called?"
   - **Capital and lowercase letters:** Using the text of a book say, "Show me a capital letter. Show me a lowercase letter."
   - **Letter concepts:** "Show me just one letter. Do you know the name of that letter? Show me another letter. What sound does that letter make?"
   - **Word concepts:** "Show me just one word. Show me two words."

4. Use the Concepts of Print Record Sheet that can be found in the Chapter 5 Resources on the website to record student answers.

5. You can also use the Qualitative Judgments of Print Concepts Record Sheet as a way to evaluate the responses which can be found in the Chapter 5 Resources on the website.

Teaching Strategy 5.3: Morning Message

Purpose: The Morning Message is a daily routine that provides a meaningful context for reading and writing. The teacher writes a message to students to share important information about the upcoming day and concludes by asking students a related personal question. The teacher can use this message to show students that they can learn about the day through reading.

Procedures:

1. Before students arrive in class, write a short message on chart paper or on the board that communicates your plans for the day. Use short, readable sentences. The message should conclude with a question that students can think about and answer in writing or in conversation. An example follows:

> Dear Students,
>
> Today is art day. We will be painting pictures this morning of our class garden. We will use blue, green, brown, red, and yellow paint. You can also combine colors to make new colors. I like to use yellow in my pictures. What colors do you like?
>
> Mrs. Shaffer

2. Post the message prior to the students' arrival in the classroom. Provide ample time for the students to look at the message and try to read it themselves.

3. Gather the students around the message and read the message aloud pointing to each word.

4. Reread the message asking the students to join in the reading.

5. Discuss the idea communicated by the message. Remind students that they can learn about what they will do during the day by reading the Morning Message.

6. Provide time for students to answer the question you posed. Have students write the answer to the question in their journals by either drawing or writing responses.

7. Provide time for students to share their journal responses.

8. Refer to the Morning Message during the day when appropriate.

Lesson Planning: Understanding Print Concepts

If you are student teaching young children or ELs, you'll need to develop lessons that teach the concepts of print.

Standard: Demonstrate understanding of the organization and basic features of print.

Objective: Students will learn the concepts of print, including left-to-right directionality and one-to-one matching by matching print during read-alouds of a poem.

Lesson Idea: Print a familiar nursery rhyme or song, such as "The Farmer in the Dell" on chart paper. Have students read or sing the rhyme with you. After students have reviewed the rhyme, show them how the words look in print. Read the rhyme pointing to each word as you read them. Also show students how you are reading the print left to right by moving your hand across the print. Have students individually point to each word as the class reads the rhyme.

Assessment: Make observational notes on each student, recording how many print words students match to spoken words.

Scoring Criteria: Students will be expected to match 100% of the print words to spoken words.

E-BOOKS AND OTHER MEDIA. When we've been talking about concepts of print, we have been discussing print books. Well, what about **e-books**? Many young children have been exposed to both print and e-books. An e-book is a text in digital form. Sentences in e-books go from left to right as in print books. Many e-books have a read-aloud feature so students can hear fluent reading and follow along. The difference is that children can tap on words for meaning, swipe from right to left to turn a page, click to change the screen, or click on hyperlinks.

There has been a lot of discussion about how much screen time young children should have. Guernsey and Levine (2015) suggest that you use the **"Three Cs"** (**content, context, children**) to make those kinds of decisions. First consider the content on the screen. Then think about the context in which the media is used, and finally consider the needs of individual children, remembering that students will vary in how digitally savvy they are.

Connection to the Field: Digital Media Apps

Visit several classrooms and talk with teachers or parents to find out what apps they use with digital media. Develop a list of popular apps with your rating system of how valuable these apps could be to support literacy. As you rate the apps, make sure you look at how valuable they are for language and literacy learning. You might consider working with a classmate on your list of apps.

Access to Print

Children develop concepts of print when they have **access to print**, but there are wide disparities in the amount of print children experience. Some children live in what Neuman and Celano (2018) term *book deserts*. Think about the places where children might see books. They might include bookstores, drugstores, grocery stores, discount stores, and children's specialty stores. Neuman and Celano (2001) found that children from middle-income families had access to many more books than children from poor communities. Children who live in poverty do not have the same access to books as students who are more affluent (Bhattacharya, 2016).

ENVIRONMENTAL PRINT. Children begin to develop literacy knowledge through exposure to print in their environment. **Environmental print** refers to the words and phrases that children see in their neighborhoods and as they travel to other areas, such as signs, message boards, logos, billboards, and words and logos on trucks. However, the amount of environmental print children see differs based on where they live. Children from middle-income suburban neighborhoods tend to have access to print in public spaces in the form of billboards, street signs, and business signs. There tend to be many more stores, strip malls, and businesses in middle-income neighborhoods. Children from lower-income neighborhoods typically see more community murals and graffiti (Aguilar, 2000). Rural areas may have little environmental print. You can help students learn how to read environmental print through a variety of video songs such as those in Margin Note 5.6. You'll notice that the Pizza Hut song presents and reviews signs of fast food restaurants. Think about how this kind of messaging affects students as you teach them how to read environmental print.

Margin Note 5.6:
Environmental Print Songs

Pizza Hut Song

https://www.youtube.com/watch?v=qd-V953wYlc&list=PLmmTf13PcKlJF43fSiYRmeQXCKA3UIIZu

Environmental Print ABC's

https://www.youtube.com/watch?v=gLndkW-SLUc

DEVELOPING A PRINT-RICH CLASSROOM. Because the print that children see on a day-to-day basis helps them understand the purposes of print, teachers often fill their classrooms with print. When a classroom is filled with print, students can practice reading words that are familiar (Malloy, Marinak, & Gambrell, 2019). In Figure 5.4, you can see how this classroom is filled with print. When students have a classroom with lots of words, they can practice reading environmental print by **reading the room**. Students can read the room using Teaching Strategy 5.4.

Engaging with Families: Environmental Print Book

Develop an Environmental Print Book in school to take home. Have students cut out pictures of signs, labels, and store logos to glue on paper to create a book. Include extra pages so that children can add pictures at home. Have children "read" the book at school and then take it home to read to parents. Write a short letter to parents to encourage them to work with their children to add environmental print pictures to the book. The pictures can come from magazines, they can be drawn, or they could be downloaded from the internet.

Figure 5.4. Print-rich Classroom

Teaching Strategy 5.4: Reading the Room

Purpose: Students can become aware of how print is evident in the environment by reading the letters and words in the classroom.

Procedures:

1. Set up a print rich environment by posting the alphabet, pictures with labels, Big Books, word walls, learning centers, and so on. Add different signs and words to the room as you teach different units. For example, if you are teaching about weather, add words and pictures that illustrate what you have taught.

2. Point to the letters and words in the room and say them for students. Tell students that there are letters and words not only in the room but outside in their neighborhoods (e.g., environmental print).

3. Tell students that they also can "read the room." Point to a letter or word and have students say it with you.

4. Once students have read the words in the room together, tell them that they can "read the room" independently. Provide students with a pointer to point to the words as they say *the*, and perhaps give them a fun mask or glasses to use as they read the room. Have students read the room with guidance until they know the words.

5. Give students practice reading the room one at a time. Once students are comfortable with this practice, let them read the room in pairs with one student reading at a time. Tell students to ask for assistance if they are unsure of a word or letter.

SHARED READING. Children learn about concepts of print through their environment and also through **shared reading experiences**. Some children have participated in thousands of hours of shared reading with caring adults. Other children have had very little experience with books. The amount of experience children have had with books is important in their acquisition of literacy. Most children who have been read to have learned some the basics of print concepts. They may know that books are for reading, that books open from right to left, where the pictures in books are, what print is used for, and so on. Children need to understand the purpose of books and concepts about print in order for reading instruction to be effective.

Margin Note 5.7: Shared Reading: Prompting for Purpose: Reading for Meaning, Structure, and Visual

https://www.youtube.com/watch?v=pfM58VnaoD4&t=33s

Children also learn the sounds of the language and how words form sentences from hearing books read aloud. When children hear books read aloud, they gain valuable knowledge about how books work, such as words are speech written down. They learn about print stability (that the words in a story stay the same each time it is read) and they learn concepts about print that are fundamental understandings needed for reading. We encourage shared reading in various chapters in this book. Watch the example of a teacher doing shared reading with students in Margin Note 5.7 to use as a pattern for you as you read with your students. You can read the steps of leading shared reading in Teaching Strategy 5.5.

© Sergey Novikov/Shutterstock.com

Reading aloud to students promotes their forming generalizations about words and meanings.

Teaching Strategy 5.5: Shared Reading

Purpose: One of the purposes for shared reading is to introduce students to concepts about print. Many students are unfamiliar with book parts, how books are read, and the relationship between words and speech. Providing students with explicit instruction about the parts of books can help them increase their literacy knowledge.

Procedures:

1. Choose a Big Book to read to students. (A Big Book is an oversized book that is often used in shared reading because a group of students can see the print and illustrations.) Before reading the book, identify concepts about print that you want to introduce.

2. Introduce the concepts that you want to teach as you read to students as in the example that follows:

   > Teacher: Today we're going to read *Little Cloud* by Eric Carle (1996). What do you see on the cover of this book?
   >
   > Students: Clouds!
   >
   > Teacher: Yes, you see a picture of clouds. The front of the book is called the cover, and on the cover, we usually find a picture and the name of the author. What is an author?
   >
   > Students: The person who wrote the book.
   >
   > Teacher: Yes, and the author of *Little Cloud* is Eric Carle.
   > I'm going to open the cover. Now what do you see?
   >
   > Students: The same picture of clouds.
   >
   > Teacher: Yes, this page is the title page and it has a picture and the name of the author again. Now, I'm going to begin reading with my hand sweeping under the words. Notice how my hand moves from left to right as I read. This is how we read.

3. After students have participated in shared reading, reinforce the concepts you have introduced by asking students to point to the cover of the book, the illustrations, and the name of the author. Also ask students to show you how to read by sweeping their hands under the words.

4. Give all students their own books to read. Reinforce the concepts you introduced by having students point to the cover of their individual books, the illustrations, and the name of the author. Then have students move their hands under the words of the books, reading if they can.

5. Spend several sessions each week introducing concepts of print. During each session, review the previous lesson that you taught. Some students will require many exposures to print before they begin understanding the concepts you are teaching.

Margin Note 5.8:
The Alphabet Song

https://www.youtube.com/
watch?v=75p-N9YKqNo

Alphabetic Knowledge

Sing the alphabet song with us! (There's a link in Margin Note 5.8 to use in case you've forgotten the song.) The alphabet is the foundation of reading. "**Alphabet knowledge** has traditionally been defined as the recognition and naming of uppercase and lower-case letters and the paired associations between letter names and letter sounds" (Invernizzi & Buckrop, 2018, p. 86).

Children need to know the letters of the alphabet to become independent readers. As children progress beyond becoming aware of the sounds of language, such as rhyming words, they need to be able to distinguish among the letters so that they can learn how to read unknown words. It is unrealistic to think that a young reader could learn enough words by sight to be able to read a new story. Therefore, children need to learn that words are made up of letters, and they need to learn the names of the letters of the alphabet.

There are many approaches to teaching the alphabet. Some teachers introduce a letter a week through the school year. Others teach letters in the context of words, stories, and songs. There is no one right way to teach the alphabet, although some experts believe that teaching the letters of the alphabet in context is more meaningful for children (Morrow, 2015).

ALPHABETIC FEATURES. It may seem simple to teach the alphabet, but one of the assumptions about developing concepts of print is that children have been exposed to English and the English alphabet. However, it's entirely possible that you'll have ELs who have been exposed to languages that use a different alphabet from English. Let's say, for example, that you have students who learned Spanish, which is based on the Roman alphabet like English but has some different letters. You may

Margin Note 5.9:
Alphabets Currently in Use

https://www.omniglot.com/
writing/alphabets.htm

also have children from countries in which other types of alphabets are used. For example, if you have students from Russia, they might have been exposed to the Cyrillic alphabet. Students from China might know ideograms, students from the Middle East might know the Arabic alphabet, and students from India might know the Indian alphabet.

To see the different alphabets currently in use, check out the website in Margin Note 5.9. As you click on the alphabets, notice that the name of the alphabet English uses is the Latin/Roman. If you click Latin/Roman, you'll also find that there are older versions of this alphabet that might look somewhat familiar, but English uses the Modern Latin alphabet. Find out from your instructor or mentor teacher if students in your area schools use any of the other alphabets shown. If you have students from Russia, for example, they might be familiar with the modern Cyrillic script. Try writing some letters using that alphabet.

TEACHING THE ALPHABET. When should alphabet instruction begin? Should we teach letter names or letter sounds? In what order should letters be taught? In general, most educators believe that the optimal number of uppercase numbers is between 12 and 18 and lowercase letters is between 5 and 15 that end-of-preschool children should be able to name (Invernizzi, Juel, Swank, & Meier, 2015; Piasta, Petscher, & Justice, 2012). To teach the alphabet, research indicates that you need to provide both 1) direct instruction of letter names and sounds, and 2) words and sentences that use the letters you have taught. According to the research conducted by Piasta, Purpura, and Wagner (2010), teaching the letter names and sounds is necessary but insufficient for students to be able transfer letter knowledge to other areas of literacy. Jones and Reutzel (2012) developed a protocol for applying this research called enhanced alphabet knowledge (EAK). EAK has three steps for optimal transfer of learning the alphabet to literary learning. They include:

1. Naming the letters and producing the corresponding speech sounds,
2. Identifying the letter in text, and
3. Writing the letter.

This research means that you should definitely teach letter names and sounds as described in Teaching Strategy 5.6 and also show students how letters are used in context as described in Teaching Strategy 5.7.

© Sergey Novikov/Shutterstock.com

Children need to know the letters of the alphabet to become independent readers.

Teaching Strategy 5.6: Letter Actions

Purpose: Young children tend to be very active, so the Letter Actions strategy (Cunningham, 2017) has great appeal for most teachers. The strategy entails identifying an action word that begins with a specific letter and associating that letter with the action. When students are able to associate an action with the name of a letter, they more readily learn the letters of the alphabet.

Procedures:

1. Identify the name of a letter you want to teach. Write the name of a letter on one side of a large index card.

2. For each letter, think of an action that students could perform in your classroom or outside. List the action on the reverse side of the index card. For example, if you wanted to teach the letter *n*, you could write *nod* on the reverse side of the card.

3. Show students the side of the card that has the name of the letter written on it. Say the name of the letter. Have students repeat the letter name.

4. Tell students that they will be performing an action that begins with that letter. Show them the side of the card with the action written on it. Read the word.

5. Have students perform the action while saying the name of the letter. Reinforce the association by repeating the same action card more than once.

6. After students have learned several letters and actions, have one student choose a card and lead the class in performing the action.

7. The following is a sample of actions that could be used in association with Letter Actions.

argue	gallop	laugh	quack	vacuum
bounce	hop	march	run	walk
catch	itch	nod	sit	xylophone (play)
dance	jump	open	talk	yawn
eat	kick	paint	unbend	zip
fall				

8. After students have learned the alphabet names, show students the Alphabet Workout video to use movement to draw the letters of the alphabet: https://www.youtube.com/watch?v=SE-ljfAmZis.

Teaching Strategy 5.7: Identifying Letters

Purpose: Children need to learn the letters of the alphabet in correct order, and they also need to learn how to identify letters in the context of words. Some children will have difficulty making the link from saying the letters of the alphabet to identifying letters in combination with other letters to form words. Guiding children to identify letters in print will help them learn how to read.

Procedures:

1. Choose a story, the Morning Message, or one of your student's names to teach how to identify letters. The story can be one that you read to students, a dictated story, or a Big Book with which the students are familiar. Be sure the material is large enough for all students to see.

2. Read the story, message, or name aloud to students. Then have students read it with you.

3. Place several letter cards on the table in front of you. Have a student choose a letter from the stack.

4. Have the student identify the letter. If the letter is a *d*, for example, the student should say *d*.

5. Ask all students to locate any letter in the story that matches the chosen letter. In this case, students should look for words that have a *d* in them. Remind students that the letter can be any place in a word, not just the beginning letter.

6. Have one student at a time come up and identify the letter in the story. If the story does not contain the letter, have the student choose another letter.

7. Repeat until all of the letters in the stack have been selected.

8. Do this activity regularly until students are able to identify all letters in words.

Margin Note 5.10:
Teaching the Alphabet
with Movement and Song

https://www.youtube.com/
watch?v=KSsBZamFCOQ

https://www.youtube.com/
watch?v=LLegmBlkFx0

https://www.
youtube.com/
watch?v=XN
MaxVtBoZU

In this chapter we have been discussing how to teach students the alphabet and the names of the letters. You can teach the alphabet through many different modalities. Remembering that young children love to move, you might try dance, letter movements, and any kind of manipulative you can find. We've identified a few of these in the websites found in Margin Note 5.10. Take a look at the ideas presented in these websites and try to come up with other ideas that could be used to teach the letter names. As you look at these teaching ideas, you'll find that some teachers include sounds associated with letters as well as letter names. Teaching the sounds of language is called phonemic awareness which we'll present in Chapter 6. Teaching the sounds associated with letters is called phonics which we'll discuss in Chapter 7. Even though we've separated literacy skills by chapters, you'll find as a teacher that you'll combine ideas that make sense in your teaching placement.

Lesson Plan: Teaching the Alphabet

As students learn the alphabet, they should also see the letters in context. You can use the ABC match game to have students match letters with picture cards, or you can use an alphabet chart to help students think of words that begin with the letter.

Standard: Recognize and name all upper- and lowercase letters of the alphabet and connect them to the beginning letters of words.

Objective: Students will be able to understand the connection between words and their beginning letters.

Lesson Idea: The ABC match game is an online game that has students match letter cards with pictures cards that begin with that letter. Another way to teach the alphabet is to have an alphabet chart with words or pictures that are associated with each letter.

Assessment: As students play the ABC match game or use an alphabet chart, have them say the letters aloud. As students learn the letter names, encourage them to also learn the sounds associated with each letter.

Scoring criteria: The scoring criteria will depend on the level of the students. Students will be expected to learn 100% of the letter names as they progress in their schooling.

Cultural Awareness

This chapter has been about teaching the foundations of literacy, concepts of print, and the alphabet. We've included details about how language systems are different from each other, so you are aware that some children will come to you with various experiences with language. However, we'd like to caution you about making assumptions about your ELs. Just because a student speaks a different language at home doesn't mean they have not been exposed to English. There are many factors to consider. Some students are newcomers and may be in neighborhoods with little English environmental print, but some children may be from families that have English in their homes. For example, even in households that have little English, some children have older siblings who bring home English books. It's different for every student. Therefore, you might consider giving an alphabet pre-assessment to your students to gauge their familiarity with the English alphabet as in Assessment Strategy 5.2.

Assessment Strategy 5.2: Alphabet Knowledge

Purpose: This assessment contains uppercase and lowercase letters of the alphabet in nonsequential order to help assess letter-naming ability. Note that lowercase a and g appear in both manuscript and print forms.

Procedures:

1. Duplicate the Letter Name Assessment with letters of the alphabet. A full-page Letter Name Assessment can be found in the Chapter 5 Resources on the website.

B	T	R	Z	F	N	K
X	V	I	M	J	D	L
Y	Q	W	C	U	A	
O	H	S	E	G	P	

s	d	o	a	k	w	g
l	u	r	t	q	h	y
i	p	v	f	n	z	g
b	x	e	c	j	m	a

2. Place the Alphabet Knowledge Record Sheet before the student. Use index cards to block off everything but the line being read. Point to each letter and say something like the following:

    Here are some letters of the alphabet. I want to see how many of these letters you can name. Just say the name of each letter you know. If you don't know a letter, just say "skip it."

3. Continue showing the letters unless the student becomes frustrated. If that is the case, stop until you have spent more time teaching letter names.

4. Duplicate the Alphabet Knowledge Record Sheet that can be found in the Chapter 5 Resources on the website to record the number of accurate responses the student provides. Give this assessment periodically to measure student progress.

Engaging with Families: Practicing the Alphabet at Home

All children need to practice the alphabet, either by saying the names of the letters in order, identifying the letters in words, or writing the letters. Ask your mentor teacher whether you can send home individual alphabet practice with students to practice at home. Some students might get a page with the letters of the alphabet with directions to practice saying the letters, some students might get a link to an alphabet song, and others might get a page with some of the letters filled in and places for the child to write the remaining letters of the alphabet. Encourage all students to practice the alphabet at home.

What Do You Believe about Print Concepts and the Alphabet?

In this chapter you learned about print concepts and teaching the alphabet. Some of the ideas from this chapter might be new to you, but much of it probably seemed to be common sense. There are different beliefs about what to do to help students learn about print concepts and the alphabet. What do you believe?

Think about the important takeaways from this chapter and write the ones that are personally important to you on the What Do You Believe template that can be found in the Chapter 5 Resources on the website. Then write a brief paragraph about what you believe about the foundations of literacy learning as a result of what you learned.

Closing Thoughts

Children develop literate behaviors through hearing oral language and listening to others read books. Through these experiences, children learn print concepts. Children's access to print varies depending on where they live and their home situation. You can provide a print-rich environment that helps students learn what reading and writing are about.

Cody learned about Yasin's print awareness by listening to Yasin tell a story and recording his words. Through this activity, Cody was able to learn what Yasin needed to learn about the English language, and Cody was able to help his mentor teacher prepare developmentally appropriate lessons. Learning how individual students progress toward literacy is an important skill that we hope you will learn through your experiences along with the foundational learning from this chapter.

Takeaways from Chapter 5

- The physical characteristics of young children include moving, talking, and playing.
- PreK–3 children are most likely in the preoperational or concrete operational stage of cognitive development.
- Oral language is the basis of learning to read, so it should be supported and encouraged in PreK–3 classrooms.
- Students may come to you with extensive knowledge of print concepts, but you'll need to assess their knowledge and scaffold their learning, so they understand how books are read.
- Access to print varies, so you'll need to have a print-rich environment in your classroom.
- You should teach the alphabet by teaching letter names as well as how letters are used in words.
- Every child is different, and some children are socialized into an English literacy culture whereas others are not.

To Learn More about Print Concepts and the Alphabet

Books on Social and Emotional Development

Procopio, R., & Bohart, H. (2017). *Spotlight on young children: Social and emotional development*. Washington, DC: National Association for the Education of Young Children.

https://www.naeyc.org/resources/pubs/books/spotlight-social-emotional-development

As a teacher, you will have an important role in shaping students' healthy interactions while learning from and with others. Read this book to consider how you can structure your classroom routines and environment to support students' social and emotional skills.

Jennings, P. A. (2018). *The trauma-sensitive classroom: Building resilience with compassionate teaching*. New York, NY: W. W. Norton & Company.

https://wwnorton.com/books/9780393711868

We briefly discussed the social and emotional development of young children. To be a successful teacher, you'll need to know how young children act and react in order to help them learn in a classroom situation. This book provides examples of how teachers can use their classroom practices to help children from birth to third grade develop healthy behaviors, including helping children who have experienced trauma. You can also read the book on trauma-sensitive classrooms and research trauma-informed teaching practices in your area.

Strategy Books

Johnston, F., Invernizzi, M., Bear, D., & Templeton, S. (2018). *Words their way: Word sorts for letter name-alphabetic spellers* (3rd ed.). Boston, MA: Pearson.

https://www.pearson.com/us/higher-education/program/Johnston-Words-Their-Way-Word-Sorts-for-Letter-Name-Alphabetic-Spellers-3rd-Edition/PGM1100202.html

This book is filled with hands-on picture and word sorts for students who are learning letters and reading simple words. Search this book for a picture sort or a word sort that you could use with a small group of students.

Johns, J. L., & Lenski, S. D. (2019). *Improving reading: Strategies, resources, and Common Core connections* (7th ed.). Dubuque, IA: Kendall Hunt Publishing Company.

https://he.kendallhunt.com/product/improving-reading-strategies-resources-and-common-core-connections-0

We've presented a number of strategies to help young children develop literacy. After you've tried the strategies in this book, you might read through other books to add to your repertoire of strategies to teach print concepts and the alphabet. Knowing a number of ways to teach the same thing will broaden your knowledge and help you adapt lessons for your students.

World's Alphabets and Languages

 http://www.omniglot.com/writing/alphabets.htm

 http://www.omniglot.com/writing/languages.htm

As we mentioned in this chapter, not all of your students will come from a language background that uses the Latin/Roman alphabet. If you have a student from another country, use these websites to check to see what language is spoken and what their alphabet looks like. Or just check it out for fun!

Digital Media Issues

 https://www.zerotothree.org/resources/series/screen-sense-setting-the-record-straight

 https://www.naeyc.org/resources/topics/technology-and-media

 https://www.aap.org/en-us/about-the-aap/aap-press-room/Pages/American-Academy-of-Pediatrics-Announces-New-Recommendations-for-Childrens-Media-Use.aspx

How much time should children spend looking at screens? We discussed digital reading in this chapter, but there is a lot more to think about. Check out the link for Screen Time Guidelines for babies and toddlers and read the National Association for the Education of Young Children Position Statement on Technology and Interactive Media. What do you think would be the appropriate amount of digital media to use in your classroom?

Alphabet Songs

 https://www.youtube.com/watch?v=_UR-l3QI2nE

 https://www.youtube.com/watch?v=Ks_Hkx9oxiI

There are a variety of alphabet songs you could sing with your students and also alphabet videos you could show them. Using a variety of modalities when you teach the alphabet can foster student learning. You can use these links to find the alphabet songs and videos that help students learn the alphabet and the letter names.

© Iakov Filimonov/Shutterstock.com

Jump rope songs build phonemic awareness because of the attention to rhyming.

How Do I Teach Phonemic Awareness?

REAL-LIFE EXAMPLE

One month into her twice-weekly kindergarten placement, Doretha realized that the students struggled with activities that required them to orally substitute one phoneme (sound) for another. An example from her lesson was, "Change the last sound in bus to /n/. What's the new word?" Doretha had carefully planned her phonemic awareness lesson using information from her reading methods course, but the students didn't "get it," and she wasn't sure why they struggled. She thought it was an easy activity.

When Doretha talked with her mentor teacher, Mrs. Jones explained that the students were not ready for that activity yet. Given the beginning of the year literacy assessment data, most of the students in the class needed instruction on orally identifying beginning sounds and orally identifying words that begin with the same sound. Some students were still struggling with orally recognizing rhyme and orally generating rhymes, and they needed more instruction and support in that area.

Do you remember saying rhymes when you were young? The rhymes might have been nursery rhymes, poems, tongue-twisters, or jump rope rhymes. These rhymes prepared you to understand and teach phonemic awareness, like Doretha is doing in her placement. Most students in PreK–3, especially at the beginning stages of reading instruction, need substantial instruction in phonemic awareness.

In this chapter, we describe phonemic awareness and contrast it with teaching phonics. Then we explain the components of phonemic awareness and illustrate how these components build on each other. Finally, we give you ideas for ways to assess and teach this important reading skill.

What Is Phonemic Awareness?

Phonemic awareness is the ability to hear and manipulate sounds in words. A **phoneme** (sound) is the smallest unit of spoken language. The word *dog*, for example, has three phonemes: /d/, /o/, /g/. Don't count the letters in the word. The slash marks around a letter mean that's the sound of the letter, not the letter name. Say the word *dog*. What's the first *sound* you hear in the word *dog*? It's /d/. Be sure to keep the sound precise. Don't add "uh" to it because "duh" sounds different from /d/. Keep the sounds precise so students don't add "uh" after each letter as they sound out words as they write.

Margin Note 6.1:
Letters vs. Phonemes
https://www.youtube.com/
watch?v=J608Dbhs6J8

How many phonemes are in the word *fish*? Hopefully you said three: /f/, /i/, /sh/. The letters *sh* form one sound that cannot be separated. You need to listen to the **sounds** you hear in each word instead of counting letters. See Margin Note 6.1 for a short video where Louisa Moats explains the difference between letters and phonemes.

PHONEMIC AWARENESS IN YOUR LIFE. You have much more experience with phonemic awareness than you realize. Maybe you remember jumping rope on the playground to, "Teddy bear, Teddy bear, turn around. Teddy bear, Teddy bear, touch the ground . . ." or "Cinderella dressed in yellow went upstairs to kiss a fella . . .". Jump rope songs are perfect for building phonemic awareness because of the attention to rhyming. Perhaps you participated in hand clapping games to "Miss Mary Mack." Some hand clapping games turn into dancing with raps, such as "Down, down, baby; Down, down the rollercoaster . . .". These kinds of games include rhyming and attention to syllables in words. Jump rope songs, hand clapping games, and simple raps are examples of phonemic awareness activities because they involve orally playing with sounds in words. Follow the link in Margin Note 6.2 to find 25 jump rope songs and games that you could use with your students to develop and practice phonemic awareness. The link in Margin Note 6.3 explains hand clapping games and provides examples with videos, including international examples. Often, these games become raps with dancing on the playground.

Margin Note 6.2:
Jump Rope Songs and
Jump Rope Games List
https://www.kidactivities.
net/jump-rope-rhymes-
games/

Margin Note 6.3: Hand
Clapping Games
http://funclapping.com/

PHONEMIC AWARENESS IN CHILDREN'S LITERATURE. Besides hand clapping games and jump rope rhymes, another way to promote phonemic awareness is through word play in children's literature. Dr. Seuss is the master of word play, especially when you consider how he slightly alters words to make nonsense words. *There's a Wocket in my Pocket* (Seuss, 1974) is a perfect example of **word play** because throughout

the book the beginning sound is changed to make nonsense rhyming words, such as wocket and pocket. Other children's books feature rhyming words with the use of actual words, such as *Rhyming Dust Bunnies* (Thomas, 2009), in which the characters generate rhyming words. These kinds of books are fun to read aloud to students because you can talk about rhyming and think about other words that could fit the same rhyming scheme.

The examples above highlight rhyming, which is just one component of phonemic awareness. Many other components are involved, and we explore those later in this chapter because they are all essential aspects of teaching and learning phonemic awareness.

WHAT'S THE DIFFERENCE BETWEEN PHONEMIC AWARENESS AND PHONICS? It's important to remember that phonemic awareness involves word play that is **oral**, which means phonemic awareness lessons should incorporate the sounds of words. If you add printed text or say letter names, then it becomes a phonics lesson. So instead of saying the letter names, you say the letter sounds. In this book and in other professional resources, sounds are indicated with slash marks before and after a letter. So instead of saying the letter name, you would make the sound for *m* when you see /m/.

We learn about phonics in the next chapter. The major difference is that phonemic awareness is the ability to focus on and manipulate **phonemes (sounds)** in the beginning, middle, and end of spoken words. It's totally oral, which means your phonemic awareness lessons should incorporate pictures instead of printed words and will be comprised of listening and speaking activities. By contrast, phonics focuses on print, with letter-sound associations.

Why Phonemic Awareness Is Important

Phonemic awareness is one of the best predictors of learning to read and later reading achievement in typically developing children (Adams, 1990; National Reading Panel, 2000; Quinn, Spencer, & Wagner, 2016), which means you need to be able to teach it well to students who need it. Stanovich (1993) notes that phonemic awareness is more highly related to learning to read than are tests of general intelligence and listening comprehension.

English Language Arts (ELA) standards across the United States address phonemic awareness as an important reading **foundational** skill that children need to develop in kindergarten and continue into first grade. Regardless of the ELA standards required in your state, they recommend that kindergarten and first grade students demonstrate their understanding of spoken words and sounds (phonemes). Review your state's ELA standards to find out what their recommended sequence is for teaching phonemic awareness components.

WHO NEEDS PHONEMIC AWARENESS? Students enter school with vastly different skills. Not every student attends PreK and vastly different expectations appear across PreK programs. Kindergarten is still considered optional in some states. While five states require students to begin school at age five, 32 states require students to begin at age six, and the remaining states require students to begin school by age eight (Home School Legal Defense Association, n.d.).

Some students may enter PreK, kindergarten, or first grade with a firm grasp of every component of phonemic awareness, whereas others will need explicit instruction (Adams, Foorman, Lundberg, & Beeler, 1998). This discrepancy could exist for a variety of reasons, such as different levels of exposure due to poverty, developmental delays, linguistic differences, or other factors (Helman et al., 2016; Quinn, Spencer, & Wagner, 2016). Watching educational TV shows, such as *Sesame Street*, exploring educational websites or apps geared for young children, and reading and talking with others exposes students to word play. Given differences in students' experiences and skills, there is no one right way to teach reading (International Literacy Association, 2018). Consider the real-life example from the start of this chapter, where Doretha didn't realize that she needed to use assessment data to plan her instruction. Although Doretha's placement was in kindergarten, her students had different needs for phonemic awareness instruction. Doretha's mentor teacher will help her form groups of students based on their assessed learning needs, so then Doretha can plan appropriate instruction for each group. This is an example of how to use assessment to inform instruction that we discussed in Chapter 4.

Connection to the Field: Phonemic Awareness Websites and Apps

Search for websites and apps related to phonemic awareness that you could use in your classroom during literacy stations or recommend for home use. Remember that phonemic awareness practice should involve sounds, so be sure to use pictures instead of words and letters. Talk with your mentor teacher to see how they use websites and apps to enhance students' learning.

The components of phonemic awareness should be taught with students as early as PreK because phonemic awareness provides a foundation for subsequent phonics instruction. Students across grade levels may need phonemic awareness instruction, depending on their individual learning needs. Phonemic awareness is the ability to **hear and manipulate** the sounds in words. Phonemic awareness activities typically precede formal phonics instruction because students must be able to distinguish individual sounds before we introduce letter names that match those sounds (Adams et al., 1998; Copple & Bredekamp, 2009). For example, students who are unable to identify words that rhyme may be hindered in learning the sound–symbol relationships that are a foundation of phonics instruction. That means if they cannot hear rhyming in the words *bat, mat,* and *sat,* then they will later struggle with phonics in building and spelling words ending in -*at,* and remembering to say "at" when they see that chunk in words they're trying to read in text. Due to sounds in English differing from those in other languages, students who are learning English will benefit from explicit instruction in phonemic awareness (Helman et al., 2016).

Phonemic awareness lessons may not seem like real teaching, because they seem like fun. However, this kind of teaching is appropriate and necessary for students to later learn how to decode (sound out) words and read independently. Although phonemic awareness is crucial for later reading success, instruction should be intentional yet brief. For example, Stanovich (1993) recommends no more than 20 hours of phonemic awareness instruction in a school year. Instead of budgeting those hours over the course of the school year, consider what your students already know and what they need to learn. This information comes from your assessment data and will help you form your groups based on students with similar instructional needs. Keep these lessons short, spending 5 to 10 minutes per day, perhaps 4 days weekly, with each group on phonemic awareness instruction that addresses their assessed needs. As students demonstrate understanding, shift the makeup of the groups so they are flexible and based on students' learning needs. Once students understand phonemic awareness, then they no longer need instruction in this area. You need to know your students as individual learners so you can tailor instruction to meet students' learning needs. That requires being able to use appropriate assessments to determine what those needs are and then to be able to informally assess (monitor progress) through observations and interactions to further inform instruction.

The Components of Phonemic Awareness

Although English has only 26 letters, there are 44 sounds. Some languages (e.g., Finnish, Italian, Turkish) have one consistent sound per letter, which helps with predicting the pronunciation of words. However, English is comprised of letters that have **multiple sounds** (e.g., *c* as in *cat* and *cymbals*; *g* as in *gum* and *ginger*). English contains **vowel teams** that can be confusing (e.g., *ou* as in *cough, rough, cloud, would*), **consonants** that are associated with different sounds based on combinations (e.g., *s* as in *sap*; *h* as in *hot*; *sh* as in *ship*), and **vowels** that alter their sounds based on the consonants that follow them (e.g., *a* as in *pan, car, ball*). Although English is complicated, there are patterns that make it less confusing and students can learn phonemic awareness and other aspects of reading with your carefully planned instruction that attends to their learning needs. Figure 6.1 shows the 44 sounds of the English language.

Figure 6.1. 44 English Phonemes with Examples

Phoneme (Sound)	Examples
Consonants	
/b/	bat, bubble
/ch/	chop, hitch, furniture, question, righteous
/d/	duck, odd, filled
/f/	fin, bluff, phone, rough, calf
/g/	gum, egg, ghoul, guest
/h/	hip, who
/j/	jump, wage, giraffe, hedge, soldier, exaggerate
/k/	key, snack, talk, cat, acclaim, bouquet, fox, echo
/l/	lamp, chill
/m/	mint, simmer, climb, autumn, realm
/n/	nest, funny, knock, gnash, pneumonia
/ng/	ring, sang, tongue
/p/	pig, puppy
/r/	rug, parrot, wrap, rhythm
/s/	sun, miss, race, cycle, horse, science, glisten, psychology
/sh/	shop, ocean, sure, special, machine, tension
/t/	tape, kitten
Unvoiced /th/	thunder
Voiced /th/	that

Figure 6.1. *(continued)*

Phoneme (Sound)	Examples
Consonants (continued)	
/v/	van, of, hive
/w/	wet, why, choir, quilt
/y/	yarn, opinion
/z/	zebra, fuzz, raze, these, has, xylophone, scissors
/zh/	azure, treasure, fusion
Short vowels	
Short /a/	cat, plaid
Short /e/	egg, thread, heifer, said, friend, leopard
Short /i/	iguana, women, hymn, busy, built
Short /o/	olive, honest, swan
Short /u/	mud, flood, monkey, rough
Schwa /e/ (sounds like short u)	pizza, bacon, listen, again
Long vowels	
Long /ā/	cake, pay, lady, weigh, pail, straight, gauge, break, vein, prey, crochet
Long /ē/	me, free, key, these, heat, ski, people, brief, receive, grizzly
Long /ī/	idea, ride, fly, right, pie, rye, buy, island, height
Long /ō/	open, toe, float, low
Long /ü/	blue, flute, spoon, fruit, through, screw, shoe
/y/ /ü/ (2 sounds)	unicorn, you, few, view, beauty
Other vowels	
/oo/	hook, bush, wolf, could
/oi/	coin, boy
/ow/	cow, pout
R-controlled vowels	
/ā/ /r/	air, care, pear, where
/ä/ /r/	car, heart
/i/ /r/	ear, mirror, here, cheer
/o/ /r/	for, core, door, four
/u/ /r/	bird, term, burn, worm, collar, tender

Adapted from:

Bear, D. R., Invernizzi, M., Templeton, S., & Johnston, F. (2015). *Words their way: Word study for phonics, vocabulary, and spelling instruction* (6th ed.). New York, NY: Pearson.

Fox, B. J. (2014). *Phonics and word study for the teacher of reading: Programmed for self-instruction* (11th ed.). Upper Saddle River, NJ: Pearson.

PHONEMIC AWARENESS AND ENGLISH LEARNERS. Helman, Rogers, Frederick, and Struck (2016) explain that English Learners (ELs) may have difficulty hearing some of the sounds in English because those sounds may not exist in their native languages. For example, native speakers of Spanish may have difficulties with **vowels** because they have different sounds in Spanish. The English sounds /sh/ and /v/ do not appear in Spanish, and Spanish words do not begin with *s* blends (*sc, sk, sl, sm, sn, sp, st, sw*). Spanish words end with **consonants** such as *b, g, t*, but never with **consonant blends** (e.g., *ng, nk, st*). Hmong speakers may have difficulty with the sounds associated with *th, r*, and most consonant blends. In Hmong, the final letter of *b, d, g, j, m, s*, and *v* indicates the correct tones to use when speaking (Helman et al., 2016). Be patient and supportive as students learn English sounds that may be new to them. Be sure to provide extra support for all students who struggle. You can plan to provide ample modeling so that students have plenty of good examples and build in extra time for students to practice using language during lessons.

PROGRESSION OF PHONEMIC AWARENESS SKILLS. Phonemic awareness is typically considered a **progression** of skills that is typically learned by the end of first grade. However, students across grade levels may require phonemic awareness instruction, depending on their individual learning needs. Figure 6.2 shows the components of phonemic awareness that you'll need to know as a teacher.

Figure 6.2. Phonemic Awareness Components with Examples

Phonemic Awareness Components	Examples
Recognize rhyme	Which of these two words rhyme: *cat, bat, sun*?
Generate rhyme	Can you think of a word that rhymes with *hog*?
Identify phonemes	What sound is the same in *baby, bus*, and *ball*?
Isolate phonemes	Tell me the first sound in *make*.
Blend phonemes	Put these sounds together to tell me the word: /c/ /a/ /t/.
Categorize phonemes	Which word does not belong: *cat, cup, pig*?
Segment phonemes	What are the sounds in *hat*? /h/ /a/ /t/
Add phonemes	What word do you have if you add /s/ to the beginning of *top*?
Substitute phonemes	The word is *cat*. Change the /t/ to /n/. What's my new word?
Delete phonemes	What is the word *fill* without the /f/?

Adapted from Johns, J. L., & Lenski, S. D. (2019). *Improving reading: Strategies, resources, and Common Core connections* (7th ed.). Dubuque, IA: Kendall Hunt Publishing Company.

Connection to the Field: ELA Standards

Ask your mentor teacher about the ELA state standards for teaching phonemic awareness for grades PreK and above. Ask if there's a specific sequence recommended by the school or district.

Teaching Phonemic Awareness through Rhyming Words

The first group of strategies that we provide have students listen for and reproduce rhymes in words. You can modify the strategies to build in opportunities for further practice—that way, your students understand the concept through your teaching, with practice to reinforce what you taught. You will continue to add to your teaching repertoire as you gain experience. Teaching phonemic awareness requires you to direct students' attention to the **sounds** in words so they develop the ability to notice the sounds on their own. Extend students' learning by providing time for practice in learning stations and when you can during the school day. Consider how you can enhance students' learning by connecting with families for phonemic awareness practice beyond school.

Instead of using written letters and words, phonemic awareness lessons should rely on real objects or pictures. When selecting objects or pictures to use in your lessons, try to find those that will be common to the experiences of ELs. You could ask the EL students to name the objects or pictures in their native languages and then compare it to the English word to determine if the words contain similar sounds.

IDENTIFYING RHYMING WORDS. The ability to recognize rhyming words helps students establish a foundation for later phonics instruction, especially when considering that word families have the same common ending sound in different words. Teaching Strategy 6.1 focuses on helping students identify rhyming words through oral language word play. See Margin Note 6.4 for a list of rhyming picture books that you could use in your teaching.

You can determine whether students can identify rhyming words by using Assessment Strategy 6.1. Listening to students' responses during lessons and noticing their ability to identify rhyming words as you read aloud to the class can help you determine which students might need more practice.

Margin Note 6.4: Books Featuring Rhyming Words

http://www.readingrockets.org/booklists/fun-rhyming-and-word-sounds

© Monkey Business Images/Shutterstock.com

Talk about rhyming while reading aloud to students.

Teaching Strategy 6.1: I Spy Rhymes

Purpose: Being able to hear word rhymes helps students develop an understanding that word families can represent the same sound in different words.

Procedures:

1. Read a book or poem from Margin Note 6.4 aloud that contains several rhyming words. Tell students that they should be listening for words that rhyme. Remind them that rhyming words will sound alike. Say a rhyming word pair such as *bike* and *like*. Tell students that *bike* and *like* rhyme because they have the same ending sound.

2. Reread the story or poem. Draw students' attention to the words that rhyme.

3. Read a second story or poem. Tell students that when they hear a rhyming word pair, they should stand and say, "I spy _____ and _____." The students should say the rhyming word pair as in "I spy *bike* and *like*."

4. Some stories or poems that you read will have several different rhyming words. Allow students to say all the rhymes. If they miss some, reread the story or poem emphasizing the rhymes that were not heard.

5. Repeat the activity several times each week until students can identify rhyming words easily.

© DGLimages/shutterstock.com

Assessment Strategy 6.1: Rhyme Detection

Purpose: The purpose of this assessment is to determine a student's ability to hear whether two spoken words rhyme.

Procedures:

1. Practice saying the words on the list before you assess a student.

2. Say the following to the student:

   I want you to tell me if two words rhyme. When words sound the same at the end, they rhyme. Hat *rhymes with* cat. *Does* look *rhyme with* book*? Yes. Does* mat *rhyme with* bat*? Yes. But not all words rhyme.* Mice *does not rhyme with* soon *because* mice *ends with* -ice *and* soon *ends with* -oon*. Does* cat *rhyme with* pig*? No. Does* sick *rhyme with* pick*? Yes. Now, listen carefully. I'm going to say some words, and I want you to tell me if they rhyme.*

3. Say the word pairs distinctly but in a normal voice.

4. Place a check in the appropriate column, total the correct responses, and record the score in the box. If students miss more than three, consider how you can provide additional lessons and more practice for them.

Word pairs	Correct	Incorrect
bee – see		
tall – call		
jet – dog		
can – man		
him – gym		
hen – bag		
rat – sat		
broom – zoom		
back – sing		
bake – take		

Total correct

Engaging with Families: Rhyming Words

Create a short letter to parents that provides them with ideas for them to help their children identify rhyming words and generate rhyming words. In the letter, share a few examples of rhyming words (e.g., *cat/bat, jet/pet, chip/clip, dog/log, fun/run*) and provide ideas for simple rhyming activities that they can do at home. One activity could be to share nursery rhymes and point out the words that rhyme. Another activity could be to say two words and ask the child if the words rhyme. A third activity could be to say a word and ask their child to think of a word that rhymes. Show your mentor teacher the letter and ask for their permission before sending it to families.

GENERATING RHYMING WORDS. As students engage with recognizing rhyming words, they tend to automatically jump into sharing other rhyming words. Encourage students to **generate** rhyming words as you read aloud, talk about rhyming, and at other times throughout the day. Many poems and nursery rhymes provide an informal opportunity to assess a student's ability to rhyme. Note a student's ability to predict a rhyming word at the end of a line of a poem or nursery rhyme.

Lesson Planning: Generating Rhyming Words

Being able to generate rhyming words will help students learn that different words can have common ending sounds.

Standard: Generate rhyming words.

Objective: Students will be able to say words that rhyme with a given word.

Lesson Idea: Have students sit in a circle. Say a word that has many rhyming words, such as *spin*. Throw a yarn ball or other soft object such as a Beanie Baby or a beach ball to a student. The student who catches the ball should say a word that rhymes with *spin*, such as *win*. That student should toss the ball to another student or back to you. The person who has the ball should think of another rhyme. Continue until no one can think of additional words that rhyme with the original word. Then begin with a new word.

Assessment: Say a word that has many rhyming words, such as *day*. Have students draw pictures of several of the words that rhyme with the original word.

Scoring Criteria:

1	2	3
Pictures are unrelated to the rhyming word.	Pictures are loosely related to the rhyming word.	Pictures are related to the rhyming word.

Teaching Phonemic Awareness through Identifying and Isolating Phonemes

The goal of phonemic awareness is for students to be able to identify and manipulate sounds in words. The video in Margin Note 6.5 is about a picky puppet who likes a specific sound. Note how this brief lesson targets identifying phonemes in a focused way.

Margin Note 6.5: Picky Puppet

https://www.you tube.com/watch?v= FaSEVu0xgu8

The First Sounds teaching strategy (Teaching Strategy 6.2) helps students identify pictures that begin with the same sounds. This is a type of **phoneme isolation** task that helps students recognize the beginning sounds in spoken words. It also helps students develop **phoneme identity** (recognizing the same sound in different words) and **phoneme categorization** (recognizing a word in a group that begins with a different sound). It is one of the easier phoneme awareness tasks, and students find it fun. First Sounds will help students understand that words have sounds as well as meanings. Using pictures also makes the task more concrete for beginning readers.

© Warut Chinsai/Shutterstock.com

Phonemic awareness is the ability to hear and manipulate the sounds in words.

Engaging with Families: Thinking of Sounds

Send home a list of three letter sounds that you have introduced in class. In a short note, ask families if they could say one of those sounds and ask their child to say words that start with that sound. Repeat with the next sound. Be sure to state that they should not say the letter name because you want them to focus on the letter sounds. Be sure to get permission from your mentor teacher before sending home the note.

Teaching Strategy 6.2: First Sounds

Purpose: The First Sounds strategy helps students identify pictures that begin with the same sounds. This is a type of phonemic isolation task that helps students recognize the beginning sounds in words. It also helps students develop phonemic identity (recognizing the same sounds in different words) and phonemic categorization (recognizing a word in a group that begins with a different sound). It is one of the easier phoneme awareness tasks, and students find it fun. First Sounds will help students understand that words have sounds as well as meanings. Using pictures makes the task more concrete for beginning readers.

Procedures:

1. Obtain three objects. The names of two of the objects should begin with the same sound. For example, you may select a bag, a bat that is used to play ball, and a toy car.

2. Tell students that you want them to use their eyes and ears for this activity. Have them look at the bag and tell you what it is. Ask students to listen to the first sound in the word *bag*. Stress the beginning sound as you say *bbbag*. Be sure that students understand the task. You could also have students note how they form their lips to say the word.

3. Hold up the toy car and have students name it. Then ask them to listen to the first sound as you say the word, emphasizing the first sound. Repeat the instruction in step 2.

4. Hold up the two objects and have the students name each object. Then ask, "Do the words begin with the same sound?" Say the words slowly, stressing the first sound in each word. Then say something like, "You must have listened carefully. The two words do not begin with the same sound." If necessary, have students note how they formed their mouths to say each word.

5. Hold up the bat and ask students to name it. Have them listen to the first sound as you slowly say *bbbat*. Then invite students to close their eyes and listen carefully as you say two words: *bat, bag*. Ask, "Do *bat* and *bag* begin with the same first sound? Raise your hand if they do." Reinforce correct responses and then hold up both objects, name them, and say that they begin with the same first sound.

6. Then select the toy car and ask children to name it. Compare it to the first sound of bag and help students realize that the two words begin with different first sounds. Repeat this process with the car and the bat.

7. Place the three objects on a table. Review the first sounds in the words. Have the students decide which objects begin with the same first sound. The remaining object (car) is "out" because it does not begin with the same first sound as the other two words.

8. Extend the lesson by using other objects or pictures in the classroom (e.g., book, desk, basket) to help solidify the concept of first sounds in words.

9. To provide additional teaching or practice opportunities, enlarge the pictures from the Chapter 6 Resources on the website. In each row of pictures, two of them begin with the same sound as in the following example.

PHONEME ADDITION. Phoneme addition is the ability to make a new word by **adding a phoneme (sound)** to a word (Armbruster, Lehr, & Osborn, 2001), which requires students to focus closely on spoken words and to add a phoneme with an existing word. Although this task is one of the more difficult aspects of phonemic awareness, it can be taught by using plenty of examples and practice.

✍ Lesson Planning: Adding Sounds

Young students may not understand the concept of building words by adding sounds. This is similar to rhyming. However, instead of pointing out words that rhyme, you are teaching students that they can make words (real or nonsense words) by adding a beginning sound to a word family. That means they need to listen to the sound added to the word family so they can say the new word.

Standard: Add individual sounds (phonemes) to simple, single-syllable word families to make new words.

Objective: Students will be able to say the new word when a beginning sound is added.

Lesson Idea: Choose a word family, such as -*at*, -*eg*, -*ip*, -*ot*, or -*ug*. Practice adding a beginning sound to make new words. For example, add /m/ to -*ug* to make the word *mug*. Ask students to generate more words by helping you add other sounds to the start of -*ug* (e.g., *bug, hug, tug*). Choose another word family and repeat.

Assessment: Tell students that the word family is -*at*. Tell them to add a beginning sound to -*at* and to say the word they made.

Scoring Criteria:

1	2	3
Words don't use the target word family.	Words may not consistently use the target word family.	Words use the target word family.

Teaching Phonemic Awareness by Blending and Segmenting Sounds in Words

Students who can hear individual sounds in words are usually able to blend the sounds they hear into a word. **Blending sounds** is one of the components of phonemic awareness and it is an important skill for beginning readers (Ericson & Juliebo, 1998; Quinn et al., 2016). When you blend sounds, you say each sound in a word and then put those sounds together to say the word. For example, you might say, "I'm thinking of a word. The sounds are /c/ /a/ /p/. What's my word?" The students who can blend individual sounds into words would say, "*cap*." Teaching Strategy 6.3 helps students learn how to blend sounds into words.

Teaching Strategy 6.3: Put It Together

Purpose: Blending sounds is one of the components of phonemic awareness and it is an important skill for beginning readers (Ericson & Juliebo, 1998). This strategy helps students learn how to blend sounds into words.

Procedures:

1. Explain that you will be saying a word by its sounds. If you have a puppet available, say that the puppet only likes to say whole words. Tell students that you will be saying the sounds of the word and that the puppet will say the whole word.

2. Tell students to listen carefully as you say the sounds of the word. Then say the sounds of a word, such as /l/ /u/ /n/ /ch/ for the word *lunch*. Have students put the word together by blending the sounds into a whole word. If students say the word correctly, have the puppet repeat the word.

3. After students are able to blend sounds, try this strategy with other words, such as /t/ /o/ /p/ for the word *top*, /p/ /i/ /n/ for the word *pin*, and /w/ /a/ /g/ for the word *wag*.

Engaging with Families: Blending Sounds into Words

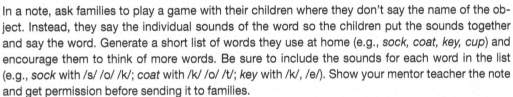

In a note, ask families to play a game with their children where they don't say the name of the object. Instead, they say the individual sounds of the word so the children put the sounds together and say the word. Generate a short list of words they use at home (e.g., *sock, coat, key, cup*) and encourage them to think of more words. Be sure to include the sounds for each word in the list (e.g., *sock* with /s/ /o/ /k/; *coat* with /k/ /o/ /t/; *key* with /k/, /e/). Show your mentor teacher the note and get permission before sending it to families.

Once students understand how to blend sounds into a word, they are ready to learn how to **orally segment** words into phonemes. Sometimes teacher candidates get confused by this terminology —blending and segmenting. For blending, think of when you make a smoothie in a blender. You gather ingredients and add them to the blender a little at a time. Once the ingredients are blended together, you have a delicious smoothie. **Blending phonemes** into a word is just the same as making a smoothie. You put the sounds together to make a word.

Segmenting is where you cut something apart. Peel an orange and you'll notice that you can pull it apart into segments. You begin with the whole orange and then you wind up with approximately 10 segments, depending on the orange. **Segmenting words** into phonemes works the same way. You start with the word and separate it into individual phonemes.

SEGMENTING SOUNDS IN WORDS. Teaching Strategy 6.4 involves Sound Boxes, which help students **segment the sounds** in a word. Sound Boxes were originally developed by Russian psychologist D. B. Elkonin (1973) and can be used to help students develop phonemic awareness in a concrete way. When students use Sound Boxes, they learn that words are made up of phonemes (sounds), and that most words contain more than one sound.

Margin Note 6.6: Sound Boxes

https://youtu.be/bd7EQyRv3YA

The short video in Margin Note 6.6 shows how Sound Boxes can be used in the classroom. However, that video focuses on words for which each sound is represented by one letter. Remember that words with digraphs (e.g., *chick*, *sheep*, *thumb*) would have one token per sound. How many sounds do you hear in the word *thumb*? You would need to slide a token for /th/, another token for /u/, and one more for /m/. The *b* is silent in the word *thumb*. The word *thumb* has three sounds. *Chick* also has three sounds: /ch/ /i/ /k/. *Chick* is tricky because *ch* makes one sound and *ck* makes one sound. Phonemic awareness is all about the **sounds**, not the letters.

Teaching Phonemic Awareness through Sound Substitution

Another phonemic awareness component is the ability to manipulate sounds by **substituting** one sound for another in a word. Teaching Strategy 6.5 is designed for students to practice making new words from an initial word and **hearing the difference** between the words. Students are asked to break up a word and make a new word. As students break and make words, they hear the sounds in word families. Be sure to emphasize the sound substitution and not the letter–sound correspondence.

Teaching Strategy 6.4: Sound Boxes

Purpose: Sound Boxes help students segment the sounds in a word. Sound Boxes were originally developed by Elkonin (1973) and can be used to help young students develop phonemic awareness. When students use Sound Boxes, they learn that words are made up of phonemes (sounds) and that most words contain more than one sound.

Procedures:

1. Select words that are familiar to students. Prepare cards with simple illustrations along with a matrix that contains a box for each sound in the word. As a variation, you may want to provide each student with the matrix and hold up a simple illustration of a one-syllable object (e.g., *cat, sock, fish, feet, mug*) for the class to see. That way the same matrix can be used multiple times. Note that the boxes represent each sound, not necessarily each letter. Secure sufficient tokens (plastic chips, paperclips, toy cars) for each student. An example of a matrix is below.

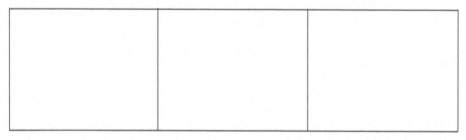

2. Slowly say the word represented by the picture and push the tokens one sound at a time into the boxes. Model the process a second time. Invite students to say the word as you move the tokens. For example, if you are using the picture of a *duck*, say the word and then the sounds: "Duck. /d/ /u/ /k/." As you say the first sound, /d/, move a token into the first box. Then say /u/ and move a second token into the second box. Finally, say the sound /k/ and move the token into the third box. Remember to say the sounds, not the letters, of the word.

3. Provide another example and begin to transfer the responsibility of identifying the sounds to the students. Encourage students to identify the picture and to pronounce the word carefully and deliberately. The goal is to emphasize each sound without distorting the word and to put a token in each box while saying each sound.

4. After students have learned how to use Sound Boxes, eliminate the boxes and have students move the tokens to the bottom of the picture or move them forward on their desks as they say each sound.

5. Pictures with sound boxes are provided in the Chapter 6 Resources on the website for additional teaching examples or practice.

Teaching Strategy 6.5: Break and Make

Purpose: Another phonemic awareness component is the ability to manipulate sounds by substituting one sound for another in a word. This strategy provides students with practice making new words from an initial word and hearing the difference between the words. Students are asked to break up a word and make a new word. As students break and make words, they hear the sounds in word families. Be sure to emphasize sound substitution, not the letter–sound correspondence.

Procedures:

1. Select a word family that has easily identifiable sounds, such as *-at*, *-et*, *-ip*, *-op*, and *-un*. Draw a picture of something that represents that word family on the board. For example, draw a *cat* for the *-at* word family, *net* for the *-et* family, *chip* for the *-ip* family, *mop* for the *-op* family, and *sun* for the *-un* family. Represent the sounds in each word with manipulatives such as tiles or tokens (e.g., paper clips, toy cars, counters). For example, you would have three tokens to represent the three sounds in the word *cat*.

2. Say the word aloud, slowly and deliberately. Then have the students say the word with you.

3. Tell students that you will make a new word by changing one sound. Break the sounds apart by moving the tokens. Replace the first token to build a new word. For example, if your first word was *cat* and you changed the first sound to /m/, you would have the word *mat*. To explain the process to the children, you might say, "The word is *cat*. If I change the /k/ to /m/, the new word is *mat*." Explain that some words are different only in one sound and that students need to listen to words carefully to distinguish between the sounds in words.

4. Invite students to participate in the Break and Make strategy using various word families. In Chapter 7, common rimes (word families) appear in Teaching Strategy 7.4.

Teaching Strategy 6.5 focuses on substituting the **initial** sound. Once students gain confidence with phoneme substitution of initial sounds, switch to substituting the **final** sound. Be sure to tell students that words are made up of **sounds**. Some sounds are in the beginning of a word, some are in the middle, and others are in the end. Explain that you've been practicing changing the beginning sound in words, but now you're going to change the ending sound instead. For example, change the word *cat* by removing the /t/ and replace it with /p/ for the word *cap*. Practice with words such as *lap* (change /p/ to /g/ for *lag*), *bed* (change /d/ to /t/ for *bet*), *pig* (change /g/ to /t/ for *pit*), *hop* (change /p/ to /t/ for *hot*), and *tub* (change /b/ to /f/ for *tough*).

Once students can substitute initial sounds and they can substitute final sounds, then you can teach them how to substitute the **medial** sound (the middle sound). This is a difficult skill, so make sure students fully understand substituting initial sounds and substituting final sounds before you teach them about substituting the medial sound. Be sure to remind students that words are made up of sounds. Some sounds are in the beginning of a word, some are in the middle, and others are in the end. Explain that you've been practicing changing the beginning sound in words and then you changed the ending sounds, but now you're going to change the middle sound in words. This is easiest to do with **short vowel sounds** that follow a CVC (consonant-vowel-consonant) pattern. For example, the word is *pat*. If we change the /a/ to /o/, then the new word is *pot*. Practice with words like *bet* (change /e/ to /a/ for *bat*), *hit* (change /i/ to /u/ for *hut*), *mop* (change /o/ to /a/ for *map*), and *fun* (change /u/ to /i/ for *fin*).

Use Assessment Strategy 6.2 to monitor students' understanding of substituting initial sounds. Once your students demonstrate understanding of initial phoneme substitution, then teach them how to change final (ending) sounds. You could use the same words in Assessment Strategy 6.2 to change the final sound, or use words like *mad* (change /d/ to /t/ for *mat*), *peg* (change /g/ to /t/ for *pet*), *hip* (change /p/ to /d/ for *hid*), *lot* (change /t/ to /g/ for *log*), and *hum* (change /m/ to /t/ for *hut*).

Connection to the Field: Sound Switching

Work with your mentor teacher to plan a sound switching activity to work on phoneme substitution. Tell students that you want them to listen to the sounds in the words that you say. Tell them that you'll be switching one of the sounds. Say a pair of words with one sound switched. You might switch the beginning consonants as in *hill* and *Bill*, you might switch the vowels such as *ball* and *bell*, or you might switch the ending sounds such as in *game* and *gate*. After saying the new words, have the students say them with you. Continue with several pairs of words.

Teaching Phonemic Awareness through Sound Deletion

The ability to recognize the word that remains when a phoneme is removed is called **phoneme deletion** (Armbruster, Lehr, & Osborn, 2001; Lane & Pullen, 2004). This type of phonemic manipulation is one of the more difficult phonemic awareness tasks, but it can be taught to students using Teaching Strategy 6.6.

Assessment Strategy 6.2: Phoneme Substitution

Purpose: Phoneme Substitution assesses the student's ability to make a new word by substituting a phoneme (sound).

Procedures:

1. Practice the words before you administer the assessment. Say the following to the student:

   Listen to the word fun. *I can make a new word. I can take the /f/ off* fun *and put on a /r/ and make* run. *Now you say the word* car. *(Have the student say the word.) Take the /c/ off* car *and put on a /j/ to make a new word. The new word is* _____ (jar).

   Use another example if you think it is needed. You could say the following to the student:

   Take the /b/ off bunch *and put on a /l/ to make a new word. The new word is* _____ (lunch).

2. Say the words below with the prompt, "Take the /_ / off _____ and put on a /_ /. The new word is _____." Place a check mark in the appropriate column after each word. Then total the correct responses and record the score in the box. If students miss two or more, consider how you can provide additional lessons and more practice for them.

Words	Answer	Correct	Incorrect
/c/ off cat and put on a /f/	fat		
/s/ off sing and put on a /w/	wing		
/r/ off red and put on a /b/	bed		
/d/ off duck and put on a /l/	luck		
/p/ off pack and put on a /b/	back		

Total correct [ ]

Teaching Strategy 6.6: Sound Bites

Purpose: The ability to recognize the word that remains when a phoneme is removed is called phoneme deletion (Armbruster, Lehr, & Osborn, 2001). This type of phoneme manipulation is one of the more difficult phonemic awareness tasks, but it can be taught to students using this strategy (Lane & Pullen, 2004).

Procedures:

1. Select a puppet and give it an alliterative name such as Tom Tiger. You could make a puppet out of a sock by drawing eyes and a mouth on it with a permanent marker. Another idea for a puppet is to cut out a picture of an animal and glue it to a strip of cardboard.

2. Explain to students that the puppet will take sound bites out of words to match the beginning sound of its name.

3. Demonstrate by saying the following:

   *This puppet is named Tom Tiger. He loves to bite the /t/ out of words. I have the word **tan**, but Tom bit out the /t/. What word do I have left? The word I have left is **an**.*

4. Continue with other words such as *table* (able), *trip* (rip), and *trot* (rot).

5. Repeat the Sound Bites activity with a different puppet to focus on target letters such as Leo Lion who bites out the /l/ in words or Mary Monkey who bites out the /m/ in words. You could also continue with your original puppet.

6. As students are able to complete this task easily with beginning sound deletions, move to deleting ending sounds which is more difficult.

7. If you wish to focus on all beginning sounds rather than targeting a single sound for deletion, you may select a puppet such as Beginning Bunny who takes a sound bite off the beginning of each word such as *slip* (lip), *cat* (at), and *bring* (ring). For ending sounds, you could use a puppet called Ending Eagle who takes a sound bite off the ending sounds of each word such as *cart* (car), *stars* (star), and *teacher* (teach).

Teaching Strategy 6.6 focuses on deleting the initial sound. Once students gain confidence with phoneme deletion of initial sounds, switch to deleting the final sound. Be sure to tell students that words are made up of sounds. Some sounds are in the beginning of a word, some are in the middle, and others are in the end. Explain that you've been practicing taking away the beginning sound in words, but now you're going to take away the ending sound instead. For example, the word *teach* without the /ch/ is *tea*. Practice with words like *dogs* (delete the /s/ for *dog*), *plant* (delete the /t/ for *plan*), and *train* (delete the /n/ for *tray*).

Use Assessment Strategy 6.3 to monitor students' understanding of deleting initial phonemes. Once your students demonstrate understanding of initial phoneme deletion, then teach how to delete final (ending) sounds. You could use the same words in Assessment Strategy 6.3 to remove the final sound, or use words like *team* (delete /m/ for *tea*), *made* (delete /d/ for *may*), *race* (delete /s/ for *ray*), and *berry* (delete /e/ for *bear*).

Informal assessments could include noticing students' responses during lessons.

Monitoring Student Progress

As you teach students how to hear the sounds in spoken language, you should be aware of students' progress. You can do this by using **informal assessments** so you can judge whether students are able to hear and manipulate sounds. Informal assessments could include noticing students' responses during lessons. You quickly jot notes about which students you think may need more practice with a specific skill and which students may be ready to move on. As you read children's literature containing language play (e.g., rhyming words), you can judge by the responses which students seem to be learning how sounds make up words.

Assessment Strategy 6.3: Phoneme Deletion

Purpose: Phoneme Deletion assesses the student's ability to produce a word part when the initial phoneme (sound) is deleted.

Procedures:

1. Practice the words before you administer the assessment. Say the following to the student:

   Listen to me say the word fun. *I can say the word* fun *without the* /f/. Fun *without the* /f/ *is* un. *Now I'll say some words, and I want you to tell me what is left when the first sound is taken away.*

   Use another example if you think it is needed. You could say the following to the student:

   Listen to me say the word make. *I can say the word* make *without the* /m/. Make *without the* /m/ *is* ake. *Now I'll say some words, and I want you to tell me what is left when the first sound is taken away.*

2. Say the words below with the prompt, "What is _____ without the /_/?" Place a check mark in the appropriate column after each word. Then total the correct responses and record the score in the box. If students miss two or more, consider how you can provide additional lessons and more practice for them.

Words	Answer	Correct	Incorrect
mad without /m/	ad		
check without /ch/	eck		
sock without /s/	ock		
fin without /f/	in		
nose without /n/	ose		

Total correct [ ]

The assessments throughout this chapter can also help you determine which students need more practice. Follow the link in Margin Note 6.7 to learn more about informal assessments. Always be sure that your phonemic awareness instruction is appropriate to your students' various levels of literacy development. That means you might need to teach phonemic awareness in small groups where the students in each group need practice with the same skill. You could also tailor their learning stations so students practice that specific skill. It is important that you **differentiate** your instruction and school experiences for students so they all have opportunities to learn. By doing this, you are providing students with an **equitable** education because you are aware of their learning needs and you are planning for their success.

Margin Note 6.7: Informal Assessment Information
http://www.readingrockets.org/teaching/reading-basics/assessment

What Do You Believe about Phonemic Awareness?

In this chapter you've learned about phonemic awareness and how to teach it. Think about the important takeaways from this chapter and write your ideas about what's important for your understanding on the What Do You Believe template that can be found in the Chapter 6 Resources on the website. Then write what you believe about teaching phonemic awareness as a result of what you learned in this chapter.

Connection to the Field: Assessing Phonemic Awareness

Your school may have a certain way of assessing students' phonemic awareness skills, so be sure to ask your mentor teacher about those assessments. See if you can watch the assessment process in action and learn what the results mean. Ask your mentor teacher how they use literacy assessment data to plan phonemic awareness lessons.

Closing Thoughts

In the beginning of the chapter, Doretha taught a phonemic awareness lesson that she learned about from her reading methods course. Her kindergartners struggled with the lesson because it was too difficult for where they were developmentally. Doretha's mentor teacher helped her understand that students' literacy assessment data helped her see what students understood and what they needed to practice. This chapter gave you an overview of the components of phonemic awareness along with teaching and assessment strategies you can use in your teaching. Remember that all components of phonemic awareness must be taught to have an impact on future reading achievement because simply focusing on rhyming is not sufficient (Reutzel, 2015). In short, phonemic awareness is a very important foundational skill for learning how to read.

Takeaways from Chapter 6

- Phonemic awareness is one of the best predictors of learning to read.
- Phonemic awareness is the ability to focus on and manipulate phonemes (sounds) in the beginning, middle, and end of spoken words.
- Components of phonemic awareness are listed below, in the order of degree of difficulty.
  - Recognize rhyme
  - Generate rhyme
  - Identify phonemes
  - Isolate phonemes
  - Blend phonemes
  - Categorize phonemes
  - Segment phonemes
  - Add phonemes
  - Substitute phonemes
  - Delete phonemes
- Phonemic awareness instruction should be intentional and provide ample opportunity for practicing word play together to solidify learning.

To Learn More about Teaching Phonemic Awareness

Strategy Books for Teaching Phonemic Awareness

Adams, M. J., Foorman, B. R., Lundberg, I., & Beeler, T. (1998). *Phonemic awareness in young children: A classroom curriculum.* Baltimore, MD: Brookes.

https://products.brookespublishing.com/Phonemic-Awareness-in-Young-Children-P317.aspx

Although we provided you with the basics for understanding what phonemic awareness is and how to teach it, this is a comprehensive guide filled with lesson planning ideas, games, and assessments. Skim the table of contents to find teaching and assessment strategies that might be appropriate for your placement. You can use this book as a resource when you are a teacher.

Blevins, W. (1999). *Phonemic awareness activities for early reading success (Grades K–2): Easy, playful activities that prepare children for phonics instruction.* New York, NY: Scholastic Professional Books.

https://shop.scholastic.com/teachers-ecommerce/teacher/books/phonemic-awareness-activities-for-early-reading-success-9780545402354.html

Phonemic awareness is an important foundational skill for learning how to read. This professional resource provides a wealth of activities that you can use in your teaching and learning stations for helping students learn phonemic awareness. Preview this book and consider how you could use the activities for independent and partner work.

Fitzpatrick, J., & Yuh, C. (2005). *Phonemic awareness: Playing with sounds to strengthen beginning reading skills.* Cypress, CA: Creative Teaching Press.

https://www.creativeteaching.com/products/phonemic-awareness-ebook

This is a professional resource devoted to ideas for teaching phonemic awareness. Games, songs, and activity ideas are included. Read the table of contents and look for teaching ideas that you could use in your placement. You can use this book as a resource when you are a teacher.

Yopp, H., & Yopp, R. H. (2010). *Purposeful play for early childhood phonological awareness*. Huntington Beach, CA: Shell Education.

https://www.teachercreatedmaterials.com/p/purposeful-play-for-early-childhood-phonological-awareness1/50665/

Phonemic awareness is essential for later reading success. This professional resource provides you with research that supports phonemic awareness, as well as lesson plans, games, and ideas for connecting with families. Preview this book for ideas about teaching phonemic awareness and consider how the authors make connections to families.

Lists for Phonemic Awareness Resources

Ideas for Teaching Phonemic Awareness

https://www.scholastic.com/teachers/articles/teaching-content/concepts-phonemic-awareness/

Scholastic provided this list of children's books arranged in sections for the different components of phonemic awareness. Skim through this website and think about how you could use these books in your teaching and for reinforcing phonemic awareness skills while reading aloud to students.

PBS Children's Books

http://www.pbs.org/parents/adventures-in-learning/2014/08/rhyming-books-kids/

PBS lists 27 children's books that could be read in school or at home to practice rhyming. Scroll through the list and consider how you could use these books in your lessons for identifying and generating rhymes.

Reading Rockets Children's Books

http://www.readingrockets.org/booklists/fun-rhyming-and-word-sounds

This list is from the Reading Rockets website and features children's books that would help you teach and practice rhyming with students. Look for these titles in your school library to become familiar with using children's books as resources for teaching phonemic awareness.

Nursery Rhymes Books

http://www.readingrockets.org/booklists/nursery-rhymes

Often, students enter school without knowing nursery rhymes. This list from the Reading Rockets website provides descriptions of books featuring nursery rhymes from around the world. Visit your library to find and survey a few of these books. Think about which ones you could use in your lessons to promote a variety of phonemic awareness skills.

Websites for Phonemic Awareness Resources

Reading Rockets

http://www.readingrockets.org/teaching/reading-basics/phonemic

The Reading Rockets website provides an overview of phonemic awareness, along with links for teachers for activities and games, links for families that you could share, and links to read research about phonemic awareness. Visit this website, open a few links, and consider how you could use the resources in your classroom as well as with families.

ReadWriteThink

http://www.readwritethink.org/classroom-resources/lesson-plans/building-phonemic-awareness-with-120.html?tab=5#tabs

This link is for phonemic awareness lesson plans, games, activities, and professional resources on the ReadWriteThink website. Go to this website and read through at least one item in each area. Modify one of the lesson plans to address your students' needs, download a game to use with your students, and consider how you could use the resources from this website in your teaching.

Florida Center for Reading Research

http://www.fcrr.org/curriculum/studentCenterActivities.shtm

This website provides a wealth of activities for you to use in centers or learning stations. Content is arranged by areas of reading. The phonemic awareness components are in the phonological awareness section. Those components are listed in parts one through five. Open one of the parts to view the activities and select one to use with your students.

© Oksana Kuzmina/Shutterstock.com

Teach students to flexibly use a variety of strategies as they read.

How Do I Teach Students to Recognize and Spell Unknown Words?

REAL-LIFE EXAMPLE

Aurleigh never really thought about how she figured out unknown words in her reading. Now that she's enrolled in a reading methods class and completing a placement in a first-grade classroom, she has become very interested in how people figure out words they don't know automatically. Aurleigh decided to keep track of what she did when encountering unknown words. Using her organic chemistry textbook, Aurleigh discovered that sometimes she skipped the unknown word and used context cues to figure out what might make sense. Sometimes she looked for parts of words that she recognized and sounded out the unknown words as she broke the word down into parts.

Aurleigh realized by engaging in this activity that as a reader she used a variety of methods flexibly as she read. There wasn't one method that always worked better than the others. Aurleigh decided that she needed to teach her students a variety of strategies and how to use them independently so they could be equipped for figuring out unknown words.

When you come to a word you don't know in your reading, what do you do? For example, you may have encountered some words or terms in previous chapters of this book, such as *miscues* or *phonemic awareness*, that were unfamiliar to you. What did you do when you encountered these words? Did you approach each of these terms the same way?

As a skilled reader, you have several strategies for reading unknown words, which is called **word recognition strategies**. You probably don't remember how you learned these strategies because that was so long ago. You might remember, however, that at times you need to read unknown words by **chunking** the words by looking at word parts. For some words you may need to apply **phonics** by figuring out the sounds that letters and letter combinations make and saying the sounds out loud to hear the word. At times you may have skipped an unknown word, read the rest of the sentences, and then went back to try to figure out the word. All of these strategies are automatic for you as a mature reader, but these strategies need to be taught to beginning readers.

Word recognition requires a sophisticated combination of strategies that encompass phonics, structural analysis, meaning cues, and syntax. In this chapter, we describe the strategies your students will need to help figure out unknown words in reading, writing, and spelling.

How Readers Figure Out Unknown Words

When readers and writers try to figure out unknown words, they use different types of information or cues to help them in that process (see Chapter 2 for a description). One type of cue relies on the letter and sound relationships. This cueing system is called the **visual** cueing system. It is sometimes called the **graphophonic** cueing system because readers look at the letters and figure out the sounds they represent. We can also use meaning or semantic cues to figure out unknown words. **Meaning cues** include using context clues, asking yourself, "what would make sense?" and considering what you already know that might help you figure out the unknown word. Meaning cues also include pictures or graphics that can help you figure out an unknown word. The **structural (or syntactic)** cueing system focuses on the structure of the English language such as word order, rules and patterns of language (grammar), and punctuation. Each of these cueing systems can help you figure out unknown words, and although they can be used individually, the cueing systems can be very effective when they are used in combination (Ayra & Feathers, 2012).

Let's think about how Aurleigh might use the cueing systems in combination as she is reading her chemistry textbook. Here is a short passage in her assigned reading:

> *The ions we have discussed so far are called monatomic ions because they are ions formed from only one atom. We also find many polyatomic ions.*

When Aurleigh encounters the word *monatomic,* she tries to sound it out by using **visual cues**. She comes up with *mon-at-om-ic,* and she doesn't recognize that as a word so she decides to read the rest of the sentence to see if the book will give her any **meaning cues** she can use to figure out the unknown word. As she reads the sentence, she sees that the textbook has provided the meaning of the word, "ions formed from only one atom." She then goes back and looks at the word again and uses visual cues to see that she can break it apart into two parts—*mon* and *atomic*—which means one atom. As she continues reading, Aurleigh sees the unfamiliar word *polyatomic*, and she uses **structural cues** to determine that the word describes atoms. She then recognizes that she can use visual cues to break that word into two parts—*poly* and *atomic*. She uses meaning cues to predict that the meaning of those two parts which leads her to infer that the word means multiple atoms. She uses meaning cues to ask herself, "Does that sound right?" and "Does that make sense?" She decides it does so she continues reading. By using the cueing systems flexibly and in combination, Aurleigh is able to figure out two of the unknown words in her chemistry reading assignment.

Now that we know what the cueing systems are that readers can use to figure out unknown words, we can do a deeper dive into each of them. We start with the visual cueing system which focuses on letter–sound relationships and includes **phonics** and **structural analysis**.

How Readers Use Visual Cues to Figure Out Unknown Words

When you use the visual cueing system, you look at the letters and consider the sounds the letters make. In other words, this cueing system relies on the ability to use phonics to **decode** or break apart words using letter–sound relationships to figure out unknown words. A simple definition of phonics is understanding that letters have sounds, and that those sounds fit together to make words. Let's think about this with an example where you encounter the word *clorx* which is not a real word, but how would you say it? Go ahead and say the word *clorx* aloud. Look at *clorx* and consider how you thought about tackling the word. Because you are a proficient reader, you probably didn't have to spend more than a few seconds on *clorx* before you said it. Maybe you started with the first two letters *cl* and thought about how you can hear both of those letter sounds at the start of the word, such as in *clean*, *cloud*, and *clam*. Next, you probably thought about the sound *or* makes, such as in *fork*, *horn*, and *cord*. Perhaps you then thought about *x* making a sound like *ks* because you know words that end in *x* make that sound, such as *flex*, *box*, and *lynx*. Finally, you put all the sounds together to say the word. In other words, you used **decoding skills** to identify the unfamiliar word because you used your knowledge of letter sounds as you looked at the letters and thought about how those letters worked together. If we asked you to spell the word *clorx*, you would probably have gone through a similar process. Instead of reading it on the page, you would have said the word to yourself and written letters to represent the sounds you heard. Reading and spelling require knowledge of phonics. Sometimes we even refer to phonics and spelling as two sides of word recognition; in **phonics** we decode or break apart a word that we see in print, and in **spelling** we encode or write a word using what we know about the sounds we hear and the letters and letter combinations that make up the word.

© Flamingo Images/Shutterstock.com

Phonics involves printed text or the act of writing, with attention to letters.

As noted previously, "phonics is the study of the relationship between sounds and letters" (International Literacy Association, 2018, p. 2). This may sound easy but think about the processes you went through to figure out how to say the word *clorx*. Although the English alphabet has 26 letters, you must be able to recognize the uppercase and lowercase forms of those letters. However, simply memorizing what each letter looks like and the name of those letters is not enough for students to learn to read because you also must consider the **sounds** that can be associated with each letter. Some letters are associated with one sound, such as *d* says /d/ as in *duck*. Some letters are associated with more than one sound, such as *c* in *cat* and *cent* and *g* in *gum* and *gym*. Some letters are associated with completely different sounds when they are paired with other letters, such as *s* and *h* making the /sh/ sound instead of /s/ and /h/. **Vowels** (*a*, *e*, *i*, *o*, *u*, and sometimes *y*) are especially tricky because they each have multiple sounds, depending on the letters surrounding them. For example, *a* has a short sound in *map*, a long sound in *late*, but has different sounds in *car*, *chair*, *call*, and *learn*.

Phonics is not something that students learn overnight; it is complex because English is not a completely phonetic language. Some languages have a one-to-one correspondence or relationship between letters and sounds, but you know that we have many letters that have more than one sound.

English Learners (ELs) in particular may be used to languages in which each letter makes a distinct sound, regardless of letter combinations. Learning the different sounds associated with each letter and the different sounds for various letter combinations takes good teaching, time, and practice. You might feel overwhelmed with all this information, and you might be worried that you can't remember everything there is to know about phonics. Take a deep breath and know that this chapter provides you with a review of phonics terms, complete with examples. This chapter also guides your thinking about how to teach the other **cueing systems** as well as other aspects of **word recognition**. In addition, you will learn more about **phonics** and how the English language works throughout your teaching career.

PHONICS AND FLUENCY. Phonics is an essential part of learning how to read and spell words. What do you do when you read? Are you just saying the words in the text, or are you reading for understanding? Phonics equips students with knowledge of sounds, letters, and how they work in words. Once students have that understanding, they become more fluent readers because students will not have to stop to figure out each sound in each word. Think about that. What would happen if you had to deliberate over every letter sound in every word as you read? Once you got to the end of the paragraph, you would be exhausted, and you probably would not even remember what you had just read! When students learn phonics, we want that learning to stick so they can apply their learning automatically, every time. For example, if you teach students that the letters *s* and *h* put together in *sh* say /sh/, then you would expect them to instantly say "/sh/" every time they see *sh* in print. You would also expect them to automatically spell /sh/ correctly as they sound out words to write. As students gain automaticity, they become more fluent in their reading and learn to recognize words at sight. Lots of reading of easy materials can help students build sight word vocabulary, confidence, and automaticity. Sight word recognition and automaticity are important for fluent reading, and they are discussed further in Chapter 8.

Fluency is key for comprehension because if you're not stopping frequently to figure out how to say the words, then you are more likely to understand what you're reading. Students need to increase the number of words known at sight so more of their attention can be devoted to comprehension. Isn't comprehension the ultimate purpose for reading? Or do you know someone who enjoys saying words on a page without thinking about the meaning? Have you read a text just to say the words? Obviously not! Because phonics helps with fluency and comprehension, it is important for reading success. Researchers agree on the importance of teaching phonics because it is a foundational skill that is essential for being able to read (Adams, 1990; Copple & Bredekamp, 2009; Kaye & Lose, 2019).

PHONICS VS. PHONEMIC AWARENESS. Phonemic awareness and phonics are different because phonemic awareness is **oral** with attention to and manipulation of sounds you hear, whereas phonics involves **printed text** or the act of **writing**, with attention to letters. As you learned in Chapter 6, if you're playing with sounds orally, then it's **phonemic awareness**. Once you say a letter name to associate with the letter sound, then it's **phonics**. The word *clorx* from the beginning of this chapter is a perfect example of phonics because it's a printed word that you had to sound out or decode, based on your knowledge of letters and the sounds they make. See the following example that illustrates the difference between phonemic awareness and phonics.

Phonemic awareness: *I'm thinking of the word* monkey. *What's the first sound that you hear in the word* monkey?

Phonics: *This is the letter* m. *It says* /m/. Monkey *is a word that starts with* m.

The easy way to remember the difference is that phonemic awareness concerns **oral sounds**. Phonemic awareness is something you can do with your eyes closed because it involves listening for and manipulating sounds in spoken words. With phonics, you must be able to see the **letters and words** to say the sounds as you read. You must also be able to use your knowledge of phonics components to **spell** words correctly. Indeed, phonics and spelling naturally go together. How good of a speller are you? It seems as if some people find spelling easier than others. Spelling words correctly in any language is a challenge, but spelling English is more difficult than spelling in many other languages. English is not a completely phonetic language, so words are not always spelled the way they sound. There are, however, rules, patterns, and relationships that govern the spelling of many words. In the next section, we highlight **phonics components** and how to teach them. As students learn these components, they often use invented, or developmental, spelling in their writing.

COMPONENTS OF PHONICS INSTRUCTION. Reading researchers (Adams, 1990; Bear et al., 2015; Kaye & Lose, 2019; Morrow, Dougherty, & Tracey, 2019) agree that phonics instruction must address teaching **letter–sound associations**, teaching students **spelling patterns** for various vowel sounds, and teaching students how to use **structural analysis** for decoding unfamiliar words. Our goal is to provide you with an understanding of phonics while giving you real world examples and ideas for how to teach phonics.

Be sure to refer to your state's English Language Arts (ELA) standards so you can see the phonics expectations by grade level. Regardless of your state, please note that the standards do not tell you *how* to teach. Standards tell you *what* to teach, but it is up to you to decide *how* to teach phonics (and everything else!). Instead of a being a cookbook, standards merely list the required ingredients.

Some states have ELA standards for PreK. Typically, PreK standards consider what should be accomplished to prepare young students for the kindergarten curriculum. Follow the link in Margin Note 7.1 to see how New York aligned their PreK ELA standards with kindergarten standards.

PreK teachers shouldn't be the only ones looking to see what the standards are for the grade level ahead. Teachers of every grade level should do this to see what's called vertical alignment. Vertical alignment helps you understand what students were supposed to learn in the previous grade level, which is useful in considering how to provide review and build on that prior learning. Vertical alignment also helps you understand what students are supposed to know for the next grade level, which is useful in considering how to get students ready for those expectations.

Margin Note 7.1: Prekindergarten to Kindergarten Standards Alignment ELA

http://www.p12.nysed.gov/ earlylearning/standards/ documents/Prekindergarten toKindergartenStandards AlignmentELA_000.pdf

Connection to the Field: ELA Phonics Standards

If you are in a K–3 placement, ask your mentor teacher to discuss the ELA standards and curriculum materials with you. Ask your mentor teacher how they use ELA standards to guide their teaching of phonics. Also, ask if there is a vertical progression guide for phonics so you can see how students' learning is expanded upon at each grade level. If you are in a PreK placement, ask your mentor teacher to share the required literacy curriculum and how that guides their teaching of phonics.

Regardless of your ideal grade level or your placement grade level, be sure to review the explanations of phonics components below so you understand what they mean and how they progress across grade levels. We cannot predict which grade levels you will teach during your career. If you

are hired to teach above third grade, you will still need to know how to teach phonics because you will have some readers who may be struggling with phonics. Remember that every student is on their own trajectory to becoming a reader and a writer, so be sure you keep the developmental stages in mind while considering why students may be struggling.

LETTER–SOUND ASSOCIATIONS. Letter–sound associations refer to seeing a letter and knowing its name and the sound(s) that letter makes. As proficient readers, we do this constantly without thinking. Learning letter names and the sounds of each letter can be difficult because they look like squiggles on a page until we point out what they are and the differences between them. These **uppercase (capital)** letters have similar shapes: C/G/O/Q, E/F, I/L, M/N, U/V/W, K/X, S/Z. Brainstorm a list of **lowercase** letters that have similar shapes and think about how you could explain the differences to young children. As students write, they may confuse letters that look similar. Providing time to practice identifying letters as you read with students and noting how they are different will help clear up the confusion. Reminding students about the differences between those confusing letters before they write will help as they think about spelling the words they sound out.

Letter–sound associations include **consonants**, **digraphs**, and **blends**. See Figure 7.1 for definitions and examples of these terms.

*L*esson Planning: Explicitly Teaching Digraphs

This lesson idea demonstrates how to teach one specific element of phonics, the *sh* digraph. Phonics could be taught one skill at a time, building from individual elements to larger pieces of text. Once students grasp an element, then you could use a contrasting approach where you contrast the known element to a new one. For example, once students understand *sh* you could introduce *th* and consider how those digraphs are alike and different.

Standard: Know common consonant digraphs.

Objective: Students will be able to identify the letters *sh* for the /sh/ sound and produce a word that starts with *sh*.

Lesson Idea: Select a phonics element to teach. This lesson idea focuses on the *sh* digraph.

1. Write the element on the board (*sh*).

2. Tell students, "The letters *sh* stand for the /sh/ sound."

3. Ask students to say /sh/ as you point to the letters.

4. Present words that start with *sh* (*sheep, she, shop, shoe*) and emphasize the sound /sh/ as you say the words.

5. Ask students to say words that start with *sh* and write them on the board as they offer ideas.

Assessment: Have students write the digraph *sh* and a word that starts with *sh* on their papers. They could draw a picture of the word. If students are unsure of words that start with *sh*, repeat the lesson and point out *sh* words throughout the day.

Scoring Criteria:

Incorrect	Correct
The word does not start with *sh*.	The word starts with *sh*.

Figure 7.1. Definitions and Examples of Consonants, Consonant Digraphs, and Blends

Term	Definition	Example
Consonants	Letters left over when you remove the vowels (a, e, i, o, u)	b, c, d, f, g, h, j, k, l, m, n, p, q, r, s, t, v, w, x, y, z
Consonant digraphs	Two consonants that make a new, different sound when they are put together: ch, ph, sh, th	In the word *ship*, you do not hear /s/ and you do not hear /h/ because *sh* makes a new sound.
	wh is a consonant digraph, but dialect may interfere with hearing subtle differences between words like *when* and *win*, or *whale* and *wail*.	
	gh is a consonant digraph that makes a different sound when it appears at the end of a word, such as *rough*. With the word *rough*, you hear /f/ instead of /g/ or /h/. When *gh* appears at the start of a word, you hear /g/ as in *ghost* and *ghastly*.	
Consonant blends	Two consonants that make their individual sounds when they are put together	**bl**ue, **br**im, **cl**ap, **cr**eek, **dr**op, **dw**ell, **fl**ip, **fr**ost, **gl**ue, **gr**een, **pl**ane, **pr**ize, **sc**an, **sk**ip, **sl**ip, **sm**ell, **sn**eeze, **sp**in, **st**op, **sw**im, **tr**ade, **tw**eed
		pa**ct**, ra**ft**, wo**lf**, me**lt**, lea**pt**, tu**sk**, ra**sp**, be**st**
Consonant blends: Preconsonantal nasals	Some consonant blends are not silent, but they are difficult to distinguish because of where the sound is produced in the mouth.	fu**nd**, si**nk**, pa**nt**, ju**mp**, si**ng**
Consonant cluster blends	Three consonants at the start of words where each consonant makes their individual sounds when they are put together	**scr**ape, **spl**at, **spr**int, **str**ing
Consonant clusters with digraphs	Three letter consonant clusters with digraphs, where a digraph is combined with another consonant. Although the digraph makes one sound, the other consonant makes its individual sound.	**sch**ool, **shr**ub, **thr**ee, be**nch**
Consonant pairs with silent letters	Consonants that make one of the letter sounds when put together	**gn**at, **kn**ow, **wr**ite
		lu**ck**, lo**dge**, lam**b**, wa**tch**

Adapted from Bear et al. (2015), Fox (2014), the International Literacy Association (2018), and Kaye and Lose (2019).

Figure 7.2 provides a grade-level progression of phonics for kindergarten through grade 2, based on a broad survey of ELA standards from across the United States. Third grade is not included with this component because standards indicated that students are expected to know these skills by the end of second grade. However, some students will not have gained control over these standards whereas others will have mastered these standards. Hence, you should consider the standards as a **continuum** and teach your students the skills they need. To assess your students' ability to identify consonants in the beginning of words you can use the Beginning Consonants in Assessment Strategy 7.1. Also, consider how your students are using these phonics skills in their **writing**. Teaching Strategy 7.1 shows you how to teach one element of phonics within the context of real reading.

Assessment Strategy 7.1: Beginning Consonants

Purpose: This strategy helps assess students' knowledge of beginning consonants in words.

Procedures:

1. Gather two 5" x 8" index cards, a copy of the letters for the student, and the checklist below for recording responses. Refer to the Chapter 7 Resources on the website for a printable version of the letters and the checklist.

2. Cover the letters on the student's copy except for the first row (*o, x, d, n, k*). Then say:

   I will say a word. I want you to point to the letter that you hear at the beginning of the word I say. Be sure to listen for the sound at the beginning of the word.

3. Say the word and circle the student's response on the checklist. The correct response is in bold type. Then cover the line of letters, expose a new line of letters, and say the next word. If necessary, repeat the basic instruction, "Point to the letter you hear at the beginning of _____." The words are *duck*, *hand*, *kitten*, *mouse*, and *table*.

4. If the student misses more than one, consider how you will strengthen their knowledge of beginning consonants.

Words	Letters as they appear on the student's copy				
duck	o	x	**d**	n	k
hand	n	d	a	g	**h**
kitten	f	**k**	r	x	t
mouse	**m**	s	p	t	h
table	l	v	**t**	j	n

Total Correct [   ]

Teaching Strategy 7.1: Whole-Part-Whole Phonics

Purpose: Whole-Part-Whole Phonics focuses on teaching phonics within the context of meaningful text. This approach allows students to see the use of phonics skills in real reading situations. Typically, a Big (oversized) Book is used as the focus of this strategy.

Procedures:

1. Select a Big Book that contains the phonic element you want to teach. For example, you might use the Big Book *I Went Walking* (Williams, 1989) to teach the initial /w/ sound.

2. Read the book aloud to students. Discuss the story.

3. On chart paper or a white board, write several sentences from the book that contain words with the target phonic element. For example, you might show the students the following sentence and question.

   I went walking.

   What did you see?

4. Read the sentences to the students. Invite students to reread the sentences with you.

5. Point out the words with the target phonic element. Ask students to read these words with you. For example, you might want to draw students' attention to *went* and *walking*.

6. Ask students to figure out what these words have in common. Lead students to discover that the words begin with the same letter and sound. Identify the letter *w* and reinforce that *w* makes the /w/ sound.

7. Ask students to brainstorm other words that have the target letter and sound. For example, you might ask students, "What else starts with /w/?"

8. Reread the sentences containing the target words.

9. Return to the book and ask students to read along with you as you reread the book.

Figure 7.2. Grade Level Progression for Letter–sound Associations

Grade level	Expectations
Kindergarten	Identify consonant letters and know the sounds for each consonant.
First grade	Know common consonant digraphs (*ch*, *ph*, *sh*, *th*) and blends (*br*, *bl*, *sm*, *st*).
Second grade	Know consonant pairs with silent letters (*gn*, *kn*, *wr*), consonant cluster blends (*scr*, *spl*, *spr*, *str*), and consonant clusters with digraphs (*shr*, *thr*, *nch*).

Margin Note 7.2:
Teaching the Alphabet with the Best Kids Books

https://www.the-best-childrens-books.org/teaching-the-alphabet.html

USING ALPHABET BOOKS. You can display alphabet books in your reading area and read them with students, inviting their participation in saying letter names as you do so. See Margin Note 7.2 for a list of alphabet books. Be sure to carefully screen them before using them in your classroom because words appearing in the text may not be the sound you want to teach. For example, which of the following would you prefer an alphabet book to feature for the letter *c*: *cat*, *cheese*, or *cymbal*? If your students are first learning the letter names and sounds, choose the **hard *c*** in *cat* because *cymbal* features a **soft *c*** and *cheese* starts with the **digraph** *ch* in which you cannot hear the hard *c*. What about the letter *t*: *train*, *think*, or *table*? If students are learning letter names and sounds, choose the alphabet book that has *table* because *tr* does not feature a crisp sound for *t* and *th* is a digraph where you cannot hear /t/. Teaching Strategy 7.2 demonstrates how to use alphabet books in your teaching.

Engaging with Families: Poetry

Work with your mentor teacher to find a poem that contains a specific phonic element that you have taught. Read the poem to students before you send it home so they can become familiar with it. In a note, ask families to read the poem aloud and ask their children to point to the phonic element, such as the letters learned in class, as the element appears in the poem. Ask them to brainstorm other words that contain that phonic element. Secure permission from your mentor teacher before you send the note and poem home with students.

© Valeriy Velikov/Shutterstock.com

Knowledge of letter names and sounds is essential for decoding.

Teaching Strategy 7.2: Using Alphabet Books

Purpose: Alphabet books are books that have letters arranged in sequential order from A through Z. Reading alphabet books to students helps them become familiar with the names of the letters in alphabetical order. Alphabet books also provide a wide range of words that start with each letter in the alphabet, which helps students learn how to associate a letter with the sound it makes and a number of words that begin with that letter.

Procedures:

1. Choose an alphabet book to read to students. Most libraries have a large collection of alphabet books.

2. Show the students the cover of the book and read the title to them. Tell students that this book will have the letters of the alphabet and that it will be about a specific topic. Tell students what the topic of the book is. For example, *Alphabears* (Hague, 1984) is a book that shows different bears with names that begin with the letters of the alphabet in alphabetical order.

3. Before reading, invite students to recite the letters of the alphabet with you.

4. Read the alphabet book, making note of any special features. Point out that each page has a letter of the alphabet in alphabetical order.

5. After reading the book, have students recite the letters of the alphabet in order. Provide assistance as needed.

6. After reading the book several times, have students read along with you.

7. Audio-record the book and place the book and recording in a listening center for students to listen to during learning stations.

SPELLING PATTERNS FOR VOWEL SOUNDS. Vowels can be tricky because they make different sounds, depending on the letter combinations. **Vowels** are *a, e, i, o, u*, and sometimes *y*. How do you know when *y* is a consonant and when it is a vowel? *Y* is a **consonant** when it starts words like *yarn* and *year*. *Y* is a **vowel** when there are no other vowels in a word like *gym, sky*, and *my* and when it is at the end of a word or syllable like *mummy, silly*, and *bicycle*.

Do you remember learning about **silent** *e*? Maybe you learned it as the magic *e*? What happens to the vowel in a CVC (consonant, vowel, consonant) word when you add *e* to the end? An example is the word *not*. How does the word *not* change when you add the silent *e*? *Note* is a different word, so it's important for students to be able to use silent *e* in their writing, as well as recognize how to read words with silent *e* in text. How often does the CVCe rule work? Johnston (2001) studied how often the silent *e* rule was accurate in the different **vowel patterns**. She found that the vowel was long with silent *e* in the *a–e* pattern 77.7% of the time, in the *e–e* pattern 16.6% of the time, in the *i–e* pattern 74.2% of the time, in the *o–e* pattern 58.4% of the time, and in the *u–e* pattern 76.9% of the time. Although the CVCe rule does not work every time, you should teach it and be prepared to discuss why some words don't fit the rule.

*L*esson Planning: Short and Long Vowels

For this lesson idea, focus on CVC and CVCe words to point out how the silent *e* makes the vowel say its name.

Standard: Read one-syllable words with short or long vowels.

Objective: Students will be able to read and write one-syllable words and explain how they know if they contain short or long vowels.

Lesson Idea: Choose a common rime (*-ap, -at, -it, -op*) where adding an *e* makes sense to the CVC word (*cap – cape, mat – mate, bit – bite, hop – hope*). Some rimes are better choices for this than others. Draw a two-column list on the board and write the CVC words in the left-hand column. Read the words to the students. Ask them to read them with you as you read the list again. Tell students that these words have a short vowel, but you have a trick where you can turn it into a long vowel. Write the letter *e* at the top of the right-hand column and write the first word with the *e* at the end. Tell students that the *e* is silent, but it makes the vowel say its name. Read the CVC word and then read the CVCe word. As you fill in the words, ask students to read the words with you and talk about the difference between CVC and CVCe words.

CVC	CVCe
Cap	Cape
Nap	
Tap	

Assessment: Give students a piece of paper and tell them to fold it in half and in half again. When they open it, the paper will have four squares. Give students a common rime that fits the CVC pattern in which words make sense when silent *e* is added (*-ap, -at, -it, -op*). Tell students to write a word in each of the four squares with the CVC pattern and to turn it into a word with a long vowel by adding the silent *e*.

Scoring Criteria:

1	2	3
Words in the four squares are unrelated to the given rime.	Words in the four squares may be related to the given rime, but they may not make sense.	Words in the four squares are related to the given rime and make sense.

Watch the short music video in Margin Note 7.3 about silent *e* and consider how this could engage students when learning about silent *e*. Sometimes students will add an *e* to the end of every word after learning that the *e* is silent, so you will need to provide clear explanations and examples to demonstrate how silent *e* works. Supplement your demonstrations with time for students to practice writing short and long vowel words so they can see the difference as they practice writing them. Carefully review Figure 7.3 for definitions and examples of **spelling patterns** for vowel sounds that you will need to teach your students.

Margin Note 7.3:
James Iglehart—
Silent *e* Music Video

https://youtu.be/
NVeq9a4dFIU

Figure 7.3. Definitions and Examples of Spelling Patterns for Vowel Sounds

Term	Definition	Example
Vowels	Letters left over when you remove the consonants.	*a, e, i, o, u,* and sometimes *y*
Short vowels	Words with a CVC (consonant, vowel, consonant) spelling pattern contain short vowels.	*cap, bed, pig, log, rug*
Long vowels	When the vowels say their name, they are considered long vowels. A common spelling pattern for long vowels is CVCe (consonant, vowel, consonant, e).	*cape, these, fine, note, dude*
Vowel teams (Vowel digraphs)	Vowel teams, also called vowel digraphs, are two vowels that have a long vowel sound, where you hear either the first or the second vowel sound as the long vowel. Vowel teams have a CVV pattern (consonant, vowel, vowel) or CVVC pattern (consonant, vowel, vowel, consonant).	**a:** *ai (mail), ay (may)* **e:** *ee (jeep), ea (leap), ie (brief), ey (key)* **i:** *ie (pie)* **o:** *oa (soap), oe (toe)* **u:** *ue (glue), ui (fruit)*
Homophones	Words that sound alike but are spelled differently.	*tail/tale, pear/pair, two/too/to*
Homographs	Words that are spelled alike but may be pronounced differently.	*read/read* in the sentence, "I *read* a magazine yesterday, but today I will *read* the newspaper."
		duck/duck in the sentence, "Remember to *duck* as you walk under the bridge on the way to the *duck* pond."
Syllables	How many beats or hops there are in a word.	*dog* (1 syllable), *monkey* (2 syllables), *butterfly* (3 syllables)
Ambiguous vowel patterns	Sometimes when two vowels are together they make new sound, or a short vowel sound.	*al (call), au (haul), aw (saw), ea (bread), ew (few), oe (shoe), oi (boil), oo (book, moon), ow (now), oy (toy), ou (pout, dough, touch, you)*
	R-controlled vowels fit with ambiguous vowel patterns because they do not make a long or short vowel sound.	*ar (car), are (care), air (fair), er (her), ere (here, where), ear (hear, bear, learn), eer (cheer), ir (fir), or (for), ore (core), oor (door), oar (roar), our (court, hour), ur (purr), ure (cure)*

Adapted from Bear et al. (2015), Fox (2014), the International Literacy Association (2018), and Kaye and Lose (2019).

Figure 7.4 provides a grade level progression of spelling patterns for vowel sounds for kindergarten through grade 3, based on a broad survey of ELA standards from across the United States. If you do not remember what the terms mean in the expectations column, then look for those terms in Figure 7.3 so you can become more confident in your knowledge of vowels. We also provide a sample lesson plan to show you how you can teach students about silent *e* and how it makes the vowel long (i.e., says its name).

Figure 7.4. Grade Level Progression for Spelling Patterns for Vowel Sounds

Grade level	Expectations
Kindergarten	Understand that vowels have long and short sounds.
First grade	Know long vowel patterns.
Second grade	Recognize that spelling patterns and contextual information work together to inform meaning in homophones and homographs.
	Read one-syllable words with short or long vowels.
	Continue learning vowel teams.
Third grade	Read irregularly spelled words, including ambiguous vowel patterns.

STRUCTURAL ANALYSIS. Structural analysis is how a reader can make sense of words by looking for familiar parts like prefixes and suffixes within those words. **Decoding** means that you are cracking a code so you can pronounce the words. Did you ever write notes in a special code to your best friend? Perhaps you created a code in which numbers represented letters, and you could pass notes back and forth in class without discovery of what was written in your notes. Because you are a proficient reader, you probably don't have to spend much time decoding words. When was the last time you stopped reading something to try to figure out an unfamiliar word? How did you figure it out?

You used decoding earlier in this chapter with the word *clorx*, and we walked through that process already. If you forgot about *clorx*, go back to that part of the chapter to quickly refresh your memory. Decoding requires letter recognition and the ability to produce sounds that correspond to the letters when reading. However, sounding out letter-by-letter in words is not the most efficient or effective approach with many words. Thus, attention to familiar parts (chunks) of words can help students quickly decode unfamiliar words. Recognizing chunks within words is part of decoding because that requires familiarity with common spellings. Teaching students about **onsets** and **rimes** helps them remember familiar spelling patterns in words. The onset is the beginning consonant in a word and the rime is the first vowel and everything that follows. In the word *cat*, the onset is *c* and the rime is *-at*. If you keep the rime *-at* and change the onset from *c* to *m*, then you have the word *mat*. Because the only difference in the words *cat* and *mat* is the onset (the beginning consonant), students should be able to quickly decode those words if they are familiar with the *-at* rime and if they know sounds for consonants. Follow the link in Margin Note 7.4 for a list of common rimes. Note that **rimes** are also called **word families** or **phonograms**. Teaching Strategy 7.3 provides you with an example of how you could teach onsets and rimes. Learning about onsets and rimes will also help with students' spelling development because they will become familiar with how to spell words based on their knowledge of rimes.

Margin Note 7.4: List of Common Rimes: Word Families

https://tutoring.uncc.edu/sites/tutoring.uncc.edu/files/media/Word%20Families.pdf

Teaching Strategy 7.3: Word Families

Purpose: Many words are composed of an onset and a rime. The onset is the first letter or letters before the vowel, and the rime is the vowel to the end of the word (or syllable). For example, in the word *top* the onset is *t* and the rime is *-op*. There are 37 common rimes in the English language that account for over 500 words used in the primary grades (Wylie & Durrell, 1970). By teaching these rimes, students should be able to read and spell many words quickly and easily.

Procedures:

1. Select one of the rimes in the box below. Write the rime on the board or on chart paper.

Common Rimes								
-ack	-ain	-ake	-ale	-all	-ame	-an	-ank	-ap
-ash	-at	-ate	-aw	-ay	-eat	-ell	-est	-ice
-ick	-ide	-ight	-ill	-in	-ing	-ink	-ip	-it
-ock	-oke	-old	-op	-ore	-ot	-uck	-ug	-ump
-unk								

2. Explain to students that this word part is called a spelling pattern. Tell students that you will use the spelling pattern to create a word family by adding letters to the beginning of the rime.

3. For example, if you selected the rime *-all*, you could demonstrate how adding the letter *b* forms the word *ball* and adding the letter *t* forms the word *tall*. Ask students to think of other words you can form using the rime *-all*. Write the words as students share them.

4. Once you have made a list of all the words for the rime, give students a sheet with a blank home on it (see the Chapter 7 Resources on the website) and have them copy the words into the word family home. You could display the word family homes on a bulletin board or in the reading area of your classroom.

5. Repeat this strategy throughout the school year to teach and review the spelling patterns you want to teach to your students.

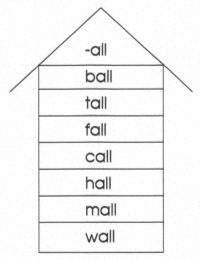

-all
ball
tall
fall
call
hall
mall
wall

Margin Note 7.5: Make a Word: Using Onsets and Rimes Video

https://youtu.be/vEwYQ8fHGak

Watch the brief video in Margin Note 7.5 to see how you can use cards with onsets and cards with rimes to help students make words and sound out words.

Sorting words is a way to help students with structural analysis because of the focus on contrasting the phonics elements being studied. If you are teaching students about digraphs, for example, you could provide word sorting experiences so students could consider the different digraph patterns as they read and sort the words. Sorting words that start with the beginning digraphs *ch*, *sh*, and *th* helps students understand how those diagraphs differ while practicing reading words that begin with those digraphs. Teaching Strategy 7.4 demonstrates how to use word sorts with students.

Engaging with Families: Word Families

Write a letter to families to explain that students are learning about word families and tell them which families you have already taught. Explain what word families are, and how to build words by adding a beginning letter. Provide families with tips as to how they can help reinforce these skills at home, such as using magnetic letters. Ask your mentor teacher to review the letter and secure permission before you send it home with students.

© matka_Warlatka/Shutterstock.com

These students are building -*at* words.

Teaching Strategy 7.4: Word Sorts

Purpose: The human brain is a pattern detector that seeks to categorize or sort information to make it more meaningful. The word sorting strategy allows students to engage in finding similarities and differences as they compare words to identify meaningful patterns and generalizations about letters and sounds.

Procedures:

1. Determine the purpose of your word sorting activity. Is it to focus students' attention on sounds, or do you want to target patterns such as word families? This example focuses on a sound sort for beginning sounds.

2. Prepare picture cards for the words you want students to sort. You can create these cards yourself, or you may wish to use the pictures provided in the book *Words Their Way* (Bear et al., 2015). Also prepare a letter card for each beginning sound students will sort for in the activity. For example, if you are targeting the letters *b* and *c*, you would prepare a letter card for each as well as approximately six to eight picture cards for each letter. For the letters *b* and *c*, you could include the pictures:

   b – ball, boy, bat, box, bed, bug, bell, bus

   c – cat, cow, cup, coat, corn, can, car, cake

3. Explain to students that they will be looking at pictures, saying the word the picture represents, and figuring out the beginning sound for the word. Model the process by saying the following.

   This is a picture of a ball. Ball *begins with the letter* b. B *makes the /b/ sound. I am going to put the picture of the ball under the letter* b *because* ball *begins with /b/.*

4. Continue with several more cards to ensure students' understanding of the process.

5. Provide a set of letter cards and pictures for students to sort the words individually or in small groups.

6. Word sorts can be adapted to match various phonics instructional goals. Some examples of other types of word sorts are listed in the box below.

Word Sort Examples
Picture sorts for beginning blends (*bl, cl, sp, dr*)
Picture sorts for beginning digraphs (*ch, sh, th, ph*)
Picture sorts for beginning short vowels
Picture sorts for medial short vowels
Picture sorts for long vowels
Word sorts for CVC words
Word sorts for CVCe words
Word sorts for r-controlled vowels
Word sorts for hard and soft *c* or *g*

Syllables. Another part of structural analysis is dividing words into syllables so that the reader can break words into meaningful parts to read them and to write them. Orally dividing words into syllables requires plenty of repetition. You will also need to recognize that linguistic differences, such as strong dialects, can pose interesting challenges. Students may pronounce words differently than you, and that's okay. Model how you say the word and explain that we all might say words differently. One example is the word *oil*. Do you pronounce *oil* as having one or two syllables? Do you say it so it sounds similar to *ul* or similar to *oy-ul*? Do you pronounce the word *crayon* as *crown* or *cray-yon*, or yet a different way? Keep in mind that **dialect** and how you say words influence spelling because you write what you hear when you sound out words to write them. Dividing words into syllables requires attention to syllable types: **open** and **closed**.

Open syllables have a vowel at the end of one of the syllables, such as *tiger* (*ti-ger*) and paper (*pa-per*). **Closed syllables** have a consonant at the end of every syllable, such as *pencil* (*pen-cil*) and *happen* (*hap-pen*). Teaching your students to recognize the difference between open and closed syllables will help them figure out how to pronounce unknown words as they read. This will also help them consider how to spell words when they write.

PREFIXES AND SUFFIXES. Understanding that words can have parts added to them helps readers think about word meanings. Chapter 9 has more about prefixes, suffixes, and root words. When thinking about phonics and parts of words, you need to teach students that adding a **prefix** or **suffix** (including **inflected endings** like *-s, -es, -ed*) changes the meaning of the word. Think about the word *preview*. The prefix *pre-* means "before" and *view* means "to see." Before you watch a movie in the theater, you sit through at least one preview. A *preview* is a sneak peek for a movie that entices viewers to want to see it. Instead of viewing the entire movie, it's a short series of clips. If you add the inflected ending *-s* to *preview*, suddenly you have more than one preview (*previews*). Although prefixes, inflected endings, suffixes, and root words relate to teaching and learning vocabulary, students need to be able to identify parts of words so they can break words into chunks for decoding. That means they need to know they can identify and read the prefix and see if there's an inflected ending or suffix they recognize before moving on to seek chunks in the rest of the word. Teaching Strategy 7.5 demonstrates how you can teach prefixes and contains information about how you can adapt the strategy to teach suffixes. Teach students that these elements should also be used in their writing.

Teaching Strategy 7.5: Prefix Removal and Replacement

Purpose: Prefixes are worth teaching because a relatively small number of prefixes are used in a large number of words. The four most common prefixes *dis-*, *in-*, *re-*, and *un-* account for 58% of the words in the English language with prefixes (Cunningham, 2017). Prefixes are consistent in their spelling and meaning, which is helpful when students are trying to identify and understand unknown words.

Procedures:

1. Select a word with a common prefix. For example, you may choose *dishonest, incomplete, remove,* or *unknown* because these words contain the most common prefixes *dis-*, *in-*, *re-*, and *un-*.
2. Display the word on the board. Tell students that the word *unknown* contains a prefix and a root word. Point out that the prefix is *un-*.
3. Ask students if what is left is a real word. In this example, it is the root word *known*.
4. Tell students that if they try to remove a prefix and a real word is left, they have found a prefix.
5. Tell students that the prefix *un-* means *not*. Discuss the meaning of the root word *known* (understood clearly).
6. Explain that the meaning of the word *unknown* is a combination of the meaning of the prefix *un-* and the root word *known*.

> un = not
> known = understood clearly
> unknown = not understood clearly

7. Put the word in a sentence and ask students if it makes sense using the meaning you identified. An example of a sentence is: There was an *unknown* amount of money missing after the bank was robbed.
8. Repeat the process with several other words. Help students realize that removing a prefix may help them decode or recognize a word. Knowing the meanings of prefixes (and suffixes) can also help them predict the meaning of the word if it is unknown to them. A list of the most common prefixes and their meanings is provided below to assist you with planning lessons on prefixes.

Prefix	Meaning	Example
dis-	not	disappear
in-	not	incomplete
re-	again	rewrite
un-	not	unlucky

9. This strategy can be adapted to teach suffixes. A list of common suffixes is provided below.

Suffix	Meaning	Example
-s or -es	plural	cats, dishes
-ful	full of	powerful
-ist	someone who does	scientist
-less	without	hopeless
-ness	state of being	happiness
-ly	in the manner of	kindly

Figure 7.5 provides definitions and examples of structural analysis for decoding unfamiliar words, which includes syllables. Figure 7.6 displays a grade level progression for structural analysis for decoding unfamiliar words for kindergarten through grade 3, based on a broad survey of ELA standards from across the United States. If you are unsure of the terminology in the explanations column, you can look at Figure 7.6 for definitions and examples.

Figure 7.5. Definitions and Examples of Components for Structural Analysis for Decoding Unfamiliar Words

Term	Definition	Example
Identify differences	Some words are spelled similarly, but have subtle differences.	*bat* and *hat* are different because *bat* starts with *b* and *hat* starts with *h*. *Bat* and *hat* are both *-at* words.
One-syllable words	Words with one beat or hop.	*cat, run, log*
Inflected endings	Suffixes that change the number or tense.	*cow - cow**s**;* *walk - walk**s**, walk**ed**, walk**ing***
Two-syllable words	Words with two beats or hops.	*fable, tablet, hopping*
	Two-syllable words can have **open syllables** where they have a vowel at the end of the syllable.	Open syllable examples: *o-pen, snea-ker*
	Syllables are **closed** if they have a consonant at the end of the syllable.	Closed syllable examples: *tab-let, hop-ping*
Common prefixes	Additions to the start of words to change the meaning of the word.	*re-* ("again"; *retell*) *pre-* ("before"; *preschool*) *un-, dis-, non-* ("not"; *unfair, dislike, nonfiction*) *mis-* ("wrong"; *mismatch*) *ex-* ("beyond"; *exclaim*) *in-* ("into"; *indoor*) *fore-* ("before"; *forehead*) *de-* ("to take away"; *defrost*) *post-, after-* ("after"; *posttest, afternoon*) *sub-* ("below"; *subway*) *pro-* ("for"; *promote*) *en-* ("causing"; *endanger*)
Numeric prefixes	Additions to the start of words to indicate how many.	*mono-, uni-* ("one"; *monotone, unicycle*) *bi-* ("two"; *bilingual*) *tri-* ("three"; *triangle*) *quar-* ("four"; *quarter*) *quint-* ("five"; *quintet*) *oct-* ("eight"; *octopus*) *dec-* ("ten"; *decathlon*)
Common suffixes	Additions to the end of words to alter the meaning of the word.	*-y* ("like"; *rainy*) *-ly* ("how" or "when"; *slowly* or *nightly*) *-ily* ("how"; *noisily*) *-ment* ("action"; *payment*) *-ness* ("state of being"; *kindness*) *-ful, -ous* ("full of"; *hopeful, dangerous*) *-less* ("without"; *restless*)

Figure 7.5. *(continued)*

Term	Definition	Example
Common suffixes *(continued)*		Comparatives: *-er (cooler)*, *-est (coolest)*
		-er, *-or*, *-ian*, *-ist* ("one who does"; *speaker*, *visitor*, *guardian*, *artist*) *-ary*, *-ery*, *-ory* (signals for adjectives or nouns; *imaginary*, *bravery*, *victory*) *-ty*, *-ity* ("quality"; *safety*, *activity*) *-al*, *-ial*, *-ic* ("related to"; *fictional*, *tutorial*, *realistic*) *-en*, *-ize*, *-ify* ("cause to be"; *sweeten*, *energize*, *beautify*) *-ion* ("action"; *selection*, *discussion*)
Common Greek and Latin prefixes	Additions to the start of words from Greek or Latin that change the meaning of the word.	*geo-* ("earth"; *geography*) *micro-* ("small"; *microchip*) *mega-* ("great"; *megabyte*) *hyper-* ("beyond"; *hyperactive*) *super-* ("above"; *superhero*) *tele-* ("distant"; *television*)
Common Greek and Latin suffixes and roots	Roots are parts of words from Greek or Latin that will help students determine meanings of unfamiliar words, while expanding their vocabulary.	*form* ("shape"; *conform*) *graph* ("writing"; *autograph*) *-logy* ("study"; *zoology*) *-scope* ("see"; *microscope*) *spect* ("to look at"; *spectator*) *port* ("to carry"; *portable*) *trans* ("across"; *transport*)
Multisyllabic words	Words with three or more beats or hops.	Three-syllable word examples: *foreshadow*, *nonfiction*, *carelessness* Four-syllable word examples: *geography*, *environment*, *information*

Adapted from Bear et al. (2015), Fox (2014), and Johns & Lenski (2019).

Figure 7.6. Grade Level Progression for Structural Analysis for Decoding Unfamiliar Words

Grade level	Expectations
Kindergarten	Identify differences in similarly spelled words.
First grade	Decode one-syllable words and understand that every syllable in a word contains a vowel sound. Read words with inflected endings.
Second grade	Decode two-syllable words with long vowels. Decode words with common prefixes. Decode words with common suffixes.
Third grade	Know the meanings of prefixes and suffixes. Decode words with common Greek and Latin prefixes, suffixes, and roots. Decode multisyllabic words.

How to Teach Phonics

You may remember learning phonics a certain way, but perhaps your mentor teacher teaches phonics in a way that differs from your prior experiences. Which way is best? It depends. The most important thing to remember is that phonics must be taught. The International Literacy Association (2018) explains that to successfully teach phonics, teachers must be **explicit** and **systematic** in their teaching.

Explicit teaching means that you explain to students what you are teaching, provide **modeling** to show students how to do it (the skill we're teaching), provide **scaffolding** to guide students as they try it out, and then provide time for practice in groups, pairs, or individually, while you step in to help as needed. The point of explicit teaching is for students to understand the skill you teach and learn to do it automatically, without your help.

Systematic teaching means that you have an organized method that you use to teach phonics so it is a **predictable routine**. You're probably wondering if you should teach one letter each week, starting with *a*. Researchers found that the letter-a-week approach and using a fixed sequence for teaching letters are methods you should avoid because the pace may be too slow and students may already know those letters (Kaye & Lose, 2019; Reutzel, 2015). So, how do you teach phonics? There are two main approaches that you should know: the synthetic and the analytic approaches.

Margin Note 7.6: Mr. Thorn Does Phonics: What Is Synthetic Phonics?

https://www.youtube.com/watch?v=FvblWW4MtVk

SYNTHETIC PHONICS. **Synthetic phonics** is rooted in the bottom-up theory of reading (see Chapter 2) in which students learn letter names and letter sounds and can use that knowledge to sound out words, **letter-by-letter**. You probably used synthetic phonics when you read the word *clorx* earlier in this chapter, where you produced each letter sound and then put it together. Watch the 1-minute video in Margin Note 7.6 to see a teacher explain and demonstrate synthetic phonics.

ANALYTIC PHONICS. **Analytic phonics** is based on a top-down theory of reading in which students may be presented with a word and asked to think of other words that begin with the same sound. An example is the word *duck*. Other words that begin with the same sound as *duck* include *dog, door*, and *down*. Another focus is on learning chunks of words, or **word families**. That way students should be able to automatically recognize these chunks of words by sight, so they don't have to sound them out. How many words can you make with *-at*? To make *-at* words, we add a consonant to the beginning of the word. If we add *b* to *-at*, we make the word *bat*. Watch the short video in Margin Note 7.7 to learn and practice *-un* words.

Margin Note 7.7: Word Family -un: Phonics Song for Kids by Jack Hartman

https://www.youtube.com/watch?v=nCF_zfflsD0

COMBINING THE APPROACHES. You can combine the synthetic and analytic approaches to form an **eclectic approach** that allows you to be flexible in how you teach phonics in order to be responsive to your students' needs. Instead of choosing sides and arguing for one approach over the other, consider an eclectic approach. Synthetic phonics might work for some students, whereas analytic phonics will work for others. We cannot possibly predict what your future students will need, so we want you to be informed and ready for anything. Your goal is to teach young students how to read and write, which means you need to be equipped with a wealth of strategies and with knowledge of different approaches to help your students. Just like T-shirts, one size rarely fits all!

AGREE TO DISAGREE. What if you don't agree with how your mentor teacher teaches phonics? You will experience many learning opportunities in your placement. Our best advice is to ask your mentor teacher questions to try to understand what is being taught and why. As a teacher candidate, your job is to learn as much as possible from your mentor teacher and placement. You may find instances when you would have done something differently than what your mentor teacher did. That's normal but remember that you are a guest in their classroom, and we want you to be a polite guest who learns from the entire experience. You may learn what to do, and you may learn what you will not plan to do in your own classroom in the future. The placement helps to shape your understanding of what happens in a real classroom, bridging what you learn in methods courses with actual teaching. If you believe something is truly ethically amiss in your placement, reach out to your university supervisor for help.

PHONICS PROGRAMS. Although we cannot predict your future teaching context or the requirements of your future school, you need to be aware of how different school districts can be with their preferred methods for teaching phonics. Some districts adopt reading programs that include phonics. You may remember the reading books, perhaps your teacher called them **anthologies**. Those are also called **basal readers** and they come with a kit that guides the teacher in teaching reading.

Some districts adopt reading programs, but they also require separate phonics programs. That means you would have those reading books as described above, but you would also have another whole set of teaching materials just for teaching phonics. Schools that require separate phonics programs tend to adopt those materials for every teacher in PreK or kindergarten through grade 3 so that teachers are consistent in their use of phonics terms and to ensure that phonics is taught the same way across grade levels. Whereas **phonics** is a focus in ELA standards for kindergarten through grade 2, **structural analysis** is a focus in grades 3 and above. Because we cannot anticipate what your students' reading needs are, you may need to teach first-grade phonics skills to third grade students who need them.

Some school districts require that teachers use specific phonics programs where they are required to follow along with a **scripted program**. Scripted programs tend to require teachers to read directly from the page (the script in the teacher's manual), without deviation. Those programs tend to be used in kindergarten through grade 3 so that phonics is taught the same way across grade levels. Thus, scripted programs do not allow for differentiation of instruction and they remove your ability to make decisions in your reading lessons (Dresser, 2012).

Some districts ask teachers to use their own **professional judgment** to teach the state ELA standards, regardless of the adopted reading program. That means the ELA standards are taught however each teacher prefers to teach them. If there is an adopted reading program in the school, the teachers who have this autonomy get to decide if and when they use those programs. Maybe they would use parts of the program but pull in other resources to supplement and enhance the programs. In these situations, the teacher is the ultimate decision maker.

Do you have a preference in the different scenarios with reading and phonics programs? Why do you think that one is your preference? You are adding to your theory of literacy learning as you think through your preferences for teaching phonics, which includes word recognition and spelling. Very soon you will be looking for your first teaching job. We strongly suggest that you start making a list of questions to ask during your job interviews, such as the following:

- How is reading taught here?
- How is phonics taught here?
- How are teachers expected to teach spelling?
- How much flexibility do teachers have in teaching the state ELA standards?

By asking those questions, you can get a sense of whether the school's required reading and phonics programs fit with your personal and professional preferences. Think of how difficult it would be to teach in a school where you weren't allowed to teach the way you want! The job interview is for you to interview them just as much as they are interviewing you.

Connection to the Field: Phonics Instruction

Ask your mentor teacher how they teach phonics and spelling, which materials they use for teaching phonics and spelling, and if there are required schoolwide phonics and spelling programs.

How Readers Use Meaning Cues to Figure Out Unknown Words

When readers encounter words they don't know, they can also use **meaning cues** to figure out what they are. As students read, they should also ask themselves the question, "Does this word make sense?" To figure out whether a word in a sentence makes sense, readers use **context clues**. (You'll learn how readers apply context clues to increase vocabulary in Chapter 9.)

There are several types of context clues that will be helpful for young readers to learn (Johns & Lenski, 2019). **Definition** or **description context clues** provide a definition right in the sentence to help the reader figure out the meaning of a challenging word. An example is provided in this sentence, "*An artisan is a person who is skilled in a specific art or craft.*" In this sentence, the reader can figure out the meaning of *artisan* by simply reading to the end of the sentence to find the definition provided in the text. A similar type of context clue is the **appositive phrase context clue** in which the author provides the definition of a challenging word in a phrase that is set off by commas. For example, "*The haberdasher, a men's shop keeper, sold suits and neckties.*" The definition of *haberdasher* is provided in the phrase *a men's shop keeper* which is set off by commas. Another type of context clue is the **linked synonyms context clue** in which the unknown word is presented in a series of known words so the reader can figure out the meaning of the unknown word. An example is in this sentence, "*He groused, grumbled, and complained about his chores every single day.*" In this example, the word *groused* may be unfamiliar to many students, but because they will likely know the words *grumbled* and *complained,* they can use this type of context clue to figure out the meaning of *groused.*

In **comparisons and contrasts context clues**, the unknown word is defined by its opposite in the sentence. In this sentence, "*Rather than eating plain rice, Kai chose the pungent rice for dinner,*" the reader can use the context to determine that the opposite of *plain* is *pungent.* This context clue can help the reader to infer that the meaning of *pungent* is flavorful or spicy because those words mean the opposite of plain. **Examples context clues** provide examples that help the reader define an unknown word. Here's a short passage that illustrates this type of context clue: "*He is fastidious about how he keeps his room. Everything is always in its place, neat and tidy.*" Because of the examples provided in the second sentence that describe the word *fastidious,* the reader can determine its meaning. **Classification context clues** help the reader to figure out an unknown word by its relationship to known words in the sentence or passage. If you are wondering what this type of context clue looks like, here's an example: "*The aggressive cat hissed and showed his claws while the calm cat sat and purred.*" In this example, the reader can classify the two cats by their different types of behaviors. One is calm and sits while purring, but the other is aggressive because it hisses and shows its claws. The **experience context clue** encourages the reader to use previous experiences to figure out the unknown word. Here's an example of an experience context clue: "*The firework show was* *mesmerizing. I could not take my eyes off of the bright colors, plumes of smoke, and flashes of light. I was frozen in amazement as I watched the show without even blinking my eyes!*" In this passage, the reader can consider how they would feel in this situation to help them figure out the meaning of the word *mesmerizing*.

Now that we've shared these different types of context clues with you, we might surprise you by saying that you don't need to worry about teaching each type separately. Rather, we offered this discussion of the different types of context clues to inform you of the range of context clues students will encounter in their reading so you have a good sense of the many different ways that readers can use context clues to figure out unknown words.

TEACHING CONTEXT CLUES. When you and your students are reading, it's the perfect time to teach and practice context clues. You can demonstrate how to use context clues during **read-alouds**, and you can guide students to use context clues during **shared reading** and **guided reading**. You can also teach students to use context clues when they are reading aloud to you or to a peer. In other words, context clues need to be taught **in the context of real reading**. As you prepare for read-alouds, shared reading, and guided reading instruction, you will want to identify context clues that you can show to students so they can see how helpful they can be in figuring out unknown words.

It's important to note, however, that not every sentence and passage will offer useful context clues to figure out challenging words. It's also a good idea to help students understand that context clues may be unavailable to help them figure out unknown words, so they will need to consider other meaning cues, such as **visual cues** (discussed previously in this chapter) or **structural cues** (discussed later in this chapter). As noted earlier in this chapter, the best approach is to use **multiple** cueing systems to cross-check the meaning of an unknown word.

TEACHING OTHER MEANING CUES. In addition to context clues, readers can use pictures and other visuals in a text to help figure out the meaning of unknown words. The question, "What would make sense here?" is a great way for students to focus their attention on meaning cues in a sentence or passage. Sometimes, asking a reader to consider what they already know about a topic can help them use that knowledge to figure out the meaning of an unknown word.

Sometimes students will substitute a word for another word in the text, but the words have highly similar meanings. For example, the student might say "yard" instead of "lawn." The words *yard* and *lawn* are not that different in terms of meaning. Students making this kind of substitution will still be able to comprehend the text because the word makes sense in the sentence.

During your reading lessons, you can teach students to attend to meaning by prompting them to consider a word that makes sense when they come across a word that they don't recognize. Model how you do this. Start by reading a sentence aloud from a Big Book and intentionally skip a word. Tell students that you don't know what that word is, but you will reread the sentence and insert a word that makes sense. An example could be the sentence, "I like to walk in the _____." Perhaps there is an illustration that shows someone walking in the forest. Point out how you are relying on pictures as clues, as well as what the sentence says. Possibilities for the blank could be *forest* or *woods*.

How Readers Use Structural Cues to Figure Out Unknown Words

Structural cues are also called **syntax**. This type of cue means that students are thinking about how the language sounds as they read and if it sounds right. You can teach students how to attend to structural cues or syntax in your reading lessons. One way to do this is by writing two sentences on the board that have slight differences in verb tense or some other slight difference that makes the sentence sound "wrong" in English. An example follows.

The cat look in the box.
The cat looked in the box.

Read the sentences to the students and ask them which one sounds right. Tell students that when they read, they need to monitor what they do when something doesn't sound right. Let them know that one strategy skilled readers use is going back to the start of the sentence and rereading it, but paying close attention to the words and whether it sounds right. Model this for students so they can hear you talk them through this process.

As we have noted throughout this book, ELs will most likely not have a foundation in the syntax of English because they have a different home language. ELs may have difficulty using structural cues to figure out unknown words because they don't know how English sounds. For example, if a student is reading the sentence, "Madison was playing on the swings," and reads *was plays* instead of *was playing*, it might not be useful for you to ask the students whether *was plays* sounds right. Instead, use a different way to help the student figure out the word, such as looking at the ending sounds of the words. The structural cueing system is very useful to teach, but possibly not for every student.

Teaching Word Recognition in the Classroom

When students (and all readers, for that matter) are reading, they will make some **miscues** where what they read is not what is written in the text. Miscues are a natural part of the reading process. Students who are relying on visual cues may look at the first part of a word and say another word that starts the same way instead of reading the entire word. That means they are saying words that are visually similar to the printed word. For example, a student might see the word *house* but say, "horse." With visual miscues the sentence does not sound right and the meaning is lost.

During reading lessons, you can teach students how to attend to visual cues by teaching them to attend to the whole word and use decoding strategies. Read a sentence aloud from a Big Book or write your own sentence on the board and read it aloud. Make a miscue so that you substitute a word that may resemble the correct word but doesn't sound like it fits. An example might be reading, "Jake put a couch on the table," instead of "Jake put a cup on the table." The word *couch* does not make sense in that sentence, but it starts with the same letter as *cup*. Tell students that sometimes you have to go back and look at the word that doesn't make sense. Demonstrate how you would look closely at the word for parts that you know. For example, if you know the beginning sound and you can sound out the other parts of the word, then you can put the sounds together. In the word, *cup* you could show them how to use your understanding of **onset** and **rime**. *C* says /k/ and you automatically know -*up* because it's from one of the word families you've learned. Plus, you know *u* says /u/ and *p* says /p/.

Teaching Strategy 7.6 demonstrates how to teach students to identify unknown words by flexibly using different cues. By taking this approach, you can help students build a toolbox of strategies to use to figure out unknown words through using and combining visual, meaning, and structure cues. Teaching Strategy 7.7 provides a way to teach students to use questions to help monitor their use of different cues while reading.

Teaching Strategy 7.6: Word Detective

Purpose: To help students use a variety of strategies to identify unknown words, teach them to become word detectives. Basically, this strategy helps students use visual cues (phonics and structural analysis) and meaning cues to help identify unknown words.

Procedures:

1. Introduce the notion of a word detective by dressing in a long coat and a hat while carrying a magnifying glass. Be creative in your approach. For each of the three cues, provide a picture or object similar to the illustrations below. You may also locate a plastic brain, a small bell, and a simple puzzle.

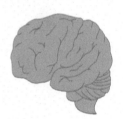  

2. Decide how to best introduce the cues. It is recommended that a different cue be introduced in consecutive lessons and that activities be developed to use the cues in combination. Begin with a cue of your choice and use the basic mode of presentation described below for the context cue.

3. Walk into the classroom dressed in detective attire. Look through your magnifying glass. Invite students to identify who you are (a detective) and what you do (solve mysteries or crimes). Then say something like the following:

    You're right! I am a detective. I'm a special kind of detective because I'm a word detective. I can help you use cues to figure out or identify unknown words in your reading. Here's the cue I'll share with you today.

    Hold up a plastic brain or enlarge the illustration of the brain above. You might also prepare a cover for a book titled *Strategies for Young Word Detectives*.

4. Invite students to identify the brain and then explain how they can use their brains to be word detectives. You might say something like the following:

    I use my brain when I'm reading to figure out meaning and see if what I read makes sense. If I come to a word I don't know, I use my brain to ask some questions so I can use meaning cues.

    Invite students to share their ideas and lead them to understand the following strategies. Use examples as appropriate.

    - I can think about a word that would make sense.
    - I can say *blank* in place of the unknown word and read to the end of the sentence. Then I can reread the sentence and ask myself, "What word would make sense in the sentence?"
    - I can read the sentence with the word I put in and ask if it makes sense. (Possible questions might be: *Does the word sound right?* Or *Is this the way someone might talk?*)
    - I can look at the pictures or illustrations to get an idea of what the word might be.

(continued)

5. Tell students that you have some other strategies in your word detective book. In subsequent lessons, introduce strategies for visual cues (phonics and structural analysis). Some of the understandings to develop are presented here. Change the statements as needed to meet students' needs and to be consistent with your instructional program.

Sounds

- Look at the beginning of the word and make the sound. Ask students, *What word begins with that sound and makes sense in the sentence?*
- Put your finger under the word and slowly say the sounds in the word. Then say the sounds faster and try to make a word you have heard before.

Parts

- Look for parts in the word that you know.
- See if the word looks like other words that you know.
- Look for two smaller words that make up the larger word.
- Separate the prefixes and/or suffixes and then try to put the pieces together.

6. Develop classroom charts with the strategies and graphics so students can refer to the cues as needed. Bookmarks with the cues can also be prepared.

7. Refer to this strategy throughout the year and add additional strategies as they are taught.

© Graphics RF/Shutterstock.com

Teaching Strategy 7.7: Cue Questioning

Purpose: As students use cross-checking, they ask themselves questions about language cues in sentences. Because many young students may have had limited experience reading independently, they may not know the types of questions to ask. Teaching students about the kinds of questions to ask and providing them with ideas for questioning cues will help them as they use cross-checking during reading.

Procedures:

1. Identify three or four of the questions from the list provided and write them on the board or on chart paper. Tell students that the questions are ones they should use as they try to figure out unknown words while they read.

2. Ask students to take out their independent reading book and read until they come to a word that is unfamiliar. Give students several minutes to read.

3. Divide the class into groups of three students. Tell students that they should ask each other questions about the words. Have one student read aloud and say, "blank" in place of the unknown word. Have other students in the group ask questions until they can figure out the missing word.

4. Repeat this strategy often using a variety of the cue questions. Tell students that they should begin asking themselves the same questions when they read and come across an unknown word.

Cue Questions

Questions for Meaning Cues
- ✓ Did that make sense?
- ✓ You said _____. What does that mean?
- ✓ What would make sense here?
- ✓ What is happening in the story? Does this word make sense in the story?

Questions for Structure Cues
- ✓ Did that sound right?
- ✓ Can you say it that way?
- ✓ Would it be correct to say _____?
- ✓ Can you think of a better word that fits?
- ✓ What word would sound right?

Questions for Visual Cues
- ✓ Does that look right?
- ✓ Do you know a word that looks like that?
- ✓ What do you notice about that word?
- ✓ Do you see a part of the word you know?

Questions for Self-Correction
- ✓ Were you right?
- ✓ What did you notice?
- ✓ What else could you try?
- ✓ What else do you know that could help you?

Teaching word recognition strategies in the classroom requires that you provide children with many opportunities to read and write so they can test and apply what they are learning to figure out unknown words in authentic literacy tasks. Because skilled readers and spellers must know how to use a variety of cues and strategies to figure out unknown words, it's important to teach students to use word recognition strategies individually as well as in combination.

Margin Note 7.8: Literacy Station Activities for PreK

https://fcrr.org/resources/resources_vpk.html

Regardless of your grade level, students need **focused instruction** on word recognition during which you help them learn to use word recognition strategies flexibly. Focused instruction means you will need to be **explicit** in your teaching. When teaching students letter and sound recognition, provide ample modeling where you tell students how you (as a reader) make sense of what you are teaching and show them how they can do the same. When teaching how to use meaning cues such as context clues, be sure to model how you use context clues, and then provide guided practice so students can begin to use context clues with your support. Build plenty of **scaffolding** into your reading lessons so you are guiding students in how to use visual, meaning, and structural cues so they can work toward using these independently in their reading and in their writing.

Margin Note 7.9: Literacy Station Activities for K–5

https://fcrr.org/resources/resources_sca.html

Many teachers implement literacy stations, sometimes called centers, in their classrooms to provide students with opportunities to read and write for real purposes. Typically, literacy stations contain games and activities that reinforce literacy concepts, including word recognition strategies you have already taught to students. See Margin Note 7.8 for PreK literacy station activities. Margin Note 7.9 contains literacy station activities for various grade levels.

The Larger Purposes for Word Recognition

We need to be able to identify unknown words in our reading and to spell them in our writing because literacy is about making meaning. We don't figure out words just to say we know a word. Rather, we use cueing systems to figure out unknown words so we can understand a passage we are reading or to communicate an idea in a written message. Although it's important to teach the cueing systems, including specific phonics skills, context clues, and grammar, they are really just tools to **construct meaning** through reading and writing.

The important thing to remember about teaching word recognition is that it is one part of the overall reading program. Although phonics is an essential part of teaching reading, teaching phonics should be brief with intentional instruction focused on your students' learning needs. The same is true for teaching students how to use meaning and structure cues as well as using cues flexibly and in combination. As a learner-ready teacher who cares about students as individuals, you need to use assessments to figure out what students already know about phonics and other word recognition strategies and what they need to learn. That way you can build on your students' prior knowledge while providing them with relevant instruction.

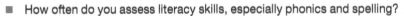

Connection to the Field: Assessing Phonics and Spelling

Talk with your mentor teacher to see if the school requires certain ways of assessing phonics. Ask the following questions:

- How often do you assess literacy skills, especially phonics and spelling?
- What materials do you use?
- How did you learn about these assessments?
- How do you use assessment information to plan instruction?

You may also want to ask if you can observe them doing the assessment.

Assessment of Word Recognition

Your school district will require specific **literacy assessments** and, when you are hired as a teacher, your school will hopefully provide you with professional development and resources for using those assessments. Approximately every 5 years, those assessment systems tend to change, but the heart of what is assessed for phonics and spelling remains fairly consistent.

ORAL READING. One way to consider students' understanding of phonics is by listening to them **read aloud** and noting which words they need help with as they read. If those words have the same features in common, then consider what you need to teach so the student can become proficient with that skill. For example, if a student is reading and every time they see a word that starts with *sh* but they attempt to sound it out letter-by-letter as /s/, /h/, then you know they need help learning that *sh* is a digraph with a special sound.

A **running record** is an **informal assessment** where the student reads aloud from a text while you follow along and note the student's reading behaviors. While doing a running record, you note which words the student reads correctly and which ones they read incorrectly. You can also determine the number of words the student reads correctly in a minute (WCPM) and their oral reading prosody (see Chapter 8 for more information on WCPM and prosody). Those words that they read incorrectly are called **miscues** because the reader misuses cues (i.e., visual, meaning, structure) and reads the words incorrectly. You can analyze the errors (miscues) students make in their oral reading by conducting a **miscue analysis** of the running record. Miscues can be related to meaning cues, structural cues, or visual cues.

By doing running records and completing miscue analysis of students' oral reading, you can determine what to teach to support your students' word recognition skill development. By attending to the different cueing systems that your students use (and do not use) during running records, you can focus your teaching on how they can improve their reading performance by monitoring which cues they use and learning how to use the cues flexibly and in combination as they read. Assessment Strategy 7.2 provides detailed instructions on how to note and analyze students' miscues as they read aloud.

Assessment Strategy 7.2: Oral Reading Miscue Analysis

Purpose: When students read orally, you can note their miscues and make observations about their reading strategies. This information can be helpful in guiding next steps in your teaching.

Procedures:

1. Select a text at the student's instructional reading level. The text can be from your usual teaching materials.

2. Meet with the student individually. Invite the student to read the text you selected. You might say something like what follows:

   I would like you to read this passage to me. When you finish reading, I'll ask you some questions (or I'd like you to tell me about what you've read).

3. When the student begins reading, begin timing with a stopwatch or your phone. Note any miscues the student makes while reading, as well as notes to indicate phrasing and repetitions. Numerous marking systems are available (Johns, Elish-Piper, & Johns, 2017), but you may find the one below easy to use. You may choose to develop your own system.

Marking	Meaning of Marking
man men	Substitution
man s/c men	Self-correction
~~men~~	Omitted word
m-- men	Partial pronunciation
men	Repeated word
small ^men	Insertion
the/men	Pause

4. When the student finishes reading, note the number of seconds that elapsed and ask comprehension questions or invite a retelling. You may refer to Chapter 8 to calculate the student's words read correctly per minute (WCPM). For this assessment, our focus is on miscue analysis.

5. The following questions and comments may provide assistance in formulating ideas for instruction.

   ■ *Does the student read accurately but have a slow rate of reading?* If the reading is accurate but slow, you will probably want to provide more opportunities for the student to read easy materials and participate in a variety of activities that focus on rereading.

- *Does the student read accurately but in a word-by-word fashion?* In addition to the above suggestion, you can mark phrase boundaries in passages by making light slash marks with a pencil to help the student see how to group words. An example follows:

    The small cat / was sleeping / under the big tree.

    Model phrasing while reading the passage aloud as the student follows along. Then ask the student to read the passage to you, attending to the phrasing you modeled. Consider using recordings of favorite books to reinforce phrasing.

- *Does the student make a number of miscues and read fast (or slow)?* Analyze the nature of the student's miscues. Miscue analysis can be done informally to gain insights into the student's general reading strategies and the impact that those strategies can have on fluency and comprehension. Some of the behaviors to look for are related to the following questions. The answers to these questions suggest strategies for instruction.

- *Are the student's miscues numerous with no particular pattern?* Many miscues suggest that the reading material may be too difficult. Consider using easier materials for instruction and recreational reading.

- *Is the student's reading generally accurate but characterized by numerous repetitions?* Repetitions may be due to habit. Record the student's reading and have them listen and comment. Ask the student why they repeat so often. Use the student's response to help plan appropriate instruction. As long as the student's comprehension is satisfactory, encourage them to reduce the repetitions.

- *Is the student's reading characterized by sounding out many words, which reduces fluency?* The student may be over-reliant on phonics. Help the student strengthen their sight vocabulary and teach how context can be used to help anticipate words. If phonics is the dominant mode of initial instruction, such behavior may be considered normal for some time until the student gains sight words. Be alert for students who seem to be stuck on sounding out letter-by-letter as they read. Remember to teach a combination of cueing systems for word identification and cross-checking. Teaching Strategy 7.6 (Word Detective) may be especially helpful.

- *Is the student's reading characterized by a moderate or fast reading rate and numerous miscues that significantly distort the meaning?* Such reading may seriously impact the student's ability to comprehend the material. You may need to use examples of the student's miscues that distort the meaning to help teach the importance of rereading when the text doesn't make sense. Teaching the student to use phonics and context as cross-checking strategies may be helpful. Help the student monitor whether the text is making sense. Questions such as, "Am I understanding?" and "Does what I'm reading make sense?" may be used. Help expand the student's sight vocabulary.

- *Is the student's reading characterized by a slow rate and numerous miscues?* Such behavior may be a strong indication that the reading materials are too difficult. Use easier materials. You can study the student's miscues to gain insights into the word identification skills that need to be taught. You may need to teach specific phonic elements, such as consonant and vowel sounds.

Margin Note 7.10: How to Take Running Records

http://scholastic.ca/education/movingupwithliteracyplace/pdfs/grade4/runningrecords.pdf

Margin Note 7.11: Running Records: Assessing and Improving Students' Reading Fluency and Comprehension

https://www.youtube.com/watch?v=ZO-4OYiJIUA

Margin Note 7.12: Fountas and Pinnell Running Record

https://www.youtube.com/watch?v=LUr1og9lPWM

Margin Note 7.13: Invented Spelling Video

https://www.youtube.com/watch?v=CDlrJqX5_q4&feature=youtu.be

Follow the link in Margin Note 7.10 for another example of step-by-step directions in how to conduct, score, and analyze a running record.

See Margin Notes 7.11 and 7.12 for video clips of teachers conducting running records with individual students. These two teachers have different approaches, but they are using the same assessment tool. In the Margin Note 7.13 video you can see the teacher noting what the student read correctly and how she analyzed the miscues as being related to meaning, structure, and visual cues.

How Students Learn to Spell

We've discussed how to teach students to recognize unknown words using the cueing systems and how to assess these skills. We'd like to also briefly discuss how students learn to spell and give you some basic parameters for teaching **spelling**. To do that, we'd like to remind you that literacy learning is a **developmental** process and learning how to spell is also developmental.

Think back to what you learned in Chapter 5 about how children learn to read and write. They learn through experience, right? Their literacy "emerges" as they experience language learning at home and at school. When children come to school, you take what they have learned and scaffold that learning to help them progress. Spelling is similar in that it is both developmental and taught.

DEVELOPMENTAL SPELLING. The term **developmental spelling** refers to a child's own way of spelling a word. When young children write, they create or invent their own spellings of words (Read, 1986). For example, when young children write *I love you*, they may spell the words using what they know about phonics at that time. The word *love* is often spelled, *L, lv,* or *luv* by young children. This developmental spelling is part of the learning process that children go through as they become **conventional** spellers (Treiman, 2018).

Developmental spelling is an important part of a child's literacy development. As children experiment with spelling, they systematically develop their own spelling rules (Richgels, 2001). These **invented** spelling rules help children communicate through writing as they are learning the rules of conventional spelling. Watch the short video in Margin Note 7.13 to see how a first-grade teacher works with students to promote their spelling development.

The goal of spelling instruction is to give students practice spelling words and to help them become conventional spellers as soon as possible. That can be accomplished by explicitly teaching phonics components and explaining how students will encounter and use those components in their reading and in their writing. The stages of spelling development can be found in Figure 7.7, and an assessment to identify a student's developmental spelling stage can be found in Assessment Strategy 7.3.

Assessment Strategy 7.3: Developmental Spelling

Purpose: Assessing developmental spelling provides a window into children's thinking about letter–sound relationships. This assessment consists of giving students challenging words to spell so that you can assess their ability to spell.

Procedures:

1. Develop a page for students to write 10 spelling words.

2. Tell students that they are going to spell some words that may be hard. Reassure students that you want them to try to write the word, spelling it as well as they can.

3. Dictate the list of 10 words. After saying each word, use it in a simple sentence. For example, for the first word in the list, you could say, "Don't drop your pencil on the floor." Continue through the entire list of words. Repeat words as needed.

1.	drop	6.	mess
2.	faster	7.	packed
3.	liked	8.	make
4.	back	9.	earn
5.	monster	10.	greet

Scoring Guide:

A student's general developmental spelling stage is determined by analyzing the student's spelling for each word on the list and then identifying the stage that appears most frequently. You can find more details about scoring in the Chapter 7 Resources on the website.

Figure 7.7. Stages of Spelling Development

Stage	Description	Example
Precommunicative stage (typically 3–5+ years old)	The child uses symbols from the alphabet by writing or copying random strings of letters but shows no knowledge of letter–sound relationships. The child may have a message in mind when writing.	ffg4koo for puppy
Semiphonetic stage (typically 4–6+ years old)	The child begins to understand letter–sound correspondences represented by letters. Spelling is abbreviated with one to three letters used to spell words. The child may know the entire alphabet and how to form each of the letters.	DG for dog
Phonetic stage (typically 5–7+ years old)	The child is able to write words with all of the letter sounds although words may be spelled phonetically rather than correctly. They often use a letter or group of letters to represent every sound that they hear in a word.	sokar for soccer
Transitional stage (typically 6–11+ years old)	The child begins to spell most common words correctly. There is a transition from relying on the sounds represented by letters to use of visual and morphological information about words.	afternewn for afternoon
Correct stage (typically 10–11+ years old)	The child knows the spelling of most words and basic spelling rules. The child can add prefixes and suffixes to root words correctly and knows the spelling of many irregular words. The child's generalizations about spelling are usually correct. Proofreading strategies are used with increasing proficiency.	

Based on Gentry, J. R. (1982). An analysis of developmental spelling in GNYS at WRK. *The Reading Teacher, 36*, 192–200.

When you think about **development stages**, it's important to remember that identifying a student's stage doesn't mean you just wait until they get to the next stage. Go back to Chapter 2 to refresh your memory about how the term **emergent literacy** came into education. When we talk about developmental spelling, we are just describing how spelling is **emerging**. To promote students' continued development, you should provide them ample opportunities to read and write. Teaching Strategy 7.8 is an example of one way you can help students think about phonics components as they learn to spell words correctly.

Teaching Strategy 7.8: Just Try It

Purpose: Students need to practice spelling words to reach conventional spelling. This strategy provides students with intentional practice spelling words.

Procedures:

1. Ask students to write a sentence or story using the best spelling they can. Encourage students to spell words using letters and sounds they know, even if the word is not spelled correctly.

2. After students finish their sentences, give them a sheet of paper with four columns. Have students identify three words that they think might not be spelled with conventional spelling. Assist students as necessary.

3. Have students write the identified words in the left-hand column the way they spelled them in the sentence as in the example below.

4. Place a checkmark above each letter that is correct in the words the students have written.

5. Show students the letters they have correct and ask them to say the word aloud, listening for additional sounds. After students say the word, ask them try to spell the word again in the next column.

6. Move around the class as students are writing words in the First Try column. Look at the word and again place checkmarks over the correct letters. If students have not spelled the words correctly, ask them to say the word again. You might help students hear sounds in the words or remind students of things they have learned about letters and sounds. Have students spell the word again in the column marked Second Try.

7. Move around the class looking at the words students have written. Congratulate students on every letter they wrote correctly. If the spelling is not correct, write the correctly spelled word in the final column. Identify the letters students got right and the ones they need to remember.

8. Encourage students to write the conventionally spelled words in their spelling notebook, which can serve as a personal spelling dictionary.

9. Tell students when they write these words, they should refer to their dictionary and spell them conventionally. Because students are still learning how to spell, they may not spell each of the identified words correctly in every situation. Encourage students to use what they have learned about letters and sounds as they try to spell new words.

Original Spelling	First Try	Second Try	Conventional spelling
✓✓✓ ✓ frnd	✓ ✓✓✓ Freend	✓✓✓✓ Frend	friend
✓✓ ✓ gonna	✓✓✓✓ ✓✓ goin to	✓ going to	going to
✓✓✓ spas	✓✓✓ Spac	✓ space	space

SPELLING INSTRUCTION. You probably remember spelling books or lists from your own elementary education. Traditionally, spelling has been taught by giving students a list of words on Monday, giving them practice exercises, and then having them take a test on Friday. You might even remember studying for spelling tests. There are now better ways to teach spelling rather than merely assigning and testing words. Indeed, this chapter is a resource that can help you consider how to explicitly teach phonic elements. You can also make direct connections from phonics instruction to spelling by telling students that you expect them to use what they know about phonics components as they write.

Engaging with Families: Spelling Development

Parents and family members sometimes don't understand that children grow as spellers when they have a chance to try to spell words during writing. These words aren't "wrong"; they are all part of a child's development. Develop a brief explanation that tells families about the stages of spelling development that are present in your grade level. Show your mentor teacher your explanation and ask if you can distribute it to parents.

EXAMINING WRITING. One way to learn what students know about words and spelling is to look at their writing. Phonics and spelling are connected because when you write, you need to know letter sounds, letter–sound associations, vowel patterns, and structural analysis. Students' writings indicate what they know about phonics and what is still confusing for them. Let's think about this as we look at the writing sample in Figure 7.8 from Madelyn, age 7.

When you look at a student's work, always look for positives and note what skills they already have, based on their use of the **visual cueing system**. That means students use their knowledge of letter–sound relationships to attempt spelling words that "look right" as they write. With Madelyn's writing sample, you can tell that she consistently spells familiar words correctly (e.g., *the, was, then, all, at, away, and, very, little*). Perhaps this is because she has learned them as **high-frequency words** (sight words). As a teacher, you want to continue to reinforce students' learning those words so they can recognize them quickly in their reading, but also so they can use them correctly in their writing.

Now look at Madelyn's writing and think about spellings that she's probably trying but aren't quite right. Did you notice how she sounded out words and spelled what she heard? You may have noticed the missing *h* in *ghost*. Do you know why the *h* is missing? When she sounded out the word, she heard /g/ /o/ /s/ /t/. The *h* is silent. Another word she used has a silent letter: *knock*. However, Madelyn omitted the *n* in *knock*. As the teacher, you may want to do a phonics lesson about silent letters.

Think about how Madelyn spelled the words *abandoned, miracle,* and *vampire. Aband* is a great start for *abandoned,* but perhaps Madelyn needs help thinking about syllables in words. With *miracle,* she sounded it out, hearing /m/ /ee/ /r/ /u/ /k/ /l/ and she wrote *meukl*. Madelyn's attempts at *vampire* aren't far off. *Vempier* and *vanpir* are close to the actual spelling. The short *a* and short *e* sounds are highly similar, as are /m/ and /n/. Think about how she spelled *tried* as *tride*. You may want to review long vowel patterns with Madelyn and teach her that long vowels can occur through different letter combinations (**spelling patterns**).

Madelyn has excellent **phonics skills** to build on and to reinforce. As the teacher, you want to focus on only one aspect of students' phonics needs at a time. Start by looking for the most basic one, based on the ELA standards. Second graders are expected to know consonant pairs with **silent letters,** so you could start with a lesson about *gh* in *ghost* and *kn* in *knock*.

Figure 7.8. Madelyn's Writing Sample: Ghosts

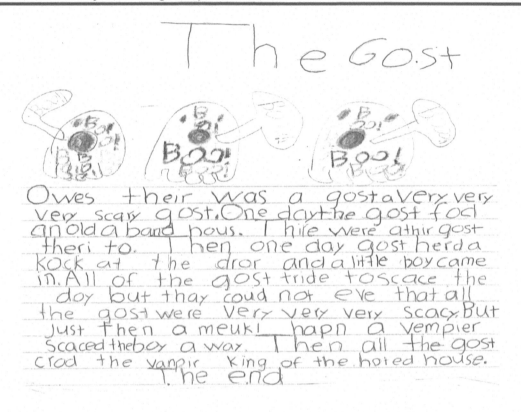

Line-by-line transcript with correct spelling and punctuation:

The Ghost

Once there was a ghost—a very, very,
very scary ghost. One day the ghost found
an old abandoned house. There were other ghosts
there too. Then one day a ghost heard a
knock at the door and a little boy came
in. All of the ghosts tried to scare the
boy but they could not, even though all
the ghosts were very, very, very scary. But
just then a miracle happened. A vampire
scared the boy away. Then all the ghosts
crowned the vampire king of the haunted house.

The end

Let's look at Anna's writing sample in Figure 7.9. How you can tell what Anna knows about phonics? Look at the beginning and endings of Anna's words. She has a good understanding of consonants, and they appear in the beginning, middle, and end of her words. Anna already spells many words correctly (e.g., *my, lost, and, of, bed*).

Figure 7.9. Anna's Writing Sample: Lost Underwear

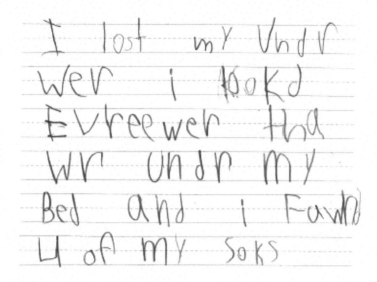

Line by line transcript with correct spellings and punctuation:
I lost my under
wear. I looked
everywhere. They
were under my
bed. And I found
4 of my socks.

What do you notice about Anna's attempts at spelling the words *underwear* and *everywhere*? It appears that Anna knows *everywhere* is a compound word. Do you think she knows that *underwear* is a compound word and she ran out of room on that line, or do you think she needs a quick lesson on compound words?

The *-er* is missing from *under*, but it is an r-controlled vowel. That means you cannot hear /e/ in *under*. The same applies for the word *were*. Anna spelled *were* as *wr* because you cannot hear the *e*. *Were* is a high-frequency word that Anna will eventually memorize or learn at sight. *They* is another **high-frequency word** that is confusing because *ey* in *they* sounds like a long *a*.

You may want to work on long vowels and **vowel teams** with Anna. The vowel team *ea* is tricky in the word *wear*. Anna used *er* in *wear*, which is close. Another tricky vowel team is *ou* in the word *found*. Anna spelled *found* as *fawnd*, which makes sense considering how the *ou* in *found* sounds like *ow*. Refer to Figure 7.3 to see the variations in sounds for the vowel teams. Other phonics elements you could teach Anna are when to use *ck* in words and the suffix *-ed*. Overall, Anna has excellent knowledge of phonics at age 5.

By thinking about Madelyn's and Anna's writing samples, we considered which phonics elements they already grasped. We also noticed how Madelyn and Anna may have been confused about specific phonics elements. We did that by noting what was present in their writing. Instead of waiting to conduct required assessments, you can look at your students' writing samples and think about what they know about phonics components. Use that information to help guide your teaching (and reteaching) of phonics elements. When you are clear in your message that learning elements of phonics helps with spelling, and you demonstrate that explicitly for students, they have a better idea of why phonics is important. Phonics is not just about reading and making sense of printed words on a page. Phonics knowledge directly connects with spelling, which is important for confidence in writing.

What Do You Believe about Teaching Students to Recognize and Spell Unknown Words?

You've learned about word recognition strategies and how readers use visual, meaning, and structural cues to figure out unknown words. You also learned a great deal about phonics, structural analysis, and context clues. You also learned about different approaches to teaching phonics and ways to assess and organize your classroom to support students' word recognition skills. Think about the important takeaways from this chapter and write the ones that are the most important to you on the What Do You Believe template that can be found in the Chapter 7 Resources on the website. Then write what you believe about teaching word recognition to young students as a result of what you learned.

Closing Thoughts

At the start of the chapter, Aurleigh was interested in how people figure out words they don't know automatically, and she decided to keep track of what she did when encountering unknown words. She realized that she figured out unfamiliar words by using visual, meaning, and structural cues. She also came to understand that she generally used multiple cues in combination to figure out unknown words that she encountered in her reading. Once she understood what she did when she encountered unknown words, she was prepared to focus on how she could help her students develop strategies to use visual cues including phonics, meaning cues, and structural cues.

Teaching word recognition will require you to know your students and to provide them with explicit instruction and frequent and meaningful opportunities for practice and application. Word recognition skills are an important foundation of reading and writing that need to be part of the literacy instruction and practice you provide in your classroom. However, it's important to remember that they are tools that readers and writers use to construct meaning, and that's the real purpose for reading and writing!

Takeaways from Chapter 7

- Word recognition is an essential part of learning how to read and spell.
- There are different approaches to teaching word recognition and phonics.
- You may need to supplement the required reading materials with additional resources, based on your students' reading needs.
- Teach students how to use meaning cues, structural cues, and visual cues flexibly as they read.
- Phonics instruction is part of the reading program, but it isn't the whole program.
- Spelling is based on students' knowledge of word recognition, phonics, and their literacy development.

To Learn More about Teaching Students to Recognize and Spell Unknown Words

Books

Adams, M. J. (1990). *Beginning to read: Thinking and learning about print.* Cambridge, MA: MIT Press.

https://mitpress.mit.edu/books/beginning-read

This classic work has had lasting influence on the teaching of reading. Read this book to learn more about the history of the debate over the right way to teach reading and the ultimate implications for instruction. As you read, consider how it compares to what you believe and add to your belief statement.

Fox, B. J. (2014). *Phonics and word study for the teacher of reading: Programmed for self-instruction* (11th ed.). Upper Saddle River, NJ: Pearson.

https://www.pearson.com/us/higher-education/program/Fox-Phonics-and-Word-Study-for-the-Teacher-of-Reading-Programmed-for-Self-Instruction-11th-Edition/PGM306288.html

As a proficient reader, you may not remember specific phonics elements. This is a self-paced guide to help boost your knowledge of phonics. Work through this book to strengthen your understanding of phonics.

Leu, D. J., & Kinzer, C. K. (2017). *Phonics, phonemic awareness, and word analysis for teachers: An interactive tutorial* (10th ed.). New York, NY: Pearson.

https://www.pearson.com/us/higher-education/program/Leu-Phonics-Phonemic-Awareness-and-Word-Analysis-for-Teachers-An-Interactive-Tutorial-10th-Edition/PGM137609.html

This professional resource serves as a tutorial for teachers so you can review phonics, phonemic awareness, and word analysis skills at your own pace. To gain deeper understanding of one of those areas, select one chapter to work through and watch the accompanying videos.

Strategy Books for Phonics and Spelling Instruction and Assessment

Bear, D. R., Invernizzi, M., Templeton, S., & Johnston, F. (2015). *Words their way: Word study for phonics, vocabulary, and spelling instruction* (6th ed.). New York, NY: Pearson.

https://www.pearson.com/us/higher-education/program/Bear-Words-Their-Way-Word-Study-for-Phonics-Vocabulary-and-Spelling-Instruction-6th-Edition/PGM199292.html

As you review this book, note how instruction is based on students' literacy development. Adapt lessons from this resource to teach phonics and spelling to small groups of students in your placement. You can use this resource for assessment and instruction.

Beck, I. L., & Beck, M. E. (2013). *Making sense of phonics: The hows and whys* (2nd ed.). New York, NY: Guilford.

https://www.guilford.com/books/Making-Sense-of-Phonics/Beck-Beck/9781462511990

Skim the table of contents for a chapter to preview. As you read that chapter, note how you will use ideas and resources for teaching and assessing phonics. Make adjustments as needed and try these ideas with a small group of students.

Cunningham, P. M. (2017). *Phonics they use: Words for reading and writing* (7th ed.). New York, NY: Pearson.

https://www.pearson.com/us/higher-education/program/Cunningham-Phonics-They-Use-Words-for-Reading-and-Writing-7th-Edition/PGM301480.html

This book provides a wealth of strategies for teaching phonics and spelling. Look through the table of contents and choose two teaching strategies to try in your placement. You can use this resource to teach whole class or small group lessons.

Cunningham, P. M. (2012). *What really matters in spelling: Research-based strategies and activities.* Boston, MA: Pearson.

https://www.pearson.com/us/higher-education/program/Cunningham-What-Really-Matters-in-Spelling-Research-Based-Strategies-and-Activities/PGM146665.html

As you read this book, note how you can use the suggested strategies, activities, and routines in your placement and in your future teaching. Choose three ideas to adapt and use with your students.

Ganske, K. (2018). *Word sorts and more: Sound, pattern, and meaning explorations K–3* (2nd ed.). New York, NY: Guilford.

https://www.guilford.com/books/Word-Sorts-and-More/Kathy-Ganske/9781462533336

Select activities from one chapter of this book that you could use with a small group of students who need to learn that skill. Note the resources for supporting ELs and sample lesson plans. Adapt the plans and activities to address your students' learning needs.

Rasinski, T. V., Rupley, W. H., & Nichols, W. D. (2012). *Phonics & fluency practice with poetry: Tapping the power of rhyming verse to improve students' word recognition, automaticity, and prosody—and help them become successful readers.* New York, NY: Scholastic.

https://www.scholastic.com/teachers/books/phonics--fluency-practice-with-poetry-by-timothy-v-rasinski/

This resource provides you with ideas for how to teach and practice phonics skills through poetry. As students practice reading the poems that feature specific phonics elements, they are on their way to becoming fluent readers. Select one aspect of phonics to teach to a small group of students. Modify the plans and routines to meet your students' learning needs. Consider how you can use poetry in your future teaching.

Online Resources

Spelling Connections: Research and Stages of Spelling Development

http://bpsassets.weebly.com/uploads/9/9/3/2/9932784/gentry.pdf

You learned about stages of spelling development in this chapter. This online resource provides more in-depth information about each stage and provides samples of students' writings to illustrate each stage. Use this resource to analyze one student's writing sample from your placement and consider what you need to teach the student based on your findings.

Teach with Phonics Skills Chart

https://www.scholastic.com/teachers/articles/teaching-content/teach-phonics-skills-chart/

Follow the link to this online chart. Explore this online resource and consider how you can use it in your teaching.

Blogs

At the Foundation of Foundational Skills: Structured Phonics

https://achievethecore.org/aligned/at-the-foundation-of-foundational-skills-structured-phonics/

Read this blog post from Achieve the Core and consider how the information compares to what you read in this chapter. Make a list of what you need to remember when teaching phonics elements to your students.

Rethinking Assessment in Word Study: Five Ready-to-Go Ideas

https://www.literacyworldwide.org/blog%2fliteracy-daily%2f2019%2f03%2f14%2frethinking-assessment-in-word-study-five-ready-to-go-ideas

This post from the International Literacy Association (ILA) *Literacy Daily: Teaching Tips* blog provides a variety of ways to assess your students' understanding of phonics components in writing that do not involve spelling tests. Read the blog and choose one method of assessment to try out in your placement classroom. Consider how you can incorporate these ideas in your future teaching.

Shanahan on Literacy: The Great American Phonics Instruction Quiz, Part I

https://www.readingrockets.org/blogs/shanahan-literacy/great-american-phonics-instruction-test-part-i

Take the test as you read this blog from the Reading Rockets website. How did you do? Reread and note how the concepts literacy expert Dr. Shanahan presented align with this chapter.

Read the follow-up blog (Part II) and think about what this means for your teaching.

https://www.readingrockets.org/blogs/shanahan-literacy/great-american-phonics-instruction-quiz-part-ii

What Are Running Records?

https://www.weareteachers.com/what-are-running-records/

Read this blog and follow the links within the blog to learn more about running records. Think about how you can use running records in your classroom to monitor students' word recognition, use of reading cues, and oral reading fluency.

Apps

Common Sense Education: Favorite Phonics Games, Apps, and Websites

https://www.commonsense.org/education/top-picks/favorite-phonics-games-apps-and-websites

Scroll through this website to read about 18 free and paid apps and websites that you could use in your literacy stations, during independent work, or recommend for home use.

Reading Rockets: Literacy Apps for Phonics

https://www.readingrockets.org/literacyapps/phonics

Read the descriptions and choose three apps from this list of 30 that you would want to use in your classroom to reinforce phonics skills. Although some are free, many are inexpensive. When you are hired as a teacher, you may want to talk with your principal about policies related to downloading apps onto school-owned devices, as well as funding for apps that require fees.

Reading Rockets: Literacy Apps for Spelling

https://www.readingrockets.org/literacyapps/spelling

Do you need apps to reinforce spelling? Browse this list of 30 apps that help students with spelling. Note that a few are free, but most are not.

Reading practice is one way to help students develop oral reading fluency.

How Do I Teach Fluency?

REAL-LIFE EXAMPLE

Caleb just started his field placement for his early clinical experience. He was working in a second grade classroom with 24 students and his mentor teacher, Mrs. Carter. Caleb remembered when his second grade teacher did one-minute fluency assessments. He recalled being nervous when reading the passage as quickly as possible—feeling like it was a race to get to the end. Caleb wondered if this was still a common activity in second grade classrooms. He knew that he would be learning about fluency in his reading/literacy methods course, and he was curious if reading fast is the most important aspect of fluency. Since Mrs. Carter told Caleb that she was happy to answer any questions he had about teaching, learning, and students, he asked her how she teaches and assesses fluency in her classroom. Caleb was surprised to learn from Mrs. Carter that reading as fast as possible is not really the goal of fluency at all!

Mrs. Carter explained that reading fluency has three components, and rate (or speed) is only one of them. Caleb was not surprised to learn that reading the words accurately is a key part of fluency, but he was unfamiliar with the importance of expression and the relationship between fluency and comprehension. Mrs. Carter assured Caleb that he would have lots of chances to observe, assist with, and even teach fluency strategies to the students during his clinical experience since developing fluency is an important goal in second grade.

Perhaps you, like Caleb, remember reading tests during which you had to read lists of nonsense words as fast as possible. Or perhaps one of your memories is hearing someone read to you who used expression in their voice and different voices for the characters in books. You may be like Caleb and feel unsure about what fluency is and how it relates to teaching reading and writing. Caleb was reassured that he would learn about fluency in his methods class and that his mentor teacher would share her knowledge with him as well.

You, too, can feel confident that, although there is much to learn, you are in the process of learning how to promote fluency as part of reading instruction. This chapter provides you with a definition of fluency that will encompass more than reading speed. We bolster this definition with research about fluency, and then we give you specific recommendations for teaching and assessing fluency.

What Is Fluency?

Let's start with the definition of fluency. **Fluency** is the ability to read a text accurately, quickly, and with proper expression and phrasing. When you listen to children read orally, you can spot the fluent readers easily. Fluent readers are able to read texts smoothly and easily with appropriate expression and phrasing. When students read texts fluently, their oral reading sounds easy and smooth—much like a normal speaking voice. To get a sense of what fluent reading sounds (and feels) like, read a page or two of a children's book aloud. Were you able read the text accurately, quickly, and with proper phrasing? How did it feel to read the text fluently? Was it relatively effortless? Did it feel almost automatic? Reflecting on your own reading fluency experiences can help you understand what reading fluency is, which you can use to help your students become fluent readers.

To understand better what oral reading fluency is, let's consider how the National Reading Panel Report (NRP, 2000) describes each of the three components of fluency. According to the NRP, fluency includes three components: accuracy, rate, and prosody. Let's look at these three components more carefully.

ACCURACY. Reading words accurately means that children can identify words and that they have solid word recognition strategies and strong sight word recognition. They can identify the words automatically with little to no effort. This ability to identify words easily allows students to devote their mental energy toward understanding what they are reading rather than laboring over the words.

RATE. Reading rate or speed is another key component of fluency; however, reading as quickly as possible is not the goal of oral reading fluency. Reading at an appropriate rate is really the goal. Hasbrouck and Tindal (2017) have done extensive research to identify the expected reading rates for children at different grade levels. These targets address both accuracy and rate and are reported as **words correct per minute**, which is often abbreviated as **WCPM**.

PROSODY. The ability to read with proper or appropriate **phrasing and expression** is called prosody. So, what does it sound like when children read aloud with prosody? Fluent readers who demonstrate prosody in their oral reading vary their voices in tone, pitch, and volume to reflect the meaning of the text. They emphasize important words and use appropriate emotion when reading dialogue.

Fluency is actually the combination of all three of these components working together—fluent readers are able to read accurately, at an appropriate rate, with proper prosody. The Common Core State Standards (CCSS) and other learning standards address fluency as an important foundational skill that children need to develop in the early elementary grades. For example, a reading standard for grades 1 through 3 is: expect students to read with sufficient accuracy and fluency and to read with comprehension.

You may be wondering what fluent reading looks and sounds like for children in first, second, and third grades. If you go to Margin Note 8.1, you can view short videos demonstrating and discussing reading fluency development and expectations in first, second, and third grades.

Margin Note 8.1: Videos of Reading Fluency at Grades 1, 2, and 3

Grade 1: https://www.understood. org/en/learning-attention-issues/ signs-symptoms/age-by-age-learning-skills/video-what-reading-fluency-looks-like-in-first-grade

Grade 2: https://www.understood. org/en/learning-attention-issues/ signs-symptoms/age-by-age-learning-skills/video-what-reading-fluency-looks-like-in-second-grade

Grade 3: https://www.understood. org/en/learning-attention-issues/ signs-symptoms/age-by-age-learning-skills/video-what-reading-fluency-looks-like-in-third-grade

Why Fluency Is Important

If children can read texts fluently, that means they are able to **say the words automatically** so they can devote their attention toward understanding what they read. Over four decades ago, LaBerge and Samuels (1974) developed the **theory of automaticity** to explain how readers must devote their attention and effort to the two major aspects of reading: word recognition and comprehension. If students have to focus too much on figuring out words, they will have limited ability to understand what they are reading. Therefore, if students have the ability to identify words automatically, they can devote most of their attention and effort to comprehension.

Fluency is often described as a **bridge that links word recognition and comprehension** (Pikulski & Chard, 2005). Although fluency does not automatically guarantee comprehension, to experience good reading comprehension, students must be able to identify words quickly and easily. If students do not read fluently, it can create additional problems. For example, if students read very slowly, it takes them much longer to read a passage than their peers. They are likely to become tired and frustrated, and it can be difficult for them to remember what happened at the beginning of a sentence or paragraph if it takes too long to read. If students struggle with fluency, they might become discouraged, develop negative attitudes toward reading, and avoid reading. This process creates a vicious cycle wherein students who struggle with fluency tend to read less which means they get less practice. When students get minimal practice reading, they are not able to improve their fluency which continues the negative cycle. For these reasons, fluency instruction must be addressed in your reading program.

Research on Fluency Instruction

The **NRP Report** (2000) was a major review of research to determine the key components of reading and effective instructional strategies. Fluency was one of the five key components of reading that the report identified. The NRP concluded that fluency can be developed through repeated readings of a text, guided reading of texts, and reading practice with a wide variety of texts. In short, reading practice is ***the best*** way to help students develop oral reading fluency. One particular instructional approach, repeated readings, has been shown in many research studies to support the fluency and comprehension development of students, including those with special needs (Therrien, 2004). Fluency is such an important foundation of reading that researchers have continued to study it in recent years. Rasinski et al. (2017) found that third grade students who struggled with reading made significant gains in their overall reading performance after receiving fluency instruction. Kuhn, Rasinski, and Young (2018) synthesized research on fluency instruction and the contributions fluency makes to reading comprehension and overall reading achievement. Based on their research synthesis, they recommend making fluency a regular part of reading instruction in the early grades.

As mentioned earlier in this chapter, oral reading fluency has three components: accuracy, rate, and prosody (Kuhn, Rasinski, & Young, 2018). Let's start with accuracy, which is the ability to identify words correctly and automatically. Words can be divided into two main groups: those that can be identified by sight and those that can be recognized using strategies such as phonics, structural analysis, and context. When students use these strategies effectively, they can add words to their sight vocabulary. Because Chapter 7 (How Do I Teach Students to Recognize and Spell Unknown Words?) addresses word recognition and both Chapters 7 and 9 (How Do I Teach Vocabulary?) address teaching words in context, we just address sight words in this chapter.

Teaching Sight Words to Promote Reading Fluency

The ability to **identify words by sight** is critical for fluent reading. If you consider the term *sight words* as the broad or general term for all words that a reader can identify automatically by sight, there is a subset of sight words that are called high-frequency words because they appear very often in written texts. Lists such as those by **Fry** or **Dolch** are examples of **high-frequency words** (see Chapter 8 Resources on the website for Dolch word lists). For emergent readers, mastering a couple of hundred high-frequency words by the end of second or third grade can help students recognize over 50% of the words in texts. Did you know that 13 words account for nearly 25% of the words children encounter in their reading? Clearly, teaching these high-frequency words so students can recognize them by sight will contribute to fluency development. Those 13 high-frequency words are provided in Figure 8.1.

Figure 8.1. 13 High-frequency Words

a	and	for	he	in	is	it	of	that	the	to	was	you

There are additional lists of high-frequency words that are important for students to be able to read automatically. You can find several lists of high-frequency words as well as phrases and sentences that contain these high-frequency words in the Chapter 8 Resources on the website.

Although high-frequency words are important, students also have to learn many words by sight that go beyond any list of high-frequency words. Instruction on sight words is important, but it's impossible to teach all the words students will encounter by sight, so that's why it's important to teach phonics, structural analysis, and use of context to figure out unknown words. In addition, plenty of opportunities to read easy texts will increase a student's sight vocabulary.

ENGLISH LEARNERS AND SIGHT WORDS. English Learners (ELs) must also learn sight words to become fluent readers, but because many ELs have had limited experiences with print texts in English and may not have target high-frequency and sight words in their listening and speaking vocabularies, additional considerations for instruction are warranted. Helman et al. (2016) concluded from a research study of ELs in three urban elementary schools that:

- Teachers need to differentiate instruction for ELs to support the level of their English language development.
- Language development activities need to be included in instruction.
- Students need to have multiple opportunities each day to read high-frequency and other sight words in connected texts.

Although these practices are offered for use with ELs, they are also appropriate for other learners who may need additional support and opportunities to learn high-frequency and other sight words. Therefore, we have embedded considerations for teaching sight words throughout the following instructional approaches and strategies.

EXPLICIT TEACHING OF SIGHT WORDS. Explicit teaching of sight words allows teachers to help their students learn important sight words in an efficient manner (Rasinski et al., 2017). By providing focused instruction on targeted sight words, children can learn to read, spell, and write the words in a relatively short period of time. See Teaching Strategy 8.1: Explicit Instruction of Sight Words for step-by-step procedures you can follow to teach your students sight words.

© Cmspic/Shutterstock.com

The ability to identify words by sight is critical for fluent reading.

Teaching Strategy 8.1: Explicit Instruction of Sight Words

Purpose: This strategy provides a procedure to teach sight words through reading, spelling, and writing. It is designed to be very efficient so you can use it regularly to help your students build their knowledge of sight words.

Procedures:

1. Select two to four targeted sight words. The words *take* and *stop* will be used as examples in this sample lesson. These words are both on the Dolch list for first grade students. The Dolch list is available in the Chapter 8 Resources on the website.

2. Say each word aloud and use it in a sentence.

   take   I will *take* one apple to eat.

   stop   The bus will *stop* so I can get on it.

3. Encourage students to use each word orally in a sentence and then write the words on the board.

4. Discuss each word and its special features. In this example, you could emphasize that both words have four letters. You can discuss the /st/ blend in the word *stop* and in the word *take* there is a silent *e* (sometimes called magic or bossy) that makes the vowel long (says its name).

5. Ask the students to spell each word aloud as you point to each letter on the board. Students can also chant the spelling of each word as you or a student points to each letter.

6. Invite students to spell the words in the air with their fingers as they orally recite the spelling of each word.

7. Have students write each word on paper and spell it aloud as they write.

8. Invite students to write each word on a note card and collect them in a file box or punch a hole in the corner of each card and store them on a metal ring. You can also have students hold up a card to indicate which of the words you say in a sentence.

9. Add these words to the Word Wall in your classroom (Margin Note 8.3).

10. Write a sentence or short paragraph with the target words on the board or chart paper or project them on a screen. Invite students to read and re-read the sentence or paragraph, emphasizing the target sight words.

11. Ask students to look for these target sight words in their reading and to use them in their writing to get additional practice.

Margin Note 8.2: Sight Word Lists

http://www.sightwords.com/pdfs/word_lists/dolch_group.pdf

http://www.uniqueteachingresources.com/support-files/fryfirst100set.pdf

CONSIDERATIONS FOR SUPPORTING ENGLISH LEARNERS. Many high-frequency and other sight words are abstract and may be difficult for some students to learn. Be sure that students have the target sight words in their listening and speaking vocabularies first. Time spent teaching the words orally will be helpful for students to link those words to their reading and writing. For example, English Learners will use sight words when they speak, even if their utterances are incomplete. Use your students' language to create phrase cards and add illustrations to help them make connections between their oral language and the written form of high-frequency words. Doing so will help them to expand their sight word vocabularies. If you label objects in the classroom using sight words and a noun, students can see the sight words in meaningful contexts that will support their learning and retention of such words. For example, the door to the classroom can be labeled *the door*. You can use a similar approach with other objects: a table, a box of books, and so on. You can link these phrases to lessons when appropriate. Your students will also benefit from time to read connected texts several times each day so they can have increased exposure to and practice with sight words in meaningful, interesting texts. You can find lists of words that students need to learn by sight in Margin Note 8.2. The words are organized by grade level and will give you a good sense of specific words that students are expected to know by sight from PreK through grade 3.

Connection to the Field: Teaching High-frequency Words

Ask your mentor teacher if there is a list of high-frequency words that students are expected to know. If so, use that list. If there is not such a list, use the Dolch or Fry list provided in Margin Note 8.2 and observe students when reading orally to see if there are words that some students do not know. Offer to work with an individual student or a small group to teach a lesson using the explicit instruction of sight words approach described above. After the lesson, reflect on how the students did with the tasks in the lesson. Observe students reading in other settings. Are they able to identify the high-frequency words you taught when reading texts?

USING A WORD WALL TO TEACH SIGHT WORDS. A **classroom word wall** is helpful for teaching sight words (Cunningham, 2017). The words are introduced and taught to students, and then they are posted on the word wall as a reference. A variety of hands-on activities are also incorporated into word wall instruction to help students learn and remember the sight words. Typically, teachers will spend a few minutes each day teaching and reviewing new word wall words over the course of a week so that using the word wall becomes a classroom routine.

Here are some ideas for implementing a word wall in your classroom. Typically, you will select up to five target sight words to teach in a week. Word lists containing high-frequency words, words that students struggle with in their reading and writing, and grade-level curriculum words are good sources for sight words for the word wall. You will introduce each word to students by writing it on an index card and using the word in a sentence. To draw the students' attention to the word wall words, write the sentence on the board and underline the word wall word. You can invite the students to suggest other sentences that use the word wall word and then discuss the meaning or use of the word.

To draw the students' attention to the actual words, you can point to each letter of the word as you spell it aloud. You can then invite students to spell the word aloud with you as you point to each letter. You can also ask students to trace around the configuration of the word using another color and discuss the shape of the word. Follow this pattern for each new word wall word. Finally, you will place the index cards for the new words on the word wall. Arrange the words by letter so all of the A words are together, all of the B words are together, and so on.

Some activities you can do on the following days with the word wall words follow.

- *Rhyme with the word wall words.* Ask students to number a piece of paper from 1 to 5. Ask them to write a word wall word that rhymes with the word you give to them. For example, for the word *my* you could say, "the word begins with *m* and rhymes with *by.* Write the word wall word." Continue this pattern for all of the new word wall words.

- *Cross-checking.* Engage students in a cross-checking activity with the new word wall words. Tell them they will need to select a word wall word that makes sense in a sentence and begins with a certain letter. For example, you could say, "The word begins with *t* and fits in this sentence, *I went ____ the store yesterday.*" Continue with this pattern for all five new word wall words. Have the students check their own words by reading each sentence again, restating the beginning letter of the word. Ask students to chant the word and then the spelling for each of the five word wall words.

Margin Note 8.3: Using Word Walls in the Classroom

https://www.readingrockets.org/strategies/word_walls

- *Word hunt.* Ask students to go on a word hunt by having them locate the new word wall words in texts. You can share a photocopied passage and provide highlighters for students to locate and highlight the word wall words, or you can provide students with small sticky notes so they can mark in a book where they see the word wall words.

For more information about how and why to use word walls to teach, review, and reinforce high-frequency words, check out the resources provided in Margin Note 8.3.

CONSIDERATIONS FOR SUPPORTING ENGLISH LEARNERS. ELs who have very limited English proficiency may be overwhelmed if too many word wall words are introduced at the same time. As a general rule of thumb, introduce no more than three words at a time for students who are very new to English. For those who are an intermediate level of English proficiency, you can introduce up to five words, and for those who are approaching proficiency, you can introduce up to seven words at a time.

Students learn high-frequency words and other sight words through frequent exposures and practice, and ELs may need even more opportunities to practice reading these words. You can encourage students to take home index cards with the word wall words they are learning. They can practice reading the word wall words with a partner at home. If you send students home with two sets of the target word wall words, they can play memory with a partner for additional practice. You can also encourage students to work with a family member to "go on a word hunt" to find the target sight words in their homes, neighborhoods, and the texts they encounter.

Games are a great way to provide opportunities for students, including ELs, to practice the sight words they need to know to develop into fluent readers. See Margin Note 8.4 to find free resources for free sight words games you can use with the students in your classroom.

TEACHING SIGHT WORDS IN THE CONTEXT OF PHRASES. Because many high-frequency words like *for, of*, and *the* lack **meaning clues**, Teaching Strategy 8.2: Associative Learning for Sight Words is designed to help students learn these words in the context of meaningful phrases. This strategy is most helpful for students (including ELs) who have difficulty learning these types of abstract words.

Because students need multiple opportunities to practice reading high-frequency words, you can extend this strategy to focus on longer phrases, sentences, and paragraphs. These longer texts will give students practice transferring their knowledge of high-frequency words to reading and writing connected texts. In Margin Note 8.5, we have provided a link to Fry's sight word phrases that you can use to teach high-frequency words in the context of meaningful phrases.

USING PATTERN BOOKS TO TEACH SIGHT WORDS. **Pattern books** provide a meaningful way for children to learn sight words in the context of real texts. As you connect sight word instruction with children's literature, students are able to see the words in the text, understand how they are used, and practice identifying the words in a meaningful context. To use this approach in your teaching, you will need to select a pattern book that emphasizes the targeted sight word(s). For young students or ELs with limited English proficiency, you will want to emphasize only one or two words at a time. For older students or ELs who are approaching proficiency, you may want to target up to five words in a single lesson.

As with any literature-based approach to teaching, you will want to read the book aloud to the students to promote enjoyment of the book. Next, you can select several pages of the book where the target sight words are used and draw the students' attention to the words by discussing their spelling, pronunciation, and meaning or use. You may then want to re-read the book using Echo Reading (see Teaching Strategy 8.3) during which you read a sentence or phrase first, emphasizing the target sight word, and then the students echo it back by re-reading the same sentence or phrase. To get the students to interact with the target sight words, you can invite them to go on a word hunt by locating one of the sight words you are targeting for the lesson. You can provide them with highlighter tape or sticky notes so they can mark the places in the book where they find the target sight word. You can then have students share where they have found the target words by asking them to read the sentence in which they found the word. You can also read the pattern book chorally (see Teaching Strategy 8.4), emphasizing the target sight words. To promote transfer of their developing knowledge of the sight words, it's important for you to remind students to look for these sight words when they read other texts and when they write.

Teaching Strategy 8.2: Associative Learning for Sight Words

Purpose: Some high-frequency sight words are function words that do not have clear meanings such as *for*, *of*, and *the*. Being able to identify these extremely common words automatically is essential for fluent reading. Therefore, this strategy focuses on teaching these words by association through the context of phrases or sentences.

Procedures:

1. Select one or two high-frequency words for instruction.
2. Present the word by using it in a phrase accompanied by a picture.
3. Underline the high-frequency word. For example, to teach the high-frequency word *of*, you could use the phrase *a box of apples*.

© brgfx/Shutterstock.com

4. Invite the students to brainstorm other possible ways to use the high-frequency word *of* in a phrase.
5. After several students share appropriate examples, distribute index cards and ask students to make their own picture card with the high-frequency word written in red and underlined. Provide time for students to share their card with others in the group. These cards can be added to the students' word banks or word rings, and you can also cue students to remember their phrase cards when they get stuck reading that high-frequency word.

Margin Note 8.6: Bilingual Books for Children: Book List

http://www.ala.org/Template. cfm?Section=Home&template =/ContentManagement/ ContentDisplay.cfm&Content ID=12952

https://www.uniteforliteracy. com/

http://en.childrenslibrary.org/

https://ccbc.education.wisc. edu/books/detailListBooks. asp?idBookLists=102

http://www.colorincolorado. org/booklist/celebrate- reading-two-languages- bilingual-booklist

CONSIDERATIONS FOR SUPPORTING ENGLISH LEARNERS. **Bilingualism is a key goal for English Learners' literacy development.** Therefore, you can use bilingual books so students can learn sight words in English as well as in their native language. To engage students' family members in their learning of sight words, you can share books in their native language because learning words in their native language will support their learning of words in English.

You can also share books that represent the students' cultures and experiences, so they find the books interesting and relevant as they read to practice their sight word vocabularies. See Margin Note 8.6 for helpful resources listing bilingual books for young students as well as access to free ebooks to use with your students.

Connecting with Families for Sight Word Practice

The more students practice sight word recognition, the more sight words they will recognize automatically. Inviting families to review sight words, play sight word games, and notice sight words in the texts they encounter in their homes and neighborhoods is a great approach to getting families involved in their children's literacy learning and to provide the practice children need to develop large sight word vocabularies. The following suggestions for sight word practice can be shared with families. You may also find it useful to share or demonstrate the activities at open house, parent–teacher conferences, or through your classroom newsletter.

Here are several easy and effective activities families can do at home to reinforce their children's sight word learning.

1. Families can play scavenger hunt with their children by looking for a specific sight word in the newspaper, in junk mail, or as they do errands in the community with their children.
2. Families can do simple activities to help their children master the 20 most frequently used words in the English language:

> the, of, and, to, a, in, is, that, it, was, for, you, he, on, as, are, they, with, be, his

Some ways families can help their children practice and learn these words are:

■ Write the words on index cards or pieces of paper. See which words the child already knows. Put those words in one pile. Read each word the child doesn't know and say a sentence that includes that word. Ask the child to read the word. If the child doesn't know the word, read it and use it in a sentence. Continue this process. Review the words often so the child will be able to learn them automatically.

■ Read a sight word aloud and ask the child to write it down. Compare how the child spelled the word and the correct spelling. If the child spelled the word incorrectly, encourage the child to rewrite the word with the correct spelling. If the child does not have ideas about how to write the word, provide two spellings—with one being the correct spelling—and encourage the child to select the correct spelling.

■ Make two sets of identical sight word cards. Play the memory game by spreading all of the sight word cards out on a table or the floor so they are face down. Take turns so that the child turns over a card, reads the word aloud, and then turns over a second card. If the cards match, the child picks up the cards and puts them into their pile. The child will continue this process until they do not draw a match or are unable to correctly read the matching words. Alternate turns with the child until all of the word cards have been matched. The winner is the person who has the most cards in their pile.

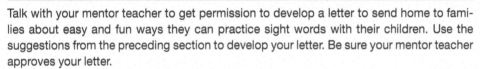

ℰngaging with Families: Sight Word Practice

Talk with your mentor teacher to get permission to develop a letter to send home to families about easy and fun ways they can practice sight words with their children. Use the suggestions from the preceding section to develop your letter. Be sure your mentor teacher approves your letter.

Assessing Sight Word Knowledge

Knowing which **high-frequency words** students know is important to help you determine which words you need to teach using the teaching strategies presented in this chapter. You can gain useful formative assessment data (i.e., assessment during instruction that is used to inform your teaching; see Chapter 3 for a more detailed discussion of formative assessment) by observing your students carefully as they read and write in authentic settings in the classroom. But because so much is always happening in a classroom, you will want to record notes about what you are seeing related to students' sight word knowledge and use. We recommend that you develop a format for anecdotal notes that allows you to capture this information easily. See Chapter 3 for more information about anecdotal notes.

In addition to observing students while reading and writing, you may want to use Assessment Strategy 8.1 which targets the 50 most common high-frequency words. This assessment strategy will allow you to quickly determine which high-frequency words your students know and which ones they still need to learn. You can then use that assessment data to make instructional decisions about teaching sight words to your students.

Assessment Strategy 8.1: High-frequency Words

Purpose: The high-frequency words assessment is a quick assessment you can use to determine a child's ability to automatically identify a sample of the most common words in English. The words for this assessment are the 50 most frequently used words in English. Two forms, 1 and 2, are provided. Each form assesses 25 high-frequency words. You can also make your own version of the assessment by selecting words from the Revised Dolch List (available in the Chapter 8 Resources on the website) or another list of high-frequency words. The results of the assessment will inform you about which words to target for instruction for the entire class, small groups, and individual students.

Procedures:

1. Select the form of the assessment you will use—1 or 2. The word lists for forms 1 and 2 are provided here. The word lists and record sheets you will need to administer this assessment are available in the Chapter 8 Resources on the website.

    Form 1 Words   the, and, a, is, it, for, he, as, they, be, at, from, I, have, but, were, all, when, their, her, we, about, said, if, would

    Form 2 Words   of, to, in, that, was, you, on, are, with, his, or, had, not, this, by, one, she, an, there, can, what, up, out, some, so

2. Duplicate the record sheet for the form you are using.

3. Cover the words with two sheets of paper so only one word is visible at a time. Place the page containing the covered words before the student and say, "I want you to read some words for me. Let's begin with this one."

4. Move one of the blank sheets of paper to reveal the first word. Ask the student to read the word.

5. Mark the words the student gets correct with a plus (+) on the record sheet. If the student makes a miscue (error), write what the student says on the record sheet.

6. If the student gets stuck on a word, encourage the student to make their best attempt.

7. If the student is unable or unwilling to read a word, ask them if they want to "skip it," and mark "skip" on the record sheet.

8. Proceed through the list of words.

9. Count the number of words read correctly.

10. Review the miscues the student made to see if there are any patterns.

11. Use the results of the assessment to plan appropriate sight word instruction for the student.

Teaching Oral Reading Fluency

Effective fluency instruction has three characteristics. It focuses on **oral reading, students re-reading texts** (sometimes called repeated readings), and **students receiving one-on-one guidance and feedback** from the teacher or a more skilled reader such as a volunteer, family member, or classmate. The following recommended teaching strategies and approaches for fluency address each of these components.

PRACTICING FLUENCY WITH TEACHER MODELING AND SUPPORT. Teaching Strategy 8.3: Echo Reading allows you to model fluent reading to students who then echo back the same text with accuracy, appropriate rate, and proper prosody. **Modeling fluent reading** is an effective way to help students develop their own oral reading fluency. Echo reading is often done with poems or song lyrics, but it can be applied to any text.

Choral reading facilitates students' oral reading fluency as they read poetry and short passages together in small or large groups. When reading with others, those who are not yet fluent readers are carried along with the pace and expression of other readers. All of the readers are able to read more accurately, smoothly, and easily because they are able to listen to readers who are more fluent and match their accuracy, rate, and prosody. Teaching Strategy 8.4: Choral Reading provides an example of how to implement this approach with your students.

READING FOR AN AUDIENCE. Reading for an audience provides authenticity and motivation to reading fluency instruction and practice. Radio reading (Greene, 1979) helps children focus on communicating a message so the audience can understand it. Pretending that they are doing a radio show, students focus on delivering the message of the text so that their listeners can understand it. Although there may be some miscues in the reading, listeners respond to the reading by discussing it, restating the basic message, and evaluating how the message was delivered. The procedure for Radio Reading is presented in Teaching Strategy 8.5.

Readers Theater provides a motivating and meaningful way for students to do repeated readings so that after practice they can perform the script for an audience. Research has shown that Readers Theater can contribute to fluency gains for all students as well as ELs (Martinez, Roser, & Strecker, 1998/1999; Samuels & Farstrup, 2006).

Teaching Strategy 8.3: Echo Reading

Purpose: Modeling is an essential aspect of effective fluency instruction. In the Echo Reading strategy, you provide a clear model of fluent reading that students can echo (or copy) as you collaboratively read a text aloud.

Procedures:

1. Select an easy text for the students to echo read with you. Poetry, nursery rhymes, and pattern books are good choices for young children. Big Books also work well for echo reading.

2. Invite students to tell you what it means to hear an echo. Explain the concept if necessary. Help students understand that when you say something, they will repeat back, or echo, the words in the same way. Try a few simple words and phrases and have the students echo them back to you.

3. Tell the students that you would like them to echo read a text with you.

4. Project the text on the screen, write it on the board, display it on chart paper, or use the text from a Big Book.

5. Read the first sentence and ask the students to echo read it back to you as you move your hand or a pointer under the words. Encourage students to focus on accuracy, rate, and prosody (expression and phrasing) so their echo reading sounds just like when you read the sentence.

6. Continue this process with the remainder of the text.

7. You may also want to discuss the text.

The students are echoing the teacher as he reads.

Teaching Strategy 8.4: Choral Reading

Purpose: The Choral Reading strategy provides a framework for students to read along as part of a group to promote reading fluency. When reading with the group, students who are not yet fluent readers are able to join in the group to match their accuracy, rate, and prosody.

Procedures:

1. Identify a poem, a short picture book, or a passage that will be of interest to the students who will be doing the choral reading.

2. Note words that may be new to the students or that they may have difficulty reading. Present those words to the students by reading them aloud and pointing out sounds or patterns that the students have previously learned.

3. Ask the students to read the text silently.

4. Read the text aloud to model fluent reading for the students. As you read, track the print with a pointer or your hand.

5. Discuss the text, asking the students to retell the story or poem or summarize the passage.

6. Conduct the choral reading using one of these formats (Trousdale & Harris, 1993):
   - Two-part arrangement: One group of voices reads alternately with another group.
   - Soloist and chorus: One voice reads and the rest of the group joins in on the refrain.
   - Unison: The whole group reads as one.

7. Experiment with volume, tempo, sound effects, and expression. Have fun!

8. Perform the choral reading for an audience, such as parents, other students, or other teachers.

Teaching Strategy 8.5: Radio Reading

Purpose: This strategy uses modeling, repeated reading practice, and performance to provide opportunities for students to develop their oral reading fluency. It also emphasizes that the most important part of oral reading is to understand and communicate the meaning of a text.

Procedures:

1. Select a radio clip that is appropriate for the age and developmental level of the students. Tell students to listen for the message of the radio clip. Play the clip for the students.

2. After listening to the clip, ask the students what they heard and what the message was about.

3. Tell the students that they will be practicing their oral reading by doing a strategy called Radio Reading. The materials selected for reading should be about a paragraph in length and should be at the students' instructional level (i.e., approximately 95% of the words are known).

4. Provide time for the students to read and re-read the text several times so they are ready to read their text to the audience.

5. Emphasize that the purpose of the strategy is to communicate the meaning of the passage to the other students in the group who are listening. If a word is unknown during the reading, the student should merely point to the word and ask, "What is that word?" You should immediately tell the student the word so the reading can proceed with limited interruptions. The other students should serve as active listeners and do not have a copy of the passage.

6. After the passage is read, invite the students who were listeners to discuss the message that was conveyed. The intent of this discussion is to confirm that an accurate message was sent and received.

Lesson Planning: Practicing Fluency with Readers Theater

Readers Theater is an authentic and fun way for students to engage in repeated reading and to perform their oral reading for an audience. In Readers Theater, students do not memorize lines or use props or staging; rather, they read from their scripts expressively to convey the meaning and emotion of the text.

Standard: Read grade level prose and poetry orally with accuracy, appropriate rate, and expression on successive readings (Grade 3 Common Core State Standards, Foundational Skills)

Objective: The student will be able to read prose fluently with appropriate accuracy, rate, and expression.

Lesson Idea: Select a script (see Margin Note 8.7 for resources to locate Readers Theater scripts) that is appropriate for your students' reading and fluency levels. Ensure that the number of parts matches the number of students in the group. Begin the lesson by reading aloud from the script to model fluent reading for the students. Match students to parts and provide time for them to read their parts silently and then to read the script aloud several times as a group, focusing on their fluency. You may need to provide time to practice over several days to allow students to improve their fluency so they are ready to perform the Readers Theater for an audience (e.g., classmates, younger students, family members, and school staff).

Assessment: Observe the students' oral reading fluency when they perform their Readers Theater for an audience. Use the fluency scale from Assessment Strategy 8.3 (provided in the Chapter 8 Resources on the website) to assess and document the fluency level of each of the students in the group.

Scoring Criteria:

Level	Description
1	Reads almost entirely word by word; monotone; little or no use of punctuation
2	Reads mostly in 2- to 3-word phrases with some word by word; monotone with some expression; some evidence of punctuation
3	Reads mostly in phrases; appropriate expression; uses punctuation most of the time
4	Reads fluently; good expression; consistently attends to punctuation

Margin Note 8.7: Free Online Resources for Readers Theater Scripts

http://www.aaronshep.com/rt/RTE.html

http://www.thebestclass.org/rtscripts.html

http://www.teachingheart.net/readerstheater.htm

https://www.thewiseowlfactory.com/readers-theater-free/

Fluency Idol is a takeoff of the TV show you might know, *American Idol*, which is popular with many children. Teaching Strategy 8.6: Fluency Idol provides meaningful, fun opportunities for repeated readings, practice, supportive feedback, and oral performance (Calo, Woolard-Ferguson, & Koitz, 2013). This strategy uses poetry as the text that students practice and perform. Fluency Idol is fun and students will be encouraged to read and re-read their poems to develop their oral reading fluency.

Teaching Strategy 8.6: Fluency Idol

Purpose: This strategy provides students a highly motivating purpose for practicing their oral reading fluency—to be declared the Fluency Idol!

Procedures:

1. Select a poem at each student's independent reading level.

2. Ask students to practice reading the poem at home for their families and provide class time for students to practice reading the poem aloud with a partner.

3. Meet with each student individually for a few minutes. Have the student read the poem aloud to you so you can offer useful feedback about improving fluency.

4. On a specific day have three students read their poem for the whole class. Record each performance so the student can see what went well and what they can work on in the future. If you have a microphone and can create a stage area of the classroom, it can add to the excitement of the Fluency Idol strategy.

5. Have the students complete a secret ballot that is focused on oral reading fluency. The winner is identified as the Fluency Idol for the week, and other performers also receive recognition for their efforts.

6. Rotate which students get to "compete" for the title Fluency Idol so everyone gets a turn and the "competition" is as fair as possible.

© Monkey Business images/Shutterstock.com

REPEATED READINGS. **Repeated readings** have been shown by multiple research studies to be an extremely effective way to build children's oral reading fluency (Therrien, 2004). By repeatedly reading the same text several times, children are able to improve their oral reading fluency. However, just reading and re-reading a text is not sufficient for many children who need guidance and feedback in order to read smoothly and easily. During the multipaired simultaneous oral reading strategy (Poe, 1986), the class is divided into pairs. Each student takes turns reading to a partner. After one student reads aloud, the partners switch roles so that all students practice reading fluently. Because most students enjoy working with a partner, this strategy is a motivating way for them to read a text multiple times in order to improve their oral reading fluency. See Teaching Strategy 8.7 for step-by-step instructions on using this approach in your classroom.

Teaching Strategy 8.8: Structured Repeated Readings (Samuels, 1979) is a research-based approach to motivating students to engage in multiple readings of the same text to track their growth. The use of technology such as iPads can provide an updated approach to this strategy (Ness, 2016) that may be highly motivating for some students. By charting and sharing their progress while participating in this strategy (see Figure 8.2 in Teaching Strategy 8.8), students can see their growth in automatic recognition of words and the reduction of miscues. This strategy is especially effective for students who find reading difficult, because they are very likely to see tangible and relatively quick progress in their oral reading fluency.

© wavebreakmedia/Shutterstock.com

This student is re-reading a favorite text, which helps to build fluency.

Teaching Strategy 8.7: Multipaired Simultaneous Oral Reading

Purpose: After you model fluent reading with a specific text, the students work with a partner to practice their fluency and provide feedback to each other.

Procedures:

1. Identify a text that will lend itself to building oral reading fluency.

2. Tell the students that they will be reading the passage to a partner. Explain the goal of their reading is to read fluently with a steady pace and good expression.

3. Model reading the passage with fluency. Read the passage expressively and at an appropriate pace.

4. Ask students to read the passage with you in a choral reading format. If there are any challenging sections, help the students say the words or read the challenging phrases.

5. Divide the group into partners and have each pair sit together. If you use this strategy regularly, you may want to alternate choosing partners and allowing students to choose partners.

6. Let the pairs set their own rules about how much each student will read—one page, one paragraph, one line, and so on.

7. Ask each pair to alternate reading the passage aloud. Monitor the activity and provide guidance as needed.

8. When a pair of students finishes reading, give each student a silent activity to complete such as writing a statement about the meaning of the text or self-evaluating their own oral reading.

9. After all of the pairs of students have completed the oral reading, discuss the students' success at reading fluently.

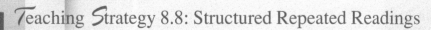

Teaching Strategy 8.8: Structured Repeated Readings

Purpose: When students read a text several times, their reading fluency improves. This strategy provides a framework for doing structured repeated readings focused on increasing reading rate as measured by words per minute (WPM). Accuracy is also considered.

Procedures:

1. Select a brief passage or story of 50–200 words for the student to read aloud. For beginning readers, a passage of approximately 50 words is sufficient for the first time the strategy is used. The passage should be at an appropriate level of difficulty. That means that the student should generally recognize more than 91% of the words. In other words, if the passage is 50 words in length, the student should generally recognize about 46 of the words. If the student misses more than 6 words in a 50-word passage, it is probably not suitable for this strategy.

2. Ask the student to read the passage orally. Using a copy of the passage, note the student's miscues and keep track of the time in seconds that it took the student to read the passage.

3. Ask the student to tell you something about the passage or to answer a question or two about the content of the passage to ensure that the student understood what was read.

4. Fill out the Reading Progress Chart (Figure 8.2) provided at the end of this teaching strategy to record the words per minute (WPM) and number of reading miscues. To calculate words per minute, record the number of seconds the student took to read the passage. Multiply the number of words in the passage by 60 and then divide by the time (in seconds) that it took the student to read the passage. For example, if the student read a 45-word passage in 58 seconds the calculation would be as follows:

    45 words in the passage × 60 seconds = 2700 divided by 58 seconds = 46 WPM

5. Encourage the student to practice re-reading the passage independently for a day or two. The reading can be done orally, silently, at school, or at home. The idea is to have the student practice the passage several times before you meet with them to repeat the process of having the student read the passage orally to you so you can calculate and record their progress on the chart in Figure 8.2. Repeat the process until the student is able to read the passage at a suitable rate. You can use the national norms for fluency (target reading rates) provided in the Chapter 8 Resources on the website or those used in the school district where you are doing your clinical experience.

6. Repeat the process with a new passage to help the student continue to improve their oral reading fluency. Consider using a slightly more difficult passage if appropriate for the student. See Figure 8.3 to see how data from multiple readings of the same text can be documented on the Reading Progress Chart.

(continued)

Figure 8.2. Reading Progress Chart

For _____ Title/Book _____

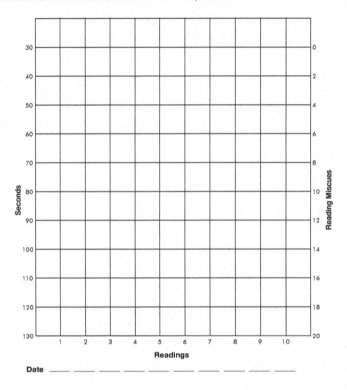

Figure 8.3. Example of Multiple Readings of a Text Documented on the Reading Progress Chart

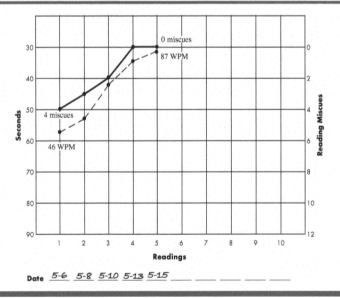

Fluency practice can easily be incorporated into centers so students can complete **self-directed fluency practice** on a regular basis (Ness, 2016). iPads can be used for Teaching Strategy 8.9: Record, Listen, Reflect. In this strategy, students work in a center to record and then play back their oral reading to reflect on their fluency and identify areas for further improvement. For younger students, a paraprofessional or classroom volunteer may need to assist with this strategy, at least in the beginning. As students have more practice with the strategy, an iPad, and the chart in Figure 8.4, they will be able to do this strategy more independently.

Figure 8.4. Fluency Chart for Record, Listen, Reflect Strategy

Name: _____

Date: _____

Text: _____

Watch your video and reflect on your reading fluency.

How was my reading accuracy?	Good	OK	Needs Work
How was my reading rate?	Good	OK	Needs Work
How was my phrasing?	Good	OK	Needs Work
How was my expression?	Good	OK	Needs Work
Overall, how was my reading fluency?	Good	OK	Needs Work

Something I did well: _____

Something I want to work on: _____

There are only so many hours in a school day so you may need to implement some large group instructional and practice activities for fluency. An effective large group fluency strategy is described in Teaching Strategy 8.10: Whole Class Repeated Reading (WCRR). This is an instructional strategy that can help increase oral reading fluency for students of all levels and abilities, especially ELs. This approach to repeated reading creates a social learning environment so all students feel comfortable in the classroom and excited to participate in reading activities and instruction with classmates (Monobe, Bintz, & McTeer, 2017).

Teaching Strategy 8.9: Record, Listen, Reflect

Purpose: By using an iPad, students can record their oral reading, listen to all aspects of their reading fluency, and reflect on how they can improve their fluency. This strategy is most appropriate for students in grade 2 and above.

Procedures:

1. Provide passages at each student's independent or instructional level that they can read with minimal assistance. You can organize these in file folders with the student's name on the outside.

2. The student will select a passage and read it orally while video recording themselves on an iPad. You can model this process for students to ensure they know how to start and stop the recording. This is very easy to do by having the student simply tap the camera icon, then tap the record button to start the recording, and then tap the record button again to stop recording.

3. The student then views their recording to note their accuracy, rate, and prosody. In this step, the student is expected to mark miscues and to note aspects of prosody such as phrasing, expression, and intonation. Students can be taught to follow a print copy of the passage to circle miscues, use the time stamp on the videos to see how quickly they read the passage, and to make notes on their prosody. If students think they can do a better job with another oral reading of the same passage, they are encouraged to do so. In fact, many students will be motivated to re-read the passage several times until they feel they have done their most fluent reading.

4. The students should then reflect on their fluency by using the chart in Figure 8.4 to identify strengths of their fluency and areas for improvement. This chart is also available in the Chapter 8 Resources on the website.

Teaching Strategy 8.10: Whole Class Repeated Readings (WCRR)

Purpose: This strategy provides an opportunity for the entire class to engage in repeated readings at the same time. Although this strategy is designed to support English Learners (ELs), it is appropriate for use with all students.

Procedures:

1. Plan to implement WCRR daily for 15 minutes. Identify words that ELs may not know. If possible, find those words in the students' first languages using free translation sites or apps such as Google Translate, iTranslate, Voice Translator, Photo Translate, or Speak and Translate. Preview these words with the students so they are familiar with them.

2. Choose a poem or song that will appeal to students but will also honor their cultural backgrounds.

3. Display the poem or song on chart paper, white board, or screen so students can easily see the text.

4. Read the text aloud using a pointer or your hand so students can follow along. Repeat this several times and then invite students to use the pointer and to be the lead voice. Students can use musical instruments or clapping to keep the rhythm or strike a pose for a specific word in the text. These opportunities for active engagement benefit all students but especially ELs who can engage in ways beyond just using their verbal skills.

5. Provide a copy of the poem or song for students to take home and read and discuss with their families.

6. Hold a public performance during which the whole class reads the poem or song for other students, teachers, staff members, and/or family members. You can also record the performance to share with family members via email or your classroom website.

PRACTICING PROSODY. Having students practice reading dialogue is a great way to improve their prosody. You can use Teaching Strategy 8.11: Say It Like a Character to help students practice reading dialogue with expression, phrasing, and emotion. You will ask students to think about what is happening in the story and how the character might feel so they can read the dialogue with appropriate prosody. This approach to practicing prosody through character dialogue can also be embedded in many of the other strategies. For example, students can be reminded to "Say it like a character" during repeated readings and readers theater, and you can model this for them during echo and choral readings.

Connecting with Families for Fluency Practice

Practice is important for developing oral reading fluency. You can share or adapt the letter in the box below to invite families to encourage their children to practice reading aloud at home. Be sure to ask your mentor teacher for permission and input on the letter prior to sending it home to families.

Engaging with Families: Fluency Practice

Dear Families,

We have been working on oral reading fluency in school. Fluent readers read smoothly, at a good pace, and with expression. Practice is important for developing reading fluency. Here are a few ideas you can use at home to help your child practice oral reading fluency:

■ Encourage your child to read and re-read books to you. Practice is important for developing oral reading fluency.

■ Provide a good reading model by reading aloud to your child. You can use books that your child brings home from school or books from the library or your home.

■ Read poems aloud together. By reading together, your child will be able to follow your lead to read smoothly, at a good rate, and with expression. You can use poems your child brings home from school or from the library or your home.

You can certainly use the teaching strategies described in this chapter with ELs; however, you will likely find that they benefit from additional opportunities to practice their oral reading fluency in English at home. You can prepare a bag or small backpack with a small digital recorder with an audio recording of a storybook on it and a hard copy of the storybook. In class, you can teach the students how to use the recorder and follow this format:

■ First, listen to the story while following along in the storybook.
■ Second, play the recording of the book while reading along orally. Do this at least two times.

You can then send the bag or backpack home with students for several days at a time and encourage them to listen and read along with the book several times. Doing so will give them the additional practice they need to build their oral reading fluency in English.

Teaching Strategy 8.11: Say It Like a Character

Purpose: This strategy is designed to help students develop their reading prosody by using character dialogue to "Say it like a character" by conveying emotion and meaning in their oral reading.

Procedures:

1. Select an excerpt of a story that has character dialogue in it.

2. Ask students to read the text silently. Then ask them to re-read it silently thinking about how the characters might sound when speaking.

3. Ask a student or two to read the excerpt aloud in the way they think the character would probably speak. Ask follow-up questions to help the students focus on how the character would feel and speak.

   - What emotion were you showing when you read the dialogue?
   - What clues did you use to help you determine the emotion and how the character would sound?

4. Encourage students to pay attention to events in the story and signals that the author gives, including punctuation and word choice to help the reader understand characters and their feelings.

© wavebreakmedia/Shutterstock.com

Organizing for Fluency Instruction

Fluency is a key foundation of reading, and it is a bridge to building strong comprehension. Therefore, it's important for you to find time daily to build students' oral reading fluency. If you use a literacy program framework, such as the Daily 5 (Boushey & Moser, 2014) or guided reading with centers, you can easily include fluency instruction and practice in your daily schedule. In fact, you generally need only 10–15 minutes daily to implement fluency instruction using one of the strategies in this chapter. As you may have noticed, however, many of these strategies require repetition, meaning that you may use the same strategy several days in a row or even for a week. That's okay—in fact, that's an excellent practice to implement. Fluency instruction can also be implemented across the curriculum, not just in your reading or language arts block. For example, students can do choral reading (Strategy 8.4) or readers theater (lesson planning example in this chapter) with texts aligned to social studies or science.

As you plan for fluency instruction in your classroom, Rasinski and Nageldinger (2016) suggest that you keep three big ideas in mind to ensure that students receive the instruction, support, and practice needed to develop into fluent readers. Those big ideas for fluency instruction are:

- I Do: Modeling
- We Do: Repetition (Rehearsal) and Support
- You Do: Performance

"I do" is important because students need to hear models of good fluent reading. You can be that fluency model or other students, parent volunteers, or video or audio recordings can provide such modeling. In addition, it is important to discuss what students notice (or should notice) when listening to fluent reading. This will allow them to have a clear understanding of all the aspects of fluent reading—accuracy, rate, and prosody.

"We do" is the heart of fluency development because fluency develops with practice. By reading a text several times, students can improve their accuracy, rate, and prosody. As presented in this chapter, there are many different ways that are motivating and interesting for students to re-read texts. Just like any skill, appropriate practice leads to improvement, and fluency is no different. Another dimension of the "we do" element is support. You can provide that support by reading with students, using a strategy such as echo reading (Teaching Strategy 8.3) or choral reading (Teaching Strategy 8.4) during which you provide a model for your students to follow along. Or, you can offer specific feedback to help students improve a certain aspect of their fluency.

"You do" focuses on performance which is highly motivating for students. Because they want to perform well, students are generally willing to engage in repeated readings to practice their oral reading fluency of a text. The performance doesn't need to be elaborate—it can be as simple as having a student read a rehearsed text in front of a classmate or as complex as performing a readers theater script for family members as a special assembly.

CONSIDERATIONS FOR EFFECTIVE FLUENCY INSTRUCTION. You may be wondering why we have not discussed some popular oral reading activities that you are likely to find in many elementary classrooms. **Round robin oral reading and popcorn reading** may be common, but we discourage you from using them because they are not effective for building oral reading fluency. You may remember round robin reading when you were a young student. The teacher may have gone around the room or reading group and asked each student to read a paragraph aloud. Chances are you and your classmates were trying to figure out which paragraph you would need to read, and you probably didn't pay any attention to what your classmates were reading. In addition, since you only got one chance to read in a public and potentially stressful situation without any practice, you probably didn't do your most fluent reading. Some of your elementary teachers may have used a variation—popcorn reading—where instead of the teacher telling students which paragraph to read aloud, the reader was expected to say "popcorn" and identify who the next person to read aloud would be. If you were a good oral reader, you may have enjoyed this activity, but it does not have any real value for developing oral reading fluency, and for students who are not good oral readers, the activity could be stressful, frustrating, and counterproductive.

As noted previously in this chapter, effective fluency instruction provides modeling, practice, and opportunities for performance, and neither round robin oral reading nor popcorn reading provide for any of these key components of effective fluency instruction. The teaching strategies in this chapter provide ideas for effective fluency instruction, and there is even a book, *Good-bye Round Robin* (Opitz & Rasinski, 2008), that provides 25 alternatives to round robin reading. Therefore, we urge you to abandon the traditional (and ineffective) practices of round robin oral reading and popcorn reading for the more effective and engaging teaching strategies provided in this chapter.

As you plan for fluency instruction, you will want to choose a variety of texts. Two types of text that are excellent and efficient to use for fluency instruction are poems and songs because they are short, rhythmic, and fun! Iwasaki, Rasinski, Yildirin, and Zimmerman (2013) offer a weekly schedule for using songs to teach fluency (and promote joy) in the classroom. Even if you are not a good singer or musical yourself, your students will love singing song lyrics to practice their oral reading fluency! See Margin Note 8.8 for more information about how you can use songs to teach fluency in your classroom.

Margin Note 8.8: Using Music to Improve Reading Fluency

https://www.scholastic.com/teachers/blog-posts/shari-edwards/using-music-improve-reading-fluency/

Poems are perfect texts for fluency instruction because they are usually short, lend themselves to repeated readings, and are perfect for performance. Nichols et al. (2018) argue that poems also promote word play through the rhyming and rhythmic language that invites students to dig in and have fun while developing their oral reading fluency. For practical suggestions and resources for using poetry to teach fluency, check out Margin Note 8.9.

Margin Note 8.9: Using Poetry to Improve Reading Fluency

https://www.literacyjunkie.com/blog/2018/4/27/the-dynamic-duo-poetry-and-fluency

Another important consideration for fluency instruction is how you will assess students' progress because those assessments will provide you with direction on what to teach next. In the following section, we offer some simple assessments you can use in your classroom for high-frequency words and oral reading fluency.

Assessing Oral Reading Fluency

As with any aspect of literacy, you will need to collect assessment information to help you plan appropriate instruction for your students. Assessment Strategy 8.2: The One-minute Fluency Probe provides a quick assessment of a child's reading rate by determining the number of words the child can read correctly per minute. This assessment strategy can be used with any text. You can compare a student's performance against their previous performance to see if there has been growth, and you can also compare their reading rate to national norms to get a sense of their performance in relation to other students.

Because fluency has multiple components—accuracy, rate, and prosody—you will want to assess students' overall fluency in a holistic way to get a general sense of their fluency development. By using Assessment Strategy 8.3: Fluency Scale, you can record your observations of the student's oral reading fluency and date each entry to document progress over time. You can also adapt the checklist to use with a whole class so you have fluency data for every student in your classroom.

Assessment Strategy 8.2: The One-minute Fluency Probe

Purpose: The purpose of this assessment is to determine the student's rate of reading in words correct per minute (WCPM). The student's rate can be compared to their previous performance on earlier administrations of the assessment, to other students in the classroom, or to national norms provided in the Chapter 8 Resources on the website. This assessment can be repeated at regular intervals (e.g., monthly or every 9 weeks) to determine and record the student's growth in oral reading fluency.

Procedures:

1. Select a short reading passage (approximately 100–200 words in length) that is at the student's instructional level. (See Chapter 3 for a discussion of how to determine instructional level.) Make two copies of the passage—one for the student and one for you. You will need your phone or tablet's stopwatch app or a timer.

2. Give the passage to the student. Say: "I would like you to read me this passage. When you have finished reading, I'll ask you to tell me about what you've read. You may begin." When the student begins reading, start your timing.

3. Note any miscues (mistakes) the student makes. You may use your own coding system for miscues, or you may use the markings shown on the right.

4. When the student completes the reading, stop your timing and note the number of seconds the student read.

5. Ask the student to tell you about what was read. You might want to say, "Tell me about what you read." The purpose of this part of the assessment is to gauge whether the student understood the text or was just reading words without any comprehension.

6. To determine the student's rate of reading, follow these steps.

   a. Count the number of words in the passage. Subtract the number of words the student read incorrectly.

   b. Multiply that number by 60. The resulting number will become the dividend.

   c. Divide the number of seconds that it took the student to read the passage.

   d. The resulting number is the quotient which determines the words correct per minute (WCPM).

Marking	Meaning of Marking
man men	Substitution
man s/c men	Self-correction
~~men~~	Omitted word
m-- men	Partial pronunciation
<u>men</u>	Repeated word
small ^men	Insertion
the/men	Pause

7. You can compare the student's WCPM to previous administrations of this assessment. You can also compare it to other students in the class or to national norms provided in the Chapter 8 Resources on the website.

Assessment Strategy 8.3: Fluency Scale

Purpose: This strategy uses a simple four-point scale so you can assess the student's fluency holistically. You can use the scale with an individual student or an entire classroom to monitor fluency performance and growth over time. You will use this assessment when you are observing students read orally such as in guided reading groups or during buddy reading. Therefore, you don't need to set aside time to administer this assessment—you can use it in the context of the teaching and learning activities that take place in your classroom.

Procedures:

1. Make a copy of the appropriate form for an individual student or the classroom. An example of each form is shown below. These forms are provided in the Chapter 8 Resources on the website.

Individual Fluency Scale Record Sheet

Student _____ Teacher _____ Grade _____

Level	Description
1	Reads almost entirely word by word; monotone; little or no use of punctuation
2	Reads mostly in 2- to 3-word phrases with some word by word; monotone with some expression; some evidence of punctuation
3	Reads mostly in phrases; appropriate expression; uses punctuation most of the time
4	Reads fluently; good expression; consistently attends to punctuation

Date	Level	Comments

Class Fluency Scale Record Sheet

Level	Description
1	Reads almost entirely word by word; monotone; little or no use of punctuation
2	Reads mostly in 2- to 3-word phrases with some word by word; monotone with some expression; some evidence of punctuation
3	Reads mostly in phrases; appropriate expression; uses punctuation most of the time
4	Reads fluently; good expression; consistently attends to punctuation

Student	Date	Level	Comments

2. Review the four levels of fluency on the record sheet.

3. Select a student to focus your attention on for a minute or two. Write the student's name and the date on the record form.

4. Use your professional judgment to determine the level that most accurately represents the student's fluency at that time and on that text. Jot down any notes that will help you plan instruction for this student.

5. Repeat the process periodically so you can use these data to plan appropriate fluency instruction for your students.

Take a moment and reflect on the many things we discussed in this chapter. We've looked at teaching sight words, defining and understanding fluency, considering multiple teaching approaches and strategies, and how to assess student learning related to various aspects of fluency. We encourage you to consider which teaching strategies might be appropriate for use in your placement so you can discuss these ideas with your mentor teacher. We also urge you to complete the activity in Connection to the Field so you can put some of your new learning into action while also expanding your understanding of fluency assessment and instruction.

Connection to the Field: Assessing Fluency

Select one of the assessments provided in this chapter. Ask your mentor teacher for permission to administer it to an individual student in your classroom. Reflect on your own performance by asking yourself:

1. Did I follow the administration instructions correctly?
2. Did I feel confident when administering the assessment?
3. Did I score and interpret the student's performance correctly?
4. What insights did I gain about the student's fluency?
5. How could I use the results from this assessment to plan appropriate fluency instruction for this student?

What Do You Believe about Fluency Instruction?

In this chapter you've learned what fluency is, why it's important, and how to teach it. Think about the important takeaways from this chapter and write the ones that are essential to your understanding on the What Do You Believe template that can be found in the Chapter 8 Resources on the website. Then write what you believe about teaching fluency as a result of what you learned.

Closing Thoughts

Remember Caleb from the beginning of the chapter? When he first started his placement, he thought that reading fast was the purpose of teaching and practicing oral reading fluency. As we learned in this chapter, although it is true that reading at an appropriate rate (but not necessarily as fast as you can) is certainly a component of oral reading fluency, it is not the only one. As Caleb spent more time in his placement, he had a chance to learn more about fluency and to see his students develop their fluency with regard to accuracy, rate, and prosody. He now understands that oral reading is an important foundation of becoming an effective reader who can comprehend what they read, and he realizes that accuracy, rate, and prosody are needed for fluent reading.

As you spend time in your placement, be sure to look for the ways your mentor teacher teaches and provides opportunities for students to practice their fluency. If you have questions about fluency instruction or assessment practices you are seeking in your placement, ask your mentor teacher in a way that is curious and not judgmental so you can learn the "why" behind what you see in the classroom. Doing so will help you make important connections from what you are learning in this class with what you are learning in your placement. Such connections between theory and practice are essential to becoming a learner-ready teacher.

Takeaways from Chapter 8

- Fluent readers are able to read texts accurately, quickly, and with prosody.
- Fluency is the bridge between word identification and comprehension; therefore, it is an essential part of reading instruction, especially in the early grades.
- In addition to teaching word identification strategies that use phonics, structural analysis, and context, teaching sight words is an important aspect of fluency instruction.
- If students are able to read words automatically, they can devote their attention and effort to understanding the text.
- There are many instructional strategies to develop students' oral reading fluency, but they have in common three specific characteristics—oral reading practice, re-reading texts, and one-on-one teacher guidance and feedback.
- It's important to be intentional and efficient with fluency instruction so there is more time to devote to other aspects of reading instruction.

To Learn More about Fluency Instruction

Resources for Your Professional Library

Griffith, L. W., & Rasinski, T. V. (2004). A focus on fluency: How one teacher incorporated fluency with her reading curriculum. *The Reading Teacher, 58*, 126–137.

https://doi.org/10.1598/RT.58.2.1

This article describes how a teacher taught fluency in her classroom in order to improve her students' overall reading performance. A weekly procedure is provided as well as practical discussions about finding materials, organizing for instruction, and creating a manageable schedule.

Walski, M., Smith, P., Johns, J. L., & Berglund, R. L. (2020). *Fluency: Questions, answers, and evidence-based strategies* (5th ed.). Dubuque, IA: Kendall Hunt Publishing Company.

https://he.kendallhunt.com/product/fluency-questions-answers-and-evidence-basedstrategies-0

This is a must-have resource book for teaching oral reading fluency. The book contains over 30 fluency lessons you can implement in your teaching and several informative assessments to help you plan appropriate fluency instruction for your students.

Rasinski, T., & Nageldinger, J. K. (2016). *The fluency factor: Authentic instruction and assessment for reading success in the Common Core classroom.* New York, NY: Teachers College Press.

https://www.tcpress.com/the-fluency-factor-9780807757475

The authors provide a strong, research-based rationale for teaching reading fluency along with practical teaching strategies and useful assessments. This book also provides many ideas for how to work with families to support children's reading and fluency development at home.

Rasinski, T. V., Rupley, W. H., & Nichols, W. D. (2012). *Phonics & fluency practice with poetry: Tapping the power of rhyming verse to improve students' word recognition, automaticity, and prosody—and help them become successful readers.* New York, NY: Scholastic.

https://www.scholastic.com/teachers/books/phonics--fluency-practice-with-poetry-by-timothy-v-rasinski/

This practical book provides everything you need to get started using poetry to teach fluency (and phonics) in your classroom. Dozens of sample lessons are provided, and the book even includes all the poems you need to teach the lessons.

Son, E. H., & Chase, M. (2018). Books for two voices: Fluency practice with beginning readers. *The Reading Teacher, 72*, 233–240.

https://doi.org/10.1002/trtr.1700

Using character dialogue in books, you can provide a fun and effective way for students to practice their fluency by reading with a partner. This article describes how to implement this approach with young readers and includes a list of books that work well with this approach.

Practical Tools for Teaching Fluency

Scholastic Fluency Resources

https://www.scholastic.com/teachers/collections/teaching-content/fluency-resources/

This collection of short articles provides practical ideas for teaching and assessing fluency as well as strategies to connect with families.

Teaching Strategies for Fluency (Grades K–1)

http://www.fcrr.org/curriculum/pdf/GK-1/F_Final.pdf

The Florida Center for Reading Research created this collection of lesson plans for use in K–1 classrooms. The lessons provide step-by-step instructions so they are ready for you to implement into your teaching.

Teaching Strategies for Fluency with Phrases and Chunked Text (Grades 2–3)

http://www.fcrr.org/Curriculum/PDF/G2-3/2-3Fluency_3.pdf

The Florida Center for Reading Research created this set of lesson plans for teaching oral reading fluency with phrases and chunked text for second and third grades. Each lesson plan includes all materials needed to teach the lesson.

Teaching Strategies for Fluency with Connected Text (Grades 2–3)

http://www.fcrr.org/Curriculum/PDF/G2-3/2-3Fluency_4.pdf

The Florida Center for Reading Research created these lesson plans for teaching reading fluency using connected text. Each lesson plan includes all instructional and materials needed to implement the lesson in your classroom.

Top 10 Resources on Fluency

https://www.readingrockets.org/article/top-10-resources-fluency

Reading Rockets has compiled their top 10 resources for fluency. These resources include information about using choral reading, repeated reading, and guided oral reading as well as fluency norms and ideas for assessment.

Listening to books being read aloud helps develop students' vocabulary.

© SpeedKingz/Shutterstock.com

Chapter

9

How Do I Teach Vocabulary?

REAL-LIFE EXAMPLE

Sabrina began her first placement in a second-grade classroom. She would be in the class 2 days a week. Her first 2 weeks were devoted to getting to know the 27 students, learning about the classroom community context, taking notes about the classroom environment, and observing her mentor teacher, Mr. Murphy. As a bilingual speaker herself, Sabrina was highly interested in ways English Learner (EL) students increased their vocabulary in school.

Sabrina had come to the United States when she was 6 years old. As a young child, she was articulate in her home language, Spanish, but she didn't know any English words. She started kindergarten and learned how to speak English from her friends and from the lessons in schools, but she always struggled to keep up with her classmates. She understood, even as a child, that she simply didn't know all of the words that she needed to know to make satisfactory progress in elementary school.

Sabrina was pleased to see Mr. Murphy address vocabulary instruction in multiple ways. He had a print-rich environment, gave students many language experiences, taught individual words, and taught word-learning strategies. Mr. Murphy seemed to weave vocabulary instruction effortlessly throughout the day. Sabrina wanted to know how he did it and what she could do when she began student teaching to keep vocabulary instruction at the front of her mind. Sabrina asked herself, "What do I need to know about vocabulary instruction and assessment before I begin student teaching?"

How many words do you know? Most of you know at least 35,000 words, and your vocabulary will continue to grow through your life. That's a lot of words! Children in preschool come to you knowing around 5,000 words and will learn approximately 3,000 words each year. Sabrina was interested in how children learned vocabulary and wanted to know how she would support her students as a teacher.

In this chapter we're going to discuss how children develop general and academic vocabularies and what you can do to facilitate their learning. We'll also present the principles of teaching vocabulary to PreK–3 students along with teaching strategies that illustrate the concepts.

General and Academic (School) Vocabularies

One of the primary ways children learn words is through experience. These experiences involve hearing language. The words children learn are part of their **general vocabulary**. For example, a child might say to their parent, "What's that?" and a parent might respond, "That's a butterfly." Although the child might not remember *butterfly* the first time they hear it, just hearing the word one time might heighten their awareness of the word so that when they see a picture of a butterfly, the word will be reinforced. Eventually they will remember *butterfly*, but it might take many exposures to the word before it sticks.

Words that children learn at home or at school that are common in English are part of their general vocabulary. There's another type of word that children learn, though, and these are words that are used mostly in school settings. These words are called a child's **academic (school) vocabulary**.

ACADEMIC VOCABULARY. Schools have their own discourse. When you think about it, there are also different vocabularies for other parts of a child's life. If a child attends a place of worship, there are words that are used that are unique for that setting (e.g., pews, bulletin, narthex). If a child goes to the movies, there are words used in theaters that are used for that purpose (e.g., tickets, aisle, concessions). It will be up to you to make sure that your students learn the words associated with schooling.

Since you've been part of a school community for much of your life, you might take school words for granted. Think of Amanda who is 6 years old. When Amanda comes to school, there are many new words and concepts that are part of schooling that are not part of her life in other situations. For example, you'll be giving students directions, such as, "Line up for recess." It's possible that this sentence would be new to Amanda. What does it mean to *line up* in this setting, and what is *recess?* Children will learn some of these school-specific words through experiences and others you'll have to teach or show them. When you start looking for school-specific words, you'll be amazed at how many of the words we use in schools are unknown to children. You'll find a list of school words in Margin Note 9.1. Brainstorm additional words to add to this list that you think will need special instruction.

Margin Note 9.1: Word Lists for Grades K–8

https://www.flocabulary.com/wordlists/

SUBJECT AREA VOCABULARY. Not only does school in general have its own language, but subject areas do too. Think about the different subjects you will be teaching: reading, writing, math, social studies, science, music, physical education, art, and health. Each one of these subjects has its own group of words and phrases that are part of its own vocabulary. Furthermore, subjects have **content words** and **process words**. That means that in each subject you'll need to teach words that are used in the content area, such as *country* and *continent* for

social studies, and words that are more abstract, such as *similar* and *different*. You'll need to make room in your instruction for both content and process words so that students can develop an academic vocabulary.

Dialect Differences

Language is one of the elements that defines a person's cultural identity because language is the basis for thinking and communication. Not only will you have students who speak languages other than English, you'll probably have some students who speak a dialect different from your own. A dialect is a certain variety of a language, with specific rules and vocabularies. If one of your students speaks a different dialect, they may use different vocabulary words than you are used to. For example, a cold carbonated drink might be called *tonic*, *soda*, *sodie*, *soda pop*, *sodie pop*, *pop*, or *cola*, depending on your dialect. Remember that their dialect is not wrong if it's different from yours. Honor and appreciate these differences while sharing words you would use to call an object and what they may be called in texts. By doing this, you are using culturally relevant teaching because you are valuing knowledge that students bring to school while expanding their vocabularies for future academic success. As you work with individual students, be aware that some of the words they know may be different depending on their dialect. There are 24 regional dialects in the United States. Look at the map in Margin Note 9.2 to see which dialectical region you live in. You can find out your dialect from one of many dialect quizzes. Take the quiz in Margin Note 9.3 to find out what your speech says about your dialect region.

Margin Note 9.2:
Dialect Map

https://www.washington
post.com/blogs/govbeat/
wp/2013/12/02/what-
dialect-to-do-you-speak-a-
map-of-american-english/
?noredirect=on&utm_
term=.777478e8627d

Margin Note 9.3:
Dialect Quiz

https://www.nytimes.com/
interactive/2014/upshot/
dialect-quiz-map.html

Provide Rich and Varied Language Experiences

The bedrock of your work will be to provide your students with **rich and varied language experiences**. As you learned in Chapter 5, children develop language through experiences and interactions in a print-rich environment. They will come to you with their experiences and backgrounds, and your role will be to build on the language foundation they have (Lawrence, 2017).

You've probably heard that it's critical for children to have books read to them. The experience of listening to books being read aloud helps develop their vocabulary. When listening to books being read, students hear new words in context, which can promote incidental word learning. As students learn how to read themselves, they can also read (or look through) books independently. One way to expand students' listening vocabulary is for you to read aloud to your students and then have students read books independently.

There are a couple of ways to read aloud to students. One way is to read the book without stopping so that students hear the story in its entirety before any discussion. The second option is to conduct an Interactive Read Aloud (see Teaching Strategy 9.1). With this strategy, you will stop and ask students to interact with the story as you read. An interactive read aloud can include the following activities:

- Previewing the book
- Discussing the author
- Accessing prior knowledge
- Introducing new vocabulary words in context
- Demonstrating fluent reading
- Illustrating story structure (beginning, middle, end)
- Promoting listening comprehension

Margin Note 9.4: Popular Interactive Read Aloud Books

https://www.goodreads.com/shelf/show/interactive-read-aloud

You've learned about **shared reading in Chapter 5**, which is similar to an **interactive read aloud.** The important thing for you to remember is that reading aloud to students in a variety of forms should be part of your teaching routine. Teaching Strategy 9.1 shows you how to conduct an Interactive Read Aloud with your students, and Margin Note 9.4 gives you a link to find popular books for Interactive Read Alouds. Scan the lists looking for books that would be appropriate to read with students in your placement.

Connection to the Field: Interactive Read Aloud

One of the first activities you should try in your placement is an interactive read aloud. Work with your mentor teacher to select a book that is appropriate for the class that will develop their vocabulary without being overwhelming. Identify the book, read through it looking for good stopping points, and practice reading to a friend before going into the classroom. When you read, show students the pictures as you read and stay aware of your students, pausing if needed to regain students' attention.

Take a look at this video to watch an interactive read aloud as an example https://www.youtube.com/watch?v=kCenDTrxmjc. You'll develop your own routine as you gain more experience, so don't be afraid to give read alouds your own unique flavor. You may even want to video record yourself reading to get a sense of your "presence."

Engaging with Families: Interactive Read Aloud

Develop a short video that shows how to conduct an interactive read aloud. In the video, talk about the purposes of reading aloud, where to get books, and how families can fit read alouds into their busy schedules. Then do a short interactive read aloud focusing on vocabulary building. Encourage families to read aloud at least three times a week. Show your mentor teacher the video and get permission before sending it to families.

Teaching Strategy 9.1: Interactive Read Aloud

Purpose: An Interactive Read Aloud is a systematic method of reading a book aloud with periodic pauses in reading for students to interact with the story. You are doing the reading while the students are asked to engage, think, and respond to the story. An Interactive Read Aloud can have many purposes, one of which is to provide students with experiences with new vocabulary words in context that they might not hear otherwise.

Procedures:

1. Select a picture book to read to students, such as *Stellaluna* (Cannon, 1993). Skim through the book looking for vocabulary words that students might already know but that they do not use in speaking or writing. The list could contain the following words: *search*, *scent*, *escape*, and *limp*.

2. Write the words on the board and ask students the meanings of the words. Remind students where they have seen the words in the past and scaffold student responses to fit the way the words are used in the context. For example, you might say something like the following:

   Remember, we learned the word scent *in science class when we were learning about the five senses. Who remembers what the word* scent *means? Yes, it means a smell and is usually used in a positive way, such as a sweet scent.*

3. Read the story, emphasizing the vocabulary words that you have written on the board. In *Stellaluna*, for example, the sentence that contains the word *scent* is, "One night, as Mother Bat followed the heavy scent of ripe fruit, an owl spied her."

4. After you have read the entire book, return to the sentences containing the new words. Write the sentences on the board if necessary. Invite students to read the sentences with you, emphasizing the new words.

5. Write the new words on a word wall and invite students to look for meaningful opportunities to use the words in their conversations and written work.

Class Discussions Develop Vocabulary

Another way to provide students with language experiences is through **classroom discussions**. Students come to your class with vastly different experiences hearing words. As you observe or teach your first group of students, you will begin noticing the variability of each child's ability to use language. There is a classic study that you should know conducted by Hart and Risley (1995). These researchers found that, on average, children from different backgrounds were exposed to a vastly different number of words. Children from low-income families heard about 616 words per hour, whereas those from working class families heard around 1,251 words per hour, and those from professional families heard roughly 2,153 words per hour. Even though this research has drawn criticism because it seems to make cultural value judgments, there are some principles that are helpful for you as a new teacher. It's important to remember that your students will have heard and will know a different number of words, and some of your students will know many more words than other students.

✐esson Planning: Applying Rich and Varied Language Experiences

As you provide students with a variety of language experiences, you might consider developing a lesson plan that encourages students to use words and phrases they have heard. This activity can promote one of the vocabulary Language Standards.

Standard: Use words and phrases acquired through conversations, reading and being read to, and responding to texts.

Objective: Students will be able to orally or in writing fill in words in a sentence frame following the patterns of If–Then sentences.

Lesson Idea: Have students write a pattern book from a read aloud, such as *If You Give a Mouse a Cookie* (Numeroff, 2010), to learn how to use an If–Then sentence.

Assessment: Using the sentence frame "If you give a mouse a _____, he's going to ask for a _____. When you give him the _____, he's going to ask for a _____."

Scoring Criteria:

1	2	3
Words in sentence frame are unrelated.	Words in sentence frame are loosely related.	Words in the sentence frame are related and make sense.

Receptive and Expressive Vocabularies

Before we get to how to teach students new words, we need to think about what it means to actually know a word. Your instruction will depend on how you want students to use words. There are words that you may know when you hear or read them that you don't use in speaking or writing. For example, you may have heard and know the word, *congruent*, but you may not use if very often when you speak. That's because knowing words when you hear them is different than being able to use words in sentences. Did you ever have the experience in your own schooling in which you had to learn a list of words by defining them and using them in a sentence? Do you remember how difficult it was to use a new word in an appropriate sentence? That's because learning words is incremental. Typically, you need to hear and see a word (**receptive vocabulary**) many times, possibly 40 or more, before you can use it in speaking or writing (**expressive vocabulary**).

Knowing words involves four different vocabularies: reading, listening, speaking, and writing. **Reading and listening are receptive vocabularies**. When you teach word meanings, your first goal is for students to be able to understand new words when they hear them in speech or when they encounter them in reading. After you teach and review vocabulary words, students should eventually be able to understand sentences that contain these new words. Being able to use words in speaking and writing represents an entirely different goal. **Speaking and writing are part of expressive vocabularies**. Since learning words tends to be incremental, students may learn a new word well enough for their receptive vocabulary but need further instruction and experience in order for them to use the word themselves. It is unreasonable to expect students to use every word that you teach in their speaking and writing until they have practiced it many times. We all have larger receptive vocabularies than expressive vocabularies.

VOCABULARY GAP. Although it may not be important to know the exact number of words each student knows, it is important to be aware of how comfortable children are using both general and academic vocabularies. Another seminal research study found that the gap between students grows unless there is instructional intervention (Stanovich, 1989). Stanovich called this the Matthew Effect. Stanovich (1989) posited the Matthew Effect theory more than 30 years ago stating that the rich get richer and the poor get poorer in regard to reading achievement. In most cases, students who begin with lower knowledge at the beginning of the year will end up in the same place at the end of the year, thus perpetuating the opportunity gap. One of your goals as a teacher should be to accelerate learning for students who begin with less knowledge of words than their classmates.

You can find out whether a word is in a student's receptive or expressive vocabulary with the Knowledge Rating Guide (Blachowicz, 1986) shown in Assessment Strategy 9.1. This assessment can also be used for instruction.

VOCABULARY OF ENGLISH LEARNERS. During your career as a teacher, it is most likely that you'll be teaching a significant number of children who are learning English as a new language. According to the U.S. Census for 2016, the white (non-Hispanic) proportion of the population is dropping to about 61%, whereas percentages for persons of color are rising. Much of the increase in diversity is due to immigration. It is estimated that 13% of American residents are foreign born (U.S. Census, 2016), many of whom will be learning English in schools. These students will come to you with a varying amount of knowledge about their home language as well as English. Some English Learners (ELs) will come to you as newcomers who don't know any English words at all.

Margin Note: 9.5: Five Stages of Second Language Acquisition

https://education.cu-portland.edu/blog/classroom-resources/five-stages-of-second-language-acquisition/

ELs may need time to just listen to English and develop their receptive vocabulary without saying much. This is commonly called the preproduction or silent stage of language development. Encourage your students to try to speak English but respect their need to listen without talking. Remember to give them as many experiences listening to language as possible (Gibson, 2016). You can find the five stages of second language acquisition in Margin Note 9.5. Examine the stages so you're familiar with how students acquire another language as you think about how to teach ELs English vocabulary words.

Assessment Strategy 9.1: Knowledge Rating Guide

Purpose: A Knowledge Rating Guide (Blachowicz, 1986) can help students understand to what degree they initially know a specific word. It can also provide a vehicle for a class discussion that allows students to expand their background knowledge of the words. You can use this strategy to determine how well students report that they know a word.

Procedures:

1. Prepare a list of six to eight words that you want to assess.
2. Next to each word, draw three columns similar to the example below.

Word	Can Define	Have Seen or Heard	No Clue!
Glacier			
Avalanche			

3. Ask students to place a check in the column that best describes how well they know the word. If they are unclear about the directions, model the procedure for them. For example, you could say something like the following:

   The first word on this list is glacier. *I know that a glacier is made of ice, and I have heard the word, but I'm not exactly sure if I could define it. I think I'll place a check under the column* Have Seen or Heard. *On the other hand, I do know what an* avalanche *is. It's falling rock or snow. I'll check* Can Define *for that word.*

4. After students have filled out the Knowledge Rating Guide, discuss the words with them. Ask which words were difficult, which were easy, which most of the students knew, and which words few students knew. As you discuss the words, ask students to share their background knowledge and experiences with the words. The discussion will help students expand their knowledge about these words.

5. From the class discussion, ask students to make predictions about further meanings of the words and how they would be used in a text. If students are unfamiliar with a specific word, you can teach it explicitly.

How to Teach Vocabulary

Now that you've learned some basic background, we're now going to focus on how to teach vocabulary. The most important principle to remember is to actually teach vocabulary words rather than just assigning words for students to memorize. Perhaps you can remember vocabulary lists when you were in school. Most likely you were given a list of words with their definitions to memorize. This kind of teaching approach is not very effective for improving students' vocabulary (Biemiller, 2003).

Researchers have developed better ways to help students develop the number of words they know and can use. First, teachers need to spend time teaching new words and reviewing words they have taught every day. This instruction can take place in short mini lessons at various times during instruction and even while students are waiting in line. Having vocabulary instruction at the forefront of your mind when you teach will help you incorporate vocabulary lessons in new ways. Graves (2016) suggests that teachers organize their instruction by teaching individual words, teaching words in context, exploring word relationships, teaching word-learning strategies, and fostering word consciousness.

TEACH INDIVIDUAL WORDS. Most of the words that children know are probably learned implicitly, which means that the words are learned though experiences with language. In addition to learning words through experience, children learn words that are taught to them. Before they come to school, adults teach words to children directly. Think about times in your life when you've seen this happen. For example, a child may ask an adult, "What's that?" and the adult answers, "That's a giraffe." The child might continue, "What's a giraffe?" and so on. Adults teach children individual words and scaffold their learning to help them remember new words.

As a teacher, you should also introduce and review individual words, remembering that students will learn only a portion of their vocabulary this way (Wright & Cervetti, 2017). Teaching words is critical, but don't pressure yourself into thinking this is the only way your students will learn new words.

As you consider the strategies and techniques for teaching individual words, you might keep in mind that students need to do all of the following before they will have the word solidly in their **expressive vocabulary**:

- Hear the word pronounced
- See the word written down
- Pronounce the word several times themselves
- Hear an age-appropriate definition
- Hear and see the word in context
- Try out the word in speech or writing

All of the steps for learning a new word won't happen in one lesson. Words need to be introduced and then reviewed many times before your students will remember them. You can see a teacher demonstrate supports for learning words in Margin Note 9.6. Watch the video and take note of the different ways this teacher introduces new vocabulary. Teaching Strategies 9.2 and 9.3 can be used to introduce and review individual words.

**Margin Note 9.6:
Vocabulary Demonstration**

https://www.teaching
channel.org/video/
improving-student-
vocabulary

Teaching Strategy 9.2: Four-square Vocabulary

Purpose: This strategy, based on the Frayer model (Frayer, Frederick, & Klausmeier, 1969), helps students develop personal understandings for key vocabulary words and concepts.

Procedures:

1. Draw a sample Four-square Vocabulary grid on the board to model the process for students. Select a word they already know. For example, if you use the word *glad*, the grid could look like the following:

Word	Makes me think of . . .
Glad	Playing with my friends
Meaning	**Opposite**
Happy	Sad

2. Have students fold a sheet of paper in half in length and then in width to form four boxes. Have students label each of the boxes similar to the example with *Word, Makes me think of . . ., Meaning,* and *Opposite*. Make sure students know the meanings of each of the words used for labels.

3. Provide students with a key vocabulary word that you want them to learn from their reading, discussions, or activities.

4. With support, have students fill out the Four-square Vocabulary grid. For younger students, you might have them draw pictures rather than writing words or phrases.

5. If you have English Learners, you might have them fill in one or more of the boxes with words from their home language.

6. Provide time for students to share their grids with their classmates. Discuss how and why students may have filled out each of the boxes. Discuss the importance of making words personal by connecting them to students' lives. A reproducible Four-square Vocabulary grid and an adapted grid for ELs can be found in the Chapter 9 Resources on the website.

Teaching Strategy 9.3: Vocabulary Mapping

Purpose: The Vocabulary Mapping strategy helps students brainstorm and associate words that are related to a key concept. By discussing and visually mapping a key concept and associated words, students are able to develop a deeper understanding of the meaning of a word.

Procedures:

1. Select a word that represents a key concept from a text or a unit that students must understand as in the example, *plants*.

2. Write the word on the board.

3. Explain to students that the word is very important to learn, and that they will be developing a Vocabulary Map to understand the word's meaning.

4. Ask students to brainstorm any words they can think of that are related to the word. For example, students could suggest the words flowers, roots, stem, vegetables, trees, grass, grow, water, and dirt.

5. Write the words on the board. As students share words, ask them to define or explain the word they brainstormed.

6. After students have shared all of the words they can think of that are related to the key concept, add any related words you want students to learn, such as *stamen, pistil, seed, bud,* and *oxygen*.

7. Work with students to develop a Vocabulary Map that shows the key concept and related words. As you complete this step, ask students to define, explain, or give examples for each of the words. Group related words together under the headings.

8. After you have completed the Vocabulary Map, invite students to share other words they can think of related to the headings on the map as in the following example:

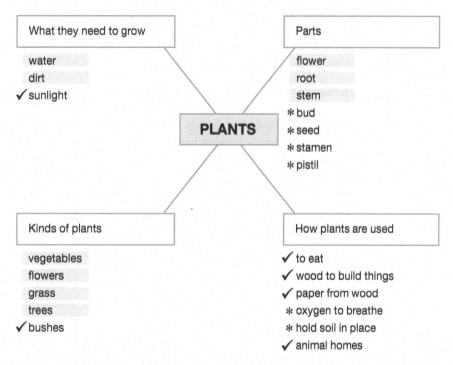

Note: Words that are highlighted were brainstormed by children. Words that are marked with an asterisk * were added by the teacher, and words that are marked with a ✓ were added by children after the Vocabulary Map was created.

Send home a list of three new vocabulary words that you have introduced in class. In a short note, ask families if they can reinforce these words at home by saying the words in sentences every day for a week. As always, get permission from your mentor teacher before sending home the note.

SELECTING WORDS TO TEACH. Before we discuss some of the additional concepts about teaching vocabulary, it might be helpful to think about how to decide what words to teach. Many of the teacher's manuals for reading suggest vocabulary lists of words to teach. These lists are a good starting place, but you will also need to use your professional judgment about how many words your students should learn for each story or unit. Often teacher's manuals introduce too many words and don't provide students with enough practice on words they are learning.

You can, however, focus on specific words that have high usability for students to learn deeply. Vocabulary words are often divided into **tier 1, tier 2,** and **tier 3 words** (Beck, McKeown, & Kucan, 2013). Tier 1 words are those words that students already know and are most likely in both their receptive and expressive vocabularies. Tier 2 words are the words that many students do not already know but that they need to learn to be able to read with comprehension at their grade level and beyond. Tier 3 words are those words that you may want to teach so that students are able to understand a particular unit of study but that will be rarely used again. If you want students to build their speaking and writing vocabularies, you will want to focus your instruction on tier 2 words. Many teachers ask how they will know which words are tier 2 words. To answer that question, you should consider whether deep knowledge of the word is critical for students to learn and understand grade level material. You should also think about whether students will most likely hear this word again in the future. For example, the word *ogre* might be a word that is fun to say and to teach for a specific story, but it's a word that students probably won't use very often in the primary grades. *Ogre*, therefore, might be a word that you teach just enough so students understand it in a lesson or story, but you may not want to spend the time and effort to teach the word so that students use it in speaking and writing.

Margin Note 9.7: The Most Useful Spanish Cognates

https://www.duolingo.com/comment/5508808/The-Most-Useful-Spanish-Cognates

TEACH COGNATES OF ENGLISH. Some of your ELs may have some experience reading and writing in their home language. If that is the case, you might use cognates, or words that are similar in spelling in English as they are in the student's home language. Students who speak Spanish, for example, will find some of the same word parts in both languages although they may be pronounced differently. For Spanish-speaking learners, some of the words that are cognates are listed in Figure 9.1. You can find more English–Spanish cognates in Margin Note 9.7. Use the list in Margin Note 9.7 to find potential words to teach to the students in your placement.

Figure 9.1. English–Spanish Cognates

English word	Spanish word
alphabet	alfabeto
hospital	hospital
hotel	hotel
color	color
family	familia
television	television

Connection to the Field: Selecting Words to Teach

Don't worry right now about knowing what words to teach in your placement. When you have your own classroom, you'll have a better sense of what to do and more chances to try different things. Right now, you can work with your mentor teacher to discuss how to select words to teach. First, look at any teacher's manuals that provide vocabulary lists. Then look at the list of words your mentor teacher identifies to teach. If there are differences, ask your mentor teacher how they made those decisions. Finally, observe how students respond. Does it seem as if students are learning all of the words quickly and easily? If so, perhaps when you are student teaching you can add more challenging words. Are some students struggling? Consider differentiating the list when you have the opportunity. Take notes on what you observe so you remember when you are student teaching. You'll have a lot to think about at that time and will benefit from being able to look back at the notes you took about your ideas and insights throughout your placement.

TEACHING WORDS IN CONTEXT. When you teach individual words, you will most likely introduce the word in a sentence, so students can hear how the word is used **in context**. Some students will automatically pick this up, but others will need you to directly show them how authors can help readers know the meaning of words through other words in the text that define the unfamiliar word. Not all unfamiliar words can be understood by the context of the sentence, but using context is a strategy that students should learn to help them understand new words. You will hopefully remember that we discussed in Chapter 7 how you can teach context to help students to anticipate known words and recognize unknown words.

Think about when you learn words through their context. For example, if you came across this sentence: Kerry yelled, "I'm going to *glissade*!" If you are unfamiliar with the term *glissade*, take a moment and predict the definition of the word. It's difficult if you have no context. Now read these sentences: Kerry yelled, "This snowfield is perfect. I'm going to *glissade* down to the bottom." In this example you might be able to determine the meaning of *glissade* through the context.

Authors use a variety of ways to define words in context that you should know (see Figure 9.2). You won't need to teach these different methods to your students necessarily, but it's helpful for you to be aware of them so that when you run across words that are defined in context you can point them out to students. Additionally, *context* is an example of a term that you will want to teach in addition to teaching students how to use context to understand words that are defined in context. Teaching Strategy 9.4 can help you organize instruction around the various ways authors define words in context. To assess your students' ability to read words in context, you can use Assessment Strategy 9.2.

Teaching Strategy 9.4: Preview in Context

Purpose: To help students expand their vocabularies by learning how to find word definitions in the context of a sentence or passage.

Procedures:

1. Select two or three words from a text that you think will be unfamiliar to your students that are defined in context. Identify the sentences that contain these words in the text.

2. Copy the sentences on the board as in the following example:

   A frog is an *amphibian* that lives in the water and on land.

3. Explain to students that there are several new vocabulary words in their reading that they can define by using the surrounding words, and you want them to understand what the words mean before reading the story or passage.

4. Assist the students with figuring out the meaning of the word by using the context. You may need to ask questions to guide students' understandings. For example, you might ask, "What do you know about the word *amphibian* from this sentence?"

5. Expand word meanings by providing additional contexts for the same word; thus, students who come across the word in different contexts will make predictions about what they know about the word's meaning in another situation.

Students are discussing vocabulary words with their teacher.

Assessment Strategy 9.2: Maze

Purpose: The purpose of this assessment is to determine how students can determine whether a word makes sense in context.

Procedures:

1. Write a sentence appropriate for your students and delete a key word. Make sure the sentence provides clear context clues to help your students identify the missing word.

2. List three choices for the deleted word. One of the choices should be correct, and the other two choices should not make sense in the sentence.

3. Write the sentence on the board.

4. Read the sentence with your students. Tell them that a word has been removed from the sentence and that they are to choose a word from the list that makes sense. Two examples are provided below:

   The dog wagged its _____. (car, tail, nose)

   It was a hot and _____ day. (sunny, snowy, hungry)

5. Discuss each word and whether it makes sense in the sentence. For example, you might say the following: *The dog wagged its car. Does that make sense? Why? Which word would fit in this sentence? Explain why it makes sense.*

6. Provide students with a list of eight sentences.

7. Read the sentences to students and ask them to circle the word that makes sense in the sentence.

8. Students who get seven or eight sentences correct can be considered proficient at using context during reading.

Figure 9.2. Methods for Defining Words in Context

Definition or Description: Words are directly defined by the sentence.
- *Redwoods* are the tallest trees on Earth.

Appositive Phrase: The definition of the unknown word or the word itself is in a phrase set off by commas.
- The *flicker*, a type of woodpecker, banged on our chimney.

Linked Synonyms: The unknown word is in a series of known words.
- The gymnast was *agile*, flexible, and limber.

Comparisons and Contrasts: The word can be defined by its opposite in the sentence.
- He thought his ideas sounded *plausible*, but his reasoning was flawed.

Examples: The word can be defined by examples in sentences that follow the unfamiliar word.
- Marta felt *exuberant*. She smiled broadly and jumped up and down.

Classification: The word can be defined by its relationship to known words.
- My Uncle Jim is *fastidious*. Whenever he gets his hands or clothes even the least bit dirty, he washes them.

Experience: The word can be defined by applying previous experience to the unknown word.
- As I stepped up to the diving board, I felt *paralyzing* fear. It was so high! If I belly flopped, I would hurt myself.

Margin Note 9.8: Idioms for Kids

https://www.theidioms.com/kids/

http://examples.yourdictionary.com/idioms-for-kids.html

Margin Note 9.9: Synonyms and Antonyms

http://www.smart-words.org/list-of-synonyms/list-of-synonyms-and-antonyms.pdf

IDIOMS. Like many rules of language, there are phrases that won't make sense in context, such as the italicized phrases in the following three sentences: Making that hockey goal was a *piece of cake*. He thought he was the *class clown*. Last night it *rained cats and dogs*. These phrases are called **idioms**. An idiom is a group of words that means something different from how the individual words are used. English has many idioms that young children need to learn. Children who grow up in English-speaking households will have more exposure to idioms than many ELs so you may need to spend more time teaching idioms with ELs. Margin Note 9.8 provides you with a bank of idioms. Develop a list of idioms that is appropriate for your students. Find other lists of idioms online to use as resources. You can use Teaching Strategy 9.5 to help you instruct your students on idioms.

EXPLORE WORD RELATIONSHIPS. In addition to teaching individual words, students also need to see how words relate to each other. The English language has many words that express nuance of meanings, which are called **synonyms**. For example, the word *friend* has a slightly different meaning from *companion, buddy, classmate*, or *acquaintance*. You've probably had experience with a teacher encouraging you to use synonyms in your writing. Think about your own experiences. Did a teacher tell you not to use the word *nice* in your writing when you were young? Or did you ever hear a student use a new word inappropriately. For example, let's say you taught your students some words they could use in their writing instead of nice: *agreeable, charming, pleasant*, and *elegant*. Each of these words has subtle differences. When students are trying out these new words, they will likely make some inappropriate word uses as they try to replace *nice*, such as, "My new notebook is *pleasant*." When students misuse words, help them understand the subtle differences without embarrassing them. Let them know that all of us make mistakes using new words. Margin Note 9.9 has a list of synonyms and antonyms you can use, and Teaching Strategy 9.6 can help you as you teach students word relationships.

Teaching Strategy 9.5: Teaching Idioms

Purpose: To help students learn how to recognize idioms and what these phrases mean.

Procedures:

1. Write *Look out!* on the board and ask students to explain the meaning.

2. Help students realize that for some phrases in our language the meaning cannot be understood by the meanings of the individual words. Return to the phrase on the board and model for students by saying something like the following:

    > *The word* look *can mean to see and* out *can mean the "opposite of" or "away from the inside." These meanings will not help me understand the sentence because the words have a special meaning. They are used to indicate a warning. I might say,* Look out! *if something was falling toward you, and I wanted you to get out of the way quickly. When words are used in this way, they are called* idioms.

3. Have students share idioms they may know and discuss the meanings of expressions, such as the following: *don't be a sour puss*, *heads up*, *down in the dumps*, *take a walk*, *piece of cake*, *save face*, *laugh my head off*, *bored to tears*, and *lighten up*.

4. Be alert for idioms in materials students are asked to read and be sure to discuss their meanings, especially if the expressions are important to understanding.

5. Help students learn and appreciate figurative language by sharing and discussing with them Amelia Bedelia books by Peggy Parish or the books of Fred Gwynne, such as *A Chocolate Moose for Dinner* (Gwynne, 1988).

6. Create a bulletin board titled "Don't Be Fooled" and have students post strips of paper containing idioms and other examples of figurative language. Have students write the meaning below the phrase, as in the following example:

    "That's a piece of cake."

    This has nothing to do with cake. It means that something is easy to do.

Teaching Strategy 9.6: Word Ladder

Purpose: Students can differentiate between words when they understand how the words relate to each other. One strategy that can help students understand relationships between related words is a word ladder.

Procedures:

1. Draw a word ladder on the board like the one that follows. Tell students that you will give them a word at one extreme on the top and a word at the other extreme at the bottom.

Hottest

Coldest

2. Provide students with words that come between the two extremes, such as *warm, chilly, frigid, lukewarm, scalding,* and *cool.*

3. Discuss each of the words and ask students where they should be placed on the ladder in relation to the top word and the bottom word.

4. Have students place the words in order between the two ends of the ladder. Then discuss the words to help clarify meanings as needed.

5. When students are comfortable with arranging words in order on a word ladder, try a more interactive activity. Write a group of eight related words on large index cards, such as *sunny, partly sunny, overcast, drizzle, mist, raining,* and *thundershowers.*

6. Give one word card to each of eight students. Invite students to come to the front of the room and arrange themselves from one extreme to the other.

7. When students have finished putting themselves in order, have them explain why they placed their card in the order they did.

8. A Word Ladder reproducible can be found in the Chapter 9 Resources on the website.

TEACH WORD-LEARNING STRATEGIES. It would be impossible to teach all of the vocabulary words that students need to know, so you should also teach students **how** to figure out unfamiliar words. To do this, you'll need to include instruction on **root words, prefixes**, and **suffixes**. Do you remember what a root word is? It's a word or part of a word that can form the basis of new words by adding prefixes and suffixes. *Run*, for example, is a root word. You can add prefixes and suffixes to form the words *runs, running, rerun,* and *prerun*. Some root words can be combined to make compound words. A **compound word** is a word is made up of two or more smaller words. Each of the words can stand alone, and together the words make a new word. For example, the word *bluebird* is made up of *blue* and *bird*. Together, the word means a specific type of bird. Not all root words, however, make sense alone. Some words have Greek or Latin roots, such as *aud* for *audience* and *maze* in *amaze*.

Analyzing words using their root and prefixes or suffixes might be a skill that you learned if you studied for tests like the SAT, ACT, or GRE. It's also a skill that you use automatically when you come to an unknown word that has prefixes and suffixes. Since it's automatic for you, you may have to refresh your memory on the specifics of teaching word parts so you can teach your students effectively.

Although students will be familiar with the different forms of many words, the idea of inferring the meanings of unknown words by analyzing root words, prefixes, and suffixes may be new. Helping students understand how words can be combined is an important component of vocabulary instruction since more than half of the words in English can be analyzed through understanding these word parts (McKeown et al., 2017). Reading the article in Margin Note 9.10 can help refresh your memory about how to use root words, prefixes, and suffixes to figure out new words. Teaching Strategies 9.7, 9.8, and 9.9 can help you teach students how to learn word meanings. You can also find a list of prefixes and suffixes in the Chapter 9 Resources on the website.

Margin Note 9.10: Root Words, Roots, and Affixes

http://www.readingrockets.org/article/root-words-roots-and-affixes

© wavebreakmedia/Shutterstock.com

Foster word consciousness by engaging in word play and playing word games.

Teaching Strategy 9.7: Compound Word Cut-apart

Purpose: Compound words can be challenging for students to identity and understand because they are multisyllabic and composed of many letters. Teaching students how to divide compound words can make these words more easily identified.

Procedures:

1. Identify several compound words from reading materials and units of study students have encountered in your classroom. Some examples could be *baseball*, *airplane*, and *backpack*. A list of compound words can be found in the Chapter 9 Resources on the website.

2. Write each compound word on a sentence strip.

3. Select one word to demonstrate the Compound Word Cut-apart strategy by showing students a compound word that you could cut into two words. You might say the following:

   What is the word I have here? Yes, it's baseball. *This is a compound word because it's made up of two separate words. I'm going to cut this word into two. One word is* base *and the other is* ball. *I can put these two words together to make one word*, baseball.

4. Explain to students that they can figure out words by reading the two root words. Give students several compound words and ask them to cut them apart to find the two root words. Discuss each compound word one at a time by asking the following questions:

   - What small word do you see in this compound word?
   - Using your scissors, cut that small word from the strip.
   - What other small word do you see in this compound word?
   - What does each word mean?
   - How do the words combine to make a new word?

5. After students understand the process, tell them that sometimes they can figure out words and word meanings of compound words by looking at each word separately.

Teaching Strategy 9.8: Using Root Words to Find Meaning

Purpose: To show students how to use root words to figure out the meaning of unfamiliar words.

Procedures:

1. Tell students that some words have beginnings (prefixes) and/or endings (suffixes) and that they can figure out the meaning of the word by looking for the root word.

2. Select a root word that is familiar to students, such as *work*. Ask students to define the word and use it in a sentence.

3. Write forms of *work* on the board that have a prefix and/or suffix, such as *works*, *working*, *worked*, *rework*, and *worker*. (For your initial lesson, use words that add prefixes and suffixes without changing the spelling of the root word, such as *write* and *writing*.)

4. Demonstrate how to figure out a word meaning by finding the root word by saying something like the following:

   Let's say you came across this sentence: The teacher asked me to rework my paper, and you weren't sure what the word reworked *means. You could look to see if the word has a root word. In this case, the root word is* work. *By knowing the root word, you can probably figure out the unfamiliar word.*

5. Tell students that not all unfamiliar words have root words that they can identify, but that looking for root words is one way they can help figure out the meaning of new words.

Teaching Strategy 9.9: Prefix and Suffix Removal and Replacement

Purpose: To show students how prefixes and suffixes change word meanings.

Procedures:

1. Tell students that some words will have beginnings and endings that change word meanings. Write the words *prefix* and *suffix* on the board. Explain that prefixes are added to the beginning of a root word and that suffixes are added to the end of the word. The following video might be useful for students to remember the difference between prefixes and suffixes: https://www.youtube.com/watch?v=l-Utt Up6wCc.

2. Select a word with a common prefix. The most common prefixes are *un-*, *re-*, and *in-*.

    Examples could include *unkind*, *remove*, and *incomplete*.

3. Display the word on the board. Tell students that the word *unkind* contains a prefix and a root word. Point out that the prefix is *un-*.

4. Ask students if what is left is a real word. In this example, it is the root word *kind*.

5. Tell students that if they try to remove a prefix and a real word is left, they have found a prefix.

6. Tell students that the prefix *un-* means not. Discuss the meaning of the root word *kind* (nice; pleasant).

7. Explain that the meaning of the word *unkind* is a combination of the meaning of the prefix *un-* and the root word *kind*.

    un = not
    + kind = nice; pleasant
    _____
    unkind = not nice; not pleasant

8. Put the word in a sentence and ask students if it makes sense using the meaning you identified.

    The girl made an unkind comment that hurt the boy's feelings.

9. Repeat the process with several other words. A list of the most common prefixes and their meanings can be found in the Chapter 9 Resources on the website.

10. This lesson can also be adapted for use with suffixes. Since the meanings of suffixes are abstract, just showing examples is probably best for young students. A list of common suffixes can be found in the Chapter 9 Resources on the website.

*L*esson Planning: Determine the Meaning of a New Word

Since many words in the English language are made up of root words, prefixes, and/or suffixes, it's important to teach young children how to figure out these words.

Standard: Determine the meaning of the new word formed when a known prefix is added to a known word (e.g., *happy/unhappy, tell/retell*).

Objective: Students will be able to orally define or show through pictures how an unfamiliar word changes when a prefix is added.

Lesson Idea: Provide students with a root word, such as *happy* and have them orally define or draw a picture of the meaning of the word. Tell students that by adding a prefix they can change the meaning of the word. Explain that a prefix is a group of letters that don't make sense by themselves but that have meaning. Give students several examples, such as *un-, re-, in-,* and *dis-*. Write the word *unhappy* on the board. Tell students that the prefix *un-* means not. Have students tell you or draw a picture of the meaning of the word. Ask students to compare their first picture with the second one. Explain how the meaning of the root word is changed by adding a prefix. Give students practice showing how word meanings change by adding a prefix. Some examples could be *afraid/unafraid, tie/untie, plug/unplug,* and *pack/unpack*.

Assessment: Have students define or draw pictures of the root word and the root word including the prefix and look for accurate meanings for both words.

Scoring Criteria:

1	2	3
Word meaning with the prefix is not different from the root word without the prefix.	Meaning of the word including the prefix is inaccurate.	The meanings of both the root word and the root word with the prefix are accurate.

USING A DICTIONARY. One of the tools students need to know to supplement word-learning strategies is using a **dictionary**. When you come to a word you don't know, how do you figure it out if you have no context clues to help you? Say, for example, that you're learning how to climb and are reading instructions about climbing a specific rockface. You come across the sentence, "Use the Gaston hold on the next move to make it safely to the next pocket." What's a Gaston? You may want to look up this word, probably in a dictionary or glossary of climbing terms.

As an adult, you have the skill of understanding how to use a dictionary, either hard copy or more likely online, as a resource to learn new vocabulary terms. This skill, however, will be new to your students. You'll need to introduce dictionaries to your students and explain when and why people use dictionaries. After you explain why dictionaries can be useful, you'll have to consider a variety of foundational skills students will need before they can successfully use a dictionary. First, students will need to understand alphabetical order if they are using hard copy dictionaries or glossaries. (Alphabetical order may not be needed if students are looking up single words online.) You might also need to teach students what guide words are and how to use them. Then students need to learn the parts of a dictionary entry and how to apply the correct entry to the context of the new word. Applying the correct dictionary definition is a sophisticated thinking skill that might be too difficult for your students to do with much success unless you are using a children's dictionary. This thinking skill, however, is important to practice when children are young. Using a dictionary is a complex skill. As students advance through the grades, the work you do in PreK–3 will enable them to use dictionaries and other resources independently to learn new vocabulary words. Teaching Strategies 9.10 and 9.11 can help you teach students how to use a dictionary.

Teaching Strategy 9.10: Making a Picture Dictionary

Purpose: A picture dictionary is a useful vocabulary resource for young students. Words are organized alphabetically, and pictures and/or definitions accompany each word. By making their own picture dictionaries, students are able to create a vocabulary resource that is personally meaningful while they are learning the beginning skills necessary for using published dictionaries. ELs can use their home language or English along with pictures to support their learning.

Procedures:

1. Explain to students that they will be creating a picture dictionary that contains new words that they want to learn.

2. Show a sample page from a picture dictionary. For example, you might show the following entry for the word *caterpillar*.

Caterpillar

The wormlike larva of butterfly or moth.

© Bannykh/Shutterstock.com

3. Tell students that a picture dictionary contains a new word, a picture, and sometimes a definition. Explain to students that dictionaries are resources to help them learn new words.

4. Write a vocabulary word for the picture dictionary on the board. The word should come from a book the students have read recently or a unit they are studying. For example, if students are studying a unit on amphibians, you might select the word *tadpole*.

5. Tell students that you will put the word *tadpole* on the T page because dictionaries are organized alphabetically.

6. Next, explain that you will add a picture of a tadpole to help you remember what the word means. Tell students that they can draw a picture or cut pictures from magazines for their picture dictionaries. Tell students they can add a definition if they want, or you can write a definition for them.

7. Construct the tadpole entry to demonstrate how students should go through the process of making a picture dictionary entry.

8. Invite students to suggest other choices of words to add to their dictionaries. Write the words on the board so students spell them correctly. Encourage students to select one or two words to illustrate for their own dictionaries.

9. Combine the pages in a three-ring binder or on rings so that students can add pages through the year.

*T*eaching *S*trategy 9.11: Using a Dictionary

Purpose: To teach students the foundational skills for using a dictionary as a resource.

Procedures:

1. Select a children's dictionary that is appropriate for the level of your students. If possible, have a copy for each student.

2. Ask students what they do when they don't know the meaning of a word. Their ideas may include asking someone for help, looking at illustrations, or skipping the word to see if the passage makes sense without it.

3. Tell students they can also use a dictionary to find the meaning of a word.

4. Ask students whether they have heard the term *dictionary* or seen one before. Also ask them whether they have ever seen anyone look up the definition of a word online.

5. Show students the dictionary they will be using and distribute copies to students. Let students look through their copy.

6. Ask students what they notice from the dictionaries they are previewing. Some answers may be that there are words with definitions, that words are in alphabetical order, or that there are words at the top of the page.

7. Demonstrate how words are organized in alphabetical order by having students find several words and showing them how they have been arranged. Suggest several words that students can look up.

8. Provide students with an example of a word from their reading that they needed defined, such as the word *octopus* in the following sentence:

   An octopus is a soft sea creature with eight *tentacles*.

9. Ask students to find the entry for *tentacle* in their dictionaries.

   Tentacle   /ˈtɛntɪkəl/ noun

   1 one of the long, flexible arms of an animal (such as an octopus) that are used for grabbing things and moving

   2 reaching out

   The company's *tentacles* were felt throughout the town.

10. Read the entry to students or have them read the entry themselves. Point out the parts of the entry, including the pronunciation, the part of speech, the two definitions, the picture, and the sentence using a different form of the word.

11. Have students look for other entries and identify the parts of the entries.

12. Ask students to take a closer look at the two definitions for *tentacle*. Ask which one of the definitions fits the sentence.

13. Explain to students that many words have multiple definitions and that the dictionary will often have more than one definition for a word. Tell students that they will need to determine which entry fits their needs.

14. Repeat this activity through the year until students are familiar with the components of a dictionary entry.

FOSTERING WORD CONSCIOUSNESS. Do you have a favorite word? Do you actively look for new words or words that are fun to say? Do you feel good about yourself when you use new words in your writing? You can capitalize on your natural enthusiasm for language and learning when you teach vocabulary words by fostering **word consciousness**.

If you remember that it can take up to 40 exposures to a word before students have that word firmly in their expressive vocabulary, you'll want to provide many opportunities for students to see, hear, say, and write the words you teach. Fortunately, you don't have to do all of this work yourself. You can teach your students to be on the lookout for words they have already learned and for new words to add to their vocabularies. Children are proud of the new words they are learning. Encourage them to actively notice new words and add them to their vocabularies.

According to Graves (2016), word consciousness is "an awareness of and interest in words and their meanings" (p. 8). When you encourage students to "collect words" in the same way they collect baseball cards, they are increasing their word consciousness which can lead to developing students' vocabularies (Scott, Miller, & Flinspach, 2012). You can foster word consciousness, by engaging in word play, encouraging students to keep word journals, and playing a variety of word games in the classroom. Teaching Strategy 9.12 can help students increase their vocabularies and have fun learning new words. You can use your imagination to create other opportunities for students to have fun with words, such as vocabulary bingo, graffiti walls, and other games.

Engaging with Families: Word Games

Develop a shelf of simple word games that could be played at home (e.g., My First Bananagrams, Bananagrams, Scrabble Junior, Boggle Jr., Boggle). Work with your mentor teacher to develop a sign-out procedure for the games so that students can take the games home for a week. Make sure that the students know how to play the game independently before they take it home.

© Ana Blazic Pavlovic/Shutterstock.com

Teaching Strategy 9.12: Word Storming

Purpose: The ability to brainstorm words is fun for many students. This strategy can help students have fun with words, review words they know, and intentionally learn new words.

Procedures:

1. Explain to students that Word Storming is like brainstorming, but the focus is on listing as many words as possible related to a specific category. Tell students that when they Word Storm, they are trying to build their ability to name words quickly and easily.

2. Assign each student to a partner. Have one student in each pair serve as the word stormer, and the other student in the pair serve as the recorder. Provide a category such as *vehicles*, *animals*, or *community helpers*, depending on what you have been studying in the classroom.

3. Tell the word stormer to say as many words related to the category in 1 minute as they can. The recorder in each group should tally each word that the word stormer says, providing one point for each word. (Repetitions do not count.)

4. Have students switch roles and name a related category. Have the second student in the pair brainstorm words while the other student tallies the number of words they've said.

5. Provide time for Word Storming at least once a week. Record students' progress throughout the year.

© Rido/Shutterstock.com

Students are experiencing word storming strategy.

What Do You Believe about Vocabulary Instruction?

Think about the important takeaways from this chapter and write the ones that are personally important to you on the What Do You Believe template that can be found in the Chapter 9 Resources on the website. Then write a brief paragraph about what you believe about vocabulary instruction as a result of what you learned.

Closing Thoughts

You might be thinking that helping students develop their vocabularies will take a great deal of instructional time, and you'd be correct. You'll need to schedule time in your day for teaching and reviewing vocabulary words and phrases. Think about the difference between children who understand a small number of words for their age group and those who understand more words. Children who are listening to you or other adults, or even watching TV, will benefit from having larger vocabularies. Furthermore, vocabulary instruction can impact how well students comprehend the books they read (Ash & Baumann, 2017). What that means to you is that the vocabulary strategies you learned in this chapter can help your students become better readers because they will better understand what they read. And isn't understanding the point of reading?

We introduced you to Sabrina at the beginning of the chapter. Sabrina knew that it was important to teach vocabulary explicitly to students, but she wondered how she should do it, and you probably had the same question. This chapter gave you an overview of the principles of vocabulary instruction along with Teaching Strategies and Assessment Strategies you can use in your teaching. Using these ideas can go a long way in helping your students strengthen their vocabularies.

Takeaways from Chapter 9

■ Students develop general vocabulary from experience.
■ Academic or school vocabulary needs to be taught.
■ Providing students with rich and varied language experiences can help them develop their vocabularies.
■ Students come to school with a wide range in the number of words they know.
■ Instructional principles for teaching vocabulary are the following:
  ■ Teach individual words.
  ■ Teach words in context.
  ■ Teach word relationships.
  ■ Teach word-learning strategies.
  ■ Foster word consciousness.

To Learn More about Vocabulary Instruction

Seminal Research on Vocabulary

Hart, B., & Risley, T. R. (1995). *Meaningful differences in the everyday experience of young American children*. Baltimore, MD: Paul H. Brookes Publishing.

https://products.brookespublishing.com/Meaningful-Differences-in-the-Everyday-Experience-of-Young-American-Children-P14.aspx

Summary of book:

https://www.leadersproject.org/2013/03/17/meaningful-differences-in-the-everyday-experience-of-young-american-children/

Read this book (or a summary of it) to learn more about the first study that connected children's vocabulary to socioeconomic status.

In addition to reading the original study, read the following two critiques. After reading the critiques, consider what ideas you can take away from Hart and Risley's study and what the interpretation of the study has done to contribute to teaching from a deficit perspective.

Nation, I. S. P. (n.d.). A brief critique of Hart, B., & Risley, T. (1995). *Meaningful differences in the everyday experience of young American children.* Baltimore, MD: Paul H. Brookes Publishing.

https://www.victoria.ac.nz/lals/about/staff/publications/paul-nation/Hart_and_Risley_critique.pdf

Bahena, S. (2016). Differences as deficiencies: The persistence of the 30 million word gap.

https://www.idra.org/resource-center/differences-as-deficiencies/

Strategy Books for Vocabulary Instruction and Assessment

McKeown, M. G., Deane, P. D., Scott, J. A., Krovetz, R., & Lawless, R. R. (2017). *Vocabulary assessment to support instruction: Building rich word-learning experiences.* New York, NY: Guilford Press.

https://www.guilford.com/books/Vocabulary-Assessment-to-Support-Instruction/McKeown-Deane-Scott-Krovetz/9781462530793

We've presented two vocabulary assessment strategies in this chapter. You can learn many other vocabulary assessment strategies by looking at this book. Skim through the table of contents to find those strategies that might be appropriate for your placement. You can also use this book as a resource when you are a teacher.

Sprenger, M. (2017). *101 strategies to make academic vocabulary stick.* Alexandria, VA: Association for Supervision and Curriculum Development.

http://www.ascd.org/Publications/Books/Overview/One-Hundred-and-One-Strategies-to-Make-Academic-Vocabulary-Stick.aspx

Academic vocabulary is critical for students to become good students and to learn the content of schooling. There are many excellent strategies aimed specifically to teach academic vocabulary. You can use this book as a resource as you're developing lesson plans for academic vocabulary learning. Many of the strategies might be most appropriate for intermediate grade students, but you can adapt the strategies to fit your grade level.

Vocabulary Lists

Graham, S., Harris, K. R., & Loynachan, C. (1993). The basic spelling vocabulary list. *Journal of Educational Research, 86,* 363–368.

http://www.readingrockets.org/article/basic-spelling-vocabulary-list

There are many lists that you can use to decide which vocabulary words to teach. Reading Rockets published the lists from Graham, Harris, and Loynachan's research article. You can use this list as a basis for deciding words to teach. You'll notice that this list contains words that would only be used for spelling and others that would be used for both spelling and vocabulary instruction.

30 Word Core Content Vocabulary List

https://www.sealyisd.com/common/pages/DisplayFile.aspx?itemId=2339209

When you teach science, social studies, language arts, and math, you'll be introducing content area words, or academic vocabulary. This list contains 30 words for each of the content areas in each grade levels K–12. You can use this list as you prepare lesson plans for these content areas and to select words that students may need to learn.

Vocabulary Development Programs

Thirty Million Word Initiative

https://cri.uchicago.edu/portfolio/thirty-million-words/

https://www.ncfr.org/zippy-news/weekly-videos/30-million-words

You may hear of programs like the Thirty Million Word Initiative in your placements or as you learn more about vocabulary teaching. These programs are designed to help bridge the gap between the number of words young children know. As you look at these programs, remember that you need to address all learning gaps from an assets perspective rather than a deficit perspective.

Talking is Teaching

http://talkingisteaching.org/

This program encourages intentional talk to children to build their vocabularies. You might be able to use some of these ideas in your classroom routines.

Apps

Reading Rockets: Literacy Apps for Vocabulary

https://www.readingrockets.org/literacyapps/vocabulary

Read the descriptions of the 21 vocabulary apps listed in this website and consider which ones you might use in your future classroom. A variety of age ranges is presented for each app. Although some are free, many require purchase. When you are hired as a teacher, you may want to talk with your principal about policies related to downloading apps onto school-owned devices, as well as funding for apps that require fees.

© Monkey Business Images/Shutterstock.com

Help students learn how to read or to listen so they have a deep understanding of the text.

How Do I Teach Reading Comprehension?

REAL-LIFE EXAMPLE

Trevor had been observing in his second-grade placement for a month and was taking observational notes and forming impressions about students' reading abilities. His mentor teacher, Miss Eva, spent most of the literacy block teaching phonics, as was called for in the district curriculum, and Trevor was concerned that the students didn't seem to comprehend the stories they were hearing and reading.

Trevor wanted to know Miss Eva's views on the subject, so he asked if they could meet during their next planning time to discuss whether the students were comprehending as well as they should be. Miss Eva agreed to meet the next week. In the meantime, Trevor asked whether he could do an informal passage reading assessment of three students during silent reading time.

Miss Eva agreed, and Trevor conducted the assessment during the next week. He found that, as he suspected, the students did well on the oral reading of the passages but not on the comprehension questions. Trevor brought these data to the meeting. Miss Eva was a little taken aback at the findings but wanted the best for the students, so she discussed with Trevor how to adapt the literacy block to focus more on comprehension.

Trevor volunteered to teach two comprehension strategies that he had learned in his teacher preparation program to one group of students. Miss Eva was pleased with Trevor's initiative and also with the opportunity to help improve students' reading comprehension.

Comprehension is the goal of reading, so this chapter will be crucial for all PreK–3 teachers like Trevor. Before you say, "Wait a minute, my students can't read yet," hear us out. You might be thinking that your students in PreK or kindergarten won't need much instruction in reading comprehension because you'll be focused on teaching them print concepts, phonemic awareness, and word identification strategies. It's true that you should spend a significant amount of time in your literacy block teaching about letters and sounds. However, Stahl (2016) found that primary reading programs have been overly focused on decoding skills and not providing enough comprehension instruction. She suggests that teachers spend more time providing comprehension instruction before students' needs are so complex that they become difficult to remedy.

It's important that you lay the groundwork for reading comprehension even before your students begin to read books independently (van den Brook, Kendeou, Lousberg, & Visser, 2017). To learn how to do this, we're going to present the importance of providing students with a diversity of texts, a framework for organizing comprehension instruction, how to determine the reading level of a text, and the thinking processes used in comprehension.

What Is Comprehension?

Comprehension is making sense of text. Have you ever read something and then realized that you didn't understand what you had read? We've all had that experience. Is that reading? That is a question that could be debated, but for now we just want you to think about the idea that reading is the process of making sense of print. There are degrees of comprehension. Sometimes you might read something and understand it fairly well, and other times you might have a deep understanding of what you've read. The same will be true for your students. Your job as a teacher is to help students learn how to read or to listen so they have a deep understanding of the text.

The strategies you teach will also depend on the type of reading you want students to do. Think about when you read a book for pleasure. You may just have gotten the overall plot or the general theme of the book. You are comprehending the book at a surface level. Students may read at a surface level for their pleasure reading as well, but if you want students to improve their reading ability, you need to help students conduct a close reading of texts, which we will discuss later in the chapter.

Different Kinds of Texts

Think about what you do when you read a novel. Now think about reading a book on how to train to run a marathon. You would approach those texts differently, right? That's because stories have a different text structure than informational texts. As you teach your students how to comprehend different kinds of texts, you should also keep in mind that the standards you use and the strategies you teach will be slightly different.

NARRATIVE TEXTS. Most learning standards, including the Common Core State Standards (CCSS), are divided into **literary texts** and **informational texts**. The term "literary texts" means **narratives**, or stories. Most of your students will be very familiar with **narrative text structure**. These include stories, fairy tales, fables, folktales, and myths.

Narrative texts have a beginning, middle, and end. The plot most often has events in a series that builds to a climax and ends in a conclusion. Figure 10.1 has an example of a plot outline that is most common in the stories you will read to your students or that they will read themselves. Refresh your memory of the plot outline by viewing the video in Margin Note 10.1. Then use the plot outline to

Figure 10.1. Plot Outline Diagram

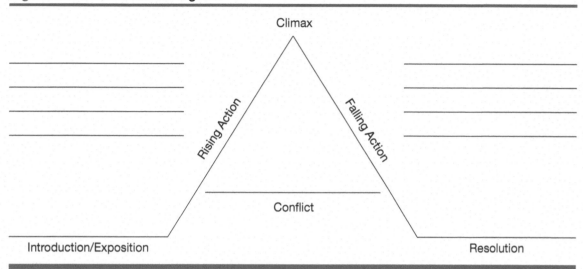

describe a well-known children's book, such as *Where the Wild Things Are* (Sendak, 1963).

Margin Note 10.1: Plot Mountain

https://www.youtube.com/watch?v=NpWHZJZQDSE

INFORMATIONAL TEXTS. Informational texts are works in which "the author purports to tell us about the real world, a real experience, a real person, an idea, or a belief" (Beers & Probst, 2016, p. 21). Informational texts are different from narrative texts in that their purposes are to inform, to persuade, to describe, and to advise. They can come in a variety of different forms. Informational texts can have narrative structures that tell a story or have events in a series. Examples of informational texts with narrative structures are biography, autobiography, literary nonfiction, and memoirs. These kinds of informational texts will be easy for your students to understand.

Informational texts also can have **expository text structures**, such as textbooks, articles, essays, speeches, documents, news articles, descriptions, and reports. Expository text structures are typically description, sequence, comparison, cause and effect, and problem and solution. Most informational texts include more than one type of structure which can make them more challenging to comprehend. Informational texts with expository structures play a large role in intermediate grade through adult reading. You probably read informational texts, possibly on the internet, to plan vacations, decide which car to buy, and evaluate childcare options. Expository text structures are also the kind of writing in textbooks that students often begin reading in the primary grades. Examples of informational texts that are appropriate for young children are *A Tree Is a Plant* (Bulla, 2001) and *Amazing Whales!* (Thomson, 2006).

Most students will need instruction on expository text structures because they are not as familiar to them. In fact, two decades ago, Nell Duke (2000) found that a group of first grade teachers spent on average 3.6 minutes per day teaching informational text. Since that study was published, there has been an effort for PreK–3 teachers to use more informational texts in the classroom. As you choose books to teach, for read alouds and for students to read independently, it's important to balance narrative texts with informational texts (McClure & Fullerton, 2017). Browse through the list

Margin Note 10.2: Reading A–Z: Informational Texts

https://www.readinga-z.com/commoncore/informational-text/

of informational texts for books in Margin Note 10.2 and develop your own list of books that is appropriate for your placement.

POETRY. **Poetry** is a third type of text that you'll teach your students. Poetry is a type of writing that appeals to a reader's imagination or emotions. The words of a poem are arranged according to meaning, sound, and rhythm, rather than in sentences. Young children probably have more experiences with poetry and rhymes than some older students. If you've been using the phonemic awareness strategies in Chapter 6, your students will be very familiar with **rhyming poetry**. You may notice that it's rather difficult to make sense of some jump rope rhymes and nursery rhymes. Some rhymes are best to be read aloud and to relish in the sound of the words rather than focus on meaning. Other poetry, however, can have a message or a meaning. For PreK–3 classrooms, reading poetry regularly and asking students what it means is all you need to do to give them the foundation for more enriched comprehension as they get older.

*C*onnection to the Field: Teaching Poetry

Select a poem from the poetry lists that follow to share as a read aloud in your placement. Decide if there is a message in the poem. For example, read the poem by Nikki Giovanni (1988) "Knoxville, Tennessee." A reading of the poem might show that the message is about the joys of summer. Find a poem like this for your class that has a message. Read the poem to your students and ask them what they think the message is. Encourage many ideas, remembering that your goal is to help students comprehend poetry at a basic level.

Some resources for poetry are: Ken Nesbitt's Poetry4kids, https://www.poetry4kids.com/poems and the Poetry Foundation: Poetry for children and poetry videos, https://www.poetryfoundation.org/learn/children

Providing a Diversity of Texts

Now that we've described the types of texts you'll use as a PreK–3 teacher (i.e., narrative, informational, and poetry), let's consider the content or topic of the texts. As a teacher, you'll want to provide your students with a range of experiences through texts that they might not have outside of school. **Literature** can be a mirror for students who see their own lives reflected on the pages of the books. Martinez, Koss, and Johnson (2016) remind us that many popular books have main characters who do not reflect the diversity of our classrooms. In a study of award-winning **Caldecott books**, these researchers found that most of the main characters were white and male. Because characters in literature can be a powerful influence in our students' lives, it makes sense to look for diversity among the characters in the books that students read.

Think about what you've learned about other places and people through books. For example, maybe you've read or seen the film, *Into the Wild* (Krakauer, 1996). If you've read this book, you might have learned about a young man who tried to live in Alaska on his own. Think about what you learned from this book, not only about the main character and his decisions but about the setting. Perhaps you didn't realize how fierce the living conditions were in Alaska. Reading books outside your experience helps you broaden your knowledge of people and the world.

Taking this a step further, let's think about the **diversity** in your classroom. We've stated in earlier chapters that the diversity in North America is increasing. Even if that's not the case where you live, your students will most likely live in an increasingly diverse world. As you select books to read aloud and for students to read, you'll want to have diversity in the authors you select, the setting of your books, and the main characters or topics. You should also consider the diversity of your classroom. For example, if you have a number of students from Ukraine, you might include books set in that country. But don't stop there. You want to expand the experience of all students, including students from other countries. So, include books that include a diversity of cultures and places. Browse the website on multicultural books in Margin Note 10.3. Create a shared document with your classmates that lists books that would be appropriate and interesting for the students in your placement.

Margin Note 10.3:
50 Multicultural Books Every Child Should Know

https://ccbc.education.wisc.edu/books/detailListBooks.asp?idBookLists=42

BILINGUAL CHILDREN'S BOOKS. If you are teaching English Learners (ELs), you might wonder whether you should encourage them to read in their home language as well as English. We recommend that the first thing you do is check with your mentor teacher to find out whether your state or province has regulations and guidelines. As you move through your teaching career, this will be a topic that you should learn more about. Then you can form your own opinion.

Connection to the Field: Learn about Your Students

If your state or province uses a teacher performance assessment, you may already be developing a classroom context description to use as you plan instruction. Teachers need to know about their students so they can develop targeted lesson plans. If you haven't already done so, create a list of students who speak other languages. Also, find out whether these students are getting support inside or outside the classroom. Talk with your mentor teacher about the best way to gather this information.

Our review of reading research indicates that having students listen to and read books in their home language can support their reading development (Wright, 2019). Unless you are teaching in a dual language program, however, your priority will be for your students to read English. We have found that books written in two languages can be very useful for these purposes. Students can listen to or read books in a familiar language, and they can also read that same book in English. Often these books are written with one page in Spanish, for example, and the facing page translated into English.

As you are looking for ways to support your ELs, you might consider using or adapting Teaching Strategy 10.1 to help your students develop a foundation for comprehension.

Cultural Wealth

Knowing a language other than English is an asset in our society. According to Yosso (2005), families from other countries bring with them the cultural knowledge, skills, abilities, and contacts that are valuable assets to your learning community which she calls **cultural wealth**. One of the forms of cultural wealth is the ability to speak a language other than English. Children who hear a different language at home have a gift that monolingual children do not. Browse through a bookstore or look at the website on Margin Note 10.4 to develop a list of bilingual children's books that would be appropriate for your students.

Margin Note 10.4: Bilingual Books for Children

https://www.ala.org/ala/alsc/alscresources/booklists/bilingualbooks.htm

Teaching Strategy 10.1: Process Drama: Acting Out the Story

Purpose: The purpose of acting out stories is not to develop a script for a production for an audience but for students to informally make sense of the story. There are many ways to act out stories, including ones that have you, as the teacher, either play a role or to be the "producer." You can ask students to act out the story in their home language or in English to help them build comprehension.

Procedures:

1. Select a book that has an obvious plot and characters that would be appropriate to act out. You might use the resource Story Books for Drama Teaching: https://dramaresource.com/story-books-for-drama-teaching/

2. Read the book to students or have them read it in groups.

3. Identify the roles in the book, including a narrator. List them on the board.

4. Ask students to volunteer to play a role in the drama. Assign roles to students.

5. Have students listen or read the story again, paying close attention to their role.

6. Have students act out the story, providing assistance as needed.

7. Give other students the opportunity to act out the story a second time.

© spass/Shutterstock.com

These students are acting out a story.

CULTURAL APPLICATION. Perhaps the **plot outline diagram** in Figure 10.1 (page 265) will be familiar to most of your students, but not all. Text structures are culturally developed, which means the plot outline that you know is typical for North America. Children in North America are exposed to a linear plot outline through the stories that they hear as well as television, movies, and books. When you teach comprehension strategies to students familiar with this story structure, it will seem natural to them. However, some ELs (but not all) will have had a different story pattern in their experience. Young children who have been told stories all their lives by their elders may be familiar with a different story pattern that does not follow a linear plot outline. Think about the last time you saw a foreign film. Were you surprised how the story developed and perhaps didn't end with a neat conclusion? Different cultures have preferred structures to their stories and informational texts.

Researchers Kaplan (1996) and Hill (1997) found that different cultures tend to have different kinds of story structures. North American and many English language stories are linear, to the point, and in a sequence. Semitic writing (Jewish, Arabic, Armenian) presents the argument in parallel propositions, or embedded in stories, not in hierarchical progression. Asian writing approaches the argument in a circular, respectful, indirect, nonassertive, but authoritative way. Romance (and German) writing favors a digressive style that requires readers to follow the argument to its conclusion. Russian writing follows the romance model, but with more freedom for dividing the pieces of the argument as the author proceeds to the conclusion. Native American writing tends to come at an argument from several directions, all moving toward a central idea.

What does this mean for you? Some of your ELs, especially newcomers, may not be familiar with the ways that the stories you teach are organized. They may need more experiences with stories and explicit instruction on what is the beginning, middle, and end of a story and with sequencing tasks. It's important to remember, however, that you can't assume an EL has less experience hearing linear stories than other students. To assess whether your students have a strong sense of story as is taught in North American schools, consider administering Assessment Strategy 10.1: Retelling a Story.

Assessment Strategy 10.1: Retelling a Story

Purpose: Some students will have a difficult time identifying the beginning, middle, and end of the story. To determine which students will need additional instruction in narrative structure, informally assess students on their knowledge of basic story structure.

Procedures:

1. Choose a short book that is new to the student. The book should have an obvious plot with named characters. You may choose to use props or puppets with the story if you think visual aids could help the student, particularly if the student's home language is not English.

2. Before reading the book say, "I'm going to read a story to you. After I'm finished reading, I will ask you to tell me the story as if you were telling it to someone who has not read the story. As you listen, try to remember as much of the story as you can."

3. Read the book aloud to the student.

4. After you have read the book, say, "Now tell me as much of the story as you can." If the student hesitates, ask probing questions such as, "What was the story about?" or, "Who was in the story?" or, "What happened first?" You may want to record the retelling for future reference.

5. To score student's responses, use the Narrative Retelling Record Sheet that can be found in the Chapter 10 Resources on the website.

6. Give the student another opportunity to retell a story in 3 or 4 weeks to monitor their progress.

Students are retelling a story with their teacher.

Comprehension Instruction

There are many ways to organize **comprehension strategies**. Since you probably will be using standards to develop lesson plans, we've decided to divide the strategies into the categories used in the CCSS. Even if your state isn't using the CCSS, you are most likely using some kind of learning standards that are similarly organized. As you read through these sections, compare the topics in this chapter to those your state or province uses.

We've divided the comprehension standards into four categories: key ideas and details, craft and structure, integration of knowledge and ideas, and range of reading and text complexity. As you have learned in previous chapters, there are anchor standards that are the ultimate goal at the end of high school. The standards are divided into grade levels beginning at kindergarten. As we discuss the standards, we'll also give suggestions for what they mean for PreK. Again, if the standards you are using are organized differently, just look at the standards individually. What's important is that you teach a variety of different kinds of comprehension strategies to your students (Cecil, Baker, & Lozano, 2017).

Key Ideas and Details

As we think about comprehension, you can ask yourself the following questions about teaching. How do I teach students to identify the key ideas and details of the text? There are three topics that will help you instruct students in this skill:

- Identify details in the text,
- Determine the central message or main idea, and
- Describe characters in the text.

You'll notice that these three topics focus on how to help students comprehend the key ideas and details of both narrative and informational texts. These topics can be addressed from PreK–3 through read alouds as well as through using texts in instruction.

IDENTIFY DETAILS IN THE TEXT. The first topic in this category requires students to refer to the **details** specifically in the text. This means as you read a book aloud or have students read a short passage, you'll be asking them to identify what they learned from the text, not their experiences. We know that young children often offer their own stories when you read a book. Although that's fine in general, you also need to make students aware of what is in the text and what is not. This is the basis for **close reading**.

WHAT IS CLOSE READING? When you read different books, you approach them differently, right? For example, when you are reading this textbook, you may be highlighting or taking notes so that you can apply the ideas to your own teaching. When you read the latest Stephen King novel, however, you read for the story. You comprehend each of the texts, but differently. As you teach students, you want to give them both experiences. This learning standard asks students to read for the details of the text. That's what we mean by close reading.

Reading closely means that you look for details in the text and that your experiences and background knowledge take a back seat to the information in the text. The reader asks, "What does the text say?" because the assumption is that the text carries the meaning. Comprehension, or an understanding of the text, varies with every reader, based on background knowledge, but meanings need to be justifiable. When reading a text closely, students become "meaning detectives," or readers who

Margin Note 10.5: Text-Dependent Questioning

https://www.youtube.com/
watch?v=0M8acO10wpE

are looking for clues in the text to back up their interpretations. Comprehension, then, can be different for every reader, but the reconstructed meaning needs to be supported by the text. To do this, you'll need to ask **text-dependent questions** in read alouds and when you're teaching. The video in Margin Note 10.5 describes text-dependent questions for you. Consider developing a list of text-dependent questions for a story that you might teach in your placement.

DETERMINE THE CENTRAL MESSAGE. The stories and informational books that you read to your students or that they read will have a **central message**. In literary texts this is called **the theme**. Writers use their stories to explore ideas and to present them to their readers. Often readers first read a story for the plot, which is what characters do in the story. The overall story, however, has one or more lessons or morals underlying the plot. That's the theme of the story. The theme is the message that describes the author's ideas about life, human nature, or society. The theme lies behind the story as a whole, which the author conveys through writing and what the reader learns through the story.

You can think back to your own experiences in English classes as you explored the themes of literature or the main ideas of informational text. That's what you'll want your students to be able to do when they are more experienced readers. Right now, however, you just want to help students look for these big ideas with your support and independently by second or third grade. You don't even have to use the word "theme" when you teach this standard unless you think your students are ready to learn the term. You can, however, ask students, "What's the big idea of this story?" or, "What's the moral of the story?" Teaching Strategy 10.2 is one strategy to help you teach students how to identify theme in a story.

MAIN IDEA FROM INFORMATIONAL TEXTS. Informational texts will have a **main idea** rather than a theme. You might remember underlining main ideas of paragraphs when you were in school. Did you think it was difficult? Many students have a hard time finding main ideas from paragraphs and longer texts. This is the kind of thinking you'll want students to be able to do when they have more experience. For now, you'll want to build the foundation for this skill by asking students what they think the passage was about. Giving students many examples of main idea when you read informational texts will help them as they progress in their reading development. Teaching Strategy 10.3 can help you develop instruction to help students find main ideas in text.

*T*eaching *S*trategy 10.2: Message in a Bottle

Purpose: The Message in a Bottle strategy helps students identify the main point, or theme, of a narrative in a fun way. Even if students have not heard of the idea of putting a message in a bottle and heaving it out to sea, they can enjoy the concept of writing down a message and having another student read it at a later date.

Procedures:

1. Ask students whether they've heard the expression, "message in a bottle." If students haven't heard this expression, explain what it means by saying something like the following:

   One of the types of stories in books and television is having someone get stranded on an island. The character tries to communicate with the outside world by writing a message on a slip of paper and putting it in a bottle that is put in the water with the hopes that someone will find it and rescue them. This idea is used in other ways as well. For example, sometimes people put messages on or in balloons and let them go to see where they land.

2. Tell students that they will be sending a message in a bottle, but their message will be from the characters in one of their books.

3. Collect empty liter bottles, clean them, and dry them to use for this project.

4. Give students bottles and have them decorate them.

5. Divide the class into groups of three or four students who have read a common story.

6. Tell the students that the main character wants to share what he or she has learned.

7. Share an example from a familiar story so students understand what they are being asked to do.

8. Distribute strips of paper to students. Have students write a sentence or two from the character's point of view about what was learned. Insert the note into the bottle.

9. Put the bottles on a shelf. At random times during the next week, give a bottle to another student to read.

10. Remind students that when they read they should be looking for a big idea from the story.

Teaching Strategy 10.3: What's the Point?

Purpose: This strategy helps students find the main idea of an informational book. Although the strategy is simple, it can build the foundation for finding main ideas in short texts.

Procedures:

1. Select an informational text that is of interest to your students. One such text is *Buildings in Disguise: Architecture that Looks Like Animals, Food, and other Things* (Arbogast, 2004).

2. Determine the main point of the book. In this example, the main point is that there are many buildings in the United States that are built to look like other things.

3. Read the book to students or have them read it in groups. Ask students to think about the main point of the book by asking, "What's the point?"

4. Discuss what the students think is the main point of the book. Guide students to write a main idea sentence such as the following:

   Some buildings look like other objects such as animals, teapots, and teepees.

5. Encourage students to think about main points of informational texts as they read independently.

© spass/Shutterstock.com

The teacher is talking about the main idea of a story with her students.

DESCRIBE CHARACTERS AND MAKE CONNECTIONS TO IDEAS IN A TEXT. One of the most appealing aspects of fiction is the **characters** that the author creates. Students often respond to fictional characters with an emotional reaction as if they were real people. You might even share some of your favorite novels with your classmates. Think about how you related to the characters in the books. It's probably not a problem for you to differentiate the characters in the books from your friends or real people. However, this is a skill that you'll want to help your students learn.

As you work with your students on identifying characters, you'll want to remind them that characters do not live outside the pages of the story. Authors imagine the characters and reveal who they are through explicit description and indirectly through the character's actions, thoughts, feelings, and words. Through this information, you want students to understand the characters, their motivations, and how they change in the story. Through learning about characters in fiction, students can learn important life lessons, perspectives, and worldviews outside their own experience (Harvey & Ward, 2017). Teaching Strategy 10.4 can help students of all ages understand characters in stories.

CONNECTING IDEAS IN INFORMATIONAL TEXT. It's pretty clear how to teach students about characters in narrative texts. In informational texts, the focus is on finding **sequence within a text and connections between ideas or information within a text**. Students who possess the ability to recognize or recall the sequence in a passage are often able to infer what occurred between two stated events or incidents. They can also make predictions about what might happen next in a passage based on the previous sequence of events. Sequencing demands that students use at least the literal level of comprehension. More often, however, the interpretive level as well as the application level must be used. In order to correctly sequence events, the students must interpret a print passage or a series of pictures and then anticipate which event must come next (and also which cannot). To teach sequence of events, begin with concrete experiences so that students can learn the language of sequencing (e.g., this idea happened before that one) before moving to printed materials. There are many ways to help students learn how to sequence ideas. Teaching Strategy 10.5 is one example.

© Rob Marmion/Shutterstock.com

Make connections to students' prior knowledge to deepen comprehension.

Teaching Strategy 10.4: Character on the Wall

Purpose: Understanding characters in fiction is the easiest of the aspects of a story for most students. However, using character traits and the actions the character took in a story to understand the character is more challenging. This strategy helps students record a character's traits and actions in order for them to gain a deeper understanding of the character.

Procedures:

1. Identify a story with one or more characters who are well described.

2. Read the story to students or have students read it independently. Ask students to pay particular attention to a character in the story.

3. Draw a big outline of a head and body and display it in a central location.

4. Ask students to volunteer character traits they learned in the story and write them within the outline of the character. (For example, the character could be friendly.) You might need to explain the term *character traits*.

5. Discuss what actions the character took in the story. For example, the character might have offered to help a friend. Write the actions of the character outside the outline.

6. Using the traits and actions you have listed, ask students what kind of person this would be.

7. Remind students to look for information about characters when they listen to or read stories.

Teaching Strategy 10.5: Sequencing Ideas

Purpose: Students will have some experience sequencing ideas, but they may not be aware of them. For example, most students could probably tell you the steps to make a sandwich. This strategy will help students apply the concept of sequencing to events in a story.

Procedures:

1. Identify an activity that has steps in a process in which sequencing matters.
2. Provide students with either pictures or sentences that describe each step in the process.
3. Scramble the sentences or the pictures and have students put them in the correct order.
4. Ask students to describe the events in order using words like *first*, *then*, *next*, and *finally*.

© Natpitcha V/Shutterstock.com   © B. Melo/Shutterstock.com   © thailerderden10/Shutterstock.com   © Lorelyn Medina/Shutterstock.com

5. Read a story to students that has a plot with several events leading up to the climax. Have students listen to the story and tell you what happened in the order it was written.

Lesson Planning: Determining the Moral of the Story

Students who listen to or read stories can begin to identify the theme of the story. Some fables and folktales have themes, or morals, that are explicitly identified which is good practice for understanding themes in literature.

Standard: Recount stories, including fables and folktales, from diverse cultures, and determine their central message, lesson, or moral.

Objective: The students will be able to say, write, or draw the moral of the story after hearing the Aesop's Fable, "The Tortoise and the Hare," and participating in a discussion about the fable.

Lesson Idea: Demonstrate how to find the moral of the story with an example using a different fable. Then read the "The Tortoise and the Hare" to students omitting the final sentence (http://www.storyarts.org/library/aesops/stories/tortoise.html) or show students a video of the fable, stopping before the final sentence (https://www.youtube.com/watch?v=psbCdWBL6ys&vl=en). Have students discuss what the moral of the story could be in small groups.

Assessment: Have students draw or write the moral of the story on a sheet of paper.

Scoring Criteria:

1	2	3
Moral does not relate to the story.	Moral includes ideas that distinguish between getting things done quickly or getting things done well.	Moral compares getting things done quickly *and* getting them done well.

Craft and Structure

The second organizational structure for comprehension standards is craft and structure. As you think about the standards in this section, think about the techniques the author(s) used when writing their book.

- Determine the meaning of words and phrases,
- Learn literary terms and use text features, and
- Distinguish point of view.

Some of the questions you might ask yourself to understand these topics are: What were some of the techniques the author used to craft the story? You know that each text has a structure. It could be the structure of a story, informational text, or poetry. How do you help students use the structure of the text to make meaning?

DETERMINE THE MEANING OF WORDS AND PHRASES. Authors make **specific word choices** as they write to advance their story or message. As authors write children's books, they also consider the words they use that are most appropriate for the grade level of the children. The goal of this standard is for students ultimately to be able to interpret words and phrases in texts and to be able to analyze how an author's word choice shapes meaning and tone. What does that mean for PreK–3 students?

First, there are many words in books that are new to students. You can refer to Chapter 9 for a variety of vocabulary strategies that will help students understand the meaning of words and phrases. That should be the bedrock of your instruction for this standard. In addition to helping students learn new words, you can also help students understand that authors can use words that appeal to the senses, including the rhythm and sound of language. Examples of this kind of writing are the books by Dr. Seuss who is famous for using words for their sound. Authors can also appeal to emotions by their word choice. Young children may not know very many words that express emotions, so one of the things you can do is to help students understand how words can evoke different feelings as they read as in Teaching Strategy 10.6. This knowledge can help your students as they read stories and poetry.

CONTROLLED VOCABULARY. Some books that you find in a reading program do not use authentic language and have **controlled vocabulary**. This means that the publishers have written books for beginning readers that contain only words that students have learned or are able to use their phonics skills to decode. These books generally do not have well developed plots and don't provide as many opportunities for comprehension development as authentic literature.

There is a debate over using beginning readers that use **authentic language** and books that have a **controlled vocabulary**. You can think about the advantages and disadvantages of each type of book. We recommend that your daily read alouds are authentic literature and that for some of your small group instruction, and possibly for independent reading, you use books that have controlled vocabulary, at least for kindergarten and first grade. You might ask your mentor teacher for their opinion as you consider the options. Your clinical placement is a great place to develop your own ideas. Use Margin Note 10.6 to delve into the topic of books with controlled vocabulary. Compare books with controlled vocabulary with stories using authentic language. Develop a list of benefits and drawbacks for using these types of books with the students in your placement.

Margin Note 10.6: Controlled Vocabulary

Popular Controlled Vocabulary Books
https://www.goodreads.com/shelf/show/controlled-vocabulary

https://www.librarything.com/tag/controlled+vocabulary

LEARNING LITERARY TERMS AND USING TEXT FEATURES. Each type of text has its own structure and its own terms. Your students will not necessarily know the terms **story**, **poem**, and **informational text**. You will need to teach them the terms for different kinds of texts, the differences between kinds of texts (e.g., how are a poem and story different?), and, by third grade, some of the terms used when describing texts (e.g., chapter, table of contents). All of these terms will probably be new to your students.

Have you ever given a baby or toddler a book and realized that you had to teach them how to hold the book with the spine to the left, open the cover, and turn one page at a time? These are all concepts of print that you need to show young children. As children get older and attend preschool or kindergarten, you should also continue teaching about book components, such as front cover, back cover, title, etc. As students advance through the grades, you can teach them literary terms for both narrative and informational texts such as chapters, table of contents, illustrations, and so on.

In addition to teaching terminology about texts and books, you can begin teaching students the terms that describe **story structure**. For example, you can teach young children that stories have a beginning, middle, and end. As students learn these concepts, you can expand their knowledge to include literary terms such as *plot*, *setting*, *characters*, and *theme*. Helping students gain knowledge about the terms used about books, stories, and informational texts will help them understand how authors use story structure to craft their works. You can use Teaching Strategy 10.7 to help students learn that stories have a beginning, middle, and end, or Teaching Strategy 10.8 will help students to identify the features of informational text.

Teaching Strategy 10.6: Getting the Feeling

Purpose: One of the more difficult activities for students is to identify the feelings of a character. Often students don't have the words to describe how a character could feel. This strategy helps students develop a range of words that evoke feelings.

Procedures:

1. Tell students that stories can make them feel lots of different ways and that responding to stories can include how they feel. Provide an example from your own reading such as the following:

   Last night I was reading The Africa Diaries *by Dereck and Beverly Joubert (2001). As I read, I had lots of different feelings. First, I was* amazed *at the vivid photographs the authors took of elephants. Then in the chapter on lions, I was* afraid *for the authors. They put themselves in really dangerous situations. Later in the book, I was* angry *at the poachers who killed the wild animals, and finally, I was* anxious *to see those animals before they become extinct.*

2. Develop a list of emotions that are appropriate for your students or use the list that follows. Over the course of several days, describe each of the emotions on the list so that students have a clear idea what each emotion means.

3. Select a book to read aloud to students or have them read independently. Before reading, tell students that you will be asking them how the story made them feel and to identify the part that made them feel that way. Use your own personal example and list your feelings along with the appropriate part of the story as in the following example:

Feelings	Part of Story
Amazed	Photographs of elephants
Afraid	Taking pictures of lions
Angry	People who kill animals
Anxious	Reading about animals becoming extinct

4. Read the selected book to the class or have them read it independently. After reading, ask students how the story made them feel. You might have them draw pictures or write sentences about their feelings.

5. Tell students that they can ascribe feelings to characters in books as well. When students read a story, have them think about how the character might feel.

6. You can find a list of emotions to use for this strategy in the Chapter 10 Resources on the website.

Teaching Strategy 10.7: Beginning, Middle, and End

Purpose: The first step in teaching plot to young students is to help them identify the beginning, middle, and end of a story, using those terms. When students use the terms beginning, middle, and end for a story, they will begin using the vocabulary they need to talk about plot.

Procedures:

1. Tell students that stories have a beginning, middle, and end. Write the words *beginning*, *middle*, and *end* on the board. To help students understand the concepts, say something like the following:

   Stories have a beginning, middle, and end. To understand what that means, think about our class. We have a beginning. What do we do at the beginning of class? [Answers could include taking attendance, morning message, etc.]

2. Write student responses under the word *beginning* on the board.

3. Ask students what they do in the middle and end of class and write their responses on the board under the words *middle* and *end*.

4. Remind students that stories also have a beginning, middle, and end.

5. Provide students with a story chart that can be found in the Chapter 10 Resources on the website.

6. Read a story to students, such as *The Paper Crane* (Bang, 1988). Tell students to pay attention to the beginning, middle, and end of the story. After you are done reading, ask students to draw a picture of the beginning. In this case, the students might draw a picture of a very kind restaurant owner standing by his restaurant. Then have students draw a picture of the middle of the story, such as when a stranger with old clothes walks into the restaurant and gives the owner a paper crane. Finally, have students draw a picture of the end of the story, such as when the paper crane comes to life. If students drew pictures that did not represent the beginning, middle, and end, point to the part of the story that they did not understand and ask them to revise their pictures.

7. Have students retell their stories using their pictures.

Teaching Strategy 10.8: Text Feature Chart

Purpose: To help students identify the features of informational text.

Procedures:

1. Tell students that informational texts often have features that are not found in fiction.

2. Select a text that has several of the features commonly found in informational texts. Some of the features that you should look for are on the following list.

   - Boldface text
   - Italics
   - Unusual spacing
   - Titles and subtitles
   - Charts and graphs
   - Inserts
   - Captions

3. Write two or three of the names of text features on the board. For example, you might select *boldface text*, *italics*, and *subtitles*. Define each of these terms for students and then show them examples in the text.

4. When students indicate that they know the definitions of the text features, provide them with a text feature chart that can be found in the Chapter 10 Resources on the website.

5. Tell students to look through the book, looking for text features. When students find a feature that is familiar to them, have them write the text feature in the left-hand column. Then have students list where they found the feature in the book. Ask students to be specific by putting the page number if they can and to also give additional information. In the right-hand column, have students write a short reason why and how this text feature can help them as they read the text.

DISTINGUISHING POINT OF VIEW. In the first section of the standards, identifying key ideas and details, students were supposed to focus on what is in the text. This standard helps students distinguish their own ideas from those of the author. When we read, we automatically make connections between our own experiences and beliefs that the author presents in the text. Rosenblatt (1938) argued that readers couldn't comprehend text without bringing their experience to the process of meaning-making. She suggested that meaning did not reside in the text but in the reader. Therefore, readers would ask, "What does this text mean to me?" This view of reading was eventually named **reader response theory** and rose in popularity through the 1980s and 1990s (Rosenblatt, 1978) and is still popular today.

Authors come to a text with their own experiences and ideas. As teachers, we want to help students distinguish between what the authors are saying and their own experiences. As you observe students in your placement and begin student teaching, you'll probably notice that your students want to share their own stories, whether they relate to your lesson or not. We have all had students raise their hands and tell you about their baby brother or the television program they saw, even if you were reading an informational book about polar bears. You'll want to give students time to share without disrupting the flow of your lesson. Bringing the discussion back to the story or lesson is always challenging. One teacher we know gently tells students, "That sounds like a great story. I'd love to hear about it when we have free time," and then redirects the discussion back to the topic.

It's also important to have realistic expectations of your students. Learning how to separate their own stories from those of an author's takes time and experience. Remember the idea of scaffolding that we discussed in Chapter 2? This is a good time to remember that it takes scaffolded experiences for students to see the difference between their own point of view and that of the narrator or author of a text. If you can help your young students learn how to identify what an author is saying and what they think, such as in Teaching Strategy 10.9, then your students will have the foundation for critical thinking as they get older.

Integration of Knowledge and Ideas

The first sections of the standards help students comprehend the meaning of a text and learn about some of the ways authors craft their stories. The third section, integration of knowledge and ideas, encourages students **to integrate ideas within a text and between texts**. The question you might ask yourself is: How do I help students use the knowledge and ideas from the text to make meaning? There are three standards that are included in this section:

- Combine illustrations with print to make meaning,
- Identify the reasoning that supports the main idea (informational text only), and
- Compare and contrast stories, plots, characters, and ideas between two texts.

You may find the standards in this section challenging to teach. That's because you are building a foundation for complex thinking. For example, you might lead students in kindergarten in a discussion about how illustrations in a story help them understand the plot. When students reach third grade, they might discuss ways illustrations contribute to or distract from the story. By the time students reach fourth grade, they use this skill with other digital formats, and by ninth grade students will be comparing scenes from two different types of media. Your work in PreK–3 builds the base from which these more sophisticated skills can be reached. As you prioritize the standards you teach, you may not spend as much time with these three standards as the other ones, but it is important that you address them as appropriate.

*T*eaching *S*trategy 10.9: Author's Ideas, My Ideas

Purpose: To understand that the author is narrating a story that is separate from the student's own ideas and stories.

Procedures:

1. Select a book that you want to read to your students, such as *All are Welcome* (Penford & Kaufman, 2018).

2. Read the title and name of the author and the illustrator. Ask students what the author does and what the illustrator does. Provide support as needed.

3. Remind students that we all have stories to tell and that the author is telling a story. Explain that everyone's stories are different.

4. Read the book to the class.

5. Duplicate the reproducible Author's Ideas, My Ideas that can be found in the Chapter 10 Resources on the website and distribute it to students.

6. Ask students to draw or write some of the ideas from the author, such as students with different cultural clothing who are participating in the class.

7. Then ask students to talk about their own stories welcoming new students to the class. Have students draw or write about their own experiences.

8. Divide the class into pairs. Have each student tell their own stories.

9. Remind students that the story the author tells will be different from their stories.

COMBINE ILLUSTRATIONS WITH PRINT TO MAKE MEANING. One of the joys of teaching PreK–3 is reading **picture books** to students. In fact, when you think about reading aloud to a toddler, you might go through the book showing the illustrations and perhaps not even reading the words. Let's say you are reading a book about dogs with a young child. You might open to an illustration and say, "What's that?" or, "What is the dog doing?" Now think of one of your favorite picture books, for example, *Goodnight Moon* (Brown, 1975). It's probably been a long time since you have read that book, but let's think about it now. Think of the ways the illustrations help tell the story. Picture the cow jumping over the moon. It certainly helps seeing the illustrations to make sense of that sentence. This standard may seem like common sense to you, but it formalizes actions by asking you, as the teacher, to explicitly help students understand the role illustrations have in picture books. As described earlier in this section, by doing this you are building the basis for more complex thinking in your students.

Connection to the Field: Picture Books

Familiarize yourself with picture books that are appropriate for your grade level. Find a book that you like to read and show it to students. As you read, draw students' attention to the illustrations and help them understand how the illustrations help the author tell the story. You might also have students tell a class story and have students illustrate it as a class book. You can find examples of picture books in the resources that follow.

Wordless Picture Books
http://www.readingrockets.org/booklists/our-favorite-wordless-picture-books

Best Picture Books
https://www.goodreads.com/list/show/460.Best_Picture_Books

IDENTIFYING THE REASONING THAT SUPPORTS THE MAIN IDEA FOR INFORMATIONAL TEXT. This topic does not apply to narrative texts because it deals with the reasoning authors make to support their main point. One important aspect of an author's craft in writing informational text is to make a **compelling**, **rational argument**. When we use the term argument in this sense, we mean that authors try to develop a main point with supporting points that make sense. They might do this with one of the structures used in informational text, such as description, comparison, cause/effect, sequencing, and problem/solution. Authors of informational texts for young children tend to use description more than the other structures, which are more appropriate for older students. For example, the book *Hello World: Dinosaurs* (McDonald, 2018) describes different types of dinosaurs. Students will do much more with this standard in later grades when they evaluate claims made in arguments and identify propaganda techniques. At the PreK–3 level, you are again helping students build the foundation for critical thinking by having students look for justifications or reasons that support the main idea of the text. Teaching Strategy 10.10 can help your students with this skill.

Margin Note 10.7: Popular Informational Picture Books

https://www.goodreads.com/shelf/show/informational-picture-books

There are many informational books appropriate for PreK–3 students that you can read aloud or have students read. Develop a list of books that are appropriate for your placement using the website in Margin Note 10.7 as a resource.

Teaching Strategy 10.10: Main Idea T

Purpose: To help students identify the details an author uses to develop a main idea.

Procedures:

1. Identify a piece of text that has a clear main idea with details. Remember that some informational text is written without clear main ideas so be sure to identify the main ideas before beginning this strategy.

2. Write the terms *main idea* and *details* on the board. Ask students if they know what the terms mean. Give students an opportunity to brainstorm ideas. Clarify as needed.

3. Tell students that authors use details to give more information about their main point. Tell students that they should think about whether the author gave the right amount of details to be clear.

4. Draw the Main Idea T on the board. Point out that the main idea line is horizontal, and the detail area is vertical.

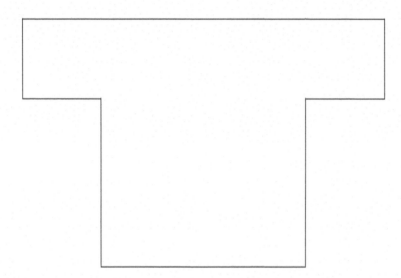

5. Read the selected text out loud to your students or have them read it independently. After reading, ask students what the author's main point was. Write it on the horizontal line.

6. Then ask students about the details the author presented. Write them on the vertical lines.

7. Explain to students that their job as a reader will be to determine whether the author presented their information clearly.

8. A reproducible Main Idea T can be found in the Chapter 10 Resources on the website.

COMPARING AND CONTRASTING STORIES, PLOTS, CHARACTERS, AND IDEAS WITHIN A TEXT AND BETWEEN TWO TEXTS. Much of the comprehension instruction that you do will be focused on helping students understand what is in the text, but this standard focuses on preparing students to **compare and contrast different stories or texts**. For younger students, you can begin by comparing characters within a text. For example, if you were reading a Frog and Toad story by Arnold Lobel, you could compare Frog and Toad within one story or compare what Frog or Toad did between two stories. For preschool and kindergarten students, you might want to begin helping students find similarities and differences between something familiar like animals. You might ask students to talk about how a cat and a dog are similar and different. This is fun to do for young children and a wonderful building block for future grades in which students ultimately are expected to analyze and compare literature and documents.

╱esson Planning: Comparing Different Texts

Students can learn to compare characters in familiar stories. There are many books with recurring characters that you read to students that can be compared. When doing this, students become more connected to the main character.

Standard: With prompting and support, compare and contrast the adventures and experiences of characters in familiar stories.

Objective: Students will be able to compare and contrast Clifford's experiences in *Clifford Goes to Kindergarten* (Bridwell, 2015) and *Clifford Takes a Trip* (Bridwell, 1966) in class discussion by using a Venn diagram.

Lesson Idea: Draw a Venn diagram on the board. Write *Clifford Goes to Kindergarten* in the left section and *Clifford Takes a Trip* on the right section. Tell students that both books are about Clifford and that you can compare Clifford's adventures between the books. Read the two books aloud one right after the other. Conduct a class discussion asking students if there were any similarities between what Clifford experienced in both books. Write those ideas in the intersecting section of the Venn diagram. Then ask students what was different. Record students' ideas in the corresponding sections of the diagram.

Assessment: Using a class list of your students, place a checkmark next to each student's name who answered correctly with a similarity or difference between Clifford's adventures. Place a minus next to students' names who answered incorrectly or off topic.

Scoring Criteria: Students who have three or four checkmarks and zero or one minus mark are able to compare and contrast a character's adventures between two books. Students who have fewer than three or four checkmarks or who have more than one minus mark need additional instruction on this standard.

Reading Levels and Text Complexity

Many states and districts have the goal of having all students read at grade level by the end of third grade, but if you are teaching preschool or kindergarten, don't worry. You'll be using **developmentally appropriate lessons** so that students can reach this goal by third grade. There will be some students who are able to comprehend by the end of third grade and some who will struggle (Allington & McGill-Franzen, 2017). An appropriate goal for kindergarten would be to "actively engage in group reading activities with purpose and understanding." For young children, your goal will be to conduct read alouds and help every student engage with the story. As you will observe in your placements, some students have a hard time paying attention when you read. Your goal in preschool and kindergarten will be for all students to be engaged in the story and to be able to answer simple questions as you read. In first grade a standard might be, "with prompting and support, read prose and poetry of appropriate complexity for grade 1." In first grade you will not be expecting all students to read first grade materials independently, but with support. You can see how the standards encourage you to scaffold student reading so that students can begin reading independently at grade level by second or third grade.

MEASURING READING LEVELS. It makes sense that students improve reading comprehension as they move through the grades, but you might be asking how reading levels are measured. As a classroom teacher probably the most common way will be for you to check the reading level on the back cover of the book. For example, the back cover might have RL 1, which means first grade reading level. Although this isn't perfect, it will give you an idea of a book's reading level.

Margin Note 10.8: The Lexile® Framework for Reading

https://www.youtube.com/watch?v=IUznnqghDAE

Reading levels on books are not the same as **leveled readers**. In general, leveled readers are described using the following: Guided Reading books run from A to Z, with A being easiest. **Developmental Reading Assessment** (DRA) begins with level A and switches to numerical numbers that range from 1–80. **Lexile®** also evaluates books for difficulty and ranges from 200L–1700L. We will discuss leveling books in Chapter 12, but it would be good for you to have an understanding about how reading levels are determined before we present those ideas. Look at the video in Margin Note 10.8 to learn about the Lexile® Framework. Talk with your mentor teacher to find out how reading levels are determined in your placement and whether Lexile® is used in your district.

ASSESSING A STUDENT'S READING LEVEL. To determine whether students can read grade-appropriate materials, your school might give **standardized tests**. Or, you can find out whether students can read at grade level by administering an **informal reading inventory**, such as the *Basic Reading Inventory* (Johns, Elish-Piper, & Johns, 2017), or you can give **Informal Graded Passage Reading** as described in Assessment Strategy 10.2. The information you get from these kinds of assessments provides you with the student's ability to read grade-level passages independently, at the instructional level, or at the frustration level as we discussed in Chapter 4. For example, if a second grade student is able to read the first grade passage independently, the second grade passage at the instructional level, and is scored at the frustration level with the third grade passage, that lets you know that this student should be able to read most second grade material with support. That student might need first grade material for free reading time. The Informal Graded Passage Reading in Assessment Strategy 10.2 can give you an approximation of how well a student can read materials at different grade levels.

Assessment Strategy 10.2: Informal Graded Passage Reading

Purpose: The Informal Passage Reading assessment is designed to give you information about a student's ability to read connected text.

Procedures:

1. Choose a passage that you think the student can read. The passages range from Easy Sight Word Passage Reading through grade 3. (Passages can be found in the Chapter 10 Resources on the website.)

2. Duplicate the corresponding Record Sheet. (Record sheets can be found in the Chapter 10 Resources on the website.)

3. Activate the student's background knowledge by saying:

   Read the title to yourself and look at the pictures. Then tell me what you think this story will be about.

4. Informally evaluate the extent of the student's background knowledge and record an X along the continuum on the record sheet.

5. Ask the student to read the story to you.

6. When the student has finished reading, ask the comprehension questions that can be found on the record sheet or invite a retelling of the story. Record a plus (+) for correct responses and a minus (−) for incorrect responses.

7. If the student was successful, present the next passage. Continue administering graded passages until the student is unable to answer more than half of the comprehension questions.

8. Use the scoring guide on the record sheet to determine the level of passage the student can read at the instructional level. This is the reading level that should be used for instructional materials. (You can review the meaning of instructional level of reading from Chapter 4.)

9. The following is a passage and record sheet for pre-primer reading.

(continued)

Pre-primer Record Sheet

My Dog

I have a dog.

My dog is Spark.

Spark is a big dog.

He plays ball.

I play with Spark.

Spark is a fun dog.

Pre-primer Word Passage Reading

Name _____ Date _____

My Dog

I have a dog.

My dog is Spark.

Spark is a big dog.

He plays ball.

I play with Spark.

Spark is a fun dog.

(Pre-primer) Activating Background:
Read the title to yourself and look at the pictures. Then tell me what you think this story will be about.

T 1. ____ What is the story mostly about? (a dog; Spark)

F 2. ____ What is the dog's name? (Spark)

F 3. ____ What does Spark do? (play ball)

E 4. ____ Why do you think Spark is a fun dog? (any logical response; because he likes to play ball)

I 5. ____ What other things might Spark like to do? (any logical response)

V 6. ____ What is a dog? (any logical response; an animal; a pet)

Questions Missed ▢

THINKING PROCESSES. As you think about how to get students engaged in reading and able to read independently, you should consider the role of thinking processes during reading. As students read, they activate prior knowledge, make predictions, and make connections. These thinking processes can be folded into any of the standards, or they can be addressed separately. All of these strategies, however, will help promote your students' comprehension development.

ACCESSING PRIOR KNOWLEDGE. Everyone, even young children, has **prior knowledge**. The ability to access that knowledge before reading can deepen comprehension. Of course, children will be building background knowledge during their lives, through school, and at home. Sometimes we hear teachers say that their students "don't have any background knowledge." What they are really saying is that the background knowledge of students, especially those from cultures different from the one represented in the curriculum, may not match that of the topics they learn in school. Moll et al. (1992) found that students bring "funds of knowledge" to learning that are valuable. **Funds of knowledge** can be defined as the skills and knowledge that families have historically and culturally developed to enable them to function in their culture. Some teachers fill out something like the Funds of Knowledge Inventory Matrix (see Figure 10.2) as a reference when they teach. For example, say Maria recently arrived from Guatemala. You might ask whether the family has any of the local currency (i.e., Quetzal) and whether they might show that currency to the class. During math, you could use the Quetzal to show different types of currency. For older students, you could explain how currency from other countries is compared to the U.S. dollar. These kinds of activities can help students feel that their prior knowledge is valued, especially if it is different from other students' knowledge. It will be up to you to respect all of the prior knowledge that students bring to school while you are helping them build knowledge that will help them develop comprehension of school texts. Teaching Strategy 10.11 can help students access prior knowledge.

Figure 10.2. Funds of Knowledge Inventory Matrix

Funds of Knowledge	Home/Community Practices	Classroom Application
Economics		
Geography		
Politics		
Agriculture		
Sports		
Technology		
Religion		
Language		
Health		
Childcare		
Art		
Cooking		
Entertainment		

Teaching Strategy 10.11: Accessing Prior Knowledge

Purpose: To help students activate their prior knowledge before reading.

Procedures:

1. Tell students that before they read they should think about what they know about the topic. Explain that they might have knowledge from watching television or movies, from their families, from school, or from other experiences.

2. Select a book that you will be reading aloud or that students will be reading, such as *Amazing Whales!* (Thomson, 2006).

3. Show students the book and say something like the following:

   > Amazing Whales! *is an informational book about whales. Since the book is about whales, I'll write the word* whales *on the board. Before I read the book to you, we need to remember as much as we can about whales. That will help us learn more when we read. Think about what you know about whales. It could be from a television program, from your family or experiences, or from school.*

4. Have students volunteer anything they know about whales. Write their prior knowledge on the board underneath the word *whales*.

5. Read the book to students.

6. After reading, discuss how the brainstormed list of prior knowledge helped students comprehend what they learned from the new text.

MAKING PREDICTIONS. Prediction strategies help increase students' comprehension of text. When students predict before reading a story, they activate their prior knowledge and form purposes for reading. During reading, prediction strategies allow students to generate many possibilities for meaning they can confirm, modify, or discard as they find more information.

Students naturally make predictions in the lives of their families. You might consider reminding students of the predictions they already make. For example, if students watch baseball on television, they might have heard a family member say, "The Cubs are going to win!" That's a prediction. Or perhaps your students have heard someone say, "I'll bet Uncle Dan will be late to Thanksgiving dinner." That's also a prediction. We make predictions all the time, and you can help students relate this natural activity to reading.

As you help students develop their ability to make predictions, remind them that they will not always be correct. One of the obstacles students encounter when making predictions is that some students don't like to be wrong. Help students feel emotionally safe when making predictions by reminding them that many predictions they make when reading will not happen. As an example, you might remind them about a family member saying, "The Cubs are going to win!" Remind them that oftentimes this prediction does not happen and to remember to make prediction while reading as in Teaching Strategy 10.12.

MAKING CONNECTIONS. Students who make a wide range of connections during reading have more possibilities for meaning making. Hartman (1992) first described how readers make connections and suggested that the most frequent connections are text-to-self, text-to-text, and text-to-world. Therefore, students who make connections to their personal experiences, to other texts, and to outside experiences often are able to build deeper comprehension of text. Making connections also builds interest and motivation. If students can find a connection from their experiences to texts, they are more likely to enjoy reading.

Making connections is a natural activity, even for young children. Think again about what happens in discussions with young children. When you talk or read a book, it's not uncommon for a child to raise their hand and tell you about a connected experience. Although making connections of text-to-self seems to be natural for children, your students may need explicit instruction in ways to connect a text with other texts or to the outside world. Teaching Strategy 10.13 can help you support students when making connections.

Engaging with Families: Bookmark for Thinking Processes

Work with your mentor teacher to develop a bookmark for families to remind students of the thinking processes they should use when reading. Identify the processes that you and your mentor teacher think would be most useful, develop a bookmark template, and have students decorate the bookmark. Prepare a lesson that shows students how to use the bookmark before sending it home.

Here are questions for a sample bookmark to consider.

I predict . . .
This reminds me of . . .
I'm picturing . . .
This is like . . .
I found out . . .
I wonder about . . .
What happened was . . .
I like the part . . .
Why did . . .?

Teaching Strategy 10.12: Directed Reading-Thinking Activity (DR-TA)

Purpose: To help students explicitly make predictions during reading.

Procedures:

1. For the Directed Reading-Thinking Activity (Stauffer, 1969), select a story or a passage that students have not read or heard. Show students the title and ask, "What do you think this story will be about?" Encourage students to draw upon their background knowledge to make predictions about the passage. Write the students' predictions on the board.

2. Select a portion of text for students to read. Choose a stopping point after reading a page or two.

3. Write the following questions on the board.

   - What has happened thus far in the story?
   - What do you think will happen next?
   - Why do you think so?

4. Have students discuss what has happened in the story up to the point where you stopped reading. Ask students, "What happened thus far in the story?" Write down some of the students' responses.

5. Then have students make predictions by asking, "What do you think will happen next?" Tell students that by answering this question they are making predictions about what will happen. Write some of the predictions on the board if appropriate.

6. Encourage students to justify their predictions by asking the follow-up question, "Why do you think so?" Encourage thinking that relates what students learned from the story thus far to their predictions.

7. Remind students that they should make predictions as they read and be prepared to revise their predictions as needed as they continue reading.

Teaching Strategy 10.13: Making Connections

Purpose: To guide students in expanding the types of connections they make before, during, and after reading both narrative and informational texts in order to expand comprehension.

Procedures:

1. Tell students that during reading they need to periodically stop and make connections, but the connections they make for stories could be different from those of informational texts.

2. Tell students that there are three main ways to make connections: text-to-self, text-to-text, and text-to-world. (Adapt wording as necessary or omit this step for young children.)

3. Begin reading a story to your students. Divide the class into pairs of students so that each student has time to share.

4. Encourage students to make connections to themselves by using the following prompts:
   - What does this remind me of?
   - What is this similar to in my life?
   - How is this different from my life?
   - Has something like this ever happened to me?
   - What were my feelings when I read this?

5. Tell students that they can connect to their lives, their families, their friends, things they have seen, feelings they have had, places they have seen, and so on. Remind students that when they make connections to themselves, the connections must be true and not made up.

6. For many students, you can then ask them to make connections to other texts. Explain to students that they can make connections using these prompts:
   - What does this remind me of in another book I've read?
   - How is this text similar to other things I've read?
   - How is this different from other books I've read?
   - Have I read about something like this before?

7. Tell students that they can make connections to characters, plots, settings, themes, and authors for stories. Students can make connections to main ideas, topics, and details for informational texts.

8. Finally, tell students that they should connect what they read to the world around them. You can do this by using the following prompts:
   - What does this remind me of in the real world?
   - How is this text similar to things that happen in the real world?
   - How is this different from things that happen in the real world?
   - How did that part relate to the world around me?

9. Remind students that "the real world" could be things they've seen on television, heard on radio, read, or heard in other conversations.

10. Encourage students to make a variety of connections when they hear stories or read on their own.

What Do You Believe about Comprehension Instruction?

Now that you've learned about comprehension instruction, consider what you believe about it. Do you think that you, as a teacher, can foster comprehension? Do you agree with the strategies that we presented in this chapter? Think about the important takeaways from this chapter and write the ones that are personally important to you on the What Do You Believe template that can be found in the Resources for Chapter 10 on the website. Then write a brief paragraph about what you believe about comprehension instruction as a result of what you learned.

Closing Thoughts

Sometimes people think that comprehension can't be taught since reading comprehension is a thinking process. We believe, however, that there are thinking processes that can be developed using the strategies we presented in this chapter. All children make predictions, for example, and when you model and demonstrate how they can make predictions when reading or listening, that helps develop reading comprehension.

In the real-life example in the beginning of the chapter, you met Trevor who was aware of the need for comprehension instruction for the students in his placement. He recognized that PreK–3 students need age-appropriate comprehension instruction to build a strong foundation for their reading development. This is what we hope you have learned from this chapter as well.

Takeaways from Chapter 10

- Comprehension, not merely pronouncing words, is the goal of all reading.
- Children need to read a variety of different kinds of texts, including narrative texts, informational texts, and poetry.
- Children benefit from reading about people and places different from themselves.
- All students come to you with background knowledge that should be valued and used in comprehension.
- Comprehension instruction should include teaching students how to read for key ideas and details, craft and structure, integration of knowledge and ideas, and text complexity.
- How difficult a text is for students to read is often measured with a reading level.
- Thinking processes, such as accessing prior knowledge, making predictions, and making connections, help students develop reading comprehension.

To Learn More about Comprehension Instruction

Close Reading

Lehman, C., & Roberts, K. (2014). *Falling in love with close reading*. Portsmouth, NH: Heinemann.
https://www.heinemann.com/products/e05084.aspx

Lapp, D., Moss, B., Grant, M., & Johnson, K. (2015). *A close look at close reading: Teaching students to analyze complex texts, grades K–5*. Alexandria, VA: Association of Supervision and Curriculum Development.

http://www.ascd.org/Publications/Books/Overview/A-Close-Look-at-Close-Reading-Teaching-Students-to-Analyze-Complex-Texts-Grades-K-5.aspx

We presented close reading as a way of having students read for key ideas and details. Close reading is one way to read that students should learn. These books show you how you can teach close reading to your students.

Children's Literature

Wooten, D. A., Liang, L. A., & Cullinan, B. E. (Eds.). (2018). *Children's literature in the reading program: Engaging young readers in the 21st century* (5th ed.). New York, NY: Guilford Press.

https://www.guilford.com/books/Childrens-Literature-in-the-Reading-Program/Wooten-Liang-Cullinan/9781462535767

We hope you accessed several of the book lists in this chapter. As a teacher, you'll need to continue to develop your knowledge of children's literature. This book provides you with ways to think about children's literature as well as examples of books you might want your students to read.

Informal Reading Inventory

Johns, J. L., Elish-Piper, L., & Johns, B. (2017). *Basic reading inventory: Kindergarten through grade twelve and early literacy assessments* (12th ed.). Dubuque, IA: Kendall Hunt Publishing Company.

https://he.kendallhunt.com/product/basic-reading-inventory-kindergarten-through-grade-twelve-and-early-literacy-assessments-0

We presented graded reading passages as a way to assess students' reading comprehension. You can learn more about how to assess students' reading using word lists and graded passages in this informal reading inventory.

Seminal Research on Informational Texts

Duke, N. K. (2000). 3.6 minutes per day: The scarcity of informational texts in first grade. *Reading Research Quarterly, 35*, 202–224.

https://www.jstor.org/stable/748074

This study was pivotal in increasing the amount of informational text taught in elementary classrooms. Before this study was published, teachers spent almost all of their time teaching narrative texts. When you read this article, you can learn about the background of teaching informational texts in the classroom. It's been 20 years or more since this study was published. Some people think things haven't changed. What do you think?

Directed Reading-Thinking Activity (DR–TA) Strategy

http://www.readingrockets.org/strategies/drta

This article describes the DR–TA strategy which we presented in this chapter. This strategy is one that has great utility. You can use it in many situations, such as when you are reading aloud and when students are reading independently. The article also has a video that shows you how you can use DR–TA in teaching.

Classroom Libraries

Creating a Classroom Library

http://www.readingrockets.org/article/creating-classroom-library

New York Public Library Around the World in 80+ Children's Books

https://www.nypl.org/blog/2014/07/22/around-world-childrens-books

How to Choose Outstanding Multicultural Books

https://www.scholastic.com/teachers/articles/teaching-content/how-choose-best-multicultural-books/

CCSS Appendix B Text Exemplars

http://www.corestandards.org/assets/Appendix_B.pdf

Most teachers have classroom libraries in addition to a school library. A classroom library gives students quick access to books at their reading level. This article and the websites give you some ideas about books to include in your own classroom library.

Apps

Reading Rockets: Literacy Apps for Comprehension

https://www.readingrockets.org/literacyapps/comprehension

Read the descriptions and choose three apps from this list of 12 that you would want to use in your classroom to reinforce comprehension skills. Although some are free, many are inexpensive. When you are hired as a teacher, you may want to talk with your principal about policies related to downloading apps onto school-owned devices, as well as funding for apps that require fees.

© Monkey Business Images/Shutterstock.com

These young children are exploring writing materials.

How Do I Teach Writing?

REAL-LIFE EXAMPLE

Sara had three children under the age of six when she began her student teaching in kindergarten, so she had lots of experiences with young children. When her children were toddlers, she gave them crayons and paper to play with. She noticed that each of her children scribbled on the paper when they were toddlers and that those scribbles changed into letters as the children learned their letters. Sara enjoyed seeing her own children develop writing skills, but she also wondered if she was doing the right thing by letting them explore and discover on their own. Sara was looking forward to watching her mentor teacher scaffold their students' writing.

When Sara got to her placement, she found that students rarely had time to write what they wanted. Instead, the students had worksheets with letters and words to trace. If students wrote their own messages, the teacher corrected the letters and the punctuation. Sara wondered whether this was a new approach to teaching young children or if her instincts were correct by letting her children grow as writers by practicing writing messages and stories.

Have you ever wondered what you would do if you couldn't communicate in writing? Think about the literacy list you created in Chapter 1 that contained the reading you do on a daily basis. Well, how about writing? Your world is filled with writing, such as text messages, your Twitter feed, or writing papers for school. Writing is the way we communicate to others when we aren't talking to them. It's a very important method of communication, one that you will be privileged to teach your PreK–3 students.

Writing can be taught in a similar method to teaching reading. You'll need to scaffold your students' experiences with writing, as you introduce them to the knowledge and skills they need. In this chapter we'll focus on the theory of emergent writing, which means that students need to explore the world through writing to grow into literacy. We'll show you how children tend to write their names as their first experience with writing and how you can leverage that experience in your classroom. From there we'll explain how you can encourage and scaffold writing through practice writing activities, writing to learn, and moving through the writing process. As you learn about how to teach writing, you might also pick up some ideas that can improve your own attitude toward writing and your writing ability. Sprinkled through this chapter you'll find examples of real student writing. We're going to start the chapter by interrogating the idea of writing and answering the question, "What is writing?"

What Is Writing?

Writing is a **method of communication that conveys meaning**. You may have heard the idea that writing is just "talk written down." In some sense, it is, but in other important ways writing is very different than talking. As you know, when we talk, we use all sorts of nonverbal cues to express our meaning. We may gesture with our hands, use facial expressions, and use the tone of our voices to get our meaning across to our listeners. Since readers can't take advantage of verbal cues, writing is different than speech and needs to more precisely convey what the writer wants to communicate.

Writing is also a **composing process** that is shaped by the decisions writers make as they identify their writing purposes, decide on format, and clarify their thoughts and ideas. Writing is like cooking soup, designing a web page, or painting a picture. It follows a process but allows for spontaneity and creativity. Writing is, therefore, both an art and a craft.

Writing is an **expression of the writer's ideas**, and it is also a **group of skills to be taught** (Britton et al., 1975). Writing can be highly creative, and, at the same time, it can be highly conventional. When writers write, words can flow so quickly that each sentence is a surprise, and the writing is thoroughly satisfying. Or writers can deliberate, mulling over thoughts and organizing ideas into carefully crafted groups of words. Often writers have moments of inspiration and moments of deliberation during the same writing event.

What that means to you as a teacher is that some students will have more facility with written language expression than others just like some students are better able to turn a somersault than others. However, all students can learn writing skills and are able to learn to write well enough to communicate their thoughts and feelings. It will be up to you to foster the language ability of students and teach them how language works so that they love writing and are able to produce "good" writing.

WHAT IS GOOD WRITING? This is one term we're not going to define. That's because **writing is personal and subjective**. If you think back to your literature classes, you might have experienced one teacher thinking Hemmingway's writing was the epitome of good writing whereas another teacher told you Jane Austen's books topped the list. What readers look for in writing can also be a function of culture. For example, Lisa Delpit (2006) writes about an African American student who wrote a narrative that black adults thought was lively and pleasing. The white adults didn't think the writing was very good because it wasn't topic centered and didn't follow a linear structure. Writing, therefore, is an individual expression that follows norms and rules that you'll be teaching to your students. You'll learn in this chapter how to facilitate your student's individual voices and also how to teach students to write in ways that follow your state or district writing standards.

WRITING APPREHENSION. One of the important ideas we want you to remember as you teach writing is that all writing is personal. When you write, you share your heart, mind, and soul in fixed symbols with another person. The personal aspect of writing makes it scary. When you write, you are committing your ideas to print for someone else to read. You could be wrong. You could be judged. You could be misunderstood. You lose your control over the way your writing will be interpreted. For those reasons, among others, many people fear writing, including some of your students.

Before we address how students feel about writing, let's take a moment to consider your experiences and feelings about writing. Even though you write a lot, as you found out in Chapter 1, you may still find writing anxiety producing. You may have heard the quote: "Writing is easy. All you do is stare at a blank sheet of paper until drops of blood form on your forehead" (Fowler, 2019). Have you ever felt that way? We imagine that some of you love to write, but others may suffer from **writing apprehension** or **writing anxiety**. Just so you know, we understand. Each of us has had anxiety about writing during at least one point in our lives. Being anxious about writing is common. To find out whether you have writing apprehension, you can take a quick test found in Margin Note 11.1.

So, what if you scored high on the writing apprehension test? As a teacher, you may have to teach students aspects of the curriculum that you feel are not your strength. If you scored high on the Writing Apprehension Test, you might consider trying to overcome your anxiety. If you have a writing center at your college or university, you can go there for assistance. For some general ideas about how to cope with writing anxiety, see the tips from the University of North Carolina's writing center in Margin Note 11.2. Read through these tips and decide which ones can help you feel more positive about writing.

Many of your students will also be anxious about writing. Words have power. They have the power to persuade, to soothe, to hurt, to encourage, and to make us laugh. Why, then, do so many students dread writing? Lucy Calkins (1986) suggests that many students fear writing because of the ways in which teachers teach writing in schools. Many teachers have not had a background in writing and have not learned how to teach it. Then they teach writing as they were taught: assigning meaningless writing assignments and then pointing out students' errors. It's no wonder many students don't like to write. In this chapter, we'll be presenting ideas on ways to teach writing so that your students love writing and become capable, competent writers.

Margin Note 11.1: Daly-Miller Writing Apprehension Test

https://www.csus.edu/indiv/s/stonerm/The%20Daly-Miller%20Test.htm

Calculate your score

https://www.csus.edu/indiv/s/stonerm/daly_miller_scoring.htm

Margin Note 11.2: Writing Anxiety Tips

https://writingcenter.unc.edu/tips-and-tools/writing-anxiety/

Emergent Writers

The term **emergent writers** covers a range of ages and abilities—from children just learning to hold a crayon and making a mark on a page to children writing letters that represent the sounds in a word they want to write. The term describes the stage of writing in which children are just learning what writing is all about and how to go about it.

Young children learn to write as they read, write, and explore language and writing materials. Scribbles and drawings are a child's first venture into writing, and they serve as an important foundation for later writing development (Calkins, 1986). Young children need the opportunity to explore, scribble, pretend to write, invent messages, copy important words, write labels, write their names, and write messages for their own purposes. Exploration is essential for young children to develop an understanding and awareness of writing and its forms and uses. Wide reading is also an important component of early writing development because it helps children learn about language, story structure, and print conventions in meaningful contexts. Children also learn a great deal about letter–sound associations in conjunction with their attempts at writing because they apply what they're learning about phonics as they sound out words and experiment with spelling. As children gain more experience with writing, they begin to write in different forms and use drawing, play, and social talk in their writing (Dyson, 2001). You can see an example of a young child's writing in Figure 11.1.

Figure 11.1. **Young Child's Writing**

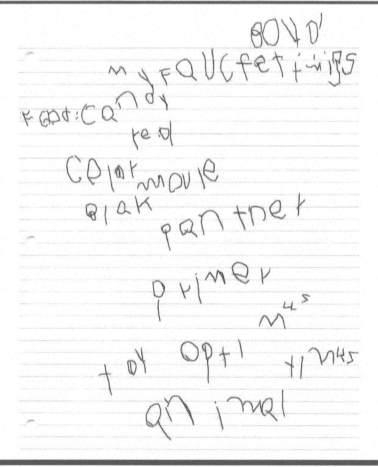

Young children experiment with writing long before they enter school. Picking up a crayon, marker, or pencil, and making scribbles on paper is fascinating for a 2- or 3-year old child. A more formal introduction to writing occurs when children enter preschool or kindergarten. They are no longer in complete control of their writing, and sometimes what is presented in lessons conflicts with concepts and ideas that they have developed at home. Because children have a definite set of unique experiences with writing before formal instruction begins, you will need to be sensitive to the tension that this can create. When teachers provide children with many examples of writing, model how to write, and think aloud as they write, young children become accustomed to more formal ways of expressing themselves (Schickedanz, 2018).

Teachers need to teach writing with the same time, energy, and resourcefulness as they do reading (Morrow & Gambrell, 2019). They need to provide young children with demonstrations of how writing works, opportunities to practice new skills, and guidance to move children along in their development. These writing experiences can help young children improve their early literacy outcomes (Hall, Simpson, Guo, & Wang, 2015). Young children also need encouragement to continue their natural desire to communicate through writing.

NAME WRITING. Researchers have found that the letters in a child's first name play an important part in their literacy development (Hildreth, 1936). **Name writing** empowers emergent writers and provides an entry point through which they gain insights into written language. According to Clay (1975), a child's "name is likely to be the most highly motivating word they want to write" (p. 46). Therefore, name writing is an excellent place to begin a children's writing instruction.

Before you begin a name writing activity, you should make sure of the name students want to be called. Many young students are called nicknames before they enter school and may not be familiar with their given name. Furthermore, you will have a class roster with a formal name, such as Reginald. Perhaps the child wants to be called Reggie. You might check with parents or family members to make sure you are using the name in name writing activities that fits the student best.

Once students know their names, they tend to write their names before attempting to write almost anything else. They first recognize the initial capital letter as "their name" and pay little attention to what comes after it. This initial letter is generally the first one that children associate with a sound. Later, as children's name writing improves, they begin to notice the other letters in their names and use them to create new words. From there, children's writing usually expands to include the names of their classmates, siblings, and other familiar words (Bloodgood, 1999).

When children enter kindergarten, a **sign-in activity**, in which students sign their names to indicate attendance, may be their first introduction to a specific purpose for writing. When teachers use the names on the sign-in sheet to check attendance, children begin to understand that writing their names represents them and their presence at school. It also demonstrates the fact that what they write can be read by others and translated into speech. You can see a demonstration of how one teacher teaches name writing in Margin Note 11.3. Teaching Strategy 11.1 shows you how to teach the sign-in strategy. A sample of a student who wrote her name can be found in Figure 11.2.

Margin Note 11.3:
Teaching Children to Write Their Names

https://www.youtube.com/watch?v=spHNSrJrdbU

Teaching Strategy 11.1: Signing In

Purpose: To have students write their names each day to practice their writing and learn that writing communicates a message; in this case, to show they are present in class.

Procedures:

1. Prepare a large, unlined sheet of paper with the date at the top. Place it on a table that is easily accessible to students. Provide plenty of sharpened pencils.

2. Explain to students that when they come into the classroom, they should write their names on a sign-in sheet. Demonstrate by holding up the paper and writing your name at the top. Tell them that you will know who is at school each day by reading the names on the sheet.

3. Since some young students are unable to write their names or may know only part of their names, be sure to stand at the table and note the order the students sign in until you are able to read or recognize each name. Read the names on the sign-in sheet aloud once students are at their desks or on the rug. Reading their names demonstrates the importance of name writing and the idea that writing can be translated into spoken language.

4. Once the sign-in strategy is routine, have students take over reading the sheet to take attendance. You may need to assist them in reading the names at first; however, this activity provides a strong incentive for students to begin to recognize classmates' names.

5. Keep the dated sign-in sheets and assess them periodically through the year. They provide valuable information on students' developing awareness of print and ability to write their names.

6. Conference with students throughout the year on what they have accomplished and show the progress they have made.

7. Once students are able to sign in with their names, ask students a question, such as, "Do you like carrots?" or, "What is your favorite color?" Draw a column to the right of their names for students to answer the question.

Figure 11.2. Name Writing

ℓ**esson Planning:** Name Writing

Some students will come to you with experience writing their names, but others will need many opportunities to write their names before they are successful. Students need to learn to write their names accurately as one of their first writing assignments in school.

Standard: Write name after being given the first letter.

Objective: The students will be able to write their names independently after being given the first letter of their name.

Lesson Idea: Create Bingo cards for the class by dividing a piece of paper into six squares. Divide the class into groups of six. Write the first letter of the name of each of the six students in one square per letter. After one student is finished, have them give the paper to another student. Ask students to write their names in the blank with the first letter of their name and repeat until all the names are written. After the Bingo cards are complete, play Bingo with the class using students' names.

Assessment: Read each of the cards to determine whether the names are spelled correctly.

---

*C*onnection to the Field: Name Writing

If you are teaching in a preschool or kindergarten, you can help students write their names in various media. For example, you could work with students to write their names in glue and color over the hardened glue to make prints. You can also have students write their names in salt or sand trays. Work with your mentor teacher to think of other ways students can get practice writing their names.

INTERACTIVE WRITING. Interactive writing provides emergent writers with the opportunity to **share the pen** and write with varying degrees of teacher support. It's a process in which the teacher and the children create a text together. This teaching strategy establishes a risk-free venue that allows children to contribute what they know and understand. It is also a means of demonstrating new strategies and skills that children may be ready to learn (McCarrier, Fountas, & Pinnell, 2018). You can watch a teacher demonstrate interactive writing in Margin Note 11.4. Teaching Strategy 11.2 provides a description of the activity.

Margin Note 11.4: Interactive Writing

https://vimeo.com/ 168991757

Teaching Strategy 11.2: Interactive Writing

Purpose: Interactive writing can scaffold young writers as they "share the pen" with the teacher. During this activity, teachers and students compose a message together with the teacher providing information about letters and sounds that are unfamiliar to the students. Students can then co-construct a text successfully that would be difficult for them to complete independently.

Procedures:

1. Choose a common experience or a familiar story to use as the basis for your interactive writing. An example might be a recent field trip, a special event such as a birthday, a visitor to the class, or a story that students have read or heard.

2. Gather a large piece of paper to tape on the board. Alternatively, you can write on a white board.

3. Suggest a topic for a text that helps students understand, summarize, or comment on an event. Ask students for ideas about what to write, such as in the following:

   We have just finished a story about a special penguin. I would like us to write about this story. Who would like to tell me what happened in the story? Marta said that Tacky saved the other penguins. Let's write that together.

4. Co-construct the letters as you write the text, drawing on the students' and your combined knowledge of the letters and sounds that comprise each word of the sentence you are writing. Here's an example of what you could say:

   Let's start with the name of the penguin, Tacky. Who knows what letter/sound Tacky begins with? That's right, Eric. Would you come up and write a T on our paper? Great. Now what comes next? What makes a sound that comes after T?

5. Scaffold students' learning by demonstrating how to stretch out each word and listen for the sounds that comprise it. Ask students to contribute what they know and help them with letters they don't know yet.

6. Continue writing with your students to complete a message or a story summary.

7. Read the piece of writing aloud with students.

ASSESSING EMERGENT WRITERS. You learned about the purposes of assessment in Chapter 4. Identifying what your students are able to do will help you prepare your teaching lessons. You might think that emergent writers need to learn so much that you don't need to assess what they can do. However, a group of emergent writers will have very different skill sets. Some of your students may have had hours of drawing and writing experience at home whereas others will have had very little. That means that your young students will need different kinds and amounts of instruction. Some may need reminders of the directionality of writing. Others will be ready for help on hearing the sounds associated with letters as they write. A short writing assessment, such as is described in Assessment Strategy 11.1, will give you this kind of information. In addition, you can give this assessment periodically to monitor your students' progress.

Practicing Writing

Students need to write every day. Writing on a daily basis encourages children to explore writing as a means of communication and expression. Daily writing, however, should not be interpreted to mean drills on letter recognition or handwriting practice. Instead, it means providing opportunities for children to learn about and use the tools they need to become writers for authentic purposes, with choices of topics that are based on their interests. Daquan eagerly writes about his pet turtle so he can share with the class, and Sheila wants to write a letter to her parents telling them why she thinks they should get a dog. Providing time to experiment with new ideas, skills, strategies, and structures helps students develop into confident, motivated writers.

Think for a moment about a skill you have learned or that you watched a child learn. For example, think about learning to play the cello. Imagine for a moment taking the cello in your arms and lifting your bow to the strings. Then imagine a teacher explaining the fingerings for the notes, how to read music, and how to move the bow across the strings. After being taught each one of these skills, would you be ready for a cello performance? Of course not. You need to practice, practice, practice. The same principle holds true for writing. Students need to practice writing in order to build the kind of writing fluency that good writers need.

Practice writing can also help students learn the **craft of writing**. When students have the opportunity to experiment with language in a risk-free environment, they are able to learn how to put letters together into words and how to use words to make sentences. When students practice, you may want to scaffold their writing by accepting their approximations and gently helping them move toward more precise communication. There are three ways you can provide students at all ages with writing practices: journal writing, writing in response to reading, and writing to learn (Lenski & Johns, 2004). You can decide which ones work best for the students you are teaching and how often you should use each one.

JOURNAL WRITING. Do you write in a journal regularly? If you do, what are your purposes for journal writing? For most journal writers, writing is not a process of communicating to an audience—it is a place to relive experiences, use their imagination, explore new worlds, and clarify personal beliefs. Journals are a spontaneous, unplanned means of understanding oneself (Giorgis, 2002).

Journal writing for emergent and developing writers has another benefit. It gives them a place to practice writing and helps develop **writing fluency**. Each time students write in journals, they are practicing language. They are learning how to formulate ideas, how to put those ideas into words, how to make sentences readable, and how to string together sentences to make thoughts comprehensible. Your students need time and opportunities to write. Before we discuss ways you can get students to write in journals, we would like to address what you should do if students divulge sensitive information.

Assessment Strategy 11.1: Assessing Emergent Writers

Purpose: To provide students with the opportunity to demonstrate their emergent writing skills and to give teachers information about what students can do. This assessment can help teachers make decisions about next steps in instruction.

Procedures:

1. Give student lined and unlined paper and a pencil or crayon. If possible, give student a choice of paper and writing instruments.

2. Depending on the student's age or ability, you may want to give separate directions for each task. "Write some letters for me." Then say, "How many words can you write?" Finally say, "Write a sentence for me." For older students you could say, "I'd like you to write some letters, words, and sentences."

3. After the student has finished, invite them to share what they have written. Jot down notes about what the student said.

4. For students who say, "I can't write," you might want to ask them to use "kid writing" or just to print anything. You could also suggest categories of words, such as the student's name, colors, foods, or names of pets.

5. Informally evaluate the student's writing using the areas on the record sheet that follows. Record an X on the continuum that represents your overall judgment. Compare the results of the student's writing to the progress of students at the same developmental stage.

6. A full page record sheet that you can use can be found in the Chapter 11 Resources on the website.

Writing Record Sheet

	Not Evident Low Seldom Weak Poor				Very Evident High Always Strong Excellent
Directionality					
Left to right	├———┼———┼———┼———┤				
Top to bottom	├———┼———┼———┼———┤				
Child's Name					
Knowledge of first (F) and last (L) name	├———┼———┼———┼———┤				
Letter–sound Relationships					
Represents sounds heard at word beginnings	├———┼———┼———┼———┤				
Represents sounds heard at word endings	├———┼———┼———┼———┤				
Represents sounds heard in word middles	├———┼———┼———┼———┤				
Uses vowels	├———┼———┼———┼———┤				
Writing Conventions					
Use of word boundaries	├———┼———┼———┼———┤				
Use of punctuation	├———┼———┼———┼———┤				

Writing (check one)

_____ Scribbles or "cursivelike" scribbles

_____ Letter-like formations

_____ Repeated letters, numbers, words

_____ Variety of letters, numbers, words

Overall Message Intent (check one)

_____ Child indicated no message intent or did not communicate a message.

_____ Child talked about but did not read or pretend to read what was written.

_____ Child was able to read what was written.

Teacher could make sense of writing independently.   yes   no

SENSITIVE INFORMATION. Sometimes your students will write sensitive information in their journals. If they do, please remember that teachers are mandatory reporters. That means that teachers are required to contact authorities with suspicions of child abuse, neglect, self-harm, or harming others. For you, that means that if you read something in a child's journal that could be evidence of abuse or neglect, you should immediately contact your mentor teacher. Your mentor teacher will determine what to do next. Although you should take everything a child writes seriously, there might be times in which a child is telling a made-up story. It is your mentor teacher's responsibility to talk with the child and decide if that is the case. If you do have this experience, you might want to document the steps you took and let one of your instructors know about the situation. You can learn more about mandatory reporters in Margin Note 11.5.

Margin Note 11.5: Mandatory Reporters of Child Abuse and Neglect

https://www.childwelfare.gov/pubpdfs/manda.pdf

SELECTING JOURNAL TOPICS. Just telling students to write in journals may not work. Some students will ask, "What do I write?" You can help students create a list of journal topics by researching what other teachers have used and applying those lists to your placement. Teaching Strategy 11.3 shows you the steps you can take to have students write in journals. You can see an example of student writing to the topic of "What do you do when it rains?" in Figure 11.3.

Figure 11.3. Student Writing

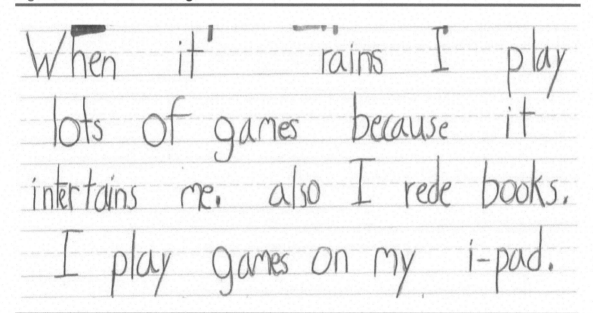

When it rains I play lots of games because it intertains me. also I rede books. I play games on my i-pad.

Connection to the Field: Developing a List of Journal Topics

You can find many lists of journal topics on the internet. Identify two or three lists that seem appropriate for the students in your placement and cull the list to 10–15 topics that you think would be motivating for your students. Show your list to your mentor teacher and ask for feedback and additional ideas. Ask your mentor teacher if you could present the list to students during journal writing time.

Teaching Strategy 11.3: Journal Writing

Purpose: Journal writing can provide students with a place and purpose to practice their writing. Teachers can give students potential topics for journal entries. Students may also come up with their own topics. Journals can be shared with others or kept private.

Procedures:

1. Tell students that they will be writing in personal journals at least three times each week. Explain that personal journals are places to record thoughts, feelings, and ideas.

2. Read the book *Diary of a Worm* (Cronin, 2003) which is an example of a journal written by a worm that describes its life.

3. Provide students with blank notebooks or have them bring them from home. Tell students that these notebooks are their own personal places to write. Explain that, even though the personal journals will be students' own private possessions, you cannot guarantee that no one will read them. Tell students that they should not write anything that is so personal that it cannot be shared with their classmates.

4. Tell students to begin keeping lists of writing topics. Help students create lists by providing them with ideas for journal topics.

5. Each week give students 10 minutes to brainstorm additional writing topics. Divide the class into groups of three or four students. Have students brainstorm ideas for their personal journals. Encourage students to add to their lists at other times during the week.

6. Provide students with 5–15 minutes three times a week to write in their personal journals. During journal writing time, provide the class with an optional journal topic. Tell students that they can write about this topic or choose one of their own. Give students a minute or two to decide on their topic before they begin to write.

7. After all students have decided on a journal topic, give them 5–15 minutes to write. Encourage students to write whatever comes to their minds.

8. Tell students that you will not be grading their journals but that you will be reading some of the entries. Develop a system in which you read each student's journal at least once a week. Consider responding to the journal entries with an encouraging message on a sticky note.

Family message journals (Woolman-Bonilla, 2000) are notebooks in which children write a message to their families each day about something they did in school, and a family member writes a message in reply. Their families learn about school experiences and are offered the opportunity to reply to the children.

RESPONDING TO READING. If you remember the **transactional theory of reading** described in Chapter 2, you'll remember that reading is a construction of meaning through an interaction with the text, the reader, and the context. Teachers often have students respond to reading through discussions, but you can also have young children respond to reading through picture drawing and writing.

When students **write in response to stories or books** that they have read or heard, they begin to listen to their hearts as they read. Stories have the power to reach our emotions, to help us understand life, and to give us ideas about how to live. As students read or hear stories, they begin to identify their thoughts and feelings with the characters and the plot. When this happens, students can reach deeper levels of comprehension about the text. Writing in response to literature, therefore, can help students construct meanings of texts while promoting writing fluency. It also helps students understand that their feelings are important as well as understanding what the author has written. They may love a story so much that they want to use it as a mentor text and create their own story using the same kinds of features, so they are attempting to write in the same style as their favorite author.

It's important for you to give students a variety of response activities to try. When engaged in different response activities, students think in different ways. For example, if students draw a picture about what a character would do next in a story, students will use their imaginations to think of potential future events. When students write a newspaper article about one of the characters, they are delving deeper into the character in the book. Figure 11.4 includes some possible response ideas. You can add to this list by thinking of ideas yourself. Teaching Strategy 11.4 shows you the steps you can take to have students respond to reading by writing a two-column response chart.

Figure 11.4. Response Ideas

1. Draw a picture about your favorite part of the story.
2. Make a storyboard about the plot.
3. Write a journal entry from one of the characters.
4. Compose a song about the story.
5. Create a collage about the story.
6. Write a letter to a friend about the story.
7. Write a different ending to the story.
8. Write a play about the main character.
9. Write a news article about one of the characters.
10. Develop a commercial for the story.

Teaching Strategy 11.4: Two-column Response Chart

Purpose: Two-column response charts are designed for students to think more deeply about specific things authors write in stories. Authors often include ideas embedded within the text. A two-column response chart provides students with an avenue to identify quotations that interest them and a chance to write their reactions to the quotations.

Procedures:

1. Tell students that different readers will construct different meanings from the same text. Tell students that they can identify and respond to sentences from texts using a two-column response chart.

2. Introduce the two-column response chart by showing students a completed chart similar to the example that follows. Point out the ideas that were chosen from the text, *Spacebusters: The Race to the Moon* (Wilkinson, 1998) and the response.

Ideas from the Text	Responses
The spacecraft was traveling 25,000 miles per hour.	I can't even imagine how fast that is. When I'm in a car traveling 65 mph, I think that's fast. What could that feel like?
Armstrong collected moon rocks and moon dust.	I wonder where the moon rocks are. Probably at the space center or in a museum. I'm going to look this up.

3. Give students a two-column chart or have them divide a piece of paper in half. On the left side of the paper have them write "Ideas from the Text" or "Quotations from the Text." On the right side, have them write "Responses."

4. Tell students that as they read, they should identify ideas or quotations that interest them and write them on their chart.

5. After students have written at least three ideas, they should write their responses to each of them.

6. When students are finished reading and writing, divide the class into groups of three or four students and have them share what they have written.

7. A full page two-column response chart that you can use with students can be found in the Chapter 11 Resources on the website.

LEARNING THROUGH WRITING. There is one more way students can practice writing, and that's through writing about what they have learned. How many of you have written exit cards at the end of class? That's when the teacher has you write a sentence or two about something you learned in class. That's an example of documenting your learning through writing. Think about what happens as you write an exit card. You have to think about the lesson, summarize your learning, and possibly answer a specific question. When young students participate in this kind of writing, they are also developing their writing skills through practice.

Having students **write in order to learn** is a powerful learning tool, both in content area learning and for writing instruction. When students write in order to learn, they wrestle with new terms and concepts and learn how to draw them or write them in sentences. Students learn to become fluent not only by writing but also in the contexts for their writing. It helps students process information. Asking students to record what they have learned helps them understand what they know (Fulwiler, 1987).

We're sure you've had this experience. You listen to a lecture or you read about a topic in your textbook, but you don't really understand until you have to write about it. That's because when you write, you are processing the information. Let's bring this back to your teaching. Let's say you are teaching about plants and show students that plants need soil, water, sunlight, and air to grow. If you ask students to write these components and draw a picture, they are more likely to remember them.

We're going to show you two strategies that you may be familiar with in other contexts. Teaching Strategy 11.5 shows you how to have young children write exit cards, and Teaching Strategy 11.6 shows you how you can have students use K-W-L (Ogle, 1986) as writing practice. You can see a student's first page of a report on penguins in Figure 11.5.

Figure 11.5. Student Report

Teaching Strategy 11.5: Exit Cards

Purpose: Exit cards provide students with an opportunity to summarize and write what they have learned from a lesson. Both the mental activity of summarizing and the act of writing are excellent methods of learning.

Procedures:

1. After students have read a text, completed a lesson, or watched a video, explain that you will be asking them to write what they have learned on an exit card. Tell students that exit cards are required for them to leave the room, hence the name.

2. Hand out index cards or small pieces of paper to students.

3. Remind students about the text they have read or the lesson you have taught. For example, if you taught students about the state you live in, tell students to think about what they learned in the lesson today.

4. If necessary, have students talk in groups to discuss and summarize what they learned. Then ask students to share their responses. Make sure that students talk only about what they learned in the lesson today.

5. Have students write one or two sentences about what they learned on their exit cards.

6. After you have collected the exit cards, sort them into groups of acceptable/correct responses and those that are not. If you have a small number of students who did not show learning, reteach the topic to those students. If many students did not understand the lesson, reteach the concept.

© stockfour/Shutterstock.com

These students are writing what they have learned on exit cards.

Teaching Strategy 11.6: K-W-L Journal

Purpose: K-W-L (Ogle, 1986) is a popular strategy to use before, during, and after a unit. Often teachers use K-W-L as a whole class activity and write student responses on a chart. You can provide students with an additional opportunity to write themselves when you have students write K-W-L responses in a journal.

Procedures:

1. Tell students that they will be writing in their journals using a new format, the K-W-L. Explain that K stands for what they already **know**, the W stands for what they **want** to know, and the L stands for what they've **learned**.

2. Select a topic for a unit that you will be teaching to demonstrate the use of the K-W-L journal. For example, let's say you were teaching about weather, specifically cloud formations.

3. Ask students what they already know about clouds. Ask probing questions such as what experiences students have had, what they know from observations, and what they might have seen on the weather channel.

4. Tell students to label the page "What I Know about Clouds." Encourage students to write what they know, either in a list or in a paragraph.

5. Then ask students what they want to know about clouds or what they wonder about. Give students several minutes to think quietly.

6. Tell students to label the next page in their journal "What I Want to Know about Clouds." Encourage students to write what they want to know on this page.

7. Tell students that as you teach about clouds, you'll be asking them to list what they have learned. Have students label the next page in their journal "What I Learned about Clouds."

8. Give students a few minutes every day you teach about clouds to write in their K-W-L journal. Have students write what they learned each day and also give them the opportunity to go back to the "What I Want to Know about Clouds" page to record additional questions.

9. After your unit is complete, have students review all of the pages they have written in their K-W-L journal. Celebrate students' learning.

The Writing Process

Writers improve their craft when they have a real purpose, a real audience, and a real motivation to write. Writing is, after all, a way for people to communicate their thoughts and ideas to someone else. These thoughts and ideas are the content of their writing. The content of writing depends on the writer's reasons for writing, the topic of the piece, and the audience for whom the piece is written.

Writing is a process that involves several steps. Graves (1983) describes writing as a series of recursive steps: prewriting, drafting, revising, editing, and publishing. Because writing is a recursive process, children will not necessarily progress through each step of the process in order. Furthermore, young children may only engage in limited work with certain steps such as revising and editing.

Writers know that completing a piece of writing is rarely as neat as many people infer from the writing process. Writing is a messy process. When writing, writers move back and forth between writing stages as necessary. Sometimes a piece of writing takes little or no revision or editing; sometimes writers begin the process by drafting; sometimes writers edit as they write. Although you should teach the steps in the writing process, remember that writing is more complex than following steps in order. It is important to remember that your students will be in different parts of the writing process at different times. That means you need to be flexible and promote that it's okay for one student to still be drafting while another is editing. If you force students to be at the same step in the writing process on the same day, then some will be bored and lose interest while others are frustrated because they feel rushed. By recognizing that this is a messy and highly individualized process, you can work to consider organization in how to keep track of where students are in the process and who needs your guidance the most, given their individual needs in learning to navigate the writing process.

We illustrate how writing can be messy by the steps we took when writing this chapter (see Figure 11.6).

Figure 11.6. My Writing Process

Procrastination

Drafting

Feeling frustrated

Walking the dog

Writing furiously: Deadline approaching

Editing, revising, turning in to team

Think of the last time you wrote a paper. What processes did you use? Think through your process and create images for each step in the process as we did in Figure 11.6. Share with your classmates and discuss how the writing process worked for you in that instance. Compare your process to the ways your students are learning the writing process in your placement.

PURPOSES FOR WRITING. Why do people write? They write for as many different reasons as there are pieces of writing. Writers usually begin composing texts by having one or more **purposes for writing**. Their purpose may be to inform a relative about a wedding shower, to explain to the public the reasons why a school bond referendum needs to be passed, or to entertain readers with a story. Writers' purposes should be a guideline that helps writers know what to say and to keep them on target.

The nature of writing, however, resists attempts to clarify purposes. Writers can set out intending to write with the primary purpose of informing and have their writing change in midstream to that of explaining. The process of writing creates its own realities as writers use initial purposes to direct the stream of words. As writers compose, purposes may change.

All writing activities should begin with some sort of real purpose, even if that purpose changes during writing. Writers need to have some reason to write, as fuzzy as it is, before they can proceed with the process of writing. In schools, however, the purposes for writing often do not go beyond completing an assignment. Writing for an assignment rarely promotes the kinds of purposes writers should bring to writing situations. Teaching Strategy 11.7 provides you with a way to help students find purposes for writing.

© kwarkot/Shutterstock.com

People write for different purposes and for different audiences.

Teaching Strategy 11.7: Finding Reasons to Write

Purpose: There are many reasons to write. We live immersed in so much print that we often take for granted the amount of writing that is in our environment. Each piece of writing was created for a purpose. Young writers can begin to learn some of the reasons they can communicate through writing.

Procedures:

1. Tell students that there are many reasons to write. Explain to students that when they begin thinking about reasons to write, they will think of more reasons on their own.

2. Begin a class chart to develop reasons for writing and potential types of writing students can do to. Write one reason to write with a few types of writing, such as the following:

Reasons to Write	Writing I Can Do
To record events	Lists, Diaries, Autobiographies, Letters, Pictures

3. Ask students if they can think of any other types of writing that records events.

4. Each week, add another reason to write on the chart with the types of writing that correspond with the writing purpose. Have students add types of writing to the chart.

5. Encourage students to add and make suggestions for the chart through the year. Remind students to refer to this chart when they are searching for purposes to write.

6. Some examples of reasons to write and types of writing follow:

Reasons to Write	Writing I Can Do
To explain	Charts, Recipes, Brochures, Invitations, Rules, Textbooks
To persuade	Instructions, Advertisements, Signs, Warnings
To predict	Forecasts, Timetables, Graphs
To command	Directions, Rules, Warnings
To entertain	Jokes, Cartoons, Bumper stickers
To narrate	Fables, Stories, Myths
To inform	Announcements, Book jackets, Labels, Catalogues
To express appreciation	Thank you notes

GENERATING WRITING TOPICS. "I don't know what to write about." This statement, echoed by many students, actually emphasizes a very important point. Content is the essence of writing. Every other part of writing—the organization, the mechanics, the style—takes a distant second place compared with the meat of writing, the content. Helping students **generate topics for writing**, therefore, is one of the key parts of writing instruction.

The advice from many authors is to write about what you know. As you think about your students' lives and funds of knowledge (see Chapters 1 and 10), help them think about what they know. One general topic for students to write about is their personal lives, such as their family, pets, and hobbies (e.g., piano lessons, sports they play, collections).

Students can also use their imagination for topics of writing. Where creative ideas originate is still somewhat of a mystery. Some people are able to take their background experiences and knowledge and organize them in unique ways. Having students imagine topics, therefore, is not an easy instructional goal to achieve. However, students need to let their imaginations take them to new places. They need to dream. They need to invent new ideas. Students also need the freedom to find topics in their imagination as well as to write about their personal experiences. You can view more ideas about having students brainstorm writing ideas in Margin Note 11.6.

Margin Note 11.6:
How-to Writing for Kids:
Brainstorming

https://www.youtube.com/
watch?v=QXuH6TUMwlg

Engaging with Families: Parent Recommended Topics

Write a short note to parents asking them to recommend topics about which their child could write. Give a few ideas such as family events, holidays, or pets. Ask your mentor teacher if you can send home the note. After the notes are returned, staple them in the students' writing folders to give them writing ideas.

IDENTIFYING AUDIENCES. If you want to give the best possible gift to a writer, give an **audience** (Elbow, 1981). An audience is any person who reads a writer's work. Audiences can be small and private, or they can be large and public.

WRITING IS PRIMARILY A SOCIAL ACT. The main purpose of writing is to be read by another person. Students need to have a variety of real audiences for their writing because it is the audience that shapes a piece of writing. As writers visualize their audience, they decide what to include in a piece of writing, what to limit, and whether their writing needs to be academic or conversational. Young children can understand these distinctions. They can understand that their writing for their parents needs to be different from a note to a classmate.

Unfortunately, most students in schools write for one audience: the teacher. When students consistently write for the teacher as their audience, they have difficulty developing a sense of audience awareness, which is when writers think about their audiences while writing. Providing students with authentic audiences for their writing can help them understand that writing is all about communicating with others. Figure 11.7 includes a partial list of audiences that might be appropriate for your students.

Figure 11.7. Audiences for Student Writing

Other students	Students in other schools	Pen pals	Last year's teachers	Administrators
School board members	Classroom displays	Hall displays	Family members	Relatives
Community newsletters	Authors of books	City officials	Local businesses	Public libraries
Local radio show hosts	Support staff in schools	Local or state representatives	Waiting rooms in dentists' or doctors' offices	Government officials

WRITING GENRE: UNDERSTANDING ORGANIZATIONAL PATTERNS OF WRITING. When we read, we often have seemingly intuitive knowledge about what will happen next in a story. The reason why we have this is through many experiences with texts. Texts are written in **organizational patterns, called genres**, that have been developed in our society over several centuries (Donovan, 2001). Writers have refined different genres over time so that, when we read, we are aware of the directions in which the text will guide our thinking. Some of the genres that have been fairly stable over time are narrative, exposition, and persuasion.

We become aware of the patterns of texts primarily through reading and writing. As we read, we subconsciously look for texts to move in predictable direction. Writing, however, is another matter. Writers generally need to be taught the genres of texts. Inexperienced writers sometimes think that writing is simply speech written down. It's not. Writing follows accepted organizational rules so that readers can comprehend content while following the train of thought represented in the text.

NARRATIVE WRITING. **Narrative writing** is a type of writing that tells a story. A writer narrates a story or shares an experience. This organizational pattern of writing is the most intuitive for students. Even young children have heard their family members tell stories and have heard books read to them. Because telling stories is a common human experience, the pattern of narrative writing will be the easiest for your students to learn.

Narrative writing can be fiction, in which writers tell stories from their imagination, or nonfiction, in which writers tell stories about themselves or others that are based on facts. The most common of the types of nonfiction narrative in schools is the personal experience story.

Personal experience stories. "Guess what happened to me?" Students burst into classrooms on a regular basis brimming with stories about their lives. That's because students' lives are filled with events and experiences they want to share. Students love to tell stories about their lives. They tell stories about themselves, their pets, their family members, and anything else they can think of. Students love to tell stories!

Personal experience stories are a natural extension of storytelling. They are the written form of stories of an author's experiences. When students write personal experience stories, they bring their personal lives into the classroom. When students share their lives with their teachers, they reveal new sides of themselves. As a teacher, you can help students develop their personal experience stories by using Teaching Strategy 11.8. Figure 11.8 shows an example of a personal experience story. You can find a writing frame and a graphic organizer for personal experience stories in the Resources for Chapter 11 on the website.

Figure 11.8. Personal Experience Story

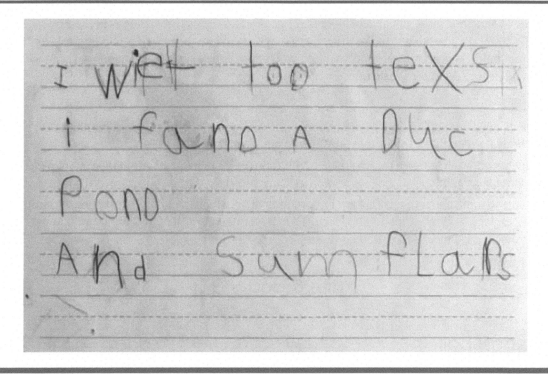

Provide students with support as they write.

Purpose: One of students' most valuable resources for generating topics for writing is in their own hearts. Nance Atwell (2002) suggests that students draw heart maps to tap into their desires and interests as possible writing topics. A heart map is simply a heart with a list of the experiences, memories, and ideas that are near and dear to the student's heart.

Procedures:

1. Tell students that they will be drawing a heart map as a resource for writing topics. Explain that a heart map is a brainstormed list of things that they care about.

2. Have students draw a heart on a piece of paper with room to write in the heart. In the center, have students write their name.

3. Ask students to think about things that are important to them which could include names of family members, hobbies, animals, friends, and so on. Then have students write those topics around their names. Provide assistance with writing as necessary.

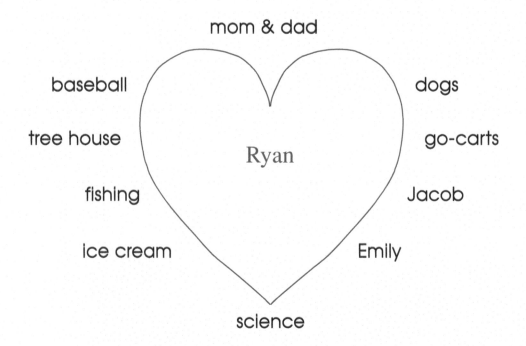

Fictional stories. **Fictional stories** have a unique structure that is similar to personal experience stories but different than expository and persuasive writing. Unlike other types of writing, fiction is not true. It is a figment of a writer's imagination. Writers can shape and develop their stories in any way they want. However, all fictional stories follow roughly the same organizational pattern.

The structure of fiction is well known to most children and adults in our society. Not only do students read and hear fictional stories, but they also view them on television and at the movies. Television stories and movies have the same elements as do print materials. Both books and movies have characters, a plot, a setting, a theme, and a point of view.

The characters of fictional stories are the people or personified animals who are the focus of the story. These characters have qualities that are revealed through their thoughts, actions, appearances, and dialogue. Stories can have a single character or many characters. The characters of fictional stories are involved in some sort of plot. The plot is the action that takes place in the story, usually in a series of events that begins with a problem to be resolved and that ends with a resolution. The problem may be as simple as deciding where to look for a lost kitten or as complex as surviving an arctic storm. Every fictional story, however, has some sort of problem to be resolved. The characters and the plot take place in a setting. The setting of a fictional story is the time and place of the story. Through the character, plot, and setting, the author of a fictional story frequently introduces a deep thought or a big idea. This thought or idea is called the theme or moral of the story. Themes also can range from simple to complex. Finally, all stories are written from a point of view. The point of view that is typically found in children's books is an outside narrator in the third person with the author relating the story using the characters' names. Some fictional stories are written as if the author is telling the story as in *Sarah, Plain and Tall* (MacLachlan, 1985). First person fictional stories seem to be true, but they're not. Teaching Strategy 11.9 will give you a way to help students outline a fictional story. Figure 11.9 shows an organizational pattern outline, writing frame, and graphic organizer for fictional stories. You can also see an example of how a student plotted a story in Figure 11.9. You can find a writing frame and a graphic organizer for fictional stories in the Resources for Chapter 11 on the website.

This teacher is helping students generate topics for writing.

Teaching Strategy 11.9: Plot Cube

Purpose: One of the most difficult aspects of writing fictional stories is organizing the elements of the genre: characters, setting, problem, action, solution, and ending. Many students begin writing but get bogged down in the details of the characters and never move on with the plot. Plot cubes can help students think about the story as a whole (and the parts that comprise it) before beginning to write.

Procedures:

1. Tell students that they will be developing the elements of a fictional story. Many students will have ideas already generated from previous lessons or from their journals. For students who are unclear about elements of fiction, show them the pictures from a wordless picture book, such as *Beaver is Lost* (Cooper, 2010). Explain to students that they can develop a story using the pictures as a guide.

2. Duplicate copies of the full-page plot cube that can be found in the Chapter 11 Resources on the website. Explain to students that they will be outlining their stories on this plot cube. Point out the areas of the plot cube: characters, setting, problem, actions, solution, and ending. Tell students that they will be using the plot cube to plan their stories.

3. Tell students that the first thing they need to consider is the setting and the characters for their story. Remind students that a setting is the time and place of the story. Have students write one or more key words for the setting on that section of the cube and then draw a picture. Then have students write key words or draw pictures of the characters.

4. Explain to students that the plot is an important component of fictional stories. Read a story to students or remind them of a story they have recently read. Discuss with students the elements of the plot, such as the problem, actions, solution, and ending.

5. Encourage students to ask questions about the elements of fictional stories.

6. Have students complete the remaining sections of the plot cube. Then have students cut the plot cube, fold the edges, and make a cube.

7. Display plot cubes in the room to illustrate fictional stories. Some students may want to write their stories after they have outlined them using a plot cube.

Figure 11.9. Storyboard of Meli at the Vet

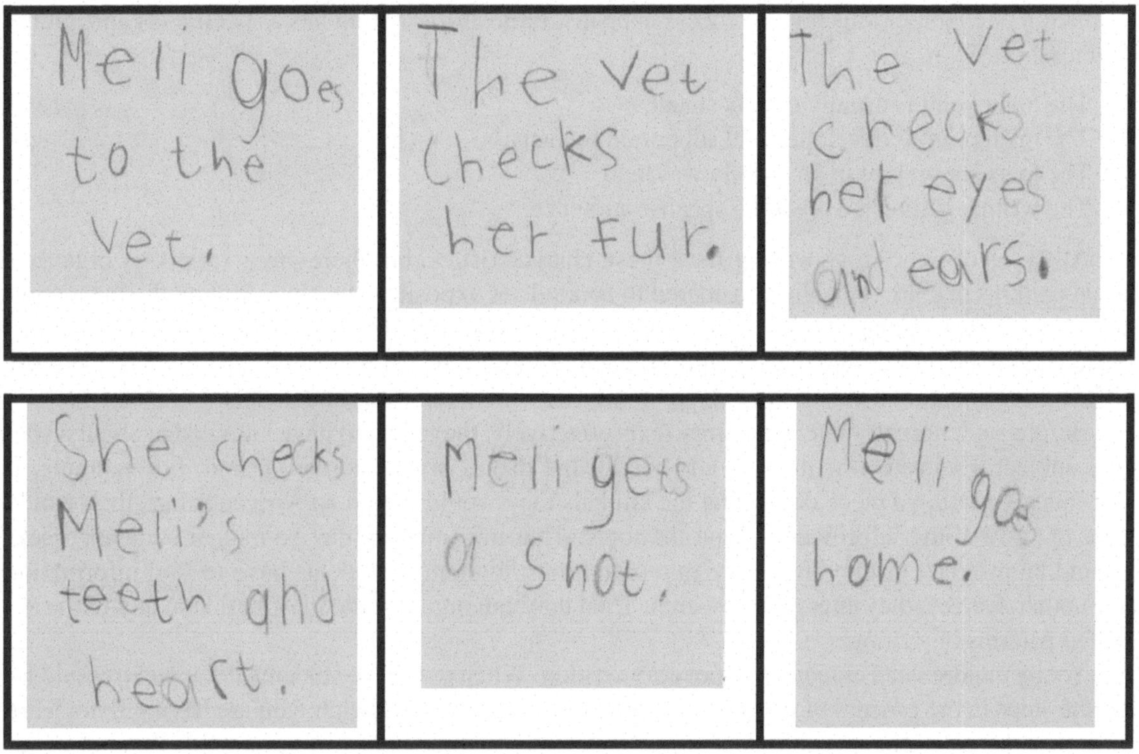

Meli goes to the Vet.

The Vet checks her fur.

The Vet checks her eyes and ears.

She checks Meli's teeth and heart.

Meli gets a shot.

Meli goes home.

Writing Frame

In this story, the problem starts when _____

_____

After that, _____

_____

Next, _____

_____

Then, _____

_____

The problem is finally solved when _____

_____

The story ends _____

_____

EXPOSITORY WRITING. **Expository writing** is what children read when they read informational texts. Expository writing is the kind of writing that gives directions, explains information, describes a situation or event, or tells how a process happens. Expository writing has a specific organizational structure.

- The main point is usually clearly stated,
- The main point is developed and supported by facts,
- The facts are present in an orderly way, and
- The writing is directed toward a specific audience.

All types of expository writing have these characteristics, but there are a variety of organizational patterns that are typically considered to be kinds of expository writing. Among the most common expository writing patterns are the simple explanation, steps in a process, compare and contrast, cause and effect, and problem and solution. Each of these types of expository writing has a slightly different organizational pattern, but all are nonfiction with main ideas and details.

Before students can write expository texts effectively, they need to have knowledge about a specific subject. Expository writing entails knowledge that is organized and shared. For example, if students are writing a piece describing the animals they would see on an African safari, they would have to know some information about the topic. That information may be part of students' background knowledge, or they may have to research information. If students have to find information from other sources, they engage in research. Then they can organize the information in any of the accepted patterns of writing.

Young children can engage in expository writing. When you have students draw pictures and label the steps in the process of making a peanut butter and jelly sandwich, you are having them learn to engage in expository writing. When students make picture books of an animal, they may "research" the animal, draw pictures, and write names or sentences. Each of these activities helps students learn the organizational patterns of expository writing. You can find a writing frame and a graphic organizer for expository writing in the Resources for Chapter 11 on the website.

*L*esson Planning: Writing Informational Texts

Students can write informational texts about specific topics that they know or have learned. Giving students experiences writing about topics helps them learn how to organize ideas into a paragraph structure.

Standard: Write informative/explanatory texts in which students name a topic, supply some facts about the topic, and provide some sense of closure.

Objective: Students will be able to write an informative text that has a topic, facts, and a conclusion.

Lesson Idea: Have students develop a brochure about a place they want to visit. It could be local, such as a park, or it could be far away from their home. Fold a piece of paper into three sections to make a trifold brochure. On the left side, have students list the place and draw a picture of it. In the center section, ask students to write three things that describe the place. On the right side, have students write one sentence about why they want to visit this place.

Assessment: Use a rubric to score the writing similar to those in Assessment Strategy 11.3.

Scoring Guidelines: Determine the score that you expect from students at this point in the school year. This cut score would represent the standard for your class at this time. Your cut score can change through the year.

PERSUASIVE WRITING. "Can we get a turtle for our classroom?" You may have heard students ask these kinds of questions without giving any rationale. If you ask them to tell you why they want a turtle and to convince you to get one, you are asking them to persuade you.

The art of persuasion and creating effective arguments is not a natural human ability but must be learned (Fulkerson, 1996). Frequently, students come to teachers with requests or opinions with little substantiating rationale. If they actually knew how to persuade, they would make a claim, offer reasons for that claim, and provide examples or details that illustrate the reasoning, and end with a powerful conclusion.

Students rarely have had these types of experiences in their lives. In addition, they rarely have read the type of persuasive essay they are expected to write in school. For these reasons, students need extra time to learn the organizational patterns of persuasive writing so they can learn to think and write using logic and reasoning. Look for books that can serve as mentor texts, such as *I Wanna Iguana* (Orloff & Catrow, 2004). Once students become comfortable with persuasion, watch out. Before you know it, you'll have a turtle for your classroom!

Persuasive writing isn't always taught in schools before third grade, but even our youngest students will want to know how to use persuasion to get their way. We're providing you with an idea for you to implement in Teaching Strategy 11.10. You can find a writing frame and a graphic organizer for expository writing in the Resources for Chapter 11 on the website.

Assessing with rubrics. **Rubrics** are often used to assess writing. Rubrics can be used to evaluate an individual piece of writing in one or more areas. Effective rubrics tend to be specific to grade and/or ability levels. The best rubrics are those you create yourself that fit your particular class and your writing standards. However, we have writing rubrics that were developed for kindergarten, first grade, and second grade that you can use as a pattern (see Assessment Strategy 11.2). By third grade most states have their own writing rubrics.

Every state chooses their **state assessment,** so different states will have different writing assessments. Check out the website in Margin Note 11.7 to find out which assessment is given to students in grades 3–8 in your state. (Some states may also give assessments to students in grades K–2.) Once you know the assessment, look at the writing assessment requirements. There you will get a sense of the kinds of writing expected for students in your state at grade 3 and higher. You can then adapt your teaching to fit the terminology of the writing genre that is assessed in your state. In addition, Margin Note 11.8 is Kathy Schrock's website of teacher resources that features a variety of different rubrics for writing and other subjects as well.

Margin Note 11.7: State Writing Assessments

http://ecs.force.com/ mbdata/mbquestrt?rep= SUM1801

Margin Note 11.8: Kathy Schrock's Guide to Everything: Assessments and Rubrics

https://www.schrockguide. net/assessment-and-rubrics. html

Teaching Strategy 11.10: Persuasive Writing

Purpose: Students are more likely to understand the genre of persuasive writing if they have the opportunity to use persuasive writing to make an actual difference. Many students do not understand that different viewpoints can have valid reasons and that explaining these reasons is the basis for persuasion.

Procedures:

1. Tell students that each person has their own opinions and these opinions may vary within a class. Explain to students that what one person believes may be different from what other people believe. Tell students that in order to persuade others, they need to explore their own thinking.

2. Choose a topic that is of interest to your students. For example, you might consider the following topics: school parties, field trips, school uniforms, use of cell phones, or pets.

3. Write the topic on the board. Ask students to develop a series of statements about the topic. For example, if the topic was school uniforms, some statements could be as follows:

   - School uniforms would restrict our independence.
   - School uniforms are boring.
   - School uniforms equalize students' appearance.
   - School uniforms could save families money on clothes.

4. Give students several minutes to write at least four statements about the topic. After students have finished their lists, divide the class into groups of two or three students and have students read each other their lists. Have students point out the similarities and differences between the lists.

5. Tell students to choose which side they want to take about the issue and to revise their lists to include only those statements that support their side of the topic.

6. Help students write a main idea sentence stating their opinion. Then have students write their statements as details of the main idea. Help students write a concluding sentence.

7. Tell students that they have just written a persuasive paragraph. Encourage students to share their paragraphs in small groups or with the class and discuss whether the reasons are strong enough to convince the reader to agree with their opinion.

Assessment Strategy 11.2: Writing Rubrics

Purpose: Writing can be assessed using rubrics in early grades in the same way they are used in grade four and higher. Rubrics provide specific categories of writing and different categories of standards.

Procedures:

1. Duplicate the appropriate number of copies of the rubrics—one for each piece of writing you will be assessing.

2. Tell students, "Today I'm going to assess your writing in two areas. The areas will include content and organization. [You can specify other areas as appropriate.] As you write, remember that your writing will be evaluated in these areas."

3. Collect the students' writing and evaluate them by circling a number in each area of assessment. If you believe the writing falls between two scores, either assign a higher score or a lower score consistently.

4. Set cutoff points to identify pieces of writing that meet your class or grade level standards, are below standard, or exceed standard. The score on a piece of writing will reflect whether a child's writing meets your grade-level expectations. You can also use the score that is at the end of each rubric. If the scoring doesn't fit your ideas of grade level standards, adjust the scores as needed.

5. Score several pieces of writing with the rubric over time. List the student's scores on a continuum to help assess whether growth is occurring.

6. You can find writing rubrics for kindergarten, first, and second grade in the Chapter 11 Resources on the website.

REVISING AND EDITING. The purpose of writing is to express ideas for an audience. The degree to which readers are able to construct meaning from a piece of writing depends on the way the piece is written. Clear writing written in a lively style that conforms to standard usage is easier to read than writing that is unclear, dull, and full or errors. In order for writers to make their meanings clear, they must pay attention to the details of writing and learn strategies for rewriting, revising, and editing.

REVISING. Writing for an audience usually needs to be completed over a period of days. **Revising** doesn't mean that students merely recopy their papers; it means that they use their initial drafts as a lens to make clear what they really want to say. Revision is revisioning or rethinking a piece of writing (Hansen, 2001). During writing, writers often put down words that do not completely capture their thoughts and ideas. Instead, these initial drafts reflect the surface thoughts of the writer. After writing an initial draft, writers often re-read their original sentences and change them to make the words express their intentions more clearly. Revising is the tough part of writing—it takes time, attention, and instruction.

Margin Note 11.9: Sentence Song

https://www.youtube.com/watch?v=h9zD7BTEstA

Even writers in preschool and kindergarten need to learn about revision. Young students should learn that pictures or written words can be changed. Students in first grade and beyond can learn how to rework, or revise, their writings. They should think of revision during drafting and after drafting. Teaching Strategy 11.11 will give you an idea about how to teach students to revise. For fun, listen to the song about revising sentences listed in Margin Note 11.9.

EDITING. **Editing** is polishing a piece of writing, putting the piece of writing into its final form by correcting its surface features, or mechanics. Correct mechanics include spelling, usage, punctuation, capitalization, paragraphing, sentence structure, and handwriting.

Most students tend to be poor editors. One of the reasons students aren't very good at cleaning up a piece of writing is that they are just learning the mechanics of the English language. However, students can learn that when they write, they may forget to put a capital letter or a period. When they edit, they can make these changes.

Margin Note 11.10: Project Based Learning: Revision Checklist

http://www.4teachers.org/projectbased/checklist.shtml

Not all papers that students write should be revised and edited (Graves, 1994). Students should write so much in schools that they simply don't have time to take every piece of writing to the sharing or publishing stage. If students are writing every day, most of their writing should not be rewritten. However, when students are writing for an audience or when their writing will be read by someone else, they need to make their writing as clear and readable as possible. That's when they need to revise and edit. Teaching Strategy 11.12 provides an idea for helping students learn to edit. Margin Note 11.10 shows an interactive website you can use to tailor your revision and editing checklist for your students.

Teaching Strategy 11.11: Grow a Sentence

Purpose: Young students can learn to revise sentences by participating in class revision activities. Grow a Sentence can help students learn how to change sentences they have written to make them more descriptive. When students learn that writing can be changed, they are more likely to understand the principles behind revision.

Procedures:

1. Write a simple sentence on the board. Use only a simple subject and a simple predicate, such as: Dogs run.

2. Tell students that you will "grow a sentence" by adding one word or phrase at a time. Emphasize the idea that after a writer finishes a part of their writing, they read over what they have written and decide whether they want to make changes.

3. Tell students that you will add one word to the sentence, such as, "Big dogs run." Explain that when you were thinking about the sentence you were not thinking about all dogs but you were visualizing a big dog.

4. Read the new sentence aloud to the class. Tell the class that you want to change the sentence some more. Have students volunteer words and phrases that would change the sentence. Write the new sentence under the second sentence.

5. After revising the sentence three or four times, draw a triangle around the sentences. Point out to students how the first sentence was changed to become the final sentence. Remind students that when writers write, they can make changes to their writing.

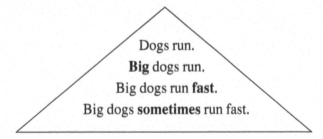

Dogs run.
Big dogs run.
Big dogs run **fast**.
Big dogs **sometimes** run fast.

Teaching Strategy 11.12: Editing Bubbles

Purpose: Young writers can learn how to edit with editing bubbles. Editing bubbles are bubbles placed over words that give directions for editing changes. When young writers use editing bubbles, they learn that writing can be changed and corrected before it is read by an audience. Since producing written text is difficult for young students, students do not have to rewrite the entire text when they use editing bubbles.

Procedures:

1. Tell students that writers often make mistakes when they write that they can correct later in the process. Explain that when writing for an audience, writers need to write as clearly and correctly as possible so their readers understand what they are trying to say.

2. Tell students that words themselves can call out for changes if they are not correct. Write a sentence on the board with one or two errors. Over the errors, draw an editing bubble as in the following example with the words, "Please change me!"

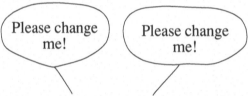

3. Divide the class into groups of three or four students. Have students discuss how to change the words that need to be changed. Ask students to volunteer the answers. When students have suggested the correct answer, change the words in the editing bubbles by writing the correct word in the bubble.

4. Create sentences with editing bubbles several times a week. After students have become familiar with editing bubbles, encourage students to edit their own writing with editing bubbles.

SELF- AND PEER-ASSESSMENT. Children should be encouraged to assume the responsibility for assessing their own writing and helping their classmates improve their writing. Such assessment requires careful modeling and scaffolding for young writers. Some teachers have the tendency to correct all errors on a student paper in an effort to help students edit. However, students need to know that the writing is theirs, and they should be allowed to make choices as writers. Teachers can help students find places in their writing to edit and still give students writing authority.

When children are taught to reflect on what they know about writing and what they have demonstrated in their writing, they begin to view themselves as writers. They also begin to appreciate and understand their progress, which increases their confidence. By learning to **self-assess**, children begin to understand their role in their own literacy development. To encourage students to re-read and edit their writing, play the song "Don't Forget to Edit" found in Margin Note 11.11. Assessment Strategy 11.3 shows a self-assessment form for young children and one for students in first through third grades to help them learn how to assess their writing.

Margin Note 11.11: Don't Forget to Edit

https://www.youtube.com/watch?v=gvKUP-U6Uq4

Organizing Writing Instruction

You might be wondering how to **organize** all of this instruction. Many teachers have used a **writing workshop approach**. Lucy Calkins (1986) popularized this idea by showing how the writing process can be applied in classrooms. When using a workshop approach, the teacher begins the writing time with a mini lesson about a skill or strategy students need to learn and then gives students time to write. As students write, the teacher confers with students to help them think through a topic, develop sentences, and spell words. After students have completed a message or story, they have the opportunity to share their writing with the class through the author's chair, which is a special chair that you use for students to sit on when they share their work.

Some teachers don't begin writing workshop until second or third grade after students have some experience with writing in school. Kissel and Miller (2015), however, suggest that, if you believe that children are emerging as literate beings, then students can communicate by writing messages and stories. Writing workshops can help fulfill this goal.

When conducting a writing workshop, students are in different places in their writing because they are writing at their own pace. For example, five students might be struggling with choosing a topic, eight students might be drafting, and 10 students might be illustrating their message or story during the same lesson. There are a variety of ways to manage these differences. One teacher decided to keep track of students' individual processes by labeling soup cans with each stage in the writing process. Then the teacher had students put their name on a popsicle stick and place their stick in the can that represented where they were in the writing process. The teacher was able to keep track of where students were, and students had to think explicitly about the writing process during writing time. See Chapter 12 for more ideas about implementing a workshop approach.

Assessment Strategy 11.3: Writing Self-assessment

Purpose: To become competent writers, students need to assess their own work. Self-assessment can be evaluative, or it can be part of the revision process. When students are taught to reflect on what they know about their writing, they begin to view themselves as writers and can set goals to make improvement.

Procedures:

1. Make copies of the self-assessment that fits the developmental level of your students. Give each student a copy of the self-assessment.

2. Have students select a piece of writing or have students take out a piece of writing from a class assignment. Older students can use more than one piece of writing to self-assess.

3. Ask students to re-read their piece and to think about what was good about the writing and what could be better.

4. If students say they don't know, help them by asking probing questions, such as, "What did you like about your writing? Did you like the part where your dog was found?"

5. Have individual conferences with each student to discuss what they thought about their writing. Encourage students to look for their strengths in writing.

6. You can find a self-assessment for young writers and one for first through third grade writers in the Chapter 11 Resources on the website.

© Dragon Images/Shutterstock.com

This student is assessing her writing by conferencing with the teacher.

What Do You Believe about Teaching Writing?

You have lots of experience writing, and you may even remember learning how to compose messages. This experience can help you as you articulate what you believe about teaching writing. Take what you know and add it to what you learned from this chapter and your clinical experience to decide what you believe about teaching writing.

Think about the important takeaways from this chapter and write the ones that are personally important to you on the What Do You Believe template that can be found in the Chapter 11 Resources on the website. Then write a brief paragraph about what you believe about writing instruction as a result of what you learned.

Closing Thoughts

As you learned in this chapter and all of the strategy chapters in this book, children's literacy emerges as they have opportunities to read and write. We provided you with many ways to give your students opportunities to write and to learn that writing carries a message to a reader. The ideas and strategies we presented, however, will take more than just implementation. Just as the teacher who labeled soup cans had to improvise to make writing workshop successful for her and her students, you will have to adapt and problem solve during your teaching to make the principles, strategies, and ideas from this chapter work for your students.

As you think about Sara from the beginning of the chapter whose instinct was to let her own children explore language through writing, you've come to teaching with your own ideas and instincts. Sometimes what you read or see in your placement will conflict with your instincts and other times it will conform to them. As a teacher, we hope you examine your deeply held beliefs in light of research and best practice and make instructional decisions that are in the best interests of your students.

Takeaways from Chapter 11

- Writing is a method of communication that conveys meaning.
- Some people are anxious when they write.
- Children's writing emerges in similar ways to reading development.
- Students need experiences practicing writing as they develop.
- The writing process is recursive and typically goes through the stages of prewriting, drafting, revising, editing, and publishing.
- Students need a purpose and audience for their writing.
- Writing includes the main genres of narrative, expository, and persuasive.
- Students need to learn how to revise and edit their work.

To Learn More about Teaching Writing

Writing Workshop

Kissel, B. (2017). *When writers drive the workshop: Honoring young voices and bold choices.* Portland, ME: Stenhouse.

https://www.stenhouse.com/content/when-writers-drive-workshop

Lucy Calkins's Unit, Tools, and Methods for Teacher Reading & Writing Workshop

http://www.unitsofstudy.com/k5writing/

We briefly presented the concept of organizing writing instruction into a workshop approach. If this idea appeals to you, we suggest you read Kissel's book to learn more about how teachers implement writing workshop. In addition, you might check out Lucy Calkins's method of teaching writing workshops. She has organized practical units and lessons for you to adapt for your classroom.

Interactive Writing

McCarrier, A., Fountas, I., & Pinnell, G. S. (2018). *Interactive writing: How language & literacy come together, K–2.* Portsmouth, NH: Heinemann.

https://www.heinemann.com/products/e09926.aspx

http://www.readingrockets.org/article/interactive-writing

Interactive writing is when you and your students jointly compose a piece of writing. We described this activity in the chapter and provided you with a demonstration video. To learn more about interactive writing, you might want to read the book and article listed above. Not only do these resources give you additional descriptions of interactive writing, they provide you with examples and lesson ideas.

Emergent Writing

Promoting Preschoolers' Emergent Writing

https://www.naeyc.org/resources/pubs/yc/nov2017/emergent-writing

How Do I Write . . .? Scaffolding Preschoolers' Early Writing Skills

http://www.readingrockets.org/article/how-do-i-write-scaffolding-preschoolers-early-writing-skills

Is emergent writing a new idea for you? If that's the case, we suggest you learn more by reading the two articles above that describe the concept in detail. In this chapter we built the case that students learn through experiences with language and that writing "emerges" in similar ways to reading. You can get a better understanding of this concept by reading these articles.

National Writing Project

https://www.nwp.org/

The National Writing Project is a network developed to improve student achievement by improving the teaching of writing and improving learning in schools. You may have heard about the National Writing Project in your schooling career. It's a great resource to learn about how to teach writing and to become involved in local writing activities. To find a site near you, check out the link below.

https://www.nwp.org/what-we-do

Strategy Book

Serravallo, J. (2017). *The writing strategies book: Your everything guide to developing skilled writers*. Portsmouth, NH: Heinemann.

https://www.heinemann.com/products/e07822.aspx

You can never have too many reading and writing strategy books. You may find that the writing strategies presented in this chapter are enough for you now, but as you enter the teaching field, you'll want additional ideas. This book will give you plenty of new strategies to try as you learn what teaching ideas fit you and your students best.

Learning about Journal Writing

Journal Writing

http://www.readingrockets.org/article/journal-writing

Kindergarten Journal Writing Lesson

https://www.youtube.com/watch?v=sqySzZp2Hrs

Journal writing is a great way for students to practice writing words and sentences on their own with help. Not only is journal writing a good activity for students to practice writing, it can be a good way for students to express themselves. You can read more about the reasons why to use journal writing in the classroom by reading the article, and the You Tube clip is a lively demonstration of kindergarten students writing in journals. What can you learn from these resources to apply in your placement?

Apps

Reading Rockets: Literacy Apps for Writing

https://www.readingrockets.org/literacyapps/writing

Look through this website for the descriptions of 24 apps related to writing. Apps in this website range from handwriting practice to publishing in digital formats. Some apps are free, whereas others require purchase. Which ones do you think you might use in your future classroom?

Section **III**

This committee is discussing options for reading program adoption.

*I*n Section II we spent a great deal of time describing the "nuts and bolts" of literacy instruction, including how to teach the various components of literacy. We gave you a close look at how to teach reading, writing, and spelling, and we shared many examples of teaching and assessment strategies you can use in your placement, in student teaching, and in your own classroom. However, that's not all there is to being a PreK–3 reading and writing teacher. You also need to look at literacy teaching and learning from a broader perspective.

In Section III we present how you can put all of your ideas, beliefs, and knowledge together to develop your teacher identity. You will use this sense of who you are as a teacher in making decisions about teaching, such as how to select a literacy program that fits with your beliefs and meets your students' needs. We also introduce some of the most common programs you might encounter in student teaching and as a new teacher, and we discuss how you might adapt the programs to fit what you believe about teaching and learning and what your students need. Next, we share ideas and insights about working with families, community members, and colleagues. Being a teacher is not only teaching—it's working with others to support your students' literacy learning. We encourage you to bring your identity as a teacher to this area also, by thinking of ways you can collaborate effectively with colleagues in your school, your students' families, and community partners.

How Do I Put It All Together?

Finally, we help you think through what it means for you to be a learner-ready teacher and enter the teaching profession. We present both practical suggestions you can implement in your teaching and bigger ideas for you to consider throughout your career. As you read and reflect on the ideas discussed in Section III, you will be able to put together your ideas with what you learned to help you move closer to being the learner-ready teacher your students deserve.

© Monkey Business Images/Shutterstock.com

Your beliefs will frame the decisions you make about teaching reading and writing.

How Are Reading and Writing Instruction Organized in the Classroom?

REAL-LIFE EXAMPLE

Aiden immigrated to the United States from Ireland where he had been a primary school teacher. He was now pursuing teaching credentials in the United States. Aiden was used to a country-wide curriculum with a timeline where every teacher taught pretty much the same thing on the same day. He was fascinated by the variety of reading programs available in the United States and wanted to learn as much as possible about them.

While Aiden was in his first-grade placement, he noticed that he was vaguely uncomfortable about the literacy instruction that was based on the core reading text. He wasn't sure what was wrong, but he felt something was missing. Aiden talked with his mentor teacher, Ms. Ellsworth, who agreed that the core reading program needed to be adapted. Ms. Ellsworth described to Aiden the ways she was adapting the program and encouraged Aiden to develop lesson plans that filled the gaps that they had both identified.

Perhaps you are like Aiden and in a placement where you are not completely comfortable with the main literacy program and want to learn what other literacy programs you could use. This is not uncommon. You are learning ways to teach reading and writing that may not align completely with what is happening in the school where you have your placement. You may be wondering whether what you're learning in your teacher preparation program is relevant because the students in your placement seem to be happy and learning. Well, we have good news. You are learning from your teacher education program the most cutting-edge research about literacy teaching, and in your placement, you're learning one way literacy teaching can be enacted. As a dedicated professional and learner-ready teacher, you can use what you're learning in both situations to develop your own ideas about teaching reading.

Before you can make informed judgments about reading and writing programs, you'll need to solidify what you believe about teaching reading and writing. The first thing we do in the chapter is guide you to form your own belief framework based on the beliefs you have identified in each of the chapters in this book, recognizing that your beliefs will continue to develop as you progress throughout your career. You then use these beliefs to develop your teaching identity. After that, we help you think about your beliefs in the context of guiding principles that you can use to critically evaluate reading programs. These guiding principles will be the "touch points" for you, regardless of the reading program you're using. They will help you keep your attention and effort on the most important aspects of teaching reading and writing. Next, we describe the most common reading programs and ask you to think about the assumptions that undergird those programs and determine the extent to which your guiding principles align with each program. Finally, we help you think about ways you can adapt programs to better fit what you believe about teaching reading and writing.

Developing a Beliefs Framework

You came to your teacher education program with **beliefs about teaching and learning**. Those beliefs served as a framework that filtered what you learned in your classes and helped you frame problems (Fives & Buehl, 2012). Your beliefs may have been challenged as you took classes and experienced schooling in your clinical placement. Your beliefs, as well as your teacher identity, will continue to evolve as you grow in experiences, but you do have beliefs right now, and the beliefs you hold as a teacher are considered a window into your decisions (Skott, 2015). According to Pajares (1992), "beliefs can be conceptualized as an individual's judgment of the truth or falsity of a proposition" (p. 316). That means that beliefs are opinions, so your beliefs may be different from your classmates and even from your instructor. You may agree on some things about teaching, but you will not agree on everything. Beliefs are considered to be "individual, subjectively true, value-laden mental constructs that are the relatively stable results of substantial social experiences and that have a significant impact on one's interpretations of and contributions to classroom practice" (Skott, 2015, p. 19).

Every teacher candidate will form a belief structure. Research (Levin & He, 2008) indicates that teacher candidates form beliefs on a combination of personal experiences (35%), coursework (31%), and clinical experiences (35%). This may vary for different candidates, but the point is that your belief framework will be influenced by all the activities you engage in during your teacher preparation program.

YOUR PERSONAL BELIEFS. As you move through your teacher preparation program and your clinical experiences, you will continue to form opinions and beliefs. Think about this for a moment. Do you have an opinion about reading children's books in the classroom? This is a belief. These beliefs will frame the decisions you make about students, programs, and instructional practices.

In Section I of this book, we described the foundational components of teaching reading and writing, and in Section II we showed you how to teach. Now, pull all of this together so you can develop a belief framework and a teaching identity. Remember you will grow and change as a teacher, but some of your core beliefs will stay with you through your entire career.

Locate the beliefs statements you wrote from each of the chapters. We had a template on the website for Chapters 2–11 that had you list your beliefs about the major topic in each chapter. For example, in Chapter 8, we had you think about fluency and what you believed about fluency. Maybe you listed that you believed that "fluency takes practice." That's one of your beliefs. If you didn't write belief statements in each of the chapters, do so now.

Read through what you said you believed about each of these topics. Can you see a pattern? For example, maybe you listed the following types of beliefs:

- I believe that young children need experiences with oral language to develop their emergent literacy (Chapter 5).
- I believe that children need to hear and say rhymes and rhyming words to develop phonemic awareness (Chapter 6).
- I believe that children need to experience shared reading and many books to develop reading comprehension (Chapter 10).
- I believe young children need to scribble and play with writing to develop a basis for emergent writing (Chapter 11).

You might notice that you are exhibiting a general belief that literacy emerges as children have experiences with authentic tasks. That would be one of your general belief statements. You will most likely see these patterns throughout your belief statements. Now you can develop some general belief statements that will help you define who you are as a teacher. A template you can use to develop your belief statements is provided in the Chapter 12 Resources on the website.

Developing Your Teacher Identity

Your belief framework is unique to you. Some of your classmates may have listed similar beliefs, but every person holds unique ideas about teaching. Each teacher is unique. Think of the teachers you've had in your life. If you're like most of us, you responded more positively to some teachers than others. As you think of your teachers, are you remembering each one as separate and distinct from each other? When I think about my first-grade teacher, Miss Wilson, I remember a teacher who wanted all of her students to develop a love of reading and writing. She read a chapter of a book aloud to us every day. I remember her telling us it was important to take risks and try things in learning because we learn by doing and making mistakes was part of learning. She had us try to read books that were just a little challenging for us and celebrated every time we tried something difficult. Miss Wilson was unique, as were all my teachers when I was in elementary school. That's because every teacher has their own **teaching identity**. As a candidate who is learning to become a learner-ready teacher, you are developing your own teaching identity right now!

Your teaching identity is what sets you apart and makes you recognizable (Waldon, 2016). Think about that statement. If you think about other teachers, we're sure you'll be able to identify them. But what about you? What are the characteristics that make you who you are as a teacher?

Teacher identity "is understood as a dynamic, career-long process of negotiating the teacher-self in relation to personal and emotional experiences, the professional and social context, and the micro and macro political environment" (Zembylas & Chubbuck, 2015, p. 174). What this means is that your teaching identity will change over time, dependent on contextual factors. Let's think about that for a moment. Let's say you get a new roommate in college, Renee, and she loves the opera. You've never been a fan of classical music, but you have always had an interest in fashion design. You agree to go with her to a performance. You find yourself intrigued and begin to learn more about opera, including the costuming for the performers. You decide to volunteer for local performances and help with staging a play. Your core interest in fashion morphed into a new field of interest.

In that same way, you will grow as a teacher. As you experience new methods of teaching reading and writing, get to know your students, learn from your colleagues, go to professional development sessions, work in teaching teams, collaborate with colleagues, get to know your community and students' families, and read books and articles about literacy, you will refine and revise your beliefs and even your identity as a teacher. Who you are right now will change through your career; however, it's important for you to identify who you are right now.

Margin Note 12.1: I Am a Teacher

https://www.youtube.com/watch?v=9nwu9PJkUf8

Watch the video in Margin Note 12.1. Consider the characteristics you want to demonstrate as a teacher. This combination of characteristics makes you different from other teachers and forms your teacher identity. Write a paragraph that describes you as a teacher. You might exchange your paragraphs with classmates to see how each of you have different teaching identities.

Develop Guiding Principles for Critically Examining Reading Programs and Practices

We hope you found it useful to think through your belief framework and teacher identity. Now, apply that knowledge to the kinds of reading and writing programs that you might experience as a PreK–3 teacher. We begin with a set of guiding principles that will be useful to you as you critically examine reading programs and make decisions about how you think reading should be taught.

As the authors of this book, we have developed guiding principles that help you think about a variety of literacy programs. These guiding principles are based on our shared beliefs, experiences, and our understanding of literacy research. We use these guiding principles as we observe teachers, evaluate school reading programs, and teach classes. You can find our list of guiding principles in Figure 12.1.

Figure 12.1. Guiding Principles for Reading and Writing

1. Literature and authentic reading experiences must form the heart of the literacy program.
2. Explicit instruction must be provided in the components of literacy, such as phonics, comprehension, vocabulary, phonemic awareness, and fluency.
3. Choice must be a cornerstone of the literacy program.
4. A variety of grouping practices must be used to differentiate instruction.
5. All students deserve high-quality, supportive teaching, including English Learners.
6. An equity lens is essential to teaching all students well.
7. A balanced focus on standards and developmentally appropriate practices leads to rigorous and effective instruction.
8. The I Do, You Do, We Do model of teaching forms a strong basis for students to become independent learners.

These are the principles that guide us, and we would like you to consider them as principles that can guide you as well. As you read the list of principles, think about how much you agree with each one. Consider your general beliefs that you developed earlier in the chapter and think about how they may cause you to want to include additional principles, revise some of them, or delete some.

Look at additional guiding principles, such as those we have in Margin Note 12.2. Guiding principles are like teaching identities that can vary with individual teachers. After reading our list and those in Margin Note 12.2, make your own list of guiding principles to provide a foundation for how you can think about how you intend to teach reading and writing in your own classroom.

Connection to the Field: Program Evaluation Form

As you develop your own guiding principles for reading and writing instruction, ask your mentor teacher whether the school or district has a program evaluation rubric. Bring the rubric to class and determine what the guiding principles are that the school or district uses to select and adopt literacy programs.

Organizing a Literacy Program

Your literacy program will include much more than just reading a textbook. Before we talk about specific reading programs, we want to emphasize that the way you organize your schedule, your classroom spaces, your bulletin boards or displays, and your centers (or stations) will be part of your overall literacy plan and reflects what you believe about teaching reading and writing. The bulk of your literacy program will be your reading program, and the kind of reading program you use will influence your schedule, your floor plan, your displays, and your centers. All of these decisions will be influenced by your belief framework and the guiding principles you develop and adopt.

DAILY LITERACY SCHEDULE. As a PreK–3 teacher, roughly half of your school day will be devoted to literacy-learning activities. How you decide to use this time may be influenced by outside factors such as when your students go to gym class or other special classes. If you are able, however, try to work with administrators to schedule an uninterrupted block of time for reading instruction in whole group, small group, and independent settings. Figures 12.2 and 12.3 illustrate possible literacy schedules for PreK–3 classrooms.

You'll notice that these sample literacy schedules illustrate several of the guiding principles we suggested earlier in the chapter. Foundational to each of these schedules is instruction based on authentic reading and writing experiences along with explicit teaching in reading and writing skills. Additionally, the schedule allows for a variety of grouping patterns to permit differentiation for individual students and for English Learners (ELs). Organizing literacy in this way provides a variety of grouping patterns, authentic experiences with reading and writing, choice, opportunities for differentiation, and explicit teaching. The way you organize your literacy program should reflect your beliefs.

Figure 12.2. Sample Literacy Schedule for K–3

Time	Activities	Instructional Setting
8:30–8:45	Sign in or other writing activity or free choice reading	Independent
8:45–9:15	Opening: Morning message, calendar, planning for the day Read aloud Shared reading Interactive writing	Whole group
9:15–10:15	Reading workshop: mini-lessons, guided reading groups, conferences, literacy centers	Whole group, small group, independent
10:15–10:30	Working with words	Whole and small groups
10:30–11:10	Writing workshop	Small group and independent
11:10–11:30	Read aloud	Whole group

Figure 12.3. Sample Literacy Schedule for PreK

Time	Activities	Instructional Setting
8:30–8:50	Opening: Morning message and calendar Read aloud	Whole group
8:50–9:20	Centers: Free choice and literacy centers	Small group
9:20–9:40	Story time (read aloud)	Whole group
9:40–10:00	Writing	Whole group, small group, and independent time
10:00–10:30	Centers: Free choice and literacy centers	Small group

Connection to the Field: Analyzing a Classroom Literacy Schedule

Write down the general or typical literacy schedule of the classroom where you have your placement. Note that on some days the schedule may be interrupted or changed, but you can still record the basics of the class literacy schedule. Include all times students are reading and writing. Bring the schedule to class and compare it with your classmates' classroom schedules. Try to infer what the guiding principles of the classroom teacher are from the schedule.

ARRANGING THE PHYSICAL SPACE. As you prepare to teach your students, you will also need to prepare the spaces in your classroom to facilitate learning and to help you and your students feel organized and able to move through the day with purpose and order. Let's first consider a key element: arranging the **floor plan in your classroom.**

THE FLOOR PLAN. Most of the classrooms where you'll work will not be as large as you'd like. However, if you are creative and sketch out your ideas before you start moving furniture, you will be able to make the most of the learning spaces you have.

It may seem strange to suggest this, but the way you arrange your classroom speaks to your beliefs about literacy learning. For example, if you embrace social constructivism, you will situate your students' desks or tables in groups so they can learn through social interaction. You may also decide to position your own desk on the side or in the back of the room, supporting your belief that the teacher is the orchestrator versus the dispenser of knowledge in the classroom. Lapp, Flood, and Goss (2000) wrote, "Desks don't move—students do in effective classroom environments" (p. 31) to explain their advocacy for active engagement in a busy, productive learning setting. Figure 12.4 displays one example of a kindergarten classroom's furniture arrangement. In that classroom, students are expected to collaborate throughout the day and the tables enhance collaboration. Materials are in bins that students can easily move from shelves to the tables and rug areas.

Figure 12.4. Example of a Kindergarten Classroom's Furniture Arrangement

Margin Note 12.3:
Classroom Architect

http://classroom.
4teachers.org/

Just like in real life, we can't always arrange our furniture the way we want. Often, we just don't have the right-sized room or enough space. Most likely you won't be able to use this ideal classroom floor plan when you get your own classroom, but having the opportunity to draw your dream space will help you remember your priorities when you get your own classroom. In Margin Note 12.3 you will find a website that lets you design a classroom floor plan. Use the website to draw a floor plan that is consistent with your beliefs. Some factors to consider are furniture placement including student seating, group work areas, traffic flow, comfort, use of wall space, materials, storage, areas for centers, reading spaces, and your desk.

BULLETIN BOARDS. Remember discussing a print-rich environment in Chapter 5? Bulletin boards, displays, and anchor charts are places where you can show students what you believe about literacy. Bulletin boards play an important role in your classroom space as you use them for student learning, student work, and organizational functions. Giving students ownership of bulletin boards can help foster the kind of collaborative environment you want and signals your belief in the social construction of knowledge as well as shared power in the classroom. The website in Margin Note 12.4 provides examples of interactive bulletin boards that you could use in your classroom to extend students' learning.

Margin Note 12.4: Interactive Bulletin Boards

https://www.weareteachers.com/interactive-bulletin-boards/

Engaging with Families: Home Literacy Bulletin Board

Consider reaching out to families to see if they can share photographs showing how they use reading and writing at home. You could create a bulletin board featuring these photographs with families' descriptions. By doing this, you make connections with students' literate lives beyond school.

WORD WALLS. You might want to devote one of your bulletin boards to a **word wall**, which is described in Chapter 8. That chapter describes how word walls serve as a reference tool for helping students learn sight words. Remember to only display words on the word wall after they have been taught. If you start the school year with all the sight words already posted on the word wall, then it's not a collaborative effort and students may view it as wallpaper instead of a valuable reference tool. One example of a word wall from a kindergarten classroom appears in Figure 12.5. See Margin Note 12.5 for a blog filled with ideas about how to build a better word wall.

Margin Note 12.5: Building a Better Word Wall

https://www.edutopia.org/article/building-better-word-wall

Figure 12.5. **Kindergarten Word Wall Example**

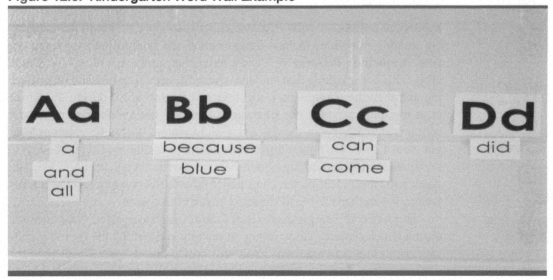

Often, we teach units that feature words that are specific only to a particular content area. You learned about teaching tier 2 and tier 3 words in Chapter 9. Instead of posting those highly specific words to the word wall, consider creating posters that feature the unit vocabulary words and display them until the end of the unit. For example, a unit on plant life cycles may feature words such as *chlorophyll*, *photosynthesis*, *germinate*, *biennials*, *perennials*, and *pollination*. Although those words may be important for understanding the plant life cycle, they are not words that students will use in their everyday reading and writing.

ANCHOR CHARTS. **Anchor charts** are charts that serve as reference tools for students to revisit when they need reminders about processes, such as how to choose a writing topic, how to use context clues to figure out an unknown word, and other strategies. "Traditionally, anchor charts are created with the whole class. The teacher documents modeled steps, or thinking processes, on large chart paper to anchor student learning" (Bacchioni & Kurstedt, 2019, p. 653). Anchor charts provide concrete reminders about learning and should be considered as a scaffold for learning. When you create such charts with your students, they provide evidence that anchor charts are important reference tools that students can revisit as needed. "The co-creation of anchor charts engages students as active participants in learning. Once created, an anchor chart is hung around the room for students to use while working independently" (Bacchioni & Kurstedt, 2019, p. 653). One example of an anchor chart from a third-grade classroom appears in Figure 12.6. Margin Note 12.6 features information about how to create anchor charts and provides several examples.

Margin Note 12.6: Anchor Charts 101: Why and How to Use Them

https://www.weareteachers. com/anchor-charts-101- why-and-how-to-use-them- plus-100s-of-ideas/

Although anchor charts are typically developed in the whole class setting, Bacchioni and Kurstedt (2019) used personalized anchor charts with second graders in their small groups to tailor the use of reading strategies to each group's specific needs. We encourage you to use anchor charts to support your students' learning with the whole class and with small groups as needed. You are the decision maker in your classroom, and it's up to you to decide how to use all available resources to help your students learn to be readers and writers.

Margin Note 12.7: Morning Meeting: Morning Message in Third Grade

https://www.youtube.com/ watch?v=Rlzui3BsFHA

MORNING MESSAGE AND POEMS. Other displays that would demonstrate our guiding principles include items such as the morning message and poems. A **morning message** is a short letter that teachers write to the whole class. This is something that students can read when they arrive in the morning and then the class reads it together and talks about it during the whole class morning meeting. The message is typically written on chart paper and contains an overview of the day using sight words. Watch the video in Margin Note 12.7 to see how a third-grade teacher uses the morning message to stimulate students' thinking about their science learning. In the video, students write their ideas on the chart paper prior to the meeting and the teacher reads what students wrote to stimulate further discussion.

Margin Note 12.8: Kindergarten Morning Message

https://www.youtube.com/ watch?v=64pOi7RsNcY

The video in Margin Note 12.8 features a kindergarten class meeting during which students are working on reading and writing the morning message as an interactive activity. You will notice that the word wall is in the same area, and the class refers to it as they are spelling words in the message. This approach helps students learn to use the word wall as a reference tool. As she writes, the teacher makes intentional mistakes that the students catch, such as when to use a capital letter. She prompts students to help

Figure 12.6. Anchor Chart from Third Grade

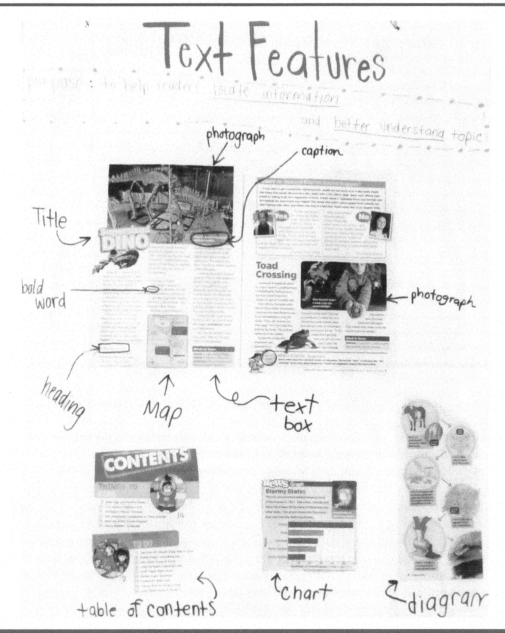

her think of the missing letters for the words in the message by making the sounds for the letters. By doing the morning message this way, the teacher reinforces prior learning about reading and writing skills. A morning message is a perfect way to practice reading and writing together in a supportive environment.

Figure 12.7 provides an example of a morning message from a kindergarten class. The teacher displays the morning message on the interactive board each morning and prompts discussion about the message after reading it to the class. Students note which letters are capitalized and why. Students point out the words they recognize, as well as how many words there are in the message. In the kindergarten setting, the morning message provides a way to share the teacher's writing for a spe-

Figure 12.7. Example of a Morning Message from Kindergarten

cific purpose while reinforcing skills related to the identification of letters and words as well as print directionality.

You will want to leave wall space open for the many charted stories and poems that you and your students will read and write together. Poems do not have to be solely ones that you and your students author. You could introduce a poem each Monday that corresponds with a topic students will explore that week. Practicing reading the poem together as a whole class reinforces sight words, fluency, and other reading skills, such as considering the author's choice of words. At the end of the week, you could provide each student with a copy of the poem so they can illustrate it and insert it in their poetry folder to take home and share with their families. When students revisit and reread poetry and other short texts, they are working toward becoming more fluent readers (Nichols et al., 2018).

Providing a print-rich environment is discussed in Chapter 5. By creating anchor charts, morning messages, word walls, and featuring poetry and other collaborative writings, students can "read the room" where they can practice reading familiar items, which builds their reading fluency.

LEARNING CENTERS (STATIONS). **Learning centers**, or **stations**, are areas of your classroom that contain materials and activities that you have assembled to teach or extend skills or concepts your students need to learn. You may be familiar with learning centers from your own schooling background. Perhaps you had a classroom with a writing center where you could compose and illustrate stories, a math center, or a science center. You may recognize that learning centers require active participation in small social settings, supporting the social constructivist stance that we are encouraging and that fit with our guiding principles.

Centers should have activities that range in difficulty from easy to challenging so that all students can succeed regardless of their development. Margin Note 12.9 features a classroom where the teacher differentiates her small group instruction during literacy centers, and she explains how she does that. Although the video in Margin Note 12.9 shows learning centers in a first-grade setting, some K–5 schools require literacy centers for all grade levels.

Margin Note 12.9: Station Rotation: Differentiating Instruction to Reach All Students

https://www.youtube.com/watch?v=Kg38A1ggYiE

Learning centers support the gradual release of responsibility model. Let's look at an example of how this works. Let's say you've taught your students about the rime (or spelling pattern) -*ack*. You instructed them in a whole group (I do), and then you had them practice making –*ack* words in small groups with your guidance (we do). You gave a formative assessment during which you observed students in small groups as they wrote –*ack* words on small white boards and read them together. As you observed, you made anecdotal notes to record which students were able to write and read multiple –*ack* words correctly and which ones struggled to do so. You found that some students could read and write many words, so they were ready to move on to learning new rimes. Some other students could read and write a few words, and a small number of students were only able to read and write the words that you had taught to the whole group and written on chart paper that you posted on a classroom wall. Because knowing how to use spelling patterns allows students to read and write many words, you decided to develop a center for students to do individual practice (you do). In the center, you provided hands-on activities for students to make words using tiles with the –*ack* rime and onsets (initial consonants and blends). You decided to differentiate in relation to both content and level of support. For students who already could read and write many –*ack* words, you provided opportunities for them to work with other rimes, such as –*ain* and –*ake*. For students who could make and read some –*ack* words, you provided activities that allowed them to add to the number of –*ack* words they could write and read. Finally, for students who needed additional instruction and practice, you provided an app on an iPad that guided them to make and read a set of –*ack* words. Because you designed this learning center to meet the needs of your students, it provided them with valuable practice learning the skill of using spelling patterns to read and write words. In fact, you can continue to change the target spelling pattern to align with your instruction so this learning center can evolve during the year to match your students' needs and your curriculum.

When you develop a learning center or station, remember to ask yourself these questions:

- What is the purpose of this center?
- What kinds of activities will students engage in at this center?
- Does this center allow for differentiation to meet the varied needs of students?
- How will students independently manage the activities at the center?
- What materials do I need?
- How will I keep records of what students do?
- How will I introduce the center, demonstrate its use, and monitor students' progress?

The types of centers you develop for your classroom will need to stem from your curriculum, your teaching goals, and your students' ability to work independently. Although centers are unique to each classroom, we have provided three kinds of centers you might consider for your classroom. Remember that your centers can be interdisciplinary, where literacy is used to explore math, science, and social studies content. Learning across the content areas cannot happen without reading and writing, so think about how you can create rich opportunities to use literacy skills while exploring the curriculum. The brief article in Margin Note 12.10 explains how to create and use learning centers in your classroom.

Margin Note 12.10: The Basics of Centers

https://www.teachervision.com/learning-centers-0

Students do well with predictable routines, so think about how you will manage an established set of centers while allowing elements of choice. For instance, you could have a center focused on word work and vocabulary, one on writing, another could be the classroom library where students listen to books on audio files and practice reading to build fluency, and a creativity or play center. In the word work center, students could engage in activities such as word sorts, building words, or practicing specific skills such as in the example described above with the *–ack* spelling pattern. In the library center, they could practice reading books of their choosing or follow along with a recorded book. Students could also have a center that is more open-ended to allow for creativity and literacy play. For instance, it could be a puppet theater one week, a restaurant another week, a maker space, and so forth. You have many decisions to make about your learning centers. The main thing to remember is that literacy centers are places for students to practice reading, writing, and learning in an environment where they can collaborate with others. The website in Margin Note 12.11 offers advice for how to get started with literacy centers, tips for organization, and includes a video of a teacher explaining how she uses literacy centers in her classroom.

Margin Note 12.11: Literacy Centers

https://www.readingrockets.org/article/literacy-centers

Margin Note 12.12: PreK Learning Center Ideas

https://www.prekinders.com/classroom-photos/

For PreK and kindergarten, it is important that students have time to explore a variety of open-ended centers such as blocks, cars, sand and water, painting, clay, kitchen, and other play centers. Although those centers can have an academic focus, we need to honor play for socialization purposes and for students learning how to navigate their worlds. Margin Note 12.12 provides examples of PreK learning center ideas with academic and open-ended stations.

Engaging with Families: Getting Input for Centers

It's important to show that we use literacy beyond school. Invite families to demonstrate how to make a simple recipe or craft for the class. If they cannot attend in person, maybe they could send a brief video or written explanations. Based on this input from families, you could create a center where students follow step-by-step directions to make the recipe with a partner.

DEVELOPING THE SOCIAL ENVIRONMENT. Think about a class you loved because you felt accepted and energized. Perhaps you were able to talk with your classmates about ideas and concepts, and you felt comfortable participating in the whole class. Perhaps you knew that your teacher cared about you and your learning, and you felt like you belonged in the community of learners. This is the kind of classroom that has a positive social environment.

As you think about developing the physical space of your classroom, you also need to think about the social environment. How will students feel about learning in your class? We know from research that giving students choices increases motivation and participation (Gambrell, 2011). We also ground our beliefs about learning in the theory of scaffolded instruction (Vygotsky, 1978) that optimizes students' opportunities to read and write. We also know that having a low-risk environment, one in which students feel like mistakes and miscues are part of learning, promotes a healthy classroom environment. These characteristics of your classroom will help students feel comfortable, safe, and motivated to learn.

As you think of ways to create a positive social environment in your classroom, don't just draw on your own personal experiences. You may have loved school! Let's think back to Chapter 2 in which we described the characteristic of young children. Some children have not had many experiences outside of their home and their families, so they may be shy and unwilling to talk in class. That's okay. Being shy and/or an introvert is one personality trait that we should respect (Cain, 2013). You may also have ELs who are new to speaking in English. As we discussed in Chapter 9, newcomers often need time to observe and listen before they speak up. If you have a low risk social environment, you will be sensitive to all children and allow them time to be ready before nudging them too much to participate in class. Having students feel comfortable in your class will help them on their literacy journey. Clearly, there are a lot of considerations for organizing your literacy program!

Connection to the Field: Adapting Individual Principles to Programs

Think of ways you can adapt the guiding principles you developed to the literacy program used in your placement. Along with your instructor, develop a list of ideas of ways you could incorporate some of what you believe into lessons while remembering that you're a guest in your mentor teacher's classroom.

Adopting and Adapting Reading Programs

Your overall literacy program will most likely include a school or district **adopted reading program**. You might have been wondering how reading programs are selected and what your role as a student teacher—and then a beginning teacher—looks like in the process. We'd like to describe for you how reading programs are selected or adopted. The adoption process is important for you to know so you understand that you will eventually be part of the decision-making process for selecting reading programs in your school or district.

When we describe some of the common reading programs, think about which kind of program fits your guiding principles most closely. It is unlikely that you will have a say in the program that you use in your first job as a teacher. However, eventually you may be able to influence the kind of program that is used in the classroom. Therefore, we're going to describe the process of selecting and adapting materials. That's why we'd like you now to think about what kind of reading program you prefer and that fits your belief system best. When your school is ready to adopt a new reading program, you'll be better equipped to provide input so that the reading program in your school aligns with your beliefs and guiding principles about reading instruction.

TEXTBOOK ADOPTION PROCESS. Some states do state-wide textbook adoption where every public school in the state has the same textbooks, and others give that responsibility to the local education agency (LEA), often referred to as a school district. Go to Margin Note 12.13 to see a listing of which states use state-wide adoption and which give that responsibility to school districts. What does your state do? If you scroll down the document further, you can see additional information about the actual process used in each state.

If your state uses a state-wide adoption process, there may be few if any opportunities for you to be involved in the selection. Some states convene teachers from around the state to offer input into textbook selection,

Margin Note 12.13: Education Commission of the States Textbook Adoption

https://www.ecs.org/ clearinghouse/01/09/23/ 10923.pdf

and others make the decision at the state education agency or state board of education. If your state uses district level textbook adoption, you'll have opportunities to be involved in the selection process. Often, school districts form a committee of teachers and administrators to review textbooks and to complete a rubric to evaluate each textbook in terms of strengths and weaknesses. Although you can use published rubrics such as the one available in Margin Note 12.14, it is important to consider district curriculum, school priorities, and your own professional guiding principles in the evaluation process. Read the short article in Margin Note 12.15 to learn more about specific considerations to address when selecting a core textbook or new reading or literacy program.

ADAPTING INSTRUCTION. You will most likely have a reading program in your placement that you'll follow during your time in your teacher education program. It's important to be familiar with this program while thinking about ways in which this program aligns with your belief framework. You won't have a choice about reading programs in your placement, but you may want to adapt your lessons to bridge your guiding principles with the goals of the program. For example, if your program is lacking in explicit instruction in sight words, you may want to develop a lesson plan that teaches sight words explicitly. As we discuss the kinds of reading programs that are commonly used, you may also want to think about what kind of reading program you'd prefer once you have your own classroom.

You may have noticed that we've been discussing adapting teaching and programs, but this is something that you may not have thought about yet. In your placement, you may have observed lessons and worked with students in small groups. Perhaps you've co-taught lessons with your mentor teacher. As you observed your mentor teacher or as you taught, did you notice that sometimes you changed what you had planned? That's called **flexibly adapting your instruction**.

Think of a specific time when you noticed a teacher adapting instruction. It may be that mentor teacher, Mr. Malone, was teaching his students how to identify the character traits from the main character in a story. Mr. Malone spent time having the class discuss the main character and how he acted and reacted in the story. The students seemed to follow along with the discussion. Then Mr. Malone asked the students to draw an outline of the main character (Teaching Strategy 10.4) and write his character traits in the center of the body. The students were stumped and looked quizzical. Mr. Malone checked in with his students to see what was hindering their progress. He realized that the students didn't know the names of character traits. Mr. Malone adapted his lesson right then to provide students with a list of 10 possible character traits that they could use for this strategy.

Mr. Malone adapted his teaching "on the fly." Teachers adapt instruction in different ways all the time. Sometimes teachers make adjustments while they're teaching (Parsons, 2012), as Mr. Malone did in the previous example. Teachers also adapt instruction based on what their students need (Duffy, 2005). These adaptations are based on formative assessment, as teachers notice students' understandings. You may want to revisit Chapter 3 for a review of formative assessment. Many teachers adapt instruction using different strategies and techniques in situations based on what students need to learn (Parsons, Dodman, & Burrowbridge, 2013). What this means is that teachers often adjust and adapt their teaching both in the moment and with intention. We're asking you to think about each of these reading programs, decide how the programs fit your guiding principles, and think of ways you might adapt instruction to align the two more closely.

There may be times when you can't adapt a program as much as you'd like. You may be required to follow the adopted curriculum. If the school district adopted a scripted program using an analytic approach to phonics (see Chapter 7), you may not be able to adapt that aspect of your teaching. What you can do is include authentic literature and story reading at times in your day outside the literacy block when you need to teach the reading program.

Margin Note 12.16: The Legal Balancing Act over Public School Curriculum

https://www.kappanonline.org/legal-balancing-act-public-school-curriculum-underwood/

The authority to determine the curriculum rests with the district, not with individual teachers. As an employee, you must carry out the adopted curriculum and abide by any restrictions. You do not have a right to use whatever teaching materials and methodologies you choose if this is contrary to school policy. To learn more about the responsibility you have for following the adopted curriculum, read the information in Margin Note 12.16. After you read this article, discuss it with your mentor teacher to learn about what their district and school require them to do to adhere to the adopted curriculum. Ask your mentor teacher what freedom and flexibility they have in their teaching.

Engaging with Families: Filling in the Gaps

Families can be helpful in filling in the gaps of a reading program. For example, if you are in a placement that has a scripted reading program with little book reading, you can ask families to read books together. If your program is light on vocabulary teaching, you can send home words for children to discuss with their families. Think of ways that families can work as partners to help you address the gaps in your reading program. Be sure to discuss what is appropriate for you to do with the students' families in your placement, and be sure to get permission from your mentor teacher.

Common Reading Programs

The reading programs most commonly used in schools span the theoretical landscape among the reading theories we described in Chapter 2. Some reading programs will align most closely with a **bottom-up approach to reading** whereas others may be more **top-down or follow the transactional/interactive theory of reading**. This might be a good time to review those theories from Chapter 2 so that you have a better understanding of the assumptions that underlie each of the programs. You will want not only to understand the programs in general but also to be able to determine the extent each program fits with your own guiding principles.

It's possible that we won't be describing the reading program that you're using in your placement, or it's possible that your mentor teacher is using a combination of approaches. If that's the case, try to find a program that is similar so that you can think about how you would adapt it to fit your guiding principles. We describe the following reading instructional approaches in this section:

- Core reading programs
- Workshop approach
- Daily 5 and CAFÉ
- Guided reading
- PreK approaches

© Michelle Baumbach/Shutterstock.com

Guided reading requires that you have books at students' instructional reading levels.

CORE READING PROGRAMS. A **core reading program** is a comprehensive literacy program that is the primary tool teachers use to teach reading. Core reading programs are published collections of materials produced for each grade level that include various supplementary materials such as workbooks, teachers' manuals, Big Books, and trade books (i.e., children's literature). The selection of passages in core reading texts varies considerably and may need to be supplemented. For example, Braker-Walters (2014) conducted a content analysis of three basal readers (sometimes called reading anthologies or literature anthologies) and found that they did not have a sufficient number and variety of informational text passages. Reutzel, Child, Jones, and Clark (2014) found that the five core reading programs they analyzed had inconsistent guidance for teachers regarding explicit instruction. That means that if you have explicit instruction as one of your guiding principles, you might want to make sure that the core reading program includes explicit instruction. Wright and Neuman (2013) also found that vocabulary instruction in kindergarten varied significantly among four different programs.

You may remember using a reading book from your own elementary school years and progressing through the levels of the book. The fundamental learning assumption that undergirds most core reading programs is that students can best be taught to read by progressing through a series of predetermined, sequenced learning steps using story selections from the text and followed by instructional activities.

Currently, there are three major publishers that produce the most commonly used core reading programs: Macmillan/McGraw Hill, Pearson, and Houghton-Mifflin. Big publishing houses often have publishers that focus on specific products, such as educational materials. You might be wondering why we're talking about publishers, but core reading texts are usually called by their name along with their publisher. For example, if you asked a teacher what reading program they used, they might say *Reading Street* or *Scott Foresman*. *Reading Street* is published by Scott Foresman/Pearson. Or they may say *Treasures* (published by Macmillan/McGraw Hill) or *Imagine It!* (published by SRA/McGraw Hill).

Core reading programs vary in their approaches, with a focus on skills-based instruction, a literature-based approach, or balanced literacy where skills are taught using literature. Publishers of core reading programs try to stay current in the field and publish books that align with current research. However, publishing a core reading program takes years of development and production, so they may lag behind developments in reading research by several years.

MATERIALS INCLUDED IN CORE READING PROGRAMS. Core reading programs, sometimes called basal reading programs, vary from one publisher to the next, but there are many common elements and features. Such programs provide all the materials needed for reading (and sometimes writing) instruction. An anthology, a collection of carefully selected and leveled texts, is usually the centerpiece of a core reading program. However, some publishers provide leveled books and other texts beyond the anthology. Typically core reading programs are organized by levels; therefore, students are grouped by reading ability to provide targeted instruction and guided reading support.

Core reading programs provide a scope and sequence framework that shows the skills and strategies to be taught at each level and how that progression builds across a school year and over the grades. For a scope and sequence chart from a core reading program, see Margin Note 12.17. As you look at this scope and sequence chart, focus on the information for PreK–3. How does this scope and sequence chart align with what you've been learning from this textbook, your methods courses, and your placement? What about your guiding principles? Do you see alignment, or would you need to adapt and augment the core reading program to ensure that your teaching addresses what you value and what your students need? If you answered "yes," think about what types of adaptations and augmentations you would need to do.

In a core reading program, a typical lesson would start with building students' background to activate their prior knowledge. Often, students make predictions after taking a picture walk and reading the title. Then students are introduced to vocabulary words. Next, the class makes predictions about the story, and guided reading begins with the teacher. Once the reading is complete, students refer back to their previous predictions and complete a comprehensive discussion, followed by extension projects and activities.

A teacher's manual is provided by such programs, and step-by-step instructions are provided for each lesson, text, and skill. Core reading programs often provide workbooks, worksheets, assessments, audio recordings, technology-based instructional materials, and materials for remediation and enhancement. To see the range of materials provided in a core reading program, check out Margin Note 12.18. As you look at the listing and description of materials, which ones do you think would be most useful for your teaching and why? Which ones do you think would be less useful?

ADAPTING CORE READING PROGRAMS. A common criticism of core reading programs is that the lesson sequence is so long that there is little opportunity to add instructional and practice activities that you design. Because most core reading programs are designed by level, students are placed into groups based on reading levels. When you combine these two concerns about core reading programs, you will find that the groups are expected to move through lessons in sequence which makes it difficult to move students from group-to-group based on their needs, development, and the focus of instruction. You may be in a situation in which you are asked to use your core reading program

Margin Note 12.17: Pearson Scope and Sequence for *Reading Street* and Prentice Hall Literature K–12

https://assets.pearsonschool.com/asset_mgr/current/201140/RS_k12_scope_sequence.pdf

Margin Note 12.18: Materials Included in *Reading Street* Core Reading Program

https://www.pearsonschool.com/index.cfm?locator=PSZu68&PMDbProgramID=71202

with fidelity, which means that you will be asked (or even required) to follow the program as it is written. According to Dewitz and Jones (2013), core reading programs should be approached with intelligent decision making. What that means for you is that you may be able to adapt a core reading program if you wish to do so, but you will need to ask for permission from your mentor teacher during your placement and from your principal when you are teaching in your own classroom. When you adapt your lessons, you should think about how well the program matches your guiding principles, and what changes or additions need to be made to improve the alignment.

Achieve the Core (2016) is a resource that offers several things you can do to help you improve or enhance a core reading program if you have concerns about the one you are expected to use in your classroom. First, they recommend that you make sure the texts in the program are worthy of your students' time and attention. In this situation, you would want to make sure each text you use from the basal is high quality and supports the learning goals you have for your students. If some of the texts don't meet those expectations, skip them or replace them with other texts that you think are more appropriate. Second, you will want to check to see if the lessons link reading, writing, listening, and speaking. If the majority of them do not, you'll need to augment the lessons to provide those linkages to support students' literacy learning. In addition, you should look at what vocabulary words are taught and how. Many basal reading programs introduce a large number of vocabulary words that may be necessary to know for a specific text, but they are not tier 2 words (see Chapter 9) that are useful across many texts. If this is the case, you will want to strategically choose the words you teach to ensure that students can learn and use them in their reading, writing, listening, and speaking vocabularies.

Finally, consider whether the basal reader provides sufficient opportunities to build students' knowledge about the topics addressed in the texts that are included. If not, you will want to add such opportunities to build students' background knowledge and to deepen their existing knowledge. As a learner-ready teacher who uses culturally relevant practices, you will want to seek ways to affirm your students' backgrounds and lives beyond school so they see themselves in the readings and the relevance of reading lessons (Toppel, 2015). Think about your guiding principles and beliefs statements from earlier chapters. Did you include something about how you will help every student learn to read and write? How will you adapt your lessons from the basal reader to help students who may be learning English? How will you supplement the basal reader to make connections with students' lives beyond school?

Connection to the Field: Teaching with Knowledge of Students' Lives

Ask your mentor teacher how they gather information about students' lives beyond school. This may include interests, home lives, languages spoken, traditions, celebrations, and more. Talk with your mentor teacher about how you can be purposeful in incorporating the information you gather about students into your lessons. This may include supplementing the reading program with children's literature that reflects your students' lives beyond school.

WORKSHOP APPROACH. **Reading and writing workshops** are designed to offer a simple and predictable structure so the teacher can focus on the complex work of observing and monitoring students' progress and teaching to meet their needs and build on their strengths. A workshop approach is based on the belief that children learn to read and write by engaging in authentic reading and writing activities (Calkins, 2015).

In a workshop approach, each session typically begins with a mini-lesson that provides explicit instruction on a specific skill or strategy that students need to learn. For young students, mini-lessons are indeed mini! They may be as short as 5 minutes and not longer than 10 minutes. As soon as the mini-lesson ends, students go off to do their own independent work, with a focus on using what they learned in the mini-lesson. Independent work takes place for 35 to 45 minutes each day. Independent work usually involves reading high-quality children's literature and writing in a variety of genres. During independent work time, the teacher confers with individual students to see how they are doing and to provide targeted, individualized instruction to help them with their reading and writing. Teachers also lead small guided reading or guided writing groups during this time. Sometimes teachers provide a brief second mini-lesson for the whole class during the independent work time to address a common need they have observed from their work conferencing with students or facilitating guided groups. Finally, the workshop ends with an opportunity for students to share what they worked on and how it went. To get more information about a workshop approach, see Margin Note 12.19 where you will be able to access a framework for Calkins's Units of Study approach to reading and writing workshop as well as a sample daily schedule. As you look at these materials, consider how well this approach aligns with your guiding principles and what modifications of additions you might need to make to address your curriculum as well as your students' needs.

Margin Note 12.19: Units of Study Model of Reading and Writing Workshop

Calkins's Units of Study Framework

http://www.unitsofstudy.com/framework

Calkins's Units of Study Overview

http://www.unitsofstudy.com/shared/resources/Overview%20of%20A%20Day's%20Reading%20or%20Writing%20Workshop.pdf

ADAPTING THE WORKSHOP APPROACH. Let's say you are in a placement where your mentor teacher is using a workshop approach. How does that fit with your own guiding principles? One of the most commonly cited benefits of using a workshop approach is the focus on reading authentic children's literature and writing for authentic purposes, but a common criticism is that explicit instruction may be too limited for students, especially those who find reading and writing difficult. Perhaps you believe there should be more explicit instruction beyond just the mini-lessons included in the workshop approach. You may also notice that students are consistently making errors in reading and writing, but you have not seen any explicit instruction provided to teach them how to address those errors. For example, you may see that students are not using context clues to figure out unknown words or they are linking together written ideas with a string of "ands" rather than writing complete sentences. You might consider asking your mentor teacher if you could teach a lesson about context clues or writing complete sentences to help ensure that they are building the skills and strategies they need to grow as readers and writers.

THE DAILY 5 AND CAFÉ. The **Daily 5** is a flexible literacy framework that provides routines for five literacy tasks that students engage in on a daily basis. If you are unsure of how to structure your literacy block, then you may want to use and adapt this framework. It was developed by two sisters, Gail Boushey and Joan Moser (2014) and it was designed to promote independence and promote engaged reading, writing, and learning. The Daily 5 and CAFÉ are different from the other reading programs discussed in this chapter because they really are just a structure and not a curriculum. In fact, Daily 5 and CAFÉ have no specific curricular content, materials, or texts. That means you bring the knowledge about how to teach reading, and they provide ideas for routines. This approach can be used in any school or district and can be the structure used to address any state standards. In the Daily 5 structure, students participate in meaningful literacy activities independently and with a partner in a center or station format. The Daily 5 structure is designed to instill behaviors of independence, engagement, and stamina, which is the ability to read and write independently for increasing

Figure 12.8. Daily 5 Components

Components	Descriptions of Component
Read to self	Students learn three ways to read a book (pictures, words, retelling), how to select good-fit books, how to manage their own independent reading materials, and how to develop reading stamina.
Work on writing	Students learn to set up a writing notebook, to select writing topics, to underline words they don't know how to spell, and to develop writing stamina.
Read to someone	Students read with a partner to practice reading, check understanding, give feedback, and coach each other.
Listen to reading	Students listen to models of fluent reading and to build comprehension.
Word work	Students learn and use spelling patterns, prefixes and suffixes, and high-frequency words to support their reading and writing development.

Margin Note 12.20: Daily 5 and CAFÉ

What Is the Daily 5 and CAFÉ?

https://www.youtube.com/watch?v=Tk1YxpGRdrk

The Daily 5 in First Grade

https://www.youtube.com/watch?v=sJaeZ06QIb0

CAFÉ Menu

https://www.thedailycafe.com/sites/default/files/Conferring_Notebook_CAFE_Menu.pdf

periods of time. Furthermore, the Daily 5 structure provides teachers with the time and structure to meet diverse student needs through whole group, small group, and individual instruction. So, what are the five activities in the Daily 5? They are listed and briefly described above in Figure 12.8 above.

The developers of the Daily 5 also created the Literacy CAFÉ System (Boushey & Moser, 2009) to provide teachers with a way to maximize student understanding of the four key components of successful reading through the use of the CAFÉ menu. CAFÉ is an acronym for comprehension, accuracy, fluency, and expand vocabulary. This part of the program focuses on teacher-led whole group, small group, and individual instruction. Typically, the teacher begins the literacy block (i.e., 90 to 120 minutes set aside for literacy instruction each day) with a whole group lesson on comprehension. The teacher then conducts guided reading groups and individual instruction to provide targeted instruction to meet students' reading needs while the other students work on Daily 5 activities independently or with a partner. The teacher also does an accuracy lesson each day, usually in a whole group, and another whole group lesson to address either fluency or expanding vocabulary. Most teachers alternate between fluency and expanding vocabulary lessons, doing one the first day and the other on the next day. To take a deeper dive into Daily 5 and CAFÉ, watch the two videos in Margin Note 12.20. The first one provides a great overview of Daily 5 and CAFÉ, and the second video shows how a first-grade teacher implements this approach in her classroom. You will also see a CAFÉ menu that shows the specific strategies that can be addressed in each of the four components of comprehension, accuracy, fluency, and expanding vocabulary. As you watch the videos and review the CAFÉ menu, consider how this approach would look if implemented in the classroom where you are doing your placement. How does this approach align with your beliefs and guiding principles? Are there things you would want to change or add to the Daily 5 and CAFÉ to align more closely with your beliefs and guiding principles?

GUIDED READING. **Guided reading** is not a program by itself, but it is a key component to most reading programs; therefore, we've decided to discuss it in this section of the chapter. Guided reading is small group, teacher-led instruction to address reading skills and strategies targeted to the development and needs of students (Fountas & Pinnell, 2012). In guided reading, teachers work with small groups of three to eight students at a table to provide brief lessons that usually last 10 to 15 minutes and address a specific skill or strategy using leveled texts. Guided reading allows the teacher to intentionally provide differentiated instruction by grouping students who have similar skill and strategy needs together for a lesson or series of lessons. Because of the small group structure, teachers can further differentiate by including work with individual students as part of the guided reading lesson (Iaquinta, 2006). Instead of the group reading aloud at the same time or taking turns reading, guided reading means each student reads quietly to themselves and at their own pace. You monitor their reading by asking each student to read just loud enough so you can hear them. Watch the video in Margin Note 12.21 to see an example of a first-grade guided reading lesson.

Margin Note 12.21: First Grade Guided Reading Lesson

https://www.youtube.com/watch?v=prT7w6ViwE0

You may be wondering how to get young students to read quietly without interfering with others' ability to concentrate. Make whisper phones for students so they can hear themselves read even when their voice is only a whisper. The directions for making whisper phones are in Margin Note 12.22. Although some teachers decorate the whisper phones, you can simply write students' names on them with permanent marker and ask students to keep their whisper phones in their desks or cubbies. You may want to occasionally run them through the dishwasher.

Margin Note 12.22: How to Make a Whisper Phone

https://blog.maketaketeach.com/how-to-make-a-phonics-phone/

Guided reading is different than traditional reading groups in that they are flexible and short-term, meaning that teachers frequently change the group composition to reflect the specific lesson to be taught and the students' evolving skills and reading levels. This small group format allows you to closely monitor students' reading needs while providing time for you to prompt students' use of strategies you learned in Section II of this book. Guided reading is not just about listening to students read in small groups. Instead, it's valuable time for coaching and guiding readers to think about how they are using strategies to become better readers. That means you need to recognize when students need help as they read and you need to know how to prompt them to use strategies (Mikita, Rodgers, Berenbon, & Winkler, 2019).

Teachers generally provide guided reading instruction every day for the readers in their classroom who may need more support. Depending on the number of students in your classroom, the number of reading groups, and the length of the literacy block, you may opt to provide guided reading instruction only 3 days a week for your readers who need less support. Watch the video in Margin Note 12.23 to learn how a first-grade teacher organizes guided reading groups, plans lessons, finds leveled texts, and uses resources. She provides links in the video information area to free guided reading resources that she discusses in the video. A typical format for a guided reading lesson is provided in Figure 12.9 on the next page.

Margin Note 12.23: What I Do for Guided Reading

https://www.youtube.com/watch?v=3S2Ny4YX4Cl

Figure 12.9. Guided Reading Format

Component	Teacher	Students
Brief book introduction	Reads title Takes students on a brief picture walk Draws attention to a few new words Ask students to make predictions about book	Participate in book introduction Comment about connection to own lives Look at pictures Make predictions
First reading	Monitors reading Listens to individual readers Offers help if needed	Read silently or in quiet voice
Second reading	Acknowledges use of strategies Asks students how they figured out words during reading	Read through the book again May participate in choral reading of book
Responding to the book	Invites conversation about the book Asks if predictions came true Makes informal assessment of comprehension	Talk about the book Discuss predictions Make connections to own lives Retell story
Focus lesson	Decides on a particular strategy or concept to use as a focus lesson	Participate in focus lesson Practice strategy
Follow-up	May invite students to extend reading through writing, art, or drama	Take part in extension activities

LEVELED BOOKS. Guided reading requires that you have books on students' instructional reading levels. You may want to revisit Chapter 3 to review running records and other forms of reading assessments. You don't want to use books that students can read independently for guided reading, and you don't want to use books that are too difficult. The instructional level is ideal because students can read those books with your help. Core reading programs tend to provide **leveled books** for guided reading as part of their kits. Some schools have sets of leveled books that teachers can check out from a book room. Regardless of where you find leveled books, you will notice that each source provides a different method of leveling. For instance, your required reading assessment system may provide a Lexile® score. Some books are leveled by **Lexile® levels**. But what if you want to use a set of books that are leveled in a different way, such as DRA, Scholastic, Reading Recovery, or other methods of leveling books? You will need a conversion guide, such as the correlation chart in Figure 12.10. Often, the challenge is to find leveled books or other kinds of texts that appeal to students' interests. See Figure 12.10 for a list of sources for free online leveled texts that are perfect for guided reading because they are short texts with a wide range of topics.

It is important to mention that we don't want to rigidly label students by their instructional reading level, or to restrict their access just to books on those levels. Texts at various levels appeal to students, based on their interests. Leveled texts are important for guided reading and for assessment purposes, but students should be able to choose from a wide range of reading materials in your classroom. For example, many of Roya's kindergartners and first graders were keenly interested in learning about the Titanic. Others were interested in reading about dinosaurs, race cars, or tigers. Students would eagerly look through books, regardless of the reading level, to gain more information about their topics of interest. Roya's students were motivated to want to read because of the wide range of materials she provided for students, based on their interests.

Figure 12.10. Links to Leveling Guides and Free Short Text

Name	Description	Website Link	QR Code
Book Level Correlation Chart	■ This chart is provided by Reading A–Z and you can choose which leveling methods to compare.	https://www.readinga-z.com/learninga-z-levels/level-correlation-chart/	
Leveled Books Database	■ Search this database by book title for the Guided Reading, Reading Recovery, and Accelerated Reader levels.	http://books.atozteacherstuff.com/leveled-books/	
America in Class	■ Primary sources for social studies topics	http://americainclass.org/primary-sources/	
DOGO News	■ Science and social studies themes ■ Teacher resources ■ Vocabulary word features	http://www.dogonews.com/	
Library of Congress	■ Primary sources ■ Lesson plans with all materials included ■ Search by topic or era	http://www.loc.gov/teachers/	
NewsELA	■ Articles have adjustable Lexile® levels ■ All curriculum areas included	https://newsela.com/	
One-page Nonfiction Reading/Thinking Passages	■ By grade level (grades 2 and above) ■ Paired nonfiction and fiction readings ■ Social studies and science passages	https://teacher.depaul.edu/Nonfiction_Readings.htm	
Tween Tribune	■ Adjustable Lexile® levels ■ Math, science, and social studies topics ■ Teacher resources included	http://tweentribune.com/	

(continued)

Figure 12.10. *(continued)*

Name	Description	Website Link	QR Code
Unite for Literacy	■ Picture books with a read aloud feature ■ All subjects represented	http://www.unitefor literacy.com/	
Wonderopolis	■ Vocabulary word features ■ Articles have a "listen" feature ■ All content areas represented ■ Search for topics	http://wonderopolis.org/ wonders	

Connection to the Field: Finding Leveled Text

Observe how and when your mentor teacher uses leveled texts with students. Ask your mentor teacher how they find leveled texts, what the levels mean, and how they know how to use which levels with students. Be sure to ask if your mentor teacher could share resources and helpful hints for finding leveled texts with you.

PREK APPROACHES. Across the United States, there are a variety of teacher licensure options. Your licensure band may be K–6, PreK–4, 1–8, or some other variation. In some states, teachers with licensure beginning with kindergarten may also be eligible to teach PreK. If this does not apply to your situation, you can skip this section. However, you may want to read about PreK approaches to better understand our youngest students' experiences with reading and writing prior to entering kindergarten.

Margin Note 12.24:
Montessori, Waldorf, and Reggio Emilia:
A Comparison of Philosophies

https://www.ourkids.net/school/montessori-vs-waldorf-reggio-emilia

What do you remember about your own PreK experiences? PreK programs vary widely in how they teach reading and writing. In Chapter 1 you learned that some states have PreK literacy standards, whereas others design learning experiences based on the kindergarten standards. PreK standards tend to be guided by the **National Association for the Education of Young Children** (NAEYC) position statement on developmentally appropriate practice and the Head Start Early Learning Outcomes Framework.

Popular approaches to teaching PreK reading and writing tend to be shaped by **Montessori**, **Waldorf**, and/or **Reggio Emilia** philosophies. All three approaches are student-centered with multiage classrooms, provide hands-on explorations, and honor students as individuals who develop at their own pace (Ourkids.net, n.d.). Refer to the website in Margin Note 12.24 to compare the three approaches in depth. Perhaps your mentor teacher uses a blend of these philosophies to teach reading and writing. Think about the subtle differences in the brief descriptions that follow.

THE MONTESSORI APPROACH uses individualized activities tailored to meet students' needs. If you were to use a **Montessori approach**, you would incorporate everyday objects in your classroom, provide multisensory learning experiences, and serve as a guide with a focus on helping each student learn. Specific to teaching and learning reading and writing, Montessori schools teach students the letter sounds before they teach the letter names because they emphasize understanding of the concepts instead of memorization. Vocabulary is taught through real-world experiences to provide students with authentic learning that connects words with actions, objects, and environments in real ways. For instance, a field trip to a farm would precede or coincide with learning farm-related words. A walk through the woods would precede learning vocabulary related to trees or the woods. Vocabulary words are also encountered and explained while reading aloud to students. With the Montessori approach, students learn to read by learning to write because the two acts are connected. Indeed, students are encouraged to experiment with writing from an early age with the understanding that expressing thoughts through writing is more important than using correct grammar or conventions. Teachers read aloud to students and encourage a love for reading for pleasure. Watch the short video in Margin Note 12.25 to learn how a public school in South Carolina transitioned to a Montessori school.

Margin Note 12.25: A Public School Transitions to Montessori

https://www.edutopia.org/video/public-school-transitions-montessori

THE WALDORF APPROACH focuses on inquiry-based, experiential learning where students learn through the arts and creative play. If you were to use a **Waldorf approach**, you would follow each student's lead. That is, you would carefully observe each student and teach based on what you noticed they were ready to learn. Specific to teaching and learning reading and writing, PreK students focus on listening to stories and poetry so they can appreciate oral language. The stories and poems are told repeatedly so students often memorize them. This builds listening skills. Instead of textbooks and leveled readers, teachers in Waldorf schools read aloud authentic children's literature. Students learn about story structure and the language associated with genres from repeated exposure to literature during story time. Students are encouraged to retell stories through creative play, such as puppet shows and reenactments. Learning to read and write typically does not formally occur until students are age 7 in Waldorf schools. Fine motor skills are developed through arts and crafts, which prepare young students for later writing. Read the blog in Margin Note 12.26 for an explanation of early literacy learning in a Waldorf school.

Margin Note 12.26: Early Literacy Learning in Waldorf Education

https://blog.waldorfmoraine.org/2019/07/early-literacy-learning-in-waldorf-education/

THE REGGIO EMILIA APPROACH encourages play-based learning, the arts, and students pursuing projects based on their interests. If you were to use the **Reggio Emilia approach**, you would help students decide which projects to pursue, how they plan to demonstrate their learning, and which materials they needed for their projects. You would follow each student's lead while serving as an advisor and documenting their progress. Specific to teaching and learning reading and writing, teachers get to know their students' interests and learning preferences. For instance, if a student is interested in dinosaurs, you would help that student design a project in which they explore resources about dinosaurs and lead them to ask questions to pursue during their project. If that student prefers to learn through building, then perhaps their project could include building a model or scene to demonstrate what they learned by pursuing their project. Teachers provide a print-rich environment with labels around the classroom, a wide variety of reading materials and genres in the classroom library, and inviting spaces for reading. For reading independently or with others, young students are drawn

Margin Note 12.27:
Education Counts
Michiana—The Reggio
Emilia Approach

https://www.youtube.com/
watch?v=fYx_aGs-DjU

to decorative rugs and beanbag chairs. Teachers read aloud to students and introduce vocabulary words as they appear in stories. In classrooms that use the Reggio Emilia approach, young students are encouraged to experiment with using a variety of writing utensils, such as pens, pencils, markers, paint, and a rubber stamp alphabet. The focus is on play-based learning, and the teacher provides scaffolding as needed, based on students' interests and specific learning needs. Watch the short video in Margin Note 12.27 to learn how a preschool in Indiana uses the Reggio Emilia approach.

What do you believe about teaching reading and writing to PreK students? How do your guiding principles align with each approach described? How could you use or adapt aspects of those approaches in your future PreK classroom?

*E*ngaging with Families: How Students Learn

Work with your mentor teacher to create a brief survey to ask families how they think their children learn best. Be sure to secure permission before sending it home with students. Use information from the responses to shape your lessons and learning center activities.

What Do You Believe about Organizing Reading and Writing Instruction?

As you reflect on the ideas presented in this chapter, consider how you plan to organize your classroom for reading and writing instruction that fits with your beliefs framework and guiding principles. Who are you as a teacher? Although room arrangement is important, think beyond the furniture. How do you plan to structure your literacy block? What might your schedule look like? What approaches do you plan to include? Which resources might you use and where will you find them? How will you adapt programs, approaches, and resources to meet your students' reading and writing needs? How do these decisions match your teacher identity? After reviewing the takeaways from this chapter and reflecting on your ideas, go to the What Do You Believe template provided in the Chapter 12 Resources on the website to record your ideas.

Closing Thoughts

Teaching students to read and write is a complex endeavor with many moving parts. Considering how to organize your reading and writing instruction requires a great deal of thought, planning, and knowing how to provide your students with skills and strategies that they need. At the start of this chapter we met Aiden who was uncomfortable with the literacy instruction in his first-grade placement. You may be in a similar situation. Now that you are aware of different programs, approaches, and you've thought about adapting instruction, we encourage you to talk with your mentor teacher. Ask your mentor teacher which programs and approaches they prefer and what advice they have for you about making adaptations to better align your instruction with your beliefs framework and guiding principles.

*T*akeaways from Chapter 12

- Your beliefs framework will continue to develop as you progress throughout your career.
- Your beliefs shape your teaching identity and inform your guiding principles.
- Your guiding principles help you keep your attention and effort on the most important aspects of teaching reading and writing.
- Organizing your schedule for teaching reading requires thinking about room arrangement and specific routines.
- Specific reading programs and approaches may be required in your school context, but you can adapt them to better fit with your beliefs about teaching reading and writing.

*T*o Learn More about Organizing Reading and Writing Instruction

Books

Boushey, G., & Moser, J. (2014). *The daily 5: Fostering literacy independence in the elementary grades* (2nd ed.). Portsmouth, NH: Stenhouse Publishers.

https://www.stenhouse.com/content/daily-5-second-edition

If you are interested in learning more about the Daily 5, this best-selling book is a great place to get started. The two sisters, Boushey and Moser, developed the Daily 5 structure based on their experiences as classroom teachers, reading specialists and coaches, and special education teachers. This book provides detailed descriptions of the approach, suggestions for implementation, and helpful tools and templates that you can use in your classroom.

Boushey, G., & Behne, A. (2019). *The CAFÉ book: Engaging all students in daily literacy assessment and instruction* (2nd ed.). Portsmouth, NH: Stenhouse Publishers.

https://www.stenhouse.com/content/cafe-book-expanded-second-edition

If CAFÉ is an approach you might like to use in your teaching, check out this book written by the developers of this approach. The authors provide easy-to-understand descriptions of each of the four components of CAFÉ: comprehension, accuracy, fluency, and extended vocabulary. They also provide strategy lessons, assessment ideas, and implementation tips to help you get CAFÉ up and running in your classroom.

Campo, N. (2008). *Literacy centers in photographs*. New York, NY: Scholastic.

https://shop.scholastic.com/teachers-ecommerce/teacher/books/literacy-centers-in-photographs-9780545278935.html

This super practical book shows you step-by-step with photographs how to organize learning centers for grades K–2, set up routines, and manage learning centers in the classroom. Examples focus mainly on literacy in areas such as poetry, listening, reading, and writing.

Fountas, I. C., & Pinnell, G. S. (2016). *Guided reading: Responsive teaching across the grades* (2nd ed.). Portsmouth, NH: Heinemann.

https://www.heinemann.com/products/e08684.aspx

This is the "must-have" book about guided reading instruction. It is overflowing with useful information about what guided reading instruction is and how to do it. In fact, the book is over 600 pages in length and a definitive resource for guided reading. It provides sample lessons and suggestions for scheduling and organizing guided reading instruction. The book also addresses matching students and books for effective guided reading lessons.

Kriete, R., & Davis, C. (2014). *The morning meeting book: K–8* (3rd ed.). Turner Falls, MA: The Northeast Foundation for Children.

https://www.responsiveclassroom.org/product/morning-meeting-book/

This teacher resource explains how to get started with morning meetings, including the morning message. Examples are provided from classroom teachers. You can use this guide to establish your classroom morning routine to build community while using reading and writing in a nurturing environment.

Southall, M. (2007). *Differentiated literacy centers*. New York, NY: Scholastic.

https://shop.scholastic.com/teachers-ecommerce/teacher/books/differentiated-literacy-centers-9780545193795.html

This book provides over 85 practical activities for use in learning centers to promote reading comprehension, fluency, word study, and writing. With a focus on differentiation, the activities can be matched with each student's needs to promote learning for all. The book also provides an easy-to-implement framework to set up centers and track student progress.

Articles

Creating a Classroom Library

https://www.readingrockets.org/article/creating-classroom-library

This short article provides step-by-step instructions on how to set up and organize a classroom library. It provides lots of pictures to show how other teachers have organized their classroom libraries. The article ends with a video that provides additional suggestions for creating a classroom library.

Dewitz, P., & Jones, J. (2013). Using basal readers: From dutiful fidelity to intelligent decision making. *The Reading Teacher, 66*, 391–400.

https://doi.org/10.1002/TRTR.01134

If you want to learn more about how you can adapt and make informed decisions about how to use a core reading program, this article is for you! The article provides practical suggestions to modify and augment a basal reading program to meet the needs of all students in your classroom.

Reutzel, D. R., & Clark, S. (2011). Organizing literacy classrooms for effective instruction. *The Reading Teacher, 65*, 96–109.

https://doi.org/10.1002/TRTR.01013

This article is written for beginning teachers to provide guidance on the classroom environment, management, assessment, instruction, parent and community involvement, and personal and professional growth. Organized in a Q/A format, the article addresses many of the questions you'll have about setting up and organizing your first classroom.

Websites and Online Resources

The Daily 5

https://www.thedailycafe.com/daily-5

This website provides articles, photos, videos, and other resources related to implementing the Daily 5 structure into your teaching. The section on the Daily 5 provides lessons and videos that you can use to plan your instruction in these five areas: read to self, work on writing, read to someone, word work, and listen to reading. The section on classroom design offers many ideas, pictures, tips, and videos to help you decide how to set up your room.

What Is Guided Reading?

http://teacher.scholastic.com/reading/bestpractices/guidedreading/whatis.pdf

This short handout provides a clear and concise description of what guided reading is, how to match students with appropriate books, and how to implement guided reading in the classroom. It also explains how guided reading supports students' reading development.

Blogs

Fountas, I. C., & Pinnell, G. S. (2019, Jan. 18). What is Guided Reading? Fountas & Pinnell Literacy Blog.

https://fpblog.fountasandpinnell.com/what-is-guided-reading

This blog offers a clear and concise description of guided reading. It includes an embedded video that shows clips of guided reading lessons in a variety of classrooms. It also provides links to other useful resources about guided reading.

Newingham, B. (2009, Oct. 17). Reading Workshop and What It Looks Like in My Classroom. *Scholastic Teaching Blog.*

https://www.scholastic.com/teachers/blog-posts/beth-newingham/reading-workshop/

This blog describes how a teacher implements reading workshop in her classroom. The blog includes a video showing reading workshop in action as well as descriptions of exactly how she and her students implement reading workshop. The blog also provides photos, lesson descriptions, and tips for organization, management, and assessment within reading workshop.

Videos

Teaching Reading K–2

https://learner.org/series/teaching-reading-k-2-a-library-of-classroom-practices/connecting-skills-to-text/?jwsource=cl

Watch this video and consider which ideas and approaches align with your guiding principles. Make note of the ideas from the video that you have seen implemented in your placement and consider which ones you would like to add to your literacy program once you have your own classroom.

Station Rotation: Differentiating Instruction to Reach All Students

https://www.youtube.com/watch?v=Kg38A1ggYiE

This video provides a great overview of how a first-grade teacher organizes her literacy instruction. It highlights how she uses centers and differentiates instruction to meet the needs of all students in her classroom.

© Iakov Filimonov/Shutterstock.com

Communication is essential for building and maintaining relationships with families.

How Do I Support My Students' Literacy Learning?

Working with Families, Colleagues, and Community Members

Joo-Hee enjoys working with her classmates on projects, and she is a member of her college's education club where she is the chair of the service committee. Last semester, she coordinated a book drive for children and families at a local homeless shelter. When she and the other committee members took the books to the homeless shelter, a staff member invited them to read a few of the books to the children. Joo-Hee was thrilled to have this chance to read with the children, and she was touched at how appreciative and kind the parents were.

Joo-Hee recently visited her Aunt Yanghee, who is a preschool teacher in another state. Her aunt has told her that to be an effective teacher she has to work with other teachers, her students' families, and community members. This information makes Joo-Hee nervous because she wonders if her future teaching colleagues will take her seriously because she is young and will be a new teacher. She is scared about talking with parents because she has never really had any experience doing so in a school setting, and she fears that because she is young, family members may not take her seriously. Joo-Hee is also surprised about the expectation that teachers work well with community members because she never thought about them playing a role in young children's schooling. Her Aunt Yanghee recently told her that teaching is all about building relationships—with students, families, colleagues, and others in the community. Joo-Hee wonders, how can I do all of this?

Like Joo-Hee, the experiences you have in class and in your daily life can form the foundation for you to work well with families, colleagues, and community members. In this chapter, we address Joo-Hee's worries by discussing the importance of connecting and communicating effectively with families, collaborating with colleagues, and building relationships with community members to help support young children's literacy learning. We also offer useful strategies and insights about how to address common challenges that new teachers face with building relationships and working effectively with families, colleagues, and community members.

Working with Families

The teacher candidates we work with often say they are worried or nervous about working with families. You have likely heard that **parent involvement** is important, but chances are you have not yet had many opportunities to interact much with students' families. Although you might be feeling inexperienced or nervous about working with students' families, they play an important role in children's learning, attitudes toward school, and educational outcomes. We will share some key ideas and useful strategies you can use during your placement as well as when you have your own classroom, so that you can get more comfortable and effective in working with your students' families. We understand that you may have limited opportunities to interact with families during your placement, so we recommend that you consider how you can use the information and strategies in this chapter once you are teaching in your own classroom.

RESEARCH ON FAMILY INVOLVEMENT IN EDUCATION. A review of over 80 research studies concluded that family involvement contributes to students' literacy achievement regardless of family income, parent education level, or ethnicity (Henderson & Mapp, 2002). Moreover, the impact is greatest for children whose families have lower incomes and lower parent educational levels. This review of research found that when children's families were involved with their schools, the children earned better grades, had better school attendance, had more positive attitudes toward school, and demonstrated better social skills and behavior than their peers whose families were not involved. In addition, this review found that children whose families were involved in their schooling were more likely to graduate from high school and pursue post-secondary education or job training. In other words, the family involvement you address in your teaching—even as an early childhood teacher— can contribute to children staying in school and graduating!

So now that you know that family involvement is important because it contributes to positive outcomes for children in all aspects of their schooling, let's turn our attention to what types of family involvement are effective for producing these positive outcomes for students. Jeynes (2012) analyzed 50 research studies and found that four specific types of family involvement activities produced the greatest achievement gains for children. Those activities were shared reading at home, teacher–family partnerships to work toward academic and behavioral goals, daily homework checking at home, and regular two-way communication. Let's now dig into what you can do as a teacher to help you work well with families.

BUILDING RELATIONSHIPS WITH FAMILIES. You have probably heard the term **parent involvement**, but we want you to consider the term more broadly. First, because families can take many forms, we prefer to broaden the term from just "parent" to "family" to include the many adults who may have caregiver or parental roles in our students' lives. Our students may live in two-parent homes, single parent homes, or they may have grandparents, aunts, uncles, siblings, cousins, or foster parents as their primary caregivers and parental role models. Some students may have a babysitter who helps with homework, attends school events, and serves in a parental-type role. Regardless of the composition, these are our students' families and our partners in their education.

Now let's look at the word "involvement." Let's use a metaphor related to dating. If you say, "we are involved," that means that you are dating or seeing one another, but if you say, "we are engaged," it shows an increased level of commitment that is much deeper and more serious (Elish-Piper, 2014/2015). Furthermore, the term involvement implies "doing to" whereas the term engagement implies "doing with" (Ferlazzo, 2011). In other words, **family engagement** is more than simply sending home an activity or making an occasional phone call. It is focused on developing meaningful relationships with families to support students' learning, growth, and success in school.

As we noted previously, many teacher candidates and new teachers are nervous about working with families. They worry family member may ask questions they can't answer or raise concerns about some of their practices or decisions. Although it may seem like family members asking questions or sharing concerns indicate a problem, we argue that it's the exact opposite! These things indicate that families understand the importance of school and want to be engaged in their children's education. In this section of the chapter, we discuss and debunk common challenges to family engagement, and we share practical suggestions for how you can communicate effectively and build collaborative relationships with families that will support students' literacy learning and school success.

COMMUNICATING WITH FAMILIES. As in any relationship, communication is an important foundation and essential component to building and maintaining a relationship. You may have some chances to communicate with families in collaboration with your mentor teacher in your placement. When you have your own classroom, you will want to get started on communicating with families as soon as you know who your students will be. You will want to introduce yourself, so families know who their child's teacher is. You can also share a bit about yourself, so they get a sense of who you are as a person. You can send a letter home, send an email introduction, share a video message, or—better yet—all three! Yes, different families prefer different types of communication, so it's important to find out from families whether they prefer notes sent home in their children's backpacks, email messages, phone calls, or another communication channel. Regardless of the format of your introduction, Currie (2015) offers three guidelines for you to consider. First, keep the message short and enthusiastic. Second, make personal connections in the communication. And, third, use the method of communication that families prefer. See Figure 13.1 for a sample introduction letter a teacher might share at the beginning of the school year.

In your communications with families (in collaboration with your mentor teacher during your placement and once you have your own classroom), you'll want to be sure to focus on the positive. In fact, some teachers find it useful to make "good news" calls or send good news notes or emails home to demonstrate that you are looking for the positive, not just concentrating on problems. An orientation toward positive communication with families shows that you are concerned about the whole child and are committed to working toward improvement. Even if a student is struggling academically or behaviorally, you can frame your communication in a positive way. For example, instead of saying, "Dontrell did not turn in his homework again so I have recorded three zeroes in my grade book." You could say, "I am concerned that Dontrell did not turn in his homework three times this week. I would like for all of us to work together to help Dontrell get on track with his homework. One idea I have is a homework checklist that Dontrell can fill out, that I can check before he goes home, and you can check it at home. Then the next day, I can recheck it when he turns in his homework. Do you think that idea would work, or do you have another idea that might work better? I'm sure if we all work together, we can help Dontrell with developing the skills he needs to

Figure 13.1. Sample Introduction Letter

Dear Families,

I am very excited to have your child in our class this year. I'm new to Porter Elementary School, and I can't wait to get to know you and your child. I enjoy sharing my love of reading and writing with my students. We will be reading lots of different types of books this year, and we will be writing lots too! We will study many interesting topics and work on important skills in reading, writing, and math. My main goal this year is for your child to develop a love of reading, writing, and school.

This summer I got a new puppy named Daisy, and I did lots of bike riding, hiking, and reading. I hope you had a fun summer and that your child is excited to get back to school. I can't wait to get to know your child and you, too!

I will be sharing a weekly update on our class website. At Open House, I'll ask you to tell me the way you prefer to communicate, and I'll share information about our classroom. Please be sure to contact me at any time with questions, concerns, or information that will help me teach your child better.

I look forward to a great year working with your child and you!

Sincerely,

Ms. Katie Norris
(123) 456-7890
knorris@porter123.org

---

complete and turn in his homework." By taking a positive, problem-solving stance, you can show families that you want to help the student succeed, and you want to work with the family to do so.

KEY CONSIDERATIONS FOR COMMUNICATING WITH FAMILIES. When you think of **communicating with families**, the first thing that comes to mind may be sending notes home in backpacks. Today's families are incredibly busy, and newsletters, homework folders, and announcements may not ever make it out of the backpack, let alone start a conversation or build engagement between teachers and families. These types of communications can be classified as "one way" because they are sent or shared, but they generally do not invite or encourage a response. That's not to say, however, that one-way communication is bad or unnecessary. In fact, some types of one-way communication can be very useful such as online parent portals where parents can view grades, attendance, and homework assignments. Other schools may use a one-way communication approach with a daily phone message listing homework assignments and dates for projects and classroom events. Although these approaches make it easy to share specific information with families, they are not sufficient to foster meaningful communication between teachers and families.

The most meaningful communication between teachers and families is "two way"—meaning that there is an expectation and a mechanism for a response as well as an invitation for further exchanges. Many teachers have found it useful to ask families how they prefer to communicate. Some options include connecting by phone, by email, in person, by text, or via notes sent to and from school. Once this is determined, you can use the preferred method of communication to connect with families.

You can even expand traditional types of teacher–family communications, such as a class handbook or weekly newsletter, by asking family members to review, respond to a question or two, and return it to you so you know that communication has actually occurred. Sending home student work in a folder on a regular schedule is also a common practice that can be made into a two-way communication by including a form for a family member to review and make comments. If you have families that speak a language at home other than English, you will need to determine which materials are essential for translation so that family members are kept informed of the most important information and expectations, and you can understand and respond to their questions and concerns. If you do not have a school staff member such as a family liaison or bilingual aide who can do the translations, options you can use include working with community groups, asking bilingual parents to help with translations, or working with bilingual students at a local high school, college, or university.

To promote face-to-face communication, some teachers set a "drop-in time" each week or month in the morning before school when parents drop off students or late in the afternoon when family members are available. With the availability of technology, these "drop in times" can be expanded to include the use of Skype or FaceTime to connect virtually. Some teachers use closed (invitation only) Facebook groups to post information, announcements, photos and videos from class, and links to useful resources, as well as providing a place to encourage family members to post comments, but not to discuss specific concerns or details about a student. Other teachers use a private Twitter group to share similar information or to have students write short tweets about what they have learned or are working on at school. Whatever methods of communication you use, the real goal is to communicate with families regularly to establish positive, productive relationships to support their children's learning. See Margin Note 13.1 for nine tips you can use to promote positive and effective communication with students' families.

Margin Note 13.1:
9 Tips for Successful Parent–Teacher Communication

https://blog.edmentum.com/9-tips-successful-parent-teacher-communication

Working Well with Diverse Families

Your students' families will represent the diversity of the community where you teach. Over the past decade, families have become more diverse, including increasing numbers of single parent homes and children living in poverty. In addition, we are seeing increased cultural and linguistic diversity in today's families (Vespa, Lewis, & Kreider, 2013). Furthermore, families report being busier and more stressed than in the past (Kremer-Sadlik & Paugh, 2007). Although these challenges exist in all school settings, working with families is essential to supporting all children's learning and school success.

To help you address these challenges and engage with your students' families in meaningful ways, we recommend that you take on an **ABC approach to reaching all families** (Elish-Piper, 2015). In this approach, *A* stands for access; *B* stands for building; and *C* stands for creativity. Let's look at each of these components and how combining the parts of the approach will allow you to work well with all types of families.

ACCESS. Access is the foundation of all family engagement efforts. Barriers to family involvement include time, language, transportation, child or elder care responsibilities, and fear or anxiety about schools. Although these barriers can be challenging to overcome, you can definitely address or at least minimize their impact. See Figure 13.2 for some suggestions on how you can address these common challenges to family involvement.

Although we've provided some suggestions for addressing challenges to family engagement, you probably have other questions and ideas. We recommend that you download the report provided in Margin Note 13.2 to learn more about the types of barriers families experience that can prevent or limit their involvement in their children's schooling. As you read the report, consider which of the suggestions seem most promising for addressing these challenges. You may also find it helpful to

Figure 13.2. Suggestions to Address Common Challenges to Family Engagement

Challenges	Suggestions
Time	■ Find out when families are available and schedule classroom events then. ■ Try scheduling conferences or events early in the morning, in the evening, or on the weekend to allow more families to participate.
Language	■ Recruit bilingual community members to translate documents and to translate at conferences and school events. ■ Learn a few words in the languages of your students' families so you can demonstrate you are interested in communicating with them.
Transportation	■ Encourage families to form carpools. ■ Arrange for school buses to pick up families at regular school bus stops to bring them to and take them back from school events. ■ Work with public transportation services in the community to get bus or train tokens that family members can use to attend school events. ■ If transportation is not available, use technology so families can attend through Skype, FaceTime, Google Hangout, or other free technology platforms.
Childcare	■ Work with a local high school child development program so high school students can provide childcare during school events. ■ Arrange for the local YMCA, park district, or houses of worship to provide volunteers for childcare during events. Be sure to check with the school for guidelines on volunteers.
Fear or anxiety about schools	■ Recruit a group of engaged family members to encourage other families to get involved. ■ Post welcome signs in multiple languages and make the school feel welcoming and warm with comfortable seating and smiling and friendly people in the office and hallways. ■ Ask engaged family members to volunteer to provide tours and to introduce new families to office staff, the principal, and other family members from the classroom or school.

talk to your mentor teacher about the types of challenges they have faced and how they have tried to overcome them. You may even be able to share some new ideas with your mentor teacher from what you are learning in this chapter and in Margin Note 13.2.

Margin Note 13.2: Reducing Barriers to Family Engagement

https://go.panoramaed.com/whitepaper/reducing-barriers-to-family-engagement

BUILDING RELATIONSHIPS. **Building relationships** with families to develop children's success should be the focus of all family engagement efforts (Ferlazzo & Hammond, 2009). First, you will need to build trusting, respectful relationships with families. Implementing two-way communication as described earlier in this chapter is a great place to start. As with any new relationship, you will need to be patient yet persistent. If you don't get a response, try another approach. And, just as you will want to adopt an equity mindset in teaching your students, you will want to adopt this same stance in your interactions and partnerships with families. Rather than focusing on how families may be different from you or your own family, consider what assets and strengths they possess. We introduced the idea of funds of knowledge (González, Moll, & Amanti, 2005) in Chapter 1 in relation to students, but it also applies

Margin Note 13.3: How to Use Funds of Knowledge in Your Classroom and Create Better Connections

https://www.notimefor flashcards.com/2018/02/ funds-of-knowledge.html

when working with families. When you adopt a funds of knowledge approach, you will be able to value and build on the skills, abilities, ideas, practices, and bodies of knowledge that families possess and use in their daily lives. See Margin Note 13.3 for specific examples of how you can use funds of knowledge to build connections with your students' families.

BEING CREATIVE. You may have heard the old adage, "If you do what you've always done, you'll get what you've always gotten." This is also true for family engagement. Some traditional practices such as print newsletters, open house, and parent–teacher conferences can be effective ways to engage some families, but others will be unlikely to participate. Therefore, you need to consider **creative ways to involve more families**. Just to get your ideas flowing, here are some ideas from teachers we have worked with in our local schools:

- Bingo for Books (evening or weekend bingo to win children's books)
- Dudes and Donuts (a before-school breakfast for students and the "dudes" in their lives)
- Family stories festival (where children and their families write or illustrate family stories and share them)
- Family craft night (so families can work together to create seasonal or themed craft projects)
- Family game night (with lots of fun learning games for families to play)

One of the most creative ideas a local school did was to involve the men in students' lives by hosting a Men in Books evening event with read alouds, games, book-themed snacks, and a reptile zoo. Yes, you read that right—a traveling reptile zoo! The event was so well attended that cars were parked up to three blocks away from the school! The teachers in that low income school were shocked at how many men were in their students' lives—fathers, stepfathers, uncles, grandfathers, cousins, neighbors, family friends, older brothers, moms' boyfriends, and so on. A big lesson that these teachers learned was if you get creative, they will probably come. Most importantly, these teachers reported increases in attendance at future school events including parent–teacher conferences. What all of these ideas have in common is that they are creative, fun, and likely to attract some family members who may be hesitant or unlikely to attend conferences or other traditional school events. What other creative ideas do you have to engage families? If you are worried about whether your creative idea will work well, you can survey families about the ways they would like to be involved in their child's learning and at school.

Connection to the Field: Creative Ideas to Engage Families

Talk with your mentor teacher about some of the creative ideas you might like to use in the future to engage families. Ask for their professional opinion of what may work and what they may need to consider before implementation. Ask them to share the most creative ideas they've used to engage families and what worked well and what could be improved.

Making Conferences, Open Houses, and Curriculum Nights More Family-focused

Some of the most common family engagement strategies used in schools are **conferences, open houses, and curriculum nights**. Every school we've worked with in our careers uses these types of activities to connect and communicate with families. And although these types of activities can form the foundation of family engagement, they are not sufficient by themselves. You will also want to build meaningful relationships with families, and implement two-way communication approaches to ensure ongoing connections and collaboration with your students' families.

CONFERENCES. Traditionally, **parent–teacher conferences** were designed to allow teachers to share information with parents about students' academic performance and behavior. That approach tended to be one-way, with the teacher presenting information and the family members listening. With the move toward family engagement wherein teachers and family members are partners in supporting students' education, some teachers have moved to three-way conferences that involve students. Let's look first at general best practices for conferences that Mrs. Patz, a kindergarten teacher, follows as well as how she implements three-way conferences to fully engage her students' families.

Mrs. Patz is one of the most amazing kindergarten teachers I (Laurie) have ever known. She is energetic, creative, kind, smart, and hardworking, but, more importantly, she is great at building relationships with her students and their families. Mrs. Patz once told me, "Just like I welcome my family members and friends into my home and want them to feel comfortable, I do the same thing when families come to our classroom for conferences." When I went on to ask her how she does this, she shared several specific ideas. First, she schedules conferences so there is time in between them if conversations need to go longer than the 15 minutes normally scheduled for conferences. She also thinks of the conference as a conversation. She typically sends home progress reports before the conference so family members can review them and then discuss them with her at the conference. She also makes sure she is not doing all (or even most) of the talking at the conference so that she can learn more about her students by listening to the perspectives of family members. Finally, Mrs. Patz makes sure to conclude every conference on a positive note and to thank family members for being her partner in the student's education.

THREE-WAY CONFERENCES. Several years ago, Mrs. Patz decided to expand her **parent–teacher conferences to include students**. Making this shift to three-way conferences transformed the purpose and benefits of conferences in her classroom. In three-way conferences, students participate in order to demonstrate what they are learning, to reflect on growth, and to set goals for continued learning. Mrs. Patz works with each of her students in advance to prepare for the conference to demonstrate a skill such as reading aloud from a text, showing a piece of writing, talking about a project, or sharing work from the student's portfolio. She often uses a template such as the one provided in Figure 13.3 to prepare for and guide three-way conferences.

Figure 13.3. Three-Way Conference Template

Student's Name _____ Date of Conference _____

Skill or Work Product to Be Shared:

Student Reflection on Learning:

Student Goal for Learning:

At the conference, Mrs. Patz talks a bit about what they have been learning in the classroom and then invites the child to demonstrate the skill or share the work they have produced. She invites the family members to share what they notice and to ask questions. She then guides the child to reflect on their learning by using questions such as, "What is something you are proud about related to your learning?" or, "What have you been working hard on in your learning?" She also invites family members to share their insights and observations. Next, she asks the child to share a goal they are working on, and she invites family members to discuss the goal and to offer ways they can be involved at home to support the child's progress toward that goal. She finds that families tend to be impressed by what their children share, and they tend to view the conferences as helpful and informative.

Some teachers worry that three-way conferences won't allow them to talk about problems or concerns related to a student but remember that conferences are not the only way you can or will communicate with families. We believe that the benefits of three-way conferences to help families understand their children's learning and how they can be supportive at home outweigh any of the concerns about this approach to conferences. If a conference leads to additional conversations with family members, we consider that a positive outcome toward building relationships and engagement with families to support students' learning (Elish-Piper, 2018/2019).

Open Houses and Curriculum Nights

Most schools have open houses near the beginning of the school year so families can learn more about what their children will be learning and doing in the classroom. Open houses invite families into the classroom to see the spaces where their children work, play, and learn and to get to know the teacher better. At open houses, teachers often share classroom expectations and upcoming projects, field trips, and units of study. **Curriculum nights** are similar to open houses, but they tend to be more focused on the actual curriculum and standards that will be addressed in the coming year. Some schools do both an open house and a curriculum night, whereas other schools do only one. We suggest that you ask your mentor teacher what they do in their school for open house and/or curriculum night. If one of these events is scheduled during the time you are in your placement, you may want to ask your mentor teacher if you can attend to observe and learn first-hand how such events are organized and implemented.

A traditional approach to open houses and curriculum nights is for the teacher to give a presentation (often supported by PowerPoint slides) that provides lots of information. That approach can be overwhelming and intimidating for many families, and they may leave the event feeling confused rather than more connected to the teacher, classroom, and school. We recommend making open houses and curriculum nights more family focused by taking a few easy but effective steps (Elish-Piper, 2008). Adding a discussion time is essential so that family members can get their questions answered. In fact, at least half of the time scheduled for open house or curriculum night should be designated for questions. Be sure to invite questions by saying, "What are your questions?" But you will also need to be prepared if family members don't initially ask questions. For example, you could say, "What do you want to know about recess or reading time or homework?" to get families started with their questions. Be sure to let families know if they have a question that is specific to their child, you will be happy to schedule a follow up conference or phone call to discuss those matters.

As you think about open houses and curriculum nights, be sure to consider what families will want and need to know to be supportive of their children's learning. For example, most families find it very useful to view student work samples and see a demonstration of how you are teaching reading or using centers in your classroom. Some teachers show short video clips of classroom instruction or routines such as cleaning up or doing circle time so that families can see what their children are actually doing in the classroom. As you think about the open houses and/or curriculum nights you will be implementing as you are teaching in your own classroom, consider how you can involve families and share the types of information that will be helpful for them to understand what their child is doing and learning.

As with any event, the timing may work for some families and not for others, so it's important to keep in mind ways that families can be involved even if they can't attend. Some teachers video record open houses and curriculum nights or prepare and share "A Day in the Life of Our Classroom" videos so family members can view these even if they can't attend. You will need to check with your building principal to determine the rules for videotaping in the classroom. Other teachers offer a drop in time for a "make-up" open house or curriculum night so that families have another chance to attend and participate.

Simple Activities to Involve Families in Their Children's Literacy and Learning

Although inviting families to come to school to participate in conferences, open houses, curriculum nights, and family events is a good way to involve families, it is not sufficient, and it will not engage all families. If you are able to encourage families to read with children at home and do learning activities at home, those types of family involvement will contribute to children's literacy learning.

FAMILY READING TIME. When families set aside a daily reading time, they can help their children develop a love of reading as well as a reading habit. In addition, family reading time shows children that reading is a valuable activity that is important in their families. Suggestions for helping families establish a family reading time are provided in Figure 13.4.

Figure 13.4. Establishing a Family Reading Time

1. Pick a 15- to 30-minute time that works well for your family. Right after dinner or before bedtime are good options.
2. Have family reading time at least five times per week.
3. Everyone reads during reading time, including adults. You can read independently, with a partner, or as a group.
4. Be sure to choose fun, interesting things to read so family reading time is enjoyable for all!

To implement a **family reading time**, families will need access to interesting reading materials such as books, magazines, newspapers, and e-texts. You can encourage families to visit their local library to get reading materials, or children can bring home texts from the school or your classroom library.

BUILDING COMPREHENSION AT HOME. Since comprehension is the purpose for reading, you can invite families to get involved in promoting their children's reading comprehension by doing simple activities with school reading assignments or in conjunction with family reading time. If you teach children these comprehension activities at school, they can take them home and share them with their families.

3-2-1 STRATEGY. The **3-2-1 strategy** (Zygouris-Coe, Wiggins, & Smith, 2004) provides a simple structure that families can use to discuss any informational text with their children. Here are the steps in the strategy:

3: Discuss three things you learned.
2: Discuss two things you found interesting.
1: Ask one question you have.

Families can use the 3-2-1 strategy after children read an informational text independently or when they read together. Parents can be encouraged to coach children to go back and re-read the text or a section of it if they can't respond to one of the prompts. The 3-2-1 strategy can also be used to develop comprehension during family read alouds, after watching a video, or viewing a TV program.

READ, COVER, REMEMBER, RETELL. The **read, cover, remember, retell** (Hoyt, 2002) strategy promotes reading comprehension through a structured retelling process. After children learn and practice the strategy at school, you can invite parents to coach their children to use the strategy at home by following the steps in Figure 13.5.

Figure 13.5. Read, Cover, Remember, Retell

Read only as much text as you can cover with your hand.

Cover the text with your hand.

Remember what you read. It's okay to look back if you need to do so.

Retell what you just read. Do this in your head or to a partner.

Continue the process until you are done with the text or section.

PRACTICING WORD RECOGNITION SKILLS AT HOME. Word recognition is a foundation of reading that requires practice, and **games are a great way to practice word recognition skills**. Board games, pencil and paper games, and online games are available that families can use with children at home. Board and dice games such as Scrabble Junior, Spill and Spell, Upwords, Boggle Junior, My First Banana-Grams, and What's Gnu? are games that are easily available at most discount stores, and some libraries even have board games that families can play or check out to use at home. Pencil and paper games, such as crossword puzzles and hangman, can also be used by families to help their children practice their word identification skills. Online games such as those listed in Figure 13.6 are fun ways for families to encourage children to practice their word identification skills.

PRACTICING SIGHT WORDS AT HOME. As we discussed in Chapter 8, **sight words** are a key foundation of fluent reading. Through at-home practice, children can build their sight word vocabularies. If you send home sight words (on index cards or slips of paper) that children have been learning at school, families can play games like Memory and Go Fish. If you teach the games at school first, then children can show their families how to play the games at home. You can also encourage families to have children go on "sight word hunts" to locate sight words in print in their homes and neighborhoods. You can also encourage families to have children write words in chalk on the sidewalk or in sand or salt in a shallow box or cookie sheet. If families have shaving cream, they can spray a little on the kitchen counter and have children write their sight words, and then erase them by smearing the shaving cream to start over to write the next sight word. Figure 13.6 on the next page

Figure 13.6. Free Online Games to Practice Word Identification Skills

Gamequarium offers a large collection of phonics games for beginning sounds, short vowels, word families, and more.	http://www.gamequarium.org/dir/Gamequarium_Junior/	
Primary Games provides phonics, spelling, and writing games and puzzles.	http://www.primarygames.com/reading.php	
Word Game Time includes many games that are organized by grade level and topic including sounds, word families, and rhyming words.	http://www.wordgametime.com/word-games	

offers word games that families can use at home.. Check out Margin Note 13.4 for several other at-home activities that families can use with their children to practice sight words at home. To ensure that families have all of the materials needed to do a specific activity at home, it's a good idea to provide them in zip top bags that children can take home.

Margin Note 13.4: Ways to Practice Sight Words at Home

http://internet.savannah.chatham.k12.ga.us/schools/gss/gradelevels/K/Shared%20Documents/ways%20to%20practice%20sight%20words%20at%20home.pdf

Engaging with Families: At-home Activity

Select one of the at-home activities described in the previous section. Talk with your mentor teacher about how you could use the activity with your students' families. Develop a letter that explains the activity and its benefit for children's literacy development. Be sure your mentor teacher reads and approves the letter before you send it home to families.

Community Resources

You have probably heard the saying, "It takes a village to raise a child." We would argue that is true for teaching children, too. New teachers often feel that they have to go it alone in their first years in the classroom, and that is absolutely not the truth. In fact, many community institutions, organizations, and resources are available to support you and your students. Get familiar with your public library. The children's library can be one of your best resources. Most public libraries will put together collections of books on topics you are teaching so you can use them in your classroom. Some libraries will even drop them off and pick them up—all for free. Libraries often have free events for children and their families, and you may be able to connect these to some of the units you are teaching. For other ways the public libraries support teachers, check out the blog in Margin Note 13.5.

Margin Note 13.5: 6 Ways Public Libraries and Schools Can Work Together

https://company.overdrive.com/2017/08/23/back-to-school/

Connection to the Field: The Public Library

Visit the public library near the school where you have your placement. Talk to the children's librarian to find out what services and programs they offer for teachers and schools. Tour the children's section to see the range of materials you can borrow for use in your classroom. You can also work with your local public library to get library card applications for students and their families.

Margin Note 13.6: 11 Ways Teachers Can Score Free School Supplies

https://thekrazycouponlady.com/tips/money/free-school-supplies-for-teachers

Margin Note 13.7: School–Business Partnerships that Work

https://www.educationworld.com/a_admin/admin/admin323.shtml

Margin Note 13.8: Use Community Resources to Improve Teaching and Learning

https://www.teachandtaketime4u.com/2018/01/13/use-community-resources-to-improve-teaching-and-learning/

Other **institutions and organizations in the community** can be great partners for teachers, too. Some examples are park districts, museums, historical societies, and arts and cultural organizations. Many of these groups offer field trips, lesson plans and activity ideas for the classroom, and family-oriented events. Since each community is different, we recommend that you do a little research to learn about the resources in the community where you are doing your placement. Investigate their websites, call and ask questions, and consider visiting sites that seem most aligned to the types of things your students are learning. Some businesses are also great supporters of schools. For example, bookstores may bring in children's authors and illustrators for special events. Some discount stores have programs where teachers can request free materials for special projects. See Margin Note 13.6 for a blog about 11 ways that teachers can get free supplies for their classrooms!

One of the most valuable community resources for teachers and their students is volunteers to help with classroom activities and projects or to read with individual children. Volunteers can certainly be parents or family members, but other community members are often willing and able to be great classroom volunteers. Retired teachers and other retired community members are often eager to help in the classroom. Be sure to find out the rules for classroom volunteers from your mentor teacher or school principal so you follow those rules for compliance as well as safety. Some businesses give their employees time each week or month to volunteer in the community, and lots of these individuals love to do volunteer work that involves children! Some schools even create partnerships with a business that will adopt the school or a classroom. For more information about how such partnerships work, see the online article provided in Margin Note 13.7.

As you learn more about the community where you are teaching, you will likely continue to find new community partners and resources that are available to help strengthen teaching and learning in your classroom and school. The tips provided in the blog in Margin Note 13.8 will give you great ideas to get started.

Collaborating with Colleagues

You probably are spending lots of time with your classmates who are also pursuing a teaching career. You may be working on projects together, reviewing each other's lesson plans and projects, and discussing how your placements are going. Once you have your own classroom as a teacher, you will be spending almost all day with your students, so you may wonder how can teaching be lonely? Well, it revolves around the fact that as a teacher, you may often be the only adult in the classroom, and although you will certainly have meaningful relationships with your students and countless interactions in a given day, you may feel lonely for adult interaction and support from other teachers. That's perfectly normal because as humans we are social beings who seek and need meaningful relationships and support from others. In fact, when teachers feel connected and supported by their teaching colleagues and principal, they tend to be happier and more fulfilled as teachers. On the other hand, when teachers feel isolated and unsupported, they tend to experience more stress and dissatisfaction with their jobs (Wolgast & Fisher, 2017). So, what types of connections, support, and collaboration are most important for new teachers?

INDUCTION. Teaching can be joyful, meaningful work, but it can be hard at times, and having the support of your colleagues will help you to feel like you are part of a team. During your teacher education program, you may find that talking to your classmates is helpful to deal with challenges, frustration, and stress as well as to share the joys and successes you are experiencing. The same is true when you become a teacher and have your own classroom.

Some schools have official **induction and mentoring programs for new teachers**. In these programs, a new teacher is part of a cohort with other new teachers who receive specific orientation sometimes called on boarding as well as professional development support during the first year to learn more about the school, curriculum, students, and teaching. This approach recognizes that learning to teach is a developmental process that takes time, and when schools invest in induction for their new teachers, it shows they want their teachers to be successful.

Induction programs are designed to make you more confident and competent as a teacher. Such programs go beyond a single day of orientation to provide the information, time, support, and relationships you will need to be successful and effective as a teacher. Induction programs provide a safe place for new teachers to ask questions, share concerns, and seek the support they need. Generally, induction programs span the first year with regularly scheduled meetings that focus on topics and issues such as school norms, curriculum, teaching and learning, assessment, collaborative planning, building relationships with students, classroom organization and management, working with parents, and work–life balance. Although you already have and will continue to learn a great deal in your teacher preparation program and during clinical experiences and student teaching, an induction program will provide the job-embedded professional development you need to make a successful transition from teacher candidate to classroom teacher.

Research by Maulana, Helms-Lorenz, and van de Grift (2015) shows that induction programs contribute to teaching improvement for new teachers across their first 3 years of teaching. They also found that teachers who participate in induction programs felt more connected to their schools and teaching as well as more empowered and confident as teachers.

Therefore, because induction is so important to new teachers' success, we encourage you to proactively research which schools in your area provide induction for teachers. Be sure to ask about it when you interview for a teaching position so you can consider induction support as you make a decision about accepting a teaching position.

If you find yourself teaching in a school that does not have an induction program, you can seek other types of support to ensure that you have a successful first year teaching. You can check with school and district administrators to learn about workshops, support groups, and study groups that may be available to new teachers. You can also check with your college or university to see if they offer support for beginning teachers. You may also find that your state has regional offices of education or education service centers that provide programs, resources, and support for new teachers. Some state departments of education even provide online modules to help new teachers address challenges they are likely to face in their first year of teaching.

MENTORING. **Mentoring may be part of an induction program** or it may be separate. Either way, **mentors are essential for beginning teachers** because these veteran teachers can serve as guides, coaches, cheerleaders, and models for you. You may have been lucky enough to have a mentor or even multiple mentors in your life so far. For example, you may have had a mentor when you were a high school student. Perhaps it was a junior or senior student when you were a freshman who had just joined the speech team, band, or a community service club. This mentor may have introduced you to others, shown you how the organization operated, provided encouragement for you to get involved or take on more responsibility, or helped you through challenges you faced. You may have had a mentor in college such as a resident assistant who helped you learn how to navigate the residence hall, dining hall, and campus activities and resources. Or, you may have a professor who

© DGLimages/Shutterstock.com

Many schools will provide an official mentor who will support, encourage, and guide you.

serves as a mentor to you right now by giving you advice, helping you deal with challenges, and guiding you to get involved in activities that will help you prepare to be an effective teacher. You may also have had a mentor at work who trained you to do the job but also cared about your success, was available to answer questions or help you solve problems, and whose advice and insights you valued for advancing in the workplace. We hope that you have had many mentors in your life so far, and we urge you to seek mentors as you enter and progress in your teaching career.

Many schools will provide an **official mentor**—a veteran teacher —who will support, encourage, and guide you, but who will not judge or evaluate you. Although it may seem ideal if a mentor teaches the same grade level as you, it is not essential. What's most important is that your mentor remembers what it was like to be a new teacher and will support and encourage you. Just knowing that you have an experienced and supportive teacher down the hall is comforting so you have a ready resource to ask questions, share ideas for feedback, and even to vent after a difficult day.

You might wonder why a busy, veteran teacher would want to be a mentor for a new teacher like you? The answer is simple: they want to have a great colleague. Investing their time, effort, and energy to helping a new teacher like you get the support needed to have a great first year or two of teaching increases the likelihood that you will grow into a great colleague and member of the teaching team. In fact, after you've been teaching for several years, you will likely begin to have opportunities to mentor teacher candidates who are placed in your classroom for early field experiences, and after you've been teaching for 5 or 6 years, you may be invited to serve as a mentor teacher for a student teacher or to mentor a newly hired teacher! Yes, the teaching community— teacher candidates like you and experienced teachers in schools—work together to ensure that new teachers enter schools with the support they need to be successful and to eventually be able to take on mentoring newer colleagues.

As mentioned earlier, asking about induction and mentoring during interviews is a great way to learn about the types of support that will (and will not) be provided if you accept a specific teaching position. For example, you might ask, "Does the school provide a mentor for new teachers?" "If I were a new teacher in your school, what could I expect in terms of mentoring support?" Asking such questions shows that you are prepared for the interview and serious about being a professional and learner-ready teacher.

What happens if you find yourself working in a school that doesn't have an official mentoring program? Well, you can always talk to the principal or to a literacy coach, instructional coach, or teacher leader in the school to ask for recommendations and introductions to veteran teachers in the school who might be willing to mentor you. Just to emphasize one more time: having a mentor (or even more than one) is important for your success and satisfaction as a beginning teacher.

PROFESSIONAL LEARNING COMMUNITIES. Another way that teachers can connect and support each other is through **professional learning communities** (PLCs). DuFour et al. (2016) describe PLCs as a process that brings teachers together to focus on student learning, collaboration, results, and hard work and commitment. PLCs also encourage inquiry and reflection so that teachers are identifying problems of practice that affect their teaching and their students' learning, studying these problems, applying what they learn, and reflecting on results to determine what to do next. This approach positions teachers as teammates working together to improve teaching and learning for all. Many schools provide time for teachers to engage in PLCs on a regular basis. In other schools, teachers may take a more grassroots approach to PLCs by organizing them during common planning times, after school, or during lunch. Maybe you've already had a chance to observe or participate in a PLC with your mentor teacher during your placement. Or, the idea of a PLC may be new to you.

So, you may be wondering exactly what happens in a PLC and why it is a productive way to work collaboratively with your colleagues. Let's begin with a brief description of a PLC in action with a team of first-grade teachers from Bethune Elementary School. The four first-grade teachers always begin their PLC meetings by asking the question, "What's happening with our students?" Sara shares her observation that some of her students are not interested in reading and can only stay engaged with reading for a few minutes at a time. The other three teachers all agree that this is a concern they have noticed too. Over the course of several PLC meetings the team decides that they will observe these students closely to learn more about what is going on and reflect on those findings. They then decide to seek resources and strategies to help build students' interest in, attention to, and engagement with reading. From all the ideas they share, they select several for implementation and discuss what each of them will implement in their classroom. They discuss how the strategies they implemented are going, and they gather observational data to see how the strategies are working. They share those findings and determine their next steps. This process continues during the year with new questions and new learning. This is a PLC in its truest form. Watch the video in Margin Note 13.9 to see how a school district has implemented PLCs into the fabric of their schools. Be sure to consider how the teachers are learning from each other and how they focus on improved learning for their students.

Margin Note 13.9: Collaborating for Kids: Professional Learning Communities

https://www.youtube.com/watch?v=053ayc0Qael

In some schools, PLCs will be organized centrally or around specific themes such as formative assessment or reading, discussing, and implementing ideas from a professional book. Even with those more organized structures for PLCs, it's important for teachers to have a chance to bring their own questions about problems of practice and to inquire into them in ways that will make a difference for their students' learning and for their own professional development as teachers. It can be as simple as asking, "What questions do we have in our own practice that relate to this topic or text?" to allow for important professional and personal connections to teacher learning.

TEACHER BOOK CLUBS. A great way that you and your colleagues can learn, grow, and collaborate is through a **teacher book club.** In this approach, you and your colleagues will choose a professional book or article to read and discuss so you can determine applications you can make to your

Figure 13.7. Teacher Book Club Discussion Protocol

1. On a scale of 1 to 10, rate the book and be prepared to explain your rating to the group.
2. Share an example of how the book relates to your teaching. Mark a specific passage from the book that you want to share with the group.
3. What questions are you still considering that you want to discuss with the group?
4. What ideas from the book do you want to incorporate into your teaching? Be as specific as you can.

Margin Note 13.10: Online Teacher Book Clubs: Promoting a Culture of Professional Development

https://www.edutopia.org/blog/teacher-book-clubs-promoting-professional-development-cheryl-boes

own teaching. Some groups prefer to read articles because they are shorter, but regardless of the length of what such clubs read, the purposes and processes are similar. The group chooses a text to read, sets a date for the meeting, and uses a protocol to guide discussion. The discussion protocol can be as simple as the one provided in Figure 13.7 or the group can create its own.

With the increased availability of technology, some teachers are even participating in online book clubs with their teaching colleagues or with teachers from other schools. See Margin Note 13.10 for suggestions about participating in an online book club for teachers. One benefit that teachers often cite about online book clubs is that they can participate at home and engage with teachers from schools outside their own district or area. One drawback that some teachers cite about online book clubs is that they miss the face-to-face interactions and because teachers work in different settings, they worry about the applicability of ideas shared. What do you think? Does the idea of an online teacher book club appeal to you? Why or why not?

Other variations on book clubs include viewing and discussing videos, following education-related Facebook pages to learn and collaborate on shared topics of interest, and participating in themed Twitter chats related to education. For resources related to Facebook pages and Twitter chats for teachers, see Figure 13.8.

TEAMS. You may have seen a team structure used in the school where you have your placement. That team organization is likely determined by the grade or age level of the children in the teachers' classrooms. Teams are often provided with a common planning time so they can meet regularly to collaborate, share, and plan instruction. Sometimes teams have to make their own time by meeting before or after school or even during lunch. A team may operate as a PLC some or all of the time, or it may be flexible and operate in different ways depending on the need and tasks to be completed. For example, a team might have some meetings reserved to review student assessment data and other times reserved to plan units of study or to discuss students with special needs.

The benefit of being part of a teaching team is that you have collaborators, partners, and resources for problem solving readily available to you. For a team to be effective it's important for all team members to feel safe to ask questions, share challenges, and discuss concerns with the others without fear of judgment. You have probably worked on lots of team or group projects in your teacher education program. What made some teams work well and others struggle? As you reflect on your experiences working on a team, what are your strengths and what are your weaknesses? In general, do you think you are good team member? Why or why not?

When teams work well, they can be a valuable resource and support system for teachers. When they don't work well, they can be frustrating and unproductive. One way a teaching team can set itself up for success is to develop a shared list of team norms for how you will work together. Doing so will allow a team to create a climate that supports its members and their work. For some sugges-

Figure 13.8. Resources for Facebook Groups and Twitter Chats for Teachers

40 Facebook Teacher Pages You Should Follow Today	https://www.weareteachers.com/teacher-facebook-pages/	
An Introduction to Twitter Education Chats	https://www.edutopia.org/blog/introduction-twitter-education-chats-robert-ward	
Education Chats (with upcoming schedule)	https://sites.google.com/site/twittereducationchats/education-chat-calendar	
50 Important Education Twitter Hashtags— with Meeting Times	https://www.teachthought.com/technology/50-important-education-twitter-hashtags-with-meeting-times/	

tions on team norms that can help a team work effectively and build trusting relationships, see the list provided in Margin Note 13.11. As you read the list, did any of the norms surprise you? Why? Are there any that you think are missing? These norms are designed for PreK teachers. Do you think they would work in the early elementary grades or do you think they might need to be modified for teams at other grade levels?

We think it's important to mention that some teaching teams develop close relationships and become friends who socialize outside of school, but that is not necessary. The most important aspect of an effective teaching team is to have respect and trust in each other so you can share, learn, collaborate, and work together.

Margin Note 13.11: Pre-K Team Meeting Norms

https://www4.esc13.net/uploads/schoolready/docs/Pre-KNorms.pdf

COLLABORATING WITH INDIVIDUAL TEACHERS. As a new teacher, you will have lots to learn, but you will also have lots to share. Your teacher education program is preparing you to teach with the most up-to-date teaching methods, technology resources, and learning theories. Just as you want to have a mentor and teaching teammates who are generous with you by sharing their time, expertise, resources, and wisdom of practice, you will want to share your knowledge, ideas, and enthusiasm. The best way to build collaborations is to ensure that they are mutually beneficial.

You will likely have students in your classroom who have an **Individual Education Program (IEP)**; therefore, you will need to work closely with the special education teacher to ensure that you understand the special needs of the student and how you can support them in your classroom. Sometimes you will even get the opportunity to co-teach with a special education teacher who is assigned to be in your classroom at certain times of the day to support specific students who have IEPs. To

Margin Note 13.12:
Six Approaches to
Co-Teaching

https://ctserc.org/
component/k2/item/50-six-
approaches-to-co-teaching

learn more about co-teaching models that may be useful for working with special education teachers, check out the resources shared in Margin Note 13.12.

You will most likely have students in your classroom who work with or receive support from a bilingual or ESL teacher, reading specialist, speech-language teacher, occupational therapist, counselor, or social worker. These professionals are important resources for not only your students but also for you. Be sure to ask questions and request their help so you can get more comfortable and confident in teaching the students they support. If possible, arrange to observe them working with your students so you can get a better idea of the approaches and strategies they are using so you can make connections with what you are doing in your classroom. If you adopt a stance that these professionals are your partners in teaching and supporting students, it will help you have positive and productive relationships with these colleagues. Is there a bilingual or ESL teacher in the school where you are doing your placement? What about a reading specialist, speech-language teacher, occupational therapist, counselor, or social worker? Ask your mentor teacher to introduce you to these educators in the school where you are doing your placement so you can get a better idea of the opportunities for collaboration with educators who provide special support for students in the school.

© New Africa/Shutterstock.com

Ultimately, your students benefit from your collaborations with other professionals.

Another great way to collaborate with teachers is to ask to visit your colleagues' classrooms to observe or discuss their teaching and to see how they organize their classrooms and manage their schedules. You can also invite them in to see what you are doing in your classroom. You may be able to do this during your planning time during the day, but you may need to talk to your principal about getting coverage for your class to allow you to observe in other classrooms.

If you are open to ideas and adopt a stance of replacing judgment with curiosity, you will be able to learn from and with teachers and vice versa. Although you can expect that you will likely develop some strong friendships with your teaching colleagues—all of the authors of this book still count, among their closest friends, the teaching colleagues from the schools where they taught early in their careers— you will likely have some colleagues with whom you do not "click." That's okay. You don't need to become best friends with every teacher in your school, but you do need to have professional, respectful relationships with the teachers in your school.

As a new teacher in a school, you will probably feel overwhelmed with meeting so many new people, but it's essential that you introduce yourself, and do your best to learn your colleagues' names and what they teach. Smile and say hello when you see them in the hallway, teachers' lunchroom, office, and parking lot. Arrive at faculty meetings and team meetings on time and give your full attention to the matters being discussed. Resist the temptation to grade papers, check your email, or look at social media posts. If you want your colleagues to see you as a professional teacher, it's important that you comport that way. This doesn't mean that you can't be yourself or show your enthusiasm or worries about being a new teacher, but it does mean that you need to understand the school's norms so you can chart your own path to being a teacher in that school. Your mentor and principal can also help you understand school norms and expectations and to build relationships by connecting you with other teachers in the school.

What does collaboration with individual teachers look like? It can be many different things, but such collaboration may help you plan a lesson, understand a process such as preparing for parent–teacher conferences, or develop a project or bulletin board together. Collaboration might mean observing each other teach the same lesson and discussing how it went. It might mean talking through a lesson plan prior to teaching it to work out some of your questions. Or, it might be talking about a challenging student situation to get a fresh perspective on what to do next. Especially as a new teacher, having others with whom to collaborate can make hard work easier or at least more enjoyable to complete. Plus, collaborations usually lead to better quality outcomes than when we work alone.

Margin Note 13.13:
10 Ways to Collaborate with your Literacy Coach

https://www.edutopia.org/discussion/10-ways-collaborate-your-literacy-coach

WORKING WITH COACHES. Some schools have **literacy coaches, math coaches,** or **instructional coaches** who provide job-embedded professional development for teachers. Coaches do not evaluate teachers, but they are a partner with whom to think and problem solve. Coaches can work with teachers to co-plan and co-teach lessons, to model a new instructional approach in the teacher's classroom, review and interpret assessment data, and observe and provide feedback on specific aspects of teaching that the teacher is working to develop (Elish-Piper & L'Allier, 2014). If your school has a coach, be sure to take advantages of their support. To understand more about what a coach can do to support your teaching, see the blog post in Margin Note 13.13.

Connection to the Field: Instructional Coach

Ask your mentor teacher if their school has a literacy, math, or instructional coach. If so, find out what these professionals do and how they support teachers in the school.

Some teachers worry that working with a coach implies that they are a weak teacher, but we argue that is it the exact opposite. When teachers engage with coaches in their schools, it shows that they are interested in improving their teaching and their students' learning. It shows their commitment to professional development and lifelong learning.

You may find that the school where you work does not have coaches, but that does not mean that you won't be able to access coaching support. A reading specialist, technology specialist, or special education teacher may be available to coach you regarding an issue that aligns with their expertise. For example, if you have a question about some aspect of your reading instruction or a student's reading, the reading specialist can be a great colleague with whom to collaborate. If you have questions about technology applications in your teaching, the technology specialist may be able to coach you through how to use it in your upcoming lesson. If you have questions about a student with special needs or specific learning or behavior issues, a special education teacher in your school can be a valuable collaborator. If you have questions about finding the "just right" books for a unit or for a student, the school librarian or even the children's librarian at the public library can be a great resource. There are collaborators all around you who will be more than happy to support you as a new teacher, but you need to be proactive and seek the support you need.

WORKING WITH YOUR PRINCIPAL. Have you met the principal at the school where you have your placement? If not, be sure to introduce yourself the next time you are there. It can be as simple as, "Hi, I'm Claire Davis. I'm doing my clinical experience here in kindergarten with Mrs. Guzowski. I'm so excited to be working in your school. Thank you for allowing me to be here this semester."

That may seem so obvious to you, but many teacher candidates don't understand the importance of working well with the school principal. Principals consider it part of their professional responsibility to host students in clinical experiences and student teaching, but they are also looking for future teachers who they would like to add to their schools. Talk to your mentor teacher to determine if there is a special project or event that you will be doing in your classroom that would be appropriate to invite the principal to attend so that they can begin to see you in action teaching in their school.

I (Laurie) recently had lunch with three principals from schools near my university where we place lots of teacher candidates for early clinical experiences and student teaching. I asked how often they did observations of the student teachers in their buildings. They all agreed it was only about 50%. They each said that they offered and were happy to do such observations, but many student teachers didn't take advantage of the opportunity. Clearly if you want to get a job in that school or district, having a principal observe you can open a door that could lead to being hired as a teacher. Even if you are not interested in being hired in the school district or area where you are student teaching, having the feedback from a principal to inform your own development as a teacher and possibly to share when you apply for a job in another district can be very helpful.

Yes, principals do evaluate teachers, but they do much more. In fact, principals are the instructional leaders in their schools. They want you to be successful! As a new teacher, you will likely interact with the principal through an induction or orientation program. But there are many other positive and productive ways for new teachers to work with their principals. As mentioned earlier, participate fully in meetings that the principal leads. Share successes in your classroom, and let the principal know how you are using the resources provided such as a mentor or coach. Volunteer to serve on a school committee or project that interests you and will be possible with your availability and other commitments. Show that you are working hard to teach and also to become a contributing member of the school community. If you are not able to get answers or advice to address important issues from your mentor, teammate, or coach, go to your principal to get their insights and guidance. For more specific suggestions on how to work well with your principal, see the blog in Margin Note 13.14.

Margin Note 13.14:
A Teacher's Guide to
Working with Principals

https://www.weareteachers.
com/working-with-
principals/

Margin Note 13.15:
15 Tips for Surviving Your
First Year of Teaching

https://www.weareteachers.
com/15-tips-surviving-first-
year-teaching-istes-young-
educator-network/

PROFESSIONAL ASSOCIATIONS. As a teacher, there is always more to learn. One great way to do that is to join a **professional association** so you will have access to journals, conferences, webinars, and other professional development resources to help you continue to grow and develop as a teacher. For a list of professional associations that will be of interest, see Figure 13.9.

All of these resources that we've discussed so far in this chapter can be helpful to you in your first year of teaching but be prepared that it will still be challenging, rewarding, and exhausting. For some practical tips for surviving your student teaching and first year of teaching, watch the video and read the blog provided in Margin Note 13.15.

What Do You Believe about Working with Families, Colleagues, and Community Members?

As you reflect on the ideas discussed in this chapter, consider how you plan to build relationships and work well with your colleagues so you can have the mentoring and collaboration you need to be successful as a new teacher. What ideas do you have about building and leveraging community re-

Figure 13.9. Professional Associations

The International Literacy Association (ILA)	ILA provides professional development resources for teachers related to reading and literacy instruction.	https://www.literacy worldwide.org/	
National Association for the Education of Young Children (NAEYC)	NAEYC offers professional development support for teachers who work with young children.	https://www.naeyc.org/	
National Association for Multicultural Education (NAME)	NAME provides a wide array of professional development resources for teachers regarding diversity and equity in education.	https://www.nameorg. org/	

sources to enhance your students' education? How do you plan to develop effective communication and relationships with families? How do you think you'd like to get families involved in school events and in supporting their children's learning at home? As you consider these questions and your future plans as a teacher, what do you believe about teachers building and maintaining productive relationships with colleagues, community members, and families? After reviewing the takeaways from this chapter and reflecting on your ideas, go to the What Do You Believe template provided in the Chapter 13 Resources on the website to record your ideas.

Closing Thoughts

You might be thinking that there are lots of important relationships for teachers to build and leverage to support their students' learning. Like Joo-Hee, who you met at the beginning of the chapter, you might have been so focused on building relationships with and teaching your students that you weren't even aware of the important role that your colleagues, community partners, and families play to support your teaching and your students' learning. We hope that after reading this chapter, you see the importance of working with others as a teacher.

Takeaways from Chapter 13

- Induction and mentoring are important supports that schools can provide for new teachers.
- Professional learning communities (PLCs) provide a framework for teachers to work together to improve student learning through shared inquiry.
- Effective teachers must work well with their colleagues and principal, and they can enhance their teaching when they work with instructional or literacy coaches who are available in their schools.
- Community resources including the public library and volunteers are great ways to get support for your teaching, classroom, and students' learning.

- Engaging families is a key consideration for effective teaching, and there are many positive outcomes for student learning associated with family engagement.
- Two-way communication with families is an important foundation for building positive working relationships.
- Although there are many challenges to family engagement, there are strategies to overcome those challenges.
- You can promote at-home learning opportunities for families by encouraging family reading time and simple learning activities.

To Learn More about Working with Families, Colleagues, and Community Members

Books about Family Engagement for Your Professional Library

Boult, B. (2016). *201 ways to involve parents: Practical strategies for partnering with families.* Thousand Oaks, CA: Corwin Press.

http://us.corwin.com/en-us/nam/201-ways-to-involve-parents/book244062

If you are looking for a resource with tons of ideas about how you can work with parents and families, this practical book is for you. This book addresses everything from recruiting and working with volunteers, communicating effectively, celebrating diversity, and using community resources. Skim through this book to find ideas that will fit your placement and could be useful in your first year of teaching.

Campano, G., Ghiso, M. P., & Welch, B. J. (2016). *Partnering with immigrant communities: Action through literacy.* New York, NY: Teachers College Press.

https://www.tcpress.com/partnering-with-immigrant-communities-9780807757215

This book provides rich descriptions of how schools and teachers can work to build partnerships with immigrant community members and families to support education. With an emphasis on multicultural education and culturally relevant pedagogy, this text will be a valuable resource for your work in diverse schools.

Edwards, P. A. (2016). *New ways to engage parents: Strategies and tools for teachers and leaders, K–12.* New York, NY: Teachers College Press.

https://www.tcpress.com/new-ways-to-engage-parents-9780807756713

This book provides helpful strategies and tools you can use to build relationships with and work collaboratively with your students' parents and families. The book addresses important challenges of working with families such as connecting with hard-to-reach families and overcoming negative experiences and attitudes toward education and schooling.

Mascott, A., & McDonald, A. (2015). *Raising a rock-star reader: 75 quick tips to help your child develop a lifelong love of reading.* New York, NY: Scholastic.

https://shop.scholastic.com/parent-ecommerce/books/raising-a-rock-star-reader-75-quick-tips-for-helping-your-child-develop-a-lifelong-love-for-reading-9780545806176.html

This book is written for families and is a great resource for you as a teacher to share with your students' families. Organized as 75 quick tips, the book addresses how families can support their children's literacy and reading development and attitudes.

Online Resources about Working with Families and Community Partners

Collaborating for Success: Parent Engagement Toolkit

https://www.michigan.gov/documents/mde/4a._Final_Toolkit_without_bookmarks_370151_7.pdf

This massive toolkit (over 100 pages) was designed by the Michigan Department of Education to offer resources for educators including materials that are ready to share with families. If you are looking for a useful, free resource, this one is for you!

Five Steps to Better School/Community Collaboration

https://www.edutopia.org/blog/school-community-collaboration-brendan-okeefe

This short blog offers step-by-step ideas for how you can locate and use community resources to support teaching and learning in your classroom.

Parent, Family, Community Involvement in Education

http://www.nea.org/assets/docs/PB11_ParentInvolvement08.pdf

This policy brief from the National Education Association provides a clear and concise description of why and how to partner with parents, families, and community resources to support your students' learning.

Project Appleseed

https://www.projectappleseed.org/encouraging-parent-involvement

This web portal provides articles, videos, and tips for working with parents. Many of the resources are for teachers and others are ready for you to share with families. Many of the items on this website are free, but some do have a cost.

Raising Readers Handouts

https://www.cedu.niu.edu/literacy-clinic/resources/raising-readers/index.shtml

These two-page handouts are written for parents and are great resources for you to share at open houses, conferences, in a classroom newsletter, or on your school or classroom website. They address a wide range of topics from how to support phonemic awareness at home to promoting a love of reading. Several of the handouts are also available in Spanish.

Videos

Building Partnerships with Families

https://www.youtube.com/watch?v=r9_U8Q5XHQY

This short video provides a clear rationale for working with families as well as several practical tips you can use to build relationships and implement strategies to get families involved in their young children's learning at school and at home.

Raising Readers Videos

https://www.youtube.com/user/TheLiteracyClinic/videos

This collection of short videos shares easy-to-implement strategies that families can use to support their children's phonemic awareness, phonics, writing, vocabulary, fluency, and comprehension development. Some videos are available in Spanish. You can share these videos with families at conferences, open houses, curriculum nights, or on a classroom or school website.

© DGLImages/Shutterstock.com

Effective teachers reflect on their teaching.

How Do I Become a Learner-ready Teacher?

REAL-LIFE EXAMPLE

Sumaira had three more classes to complete before finishing her teacher preparation program and applying for her teaching credentials. She was enjoying student teaching and was looking forward to getting her own classroom. Sumaira, however, was anxious about getting a job and beginning her first year of teaching. She was worried that she wouldn't be able to apply all that she was learning in her program, and she didn't know how to begin.

Sumaira had heard about becoming a learner-ready teacher and was familiar with the concept. She knew that she needed to continue learning, but there was so much to do and to think about that she was feeling overwhelmed. Sumaira decided to talk with one of her instructors about how to organize her thoughts and prioritize her actions as she prepared to enter the teaching profession.

Perhaps you're like Sumaira right now: you're somewhat confident in your ability to teach, but you're also anxious. You recognize how much you have learned about how to teach reading and writing to PreK–3 students, but you also know that you have just scratched the surface in learning about teaching. In fact, you may have thought you knew how to teach reading and writing before you entered your program, but you now realize how complicated it is to teach children to read and write.

In this chapter, we go back to the concept of becoming a learner-ready teacher that we presented in Chapter 1, and we suggest ways to categorize and prioritize some of the aspects of teaching that you'll need to remember going forward. To do this we present seven ideas about areas in your teaching life that you will want to consider. These are areas in which you can expand your learning and thinking.

1. Be Reflective about Your Teaching

You have probably written reflection papers for some of your classes, and you might be expected to write a reflection about lessons you teach in your placement. We bet that your instructors have told you that it's important to be a reflective practitioner. But, what does it mean to be a reflective practitioner, and how can you become one?

We've encouraged you to engage in reflection at various points throughout this book, but let's look more closely at what it means to reflect. Reflection is a cognitive, or thought, process where you think about your experiences and engage in self-evaluation and self-examination to look carefully at your teaching practice. The purpose of reflection is to improve your practice, and there are two main ways to go about engaging in reflection on your teaching (Schön, 1983). You can **reflect in action** and you can **reflect on action**. You may be wondering, what's the difference? Well, reflection *in* action means that you are reflecting as you are engaged in teaching. In other words, as you are teaching, you are thinking about how the lesson is going, how students are responding, what you can do better, and you may possibly even be making in-the-moment adjustments to improve your teaching. Reflection *on* action happens after the fact. This is probably the type of reflection that you've been asked to do by your instructors, mentor teacher, or university supervisor. In this type of reflection, you look back at your teaching and ask yourself questions such as: Did I accomplish what I set out to do? Did the students participate in the lesson and learn what I intended? What did I do well? What could I do better in the future?

To get a better sense of how reflection in action and reflection on action work, let's look at how Sumaira has used reflection during her placement. Sumaira's literacy methods instructor required her to teach several literacy lessons in her placement, and she was expected to write a reflection for each lesson to address what went well, what could be improved (and how), and what she planned to do next as a follow-up to the lesson. Because she reflected after the lesson was completed, this is an example of reflection on action. One day, Sumaira and her mentor teacher, Mrs. Chang, were talking, and she told Sumaira that she reflected on her teaching not only after a lesson was over, but while she was teaching it. Sumaira wondered if she could think about anything else while teaching because, as a teacher candidate, she felt like she had to be so focused on what she planned to do in the lesson. It's true that this might seem difficult to reflect while you are teaching, but Sumaira realized that as she got more practice teaching, she was able to begin to reflect on her teaching while she was in the act of teaching. As her mentor teacher, Mrs. Chang told her, "If you want to be an effective teacher, you have to reflect almost constantly so you can use your reflections to grow and improve as a teacher."

Skilled teachers engage in reflection regularly so they can continue to improve their teaching. They are always seeking ways to improve student engagement and student learning outcomes. They set high goals for themselves as teachers, but they also understand that they will grow and evolve as

Margin Note 14.1: 5 Quick Steps of Reflective Practice

http://www.teachhub.com/5-quick-steps-reflective-practice

Margin Note 14.2: Making Teacher Reflection Meaningful

https://www.education world.com/making-teacher-reflection-meaningful

teachers across their careers. They embrace mistakes and the occasional failed lesson as ways to think deeply and honestly about their practice to identify ways they can improve their teaching (Marzano, 2012). Does this sound like you? If so, you are well on your way to being a reflective teacher. If you don't think you are there yet, look at Margin Note 14.1 to find a five-step process you can use to engage in reflective practice. Give it a try and see if it helps you think about your teaching more deeply and provides you with useful insights for improving your teaching. In Margin Note 14.2 you'll find several ways you can engage in daily and weekly reflections. Choose one of the reflection ideas and apply it to your teaching. Was this approach to reflection helpful? Did it allow you to understand something about your teaching? Did it offer you a chance to identify a way to improve an aspect of your teaching?

You may want to reflect on specific aspects of your teaching where you have been trying to improve your practice and your students' learning. For example, you might decide to reflect on how you are addressing equity in your teaching by using questions like these developed by Milner, Cunningham, Delale-O'Connor, and Kestenberg (2019, p. 66).

- Which students were successfully engaged in learning during the lesson? How do I know?
- Which students were not engaged in learning during the lesson? How do I know?
- What might have blocked these students' engagement in the lesson?
- How could I modify the lesson to engage more students?
- What different instructional strategies might have worked better?
- Should I alter the content or do other things to promote student learning?

Because teaching is a complex process that requires you to use what you know about content, teaching strategies, assessment, and your students, there is always room for growth. As John Dewey (1933), the originator of the concept of reflective practice argued, simply getting more experience teaching will not make you a better teacher. You have to reflect on those experiences, and then you can grow and improve as a teacher.

2. Prioritize Your To-do List

As a student in a teacher preparation program, you probably have learned how to prioritize tasks that need to be done. Think about all of the times you've had competing tasks. Perhaps your mentor teacher wanted you to teach a lesson on syllables the same day that you had a big paper due for a class. What do you do? Which one do you spend most of your time on?

All of us make decisions based on a risk–reward calculation to some extent. For example, let's say that the paper you had due would make the difference for you in getting an A in the class or not. How much do you want the A? On the other hand, let's say that your mentor teacher is going to be on the hiring committee for a new first-grade teaching position, and you really want to be completely prepared for every lesson you teach. Also, your last lesson didn't go so well. You thought you were prepared, but the students didn't respond as well as you expected, and you want every student to be engaged and learning in your next lesson. You only have so much time, so which project gets most of your attention or do you decide not to sleep much that weekend?

We have a couple of comments for those of you who tend to be perfectionists and expect everything to go smoothly when you are teaching. First, students are unpredictable, and teaching is not an exact science. You will make mistakes so reflect on them and move forward. Spending more time to plan your every teaching move may not make much of a difference in the way students respond to you. As you reflect on your lessons, you will also need to prioritize what to do differently. You can't do everything all at once, so you need to make decisions based on the time you have and organize your work so that your decisions will have the most impact on student learning (Heyck-Merlin, 2012). This skill will be important throughout your teaching career.

When you're a teacher, you'll have the same situation with an overwhelming number of things to do and a lack of time to do them. Therefore, you need to prioritize your work. You can't do everything. Of course, your biggest priority will be to do what your students need. However, you will also have tasks to do for your school and the administration that are time sensitive. For example, you may have 4 hours allocated to do schoolwork over the weekend. You really want to develop a new unit using children's books on migration issues, but you also need to finish grades for the students' report cards. Because report cards have a firm deadline, you will need to prioritize that task and save the unit planning for later. There will also be times when you just can't get to some of those big projects until you have a set amount of time. Your daily work, such as planning, instructing, and assessing, will take up most of your time, especially during your first year of teaching. Of course, if you tend toward procrastination or are not very organized, you'll have to work harder to manage your time. This will be a trial and error process until you find a way to manage your time and prioritize your tasks that will work for you in your teaching situation.

Margin Note 14.3: Time Management Tips for Teachers

https://www.youtube.com/watch?v=odOq3fOgIrU

Margin Notes 14.3 and 14.4 give you ideas about ways to prioritize teaching tasks so you can manage the many things you need and want to do. Consider which of these ideas might be helpful to you and make a note to apply them when you find yourself with a long to-do list and not enough time. As you get more experience teaching, you'll be able to develop and refine your own ways to prioritize teaching tasks and get things done.

Margin Note 14.4: 7 Ways to Prioritize Teaching Tasks When Everything Seems Urgent

https://thecornerstonefor teachers.com/truth-for-teachers-podcast/7-ways-prioritize-teaching-tasks-everything-seems-urgent/

3. Learn More about Your Cultural Identity

In your teacher preparation program, you've most likely been examining your own culture as you learned how to become a culturally responsive teacher. As you consider your own cultural background, remember that you are not identified by one thing, and neither are your students. You may be white, from an impoverished background, from a family who speaks a dialect of English, and the child of the mayor of a small rural town. You have a variety of privileged and oppressed identities. The idea that you are many things is explained by a framework called **intersectionality** that describes social identities as interacting on multiple levels with a variety of privileged and oppressed identities. Kimberlé Crenshaw (1989) developed this framework with the idea that various social identities combine to place each individual at a particular social location informed by group membership such as gender, class, sexuality, race, ethnicity, ability, religion, nation, and gender identity when introducing the concept of intersectionality. What this means for you is that you should try to think about the ways that you are privileged and ways that you may be oppressed. Understanding the ways your own cultural identity is layered will help you understand your students better.

We've discussed the importance of understanding cultural aspects of your students throughout this book. Often, though, we may have seemed to talk about one of the cultural identities of your students, such as their ethnic identity or home language. As you move into your career as a teacher, we'd like you to look at your students in a more nuanced way. Your students' identities are multilayered. Let's think of some examples. You may have a student from Guatemala, Marita, who came to the United States with her family as a political refugee. Your experiences with students from Guatemala have been students who are steeped in poverty and immigrated to the United States to find work. Marita's family, however, was wealthy and her father had a high-ranking position in the government in Guatemala, and she was used to having maids and servants and has a good command of English. As you work with Marita, you need to be aware that her identity as a newcomer will be multilayered and that her cultural experiences might be different from what you expected.

Margin Note 14.5: Crenshaw Discusses Intersectionality

https://www.youtube.com/watch?v=ViDtnfQ9FHc

Margin Note 14.6: Intersectionality 101

https://www.youtube.com/watch?v=w6dnj2IyYJE

It's important to look for those layers as you get to know your students and their families. One way to do that is to remember that we are all many things. Margin Note 14.5 shows Crenshaw describing intersectionality and Margin Note 14.6 explains intersectionality. As you learn about intersectionality, think about the ways your life is both privileged and oppressed and then talk with your colleagues about how to incorporate this framework as a teacher.

As you grow and mature as both a person and a teacher, you will gain additional insights into your own identities, and you can use these insights to understand your students' identities better too. You may be noticing that the ideas we present in this chapter are all things that will characterize your teaching life throughout your career. To be an effective teacher, you always need to be learning, growing, and evolving.

4. Become More Culturally Competent

We hope you feel like you have learned how to become a culturally competent teacher and prepare culturally responsive lessons. As you begin your teaching career, one of your goals should be to continue to learn to become more **culturally competent**. You may think that you have conquered your biases, but it's very likely that you have some unconscious or implicit biases. Now is the time to embrace a mindset that is becoming more aware of ways that you could be looking at your students through your biases (Gullo, Capatosto, & Staats, 2019).

Let's give you an example. Let's say Mark came into your second-grade classroom on the first day of school 15 minutes late. He was grimy and disheveled with several days' worth of dirt under his fingernails. His clothes looked too big for him and had worn spots. Your community has a large homeless population, so after one look at Mark, you decide he could be living in the homeless camp and probably would need to have reading intervention like other students you've known in the past.

Margin Note 14.7: Implicit Bias in Education

https://www.youtube.com/watch?v=KBZPHE1oPJo

Just reading the description of Mark, did you make some assumptions about him? We all tend to jump to conclusions based on our experiences, impressions, and biases. As a teacher, however, your biases can lead to lowered expectations and reduced student achievement so it's imperative that you examine your biases on your journey to become more culturally competent (Gullo, Capatosto, & Staats, 2019). Look at the video in Margin Note 14.7 and discuss ways you might have seen implicit bias in your schooling experience.

MICROAGGRESSIONS. As you work on your own ability to be aware of implicit or unconscious bias, you might also start becoming aware of **microaggressions**. Microaggression is a term used for unintentional insults and hurts communicated toward a person of a culturally marginalized group. For example, let's say you have a student from your classroom, Ai-Ying, who is of Asian descent and was born in the United States. Another student asks Ai-Ying where she is from. That is a microaggression, an unintentional dig at her. If Ai-Ying hears that same question throughout her life, she may feel like she is an outsider in her own country. Microaggressions are common, and we're not saying that people are intentionally trying to make others feel bad. Instead, we need to think of how microaggressions could be received by our students and the hurt they may cause. Margin Notes 14.8 and 14.9 describe microaggressions in more detail. Discuss with your colleagues the times you have heard or experienced microaggressions and how you can use those insights to be a more culturally competent teacher.

Margin Note 14.8: Microaggressions in Everyday Life

https://www.youtube.com/watch?v=BJL2P0JsAS4

Margin Note 14.9: Microaggressions in the Classroom

https://www.siue.edu/facultycenter/services_resources/teaching/Microaggressions.shtml

EXAMINE YOUR ASSUMPTIONS. What should you do if you encounter bias in your own thinking or microaggressions in your classroom or even in the teachers' lounge? First, remember that becoming more culturally competent is a lifelong process. As you find a bias against a group, acknowledge that this bias is your preliminary instinct but does not need to be your mindset. Then make sure that you do not treat any student unequally because of an implicit bias (Benson & Fiarman, 2019). For example, perhaps your initial reaction to a new student from Somalia is that the student will lag in academics and be socially uncomfortable because of their religion. You can challenge your initial impression and not make any educational decision until you have more information about what that student needs.

REPLACE JUDGMENT WITH CURIOSITY. A more uncomfortable area of becoming culturally competent is when a student, teacher, or parent expresses some kind of bias, microaggression, or racial slur. What should you do? We often hear our colleagues who are experts in multicultural education say, "replace judgment with curiosity." It's a way of reorienting our thinking when we encounter someone who is different from us or who does things differently. Rather than jumping to a conclusion that anyone or anything different is deficient, they recommend that we take a stance of curiosity to learn more and to understand things from that person's perspective. This approach also allows us to build our knowledge base of different groups, cultures, worldviews, and perspectives.

TAKE A STAND. Young children are learning about themselves and others, and they may not always think about the impact of what they say on others. What should you do if a child says something that is a microaggression or worse? First, it's important to create an identity-safe classroom where everyone feels safe, valued, and supported. In that type of classroom setting, you can talk about things that people may say or do that hurt people's feelings or makes them feel unvalued or excluded. In the article, "Teaching First-graders about Microaggressions: The Small Moments Add Up" (2019), Bret Turner, a first-grade teacher, describes how he creates an identity-safe classroom and how he engages his young students. He uses children's literature like those books recommended in Figure 14.1 to introduce the concept of macroaggressions so he can engage his own students in such discussions should the need arise. He also helps children see the difference between a single unkind comment and repeated comments that build up to make a student feel excluded, unwelcome, and unvalued. Although it may be uncomfortable for you to raise such topics in your classroom, as a learner-ready

Figure 14.1. Books to Help Children Build an Awareness of Macroaggressions

Choi, Y. (2003). *The name jar.* New York, NY: Dell Dragonfly Books.

Ewart, M. (2008). *10,000 dresses.* New York, NY: Triangle Square Publishers.

Genhart, M. (2015). *Ouch moments: When words are used in hurtful ways.* Washington, DC: Magination Press.

Miller, S. (2018). *Don't touch my hair!* New York, NY: Little Brown Books for Young Readers.

Margin Note 14.10: Becoming Upended: Teaching and Learning about Race and Racism with Young Children and Their Families

https://www.naeyc.org/resources/pubs/yc/may2018/teaching-learning-race-and-racism

Margin Note 14.11: Kids Talk about Segregation

https://www.youtube.com/watch?v=Sff2N8rez_8

Margin Note 14.12: How to Be an Antiracist Educator

http://www.ascd.org/publications/newsletters/education-update/oct19/vol61/num10/How-to-Be-an-Antiracist-Educator.aspx

teacher, you must be committed to making your classroom a safe, supportive learning space for all children, and addressing microaggressions is part of creating that type of classroom with your students.

See Margin Note 14.10 to read about how you can help teach young children and their families about race and racism. As you read the article, consider what questions you have. What makes you uncomfortable? Why? How can you build your confidence with addressing race and racism in your teaching? Share your insights with your colleagues or your mentor teacher. In Margin Note 14.11, you can view a short video of young children talking about race. As you view the video, ask yourself how you can use the insights you gain to help you be more well-prepared to address race and racism in your teaching and classroom.

You may be thinking that the approach we are advocating is to not be a racist, but there is a new, bolder approach that we want you to consider. It's being antiracist. Kendi (2019) describes being an antiracist as working against racism to change structures and systems to help eliminate racism. As a teacher, how can you do that? Well, you can start in your own classroom using ideas such as those offered in the article in Margin Note 14.12. As with any instructional approach or activity, it's important to consider context. On a topic that may be considered controversial such as racism, always be sure to talk to your mentor teacher and building administrator to come up with a plan you can all agree on together.

Engaging Families: Learning about Student Identities

Talking to family members is a great way to learn more about your students and their identities. Be sure to approach such conversations with an open mind and adopt the stance of replacing judgment with curiosity. You may find that open-ended questions such as the following are helpful:

- Tell me something about your child that will help me teach them better.
- What is a fear you have for your child?
- What is a dream you have for your child?
- What do you want me to understand about your child that other teachers may not have known or understood?

Before contacting any families, be sure you have your mentor teacher's approval and support.

5. Express Your Teaching Identity

Do you know who you are? Maybe you're a parent, runner, reader, or spouse. Your identity will change throughout your life, but we imagine you have a pretty good idea of who you are right now. It's the same with your teaching identity. We asked you to think through who you are as a teacher in Chapter 12, and you added to your awareness of that identity in Chapter 13. Now we want you to solidify that identity and understand what it means for you as you interview for your first teaching job and then begin your teaching career.

INTERVIEWING. When you begin interviewing, your **teaching identity** will be the guiding framework for how you answer questions. Let's think about this for a moment. The first question of most interviews is, "Tell me about yourself." This may seem like a softball question, but it's actually very hard to answer. What should you include without telling your life story? Here's where your teaching identity comes into play. Think about who you are as a teacher and try answering the question. Here is Sumaira's answer to the question:

> I wanted to become a teacher since I was a young child. I had trouble reading, because my school used a phonics first program, and I couldn't distinguish between the sounds of the letters that the teacher taught. Although I wasn't diagnosed with a disability, I just didn't have good auditory discrimination, so I found learning to read using a bottom-up approach with a heavy emphasis on phonics really hard. My mom got me a tutor who taught me to read using a whole word approach. That worked for me. As a result, I am a voracious reader. As a teacher, and more balanced I believe strongly that students learn in different ways and that my responsibility is to find the best way to teach each child.

Can you tell something about Sumaira's teaching identity through this answer? You can see how she wove a part of her life story into the answer but highlighted who she was as a teacher in a brief answer. Margin Note 14.13 provides some guidelines for answering this question. After watching the two videos, develop an answer to the question, "Tell me about yourself." You might begin by writing your answer. Then practice with some of your classmates and seek their feedback to help you make your answer clearer and more informative.

Margin Note 14.13:

How to Answer: Tell Me about Yourself

https://www.youtube.com/watch?v=MmFuWmzeiDs

Tell Me about Yourself: A Good Answer to this Interview Question

https://www.youtube.com/watch?v=kayOhGRcNt4

ANSWERING INTERVIEW QUESTIONS. Your teaching identity will come into play as you answer other interview questions, and this is what your interviewers want to hear. As your interviewers listen to your answers, they are really wanting to know who you are as a teacher. Then they are looking to match the needs on their staff with a new teacher who fills a gap. For example, perhaps a K–2 teaching staff is strong on teaching word identification and other reading skills but isn't current on children's literature. They may be looking for someone who identifies strongly with using books to teach skills and strategies. You shouldn't try to second guess what interviewers want. You only need to make it clear who you are and what you believe.

There are many ways to answer interview questions, but we've found that thinking through your answers using the STAR technique is useful (Doyle, 2019). The STAR technique is to frame your answers around a situation, task, action, and result. As you listen to a question, try to think of a situation to describe, then explain the task you had to complete, describe the action you took to complete the task, and close with the result of your efforts. Here's an example of Sumaira's answer to the question, "How would you improve students' reading?"

When I began student teaching, I noticed that many students could not comprehend the stories that were in their core reading text (**Situation**). My mentor teacher asked me to develop a series of lessons that would help my students understand what they were reading (**Task**). Because I believe that readers need to self-monitor as they read, I developed three lesson plans with strategies on monitoring. I taught the lessons over a period of several weeks and provided guided practice for the students (**Action**). After about a month, my mentor teacher told me that she was noticing an improvement of most of the students' reading comprehension which was backed up with an informal assessment (**Result**).

You can see that Sumaira answered the question with a specific example using the STAR framework and also indicated that she believes that students need to monitor reading and that reading strategies should be explicitly taught. She didn't spend time on details of her beliefs or identity, but she opened the door to follow-up questions that interviewers might have. Her answer might be followed up with a question that probes Sumaira's beliefs about self-monitoring or teaching strategies.

Margin Note 14.14:
18 Interview Questions Every Teacher Must Be Able to Answer

https://www.weare teachers.com/most-common-teacher-interview-questions/

You don't have to use the STAR approach for every answer, but you should try to answer questions that tell a story, are brief, and express who you are as a teacher. You don't have to "hit your interviewers over the head" with your answers. Focus on answering the question with the strong knowledge of who you are as a teacher. Margin Note 14.14 provides some sample interview questions. Try answering these questions using the STAR approach with small groups of your classmates. Can you tell who your classmates are as teachers from their answers?

Connection to the Field: Interview Questions

Ask your mentor teacher or your school administrator if they have a list of interview questions that they use. Read the questions and practice answering them.

YOUR IDENTITY AS A NEW TEACHER. Once you get your first job, you will need to make sure that you know who you are as a teacher and also be ready to compromise if needed. "Wait," you might be saying, "what do you mean?" Being part of a teaching community is similar to any relationship. You need to know what you believe, but you also need to figure out ways to compromise and fit into the community.

What you need to remember is that you were hired for who you are, and that's important. However, you also need to be open to learning from your colleagues. All teachers need to reflect on their identity through their careers and change as needed. As a new teacher, you'll learn so much about teaching in your first few years (and every year after that), and your experience might point you in a slightly different direction from the beliefs you have now. For example, let's say that you're currently a firm believer in using children's literature as the basis for developing teaching lessons. As a teacher, you might find that you also need to use a supplementary text or a scope and sequence chart to explicitly teach phonics skills and strategies in addition to using books as your teaching foundation.

As you learn more, have more experience teaching, and grow as a teacher from reflecting on your practice, you will find that your teacher identity will grow along with you. Be sure to embrace this growth and development as part of your lifelong journey of becoming a teacher.

6. Practice Self-care

Teaching is not merely a job or a career, it's a way of life that is incredibly rewarding and challenging! Did you think you'd be working 8:00 am–3:00 pm with summers off? Sorry, that's definitely not going to happen. You'll be thinking of your students at all hours. You might be at dinner with a friend and suddenly have a great idea about how to help Samantha learn her sight words. You might think this is contradictory to practicing self-care, but it's an important part of the reality of being a teacher. We want you to become a teacher who loves the teaching life and still takes care of yourself. It's not just good to practice **self-care**, it's essential to your success and longevity as a teacher. Thompson (2019) even argues that lack of self-care can contribute to new teachers leaving the profession in the first several years of their careers. Therefore, we urge you to consider four main approaches to self-care that will help you take care of yourself as you manage the many demands of being a new teacher.

SET BOUNDARIES. Self-care is important so that you will have the energy to teach (Graves, 2001). Taking care of yourself physically and emotionally is essential to your success and longevity as a teacher. As we noted above, teaching is a way of life, but it's important for you to create boundaries so that teaching doesn't fill every moment of your life and leave you exhausted and frustrated. It's okay to say, "no" to extra tasks and projects at school if you simply don't have time. It's also okay to say that you won't work on Saturdays (unless there is a special school event) so you have time to spend with family and friends doing the things you enjoy. If you have your own children to care for, you may need to set boundaries, so you spend time with them after school rather than working in your classroom. In your first year of teaching you may find that you can't adhere to the boundaries you originally set because, as a new teacher, you may need more time to plan lessons, evaluate students' work, and complete teaching tasks. You may find that instead of taking off all of Saturday you might need to work some Saturday mornings so you can focus on yourself and other aspects of your life on Saturday afternoons and evenings. You'll need to figure out what works for you, and that may change as you progress in your teaching career.

ENGAGE IN HEALTHY HABITS. When you are very busy, one of the first things to go is often the healthy habits that you need more than ever! Eating healthy, exercising, getting enough sleep, and taking care of your emotional and spiritual needs are essential for your well-being as a teacher. By eating healthy foods and drinking plenty of water, your body will have the fuel and energy it needs to carry you through your busy days. No matter what form of exercise you enjoy—walking your dog, running, swimming, yoga, lifting weights, or playing a team sport—exercise will provide you with more energy and help you manage stress. Even on your busiest days, try to add some physical activity even if it's just walking around the block or dancing to your favorite song while you brush your teeth. You will probably notice that your mood will improve, and you will have a little more energy after doing so! Another key component of healthy habits is getting enough sleep. It's also important to develop sleep habits so you go to bed and get up at the same time each day so your body can get into a rhythm that will make it easier for you to fall asleep and wake up

© cristovao/Shutterstock.com

Self-care is essential to your success and longevity as a teacher.

quickly. It's also important to turn off your phone or computer at least 30 minutes before you go to bed and to sleep in a dark, cool room so you can relax and fall asleep easily.

Margin Note 14.15: How to Handle Stress: Teachers and Education Staff

https://www.education supportpartnership.org.uk/ blogs/claire-renn/how-handle-stress-teachers

MANAGE YOUR STRESS. **Stress** can creep up on us, and when it does, the effects can be very negative. You may find that stress causes you to be short-tempered and anxious. Find ways to manage your stress that work for you. You may find that deep breathing, meditation, or yoga works for you. Or, you may find that visualizing a calm, relaxing place helps you to manage your stress. Some of you may find that talking to a friend, family member, or counselor helps you manage your stress. And yet others may find that writing, singing, exercising, or doing a hobby such as gardening or painting works to reduce and help manage stress. Check out the ideas in Margin Note 14.15 and see which of them you think will be helpful for managing your stress.

ENJOY! Find at least three hobbies or activities that you enjoy and give yourself permission to engage in them on a regular basis. Maybe you enjoy having dinner with your partner, spouse, or best friend. Give yourself permission to do this every week or at least once a month. If you enjoy reading, make time to read for your own enjoyment. If you enjoy cooking, gardening, crafting, woodworking, playing video games, dancing, sewing, antiquing, hiking, etc., make time to do those things. By feeding your interests and engaging in things that give you joy, you'll be recharged and ready to be a better teacher.

7. Become a Teacher Leader

In Chapter 13 we described in detail how you need to enter the teaching profession as a learner who stays current in the field and networks with other professionals. We'd like to take this one step further and ask you to prepare to be a **teacher leader**. You might be thinking, "Wait a minute! I don't even have a job yet. How can I even think about being a leader?" We understand, but we also want you to think about the strengths you bring to the profession.

INSIDE YOUR SCHOOL. When you begin your teaching job, you'll likely find out that there are many ways to be involved in your teaching community and show your leadership ability. There are committees to join, parent organizations to participate in, special events to plan, bulletin boards to change, and so on. It's easy to become overly involved and then be too busy to do a good job in anything.

We'd like you to take a minute right now and think again who you are and what interests you. Try to identify a couple of areas that you think would be areas of strengths for you and become involved in those committees or look for opportunities to contribute in those areas. And, you may have to say, "No, thanks," to other requests. For example, Vanya loves children's literature and decided that in her first year of teaching she'd look for opportunities to be on committees that made decisions about chapter books to teach in grades 1–3, to help the school organize a book room, and to develop a list of suggested read alouds for parents. Vanya, however, was asked to be on the math committee and to organize outdoor field experience, but she was worried that these added responsibilities would take away from her teaching, so she carefully said that she couldn't take on these jobs this year but possibly would be interested in the future. Vanya wanted to be a leader in the school in the areas of her strength and decided to wait for a year or so to expand her areas of interest.

OUTSIDE YOUR SCHOOL. You are most likely in the midst of or just finishing your teaching preparation program. That means you have learned some of the newest research and cutting-edge ideas. You probably have developed large projects and studied concepts in detail. Perhaps, for example,

you did a large project on multicultural books and are a near expert in that area. This is an area in which you could be a leader in your school. There are also ways you could present what you have learned to other professionals, such as in local or state reading councils. Many reading councils provide opportunities for teacher candidates and teachers to present in roundtable discussions about areas of expertise.

Local literacy councils are often affiliates of state literacy associations. Therefore, you can most likely find a local literacy council near you by checking out your state literacy association's website and looking for local information. For example, the Oregon State Literacy Association website found in Margin Note 14.16 has a tab under which you can find the local councils. Check out your own state literacy association's website to find a local literacy council near you. Attend some meetings, volunteer to help with committees or events, and offer to present or co-present at a meeting. In this way, you'll begin to be a teacher leader.

Margin Note 14.16: Oregon State Literacy Association

https://www.oregonread.org/

What Do You Believe about Becoming a Learner-ready Teacher?

You've already developed a list of your beliefs about teaching and have described your teaching identity in Chapter 12. Now, we'd like you to finish this book by thinking about what you believe about becoming a learner-ready teacher.

To recap, a learner-ready teacher is the term that is currently being used for a new teacher who is prepared to enter the teaching field as a competent beginner and also a learner. According to a document titled, *Preparing "Learner-ready" Teachers: Guidance from NTEP States for Ensuring a Culturally Responsive Workforce* (CCSSO, 2018), you should be ready on Day 1 to be an effective teacher. This means that you have knowledge of the content to teach, the ability to prepare and deliver engaging lessons, and the understanding of what it means to teach students of diverse abilities, cultures, languages, and community values. This may seem like a tall order but becoming a learner-ready teacher also includes a final important characteristic: you know that you need to continue to learn in all areas.

We'd like you now to personalize this information and write down ways you are a learner-ready teacher. Be confident in your knowledge and abilities as you write and also acknowledge the areas where you could learn more. An example follows:

I am a learner-ready teacher and ready to begin my teaching career! I feel like I have a good knowledge of how children emerge into literacy because I am the oldest of five children and was privileged to watch my siblings grow into literacy. I also feel confident that I know the basics of how to teach print concepts, phonics, phonemic awareness, comprehension, fluency, vocabulary, and writing. I also have a talent for engaging students when I teach. Furthermore, I believe I am a learner-ready teacher because I am part of a mixed-race family and community. I have observed various cultures through my life, and I am learning how my cultural background influences my actions. Although I have much to learn, I believe I have the foundation to accept and respect students of all abilities, cultures, and backgrounds. I am not perfect by any means, but I am looking forward to learning more about myself as a cultural being, how to be more culturally competent, and how to teach my students.

Margin Note 14.17: I'm a Teacher: An Educator's Anthem

https://www.youtube.com/watch?v=RelL-PdcCSk

Closing Thoughts

As a new teacher, we'd like you to embrace who you are, showcase your strengths, and continue as a learner. One quote that concisely states this idea follows: "Who dares to teach must never cease to learn" (Dana, n.d.). That could be your motto as a teacher. Throughout your job search, your beginning years in the classroom, and your entire career, you'll never stop learning.

The purpose of this book is to help you learn how to teach reading and writing to children in grades PreK–3. We'd like to leave you with a final video in Margin Note 14.17: I'm a Teacher. Welcome to the profession!

Takeaways from Chapter 14

You can become a learner-ready teacher by focusing on the following big ideas.

- Reflect on your teaching.
- Prioritize your to-do list.
- Learn more about your cultural identity.
- Become more culturally competent.
- Express your teaching identity.
- Practice self-care.
- Become a teacher leader.

To Learn More about Becoming a Learner-ready Teacher

Books about Racism and Antiracism

Banaji, M. R., & Greenwald, A. G. (2016). *Blindspot: Hidden biases of good people*. New York, NY: Bantam Books.

http://www.randomhousebooks.com/books/8099/

Do you worry that you have implicit biases that might affect your ability to work well with all of your students and their families? This book provides a clear discussion of hidden biases about those who are different from us—race, age, gender, ethnicity, religion, social class, sexuality, disability status, and nationality. The authors delve into how we can uncover our implicit biases and how to adapt our beliefs and behaviors to overcome our blind spots.

DiAngelo, R., & Dyson, M. E. (2018). *White fragility: Why it's so hard for white people to talk about racism*. Boston, MA: Beacon Press.

http://www.beacon.org/White-Fragility-P1346.aspx

This book introduces the concept of white fragility which is explained as white people finding it difficult and uncomfortable to discuss race. They tend to avoid it which prevents them from addressing racial inequalities and racism. The authors argue that when white people claim to be color blind, they avoid the issue that racism is real, and we need to discuss and address it. This book will challenge your assumptions and encourage you to look at race and racism head-on rather than trying to avoid the topic.

Gullo, G. L., Capatosto, K., & Staats, C. (2019). *Implicit bias in schools: A practitioner's guide*. New York, NY: Routledge.

https://www.routledge.com/Implicit-Bias-in-Schools-A-Practitioners-Guide-1st-Edition/Gullo-Capatosto-Staats/p/book/9781138497061

This guide for educators addresses what implicit bias is, how to identify it, and how to overcome it in schools. The authors address a range of education topics including discipline, instruction, academic achievement, mindfulness, data collection, and culturally relevant practices.

Kendi, I. X. (2019). *How to be an antiracist*. New York, NY: One World.

https://www.penguinrandomhouse.com/books/564299/how-to-be-an-antiracist-by-ibram-x-kendi/

Kendi argues that not being a racist is not enough. We need to work to become antiracist which means that we push against racist practices, policies, and institutions. A provocative read that will challenge many of your assumptions, this is a powerful book for any educator who wants to promote antiracist education in their teaching.

Books about Self-Care for Teachers

Boogran, T. H. (2020). *180 days of self-care for busy educators (A 36-week plan of low-cost self-care for teachers and educators)*. Bloomington, IN: Solution Tree Press.

https://www.solutiontree.com/products/180-days-of-self-care-for-busy-educators.html

If you are always putting your teaching and others ahead of yourself, this book is for you. The author provides weekly themes such as creativity and time management along with daily self-care strategies and techniques you can implement right away. To be an effective teacher, you need to take care of yourself, and this book can help you get on the right path toward self-care.

Graves, D. H. (2001). *The energy to teach*. Portsmouth, NH: Heinemann.

https://www.heinemann.com/products/e00326.aspx

This slim volume provides insight, support, and hope for overcoming the fatigue that many teachers experience. With a focus on transforming energy-draining situations into energy-giving events, Graves will help you build your energy to teach.

Online Resources about Racism and Tolerance

Test Yourself for Hidden Bias

https://www.tolerance.org/professional-development/test-yourself-for-hidden-bias

Do you know what your hidden biases are? This free, online test will help you identify your hidden biases so you can address them in your teaching and in your life.

Teaching Tolerance

https://www.splcenter.org/teaching-tolerance

This website provides a large collection of free resources for educators to teach tolerance starting in kindergarten. It provides lesson plans, webinars, podcasts, and more so you can incorporate tolerance into your classroom and teaching.

Online Resources for Teacher Reflection

How to Become a Reflective Teacher: The Complete Guide for Reflection in Teaching

https://www.bookwidgets.com/blog/2019/02/how-to-become-a-reflective-teacher-the-complete-guide-for-reflection-in-teaching

If you want to learn more about how you can be a reflective teacher, this guide is for you. It offers strategies you can use to develop reflection as well as a collection of questions to guide your reflection in areas such as assessment, classroom management, and professional development. It even offers questions you can use to have your students help you reflect on your teaching and their learning.

The Reflective Teacher: Taking a Long Look

https://www.edutopia.org/blog/reflective-teacher-taking-long-look-nicholas-provenzano

This blog offers practical suggestions for reflecting on your teaching, including seeking feedback from your students, writing down your reflections, blogging about your teaching, and using video to reflect on your teaching.

Interviewing Tips and Other Tips for New Teachers

Elementary Teacher Interview Questions and Answers

https://www.youtube.com/watch?v=6X7YARR3GjY

If you are getting ready to interview for your first teaching job, check out this video made by a teacher candidate who has been involved in several interviews. You can learn about the types of questions that will likely be asked at interviews as well as things you will want to do to be prepared for interviews.

Top 10 Tips for New Teachers

https://www.youtube.com/watch?v=j3TXe5OvhME

This video offers 10 practical tips to help you navigate your first year of teaching. If you are looking for direction, encouragement, and practical ideas to help you succeed in your first year of teaching, check out this video.

References

Achieve the Core (Oct. 1, 2016). *Top five ways to improve your basal reading program.* Retrieved from https://achievethecore.org/aligned/top-five-ways-to-improve-your-basal-reading-program/

Adams, M. J. (1990). *Beginning to read: Thinking and learning about print.* Cambridge, MA: MIT Press.

Adams, M. J., Foorman, B. R., Lundberg, I., & Beeler, T. (1998). *Phonemic awareness in young children: A classroom curriculum.* Baltimore, MD: Brookes.

Afflerbach, P. (2016). An overview of individual differences in reading: Research, policy, and practice. In P. Afflerbach (Ed.), *Handbook of individual differences in reading: Reader, text, and context* (pp. 1–12). New York, NY: Routledge.

Afflerbach, P. (2018). *Understanding and using reading assessment, K–12* (3rd ed.). Alexandra, VA: ASCD/International Reading Association.

Aguilar, J. A. (2000, April). *Chicano street signs: Graffiti as public literacy practice.* Paper presented at the annual meeting of the American Educational Research Association, New Orleans, LA.

Ainsworth, L. (2015). *Common formative assessments 2.0: How teacher teams intentionally align standards, instruction, and assessment.* Thousand Oaks, CA: Corwin.

Allington, R. L., & McGill-Franzen, A. (2017). Comprehension difficulties and struggling readers. In S. E. Israel (Ed.), *Handbook of research on reading comprehension* (2nd ed., pp. 271–292). New York, NY: Guilford Press.

Almasi, J. F., & Hart, S. J. (2019). Best practices in narrative text comprehension instruction. In L. M. Morrow & L. B. Gambrell (Eds.), *Best practices in literacy instruction* (6th ed., pp. 221–249). New York, NY: Guilford Press.

Anderson, R. C. (1994). Role of reader's schema in comprehension, learning, and memory. In R. B. Ruddell, M. R. Ruddell, & H. Singer (Eds.), *Theoretical models and processes of reading* (4th ed., pp. 469–482). Newark, DE: International Reading Association.

Arbogast, J. M. (2004). *Buildings in disguise: Architecture that looks like animals, food, and other things.* Honesdale, PA: Boyds Mills Press.

Armbruster, B. B., Lehr, F., & Osborn, J. (2001). *Put reading first: The research building blocks for teaching children to read.* Washington, DC: National Institute for Literacy.

Arya, P., & Feathers, K. M. (2012). Reconsidering children's readings: Insights into the reading process. *Reading Psychology, 33,* 301–322.

Ash, G. E., & Baumann, J. F. (2017). Vocabulary and reading comprehension: The nexus of meaning. In S. E. Israel (Ed.), *Handbook of research on reading comprehension* (2nd ed., pp. 377–406). New York, NY: Guilford Press.

Atwell, N. (2002). *Lessons that change writers.* Portsmouth, NH: Heinemann.

Bacchioni, S., & Kurstedt, R. L. (2019). Personalized anchor charts: Bridging small group work to independence. *The Reading Teacher, 72,* 652– 658. doi:10.1002/trtr.1772

Bang, M. (1988). *The paper crane.* Hong Kong: South China Printing Company.

Bear, D. R., Invernizzi, M., Templeton, S., & Johnston, F. (2015). *Words their way: Word study for phonics, vocabulary, and spelling instruction* (6th ed.). New York, NY: Pearson.

Beck, I. L., McKeown, M. G., & Kucan, L. (2013). *Bringing words to life: Robust vocabulary instruction* (2nd ed). New York, NY: Guilford Press.

Beers, K., & Probst, R. E. (2016). *Reading nonfiction: Notice & note stances, signpost, and strategies.* Portsmouth, NH: Heinemann.

Benson, T. A., & Fiarman, S. E. (2019). *Unconscious bias in schools: A developmental approach to race and racism.* Cambridge, MA: Harvard Education Press.

Betts, E. A. (1946). *Foundations of reading instruction, with emphasis on differentiated guidance.* New York, NY: American Book Company.

Bhattacharya, A. (2016). The influence of poverty on individual differences in reading. In P. Afflerbach (Ed.), *Handbook of individual differences in reading: Reader, text, and context* (pp. 305–317). New York, NY: Routledge.

Biemiller, A. (2003). Vocabulary: Needed if more children are to read well. *Reading Psychology, 24,* 323–335. doi:10.1080/02702710390227297

Blachowicz, C. L. Z. (1986). Making connections: Alternatives to the vocabulary notebook. *Journal of Reading, 29,* 643–649. https://www.jstor.org/stable/40029692

Black, P., & Wiliam, D. (2009). Developing the theory of formative assessment. *Educational Assessment, Evaluation and Accountability, 21,* 5–31. doi.org/10.1007/s11092-008-90685

Bloodgood, J. W. (1999). What's in a name?: Children's name writing and literacy acquisition. *Reading Research Quarterly, 34,* 342–367. https://www.jstor.org/stable/748067

Boushey, G., & Moser, J. (2009). *The CAFÉ book: Engaging all students in daily literacy assessment and instruction.* Portsmouth, NH: Stenhouse Publishers.

Boushey, G., & Moser, J. (2014). *The daily 5: Fostering literacy independence in the elementary grades* (2nd ed.). Portsmouth, NH: Stenhouse Publishers.

Braker-Walters, B. A. (2014). Informational text and the Common Core: A content analysis of three basal reading programs. *SAGE Open.* https://doi.org/10.1177/2158244014555119

Bridwell, N. (1966). *Clifford takes a trip.* New York, NY: Scholastic.

Bridwell, N. (2015). *Clifford goes to kindergarten.* New York, NY: Scholastic.

Britton, J., Burgess, T., Martin, N., McLeod, A., & Rosen, H. (1975). *The development of writing abilities.* London, England: Macmillan.

Brown, M. W. (1975). *Goodnight moon.* New York, NY: HarperCollins.

Brown-Jeffy, S., & Cooper, J. E. (2011). Toward a conceptual framework of culturally relevant pedagogy: An overview of the conceptual and theoretical literature. *Teacher Education Quarterly, 38,* 65–84. https://eric.ed.gov/?id=EJ914924

Bulla, C. R. (2001). *A tree is a plant.* New York, NY: HarperCollins.

Burke, K. (2010). *Balanced assessment: From formative to summative.* Bloomington, IN: Solution Tree Press.

Cain, S. (2013). *Quiet: The power of introverts in a world that can't stop talking.* New York, NY: Random House.

Calkins, L. (1986). *The art of teaching writing.* Portsmouth, NH: Heinemann.

Calkins, L, (2015). *A guide to the reading workshop, primary grades.* Portsmouth, NH: Heinemann.

Calo, K. M., Woolard-Ferguson, T., & Koitz, E. (2013). Fluency idol: Using pop culture to engage students and boost fluency skills. *The Reading Teacher, 66,* 454–458. https://doi.org/10.1002/TRTR.1148

Campbell, J. R., Voelkl, K. E., & Donahue, P. I. (1997). *NAEP 1996 trends in academic progress* (NCES Publication No. 97985r). Washington, DC: U.S. Department of Education.

Cannon, J. (1993). *Stellaluna.* San Diego, CA: Harcourt Brace Jovanovich.

Carle, E. (1996). *Little cloud.* New York, NY: Scholastic.

Cecil, N. L., Baker, S., & Lozano, A. S. (2017). *Striking a balance: A comprehensive approach to early literacy* (5th ed.). New York, NY: Routledge.

Chall, J. S. (1983). *Stages of reading development.* New York, NY: McGraw-Hill.

Chomsky, N. (1975). *Reflections on language.* New York, NY: Pantheon.

Clay, M. M. (1966). *Emergent reading behaviour.* Unpublished doctoral dissertation, University of Auckland, Auckland, New Zealand.

Clay, M. M. (1975). *What did I write? Beginning writing behavior.* Exeter, NH: Heinemann.

Clay, M. M. (1985). *The early detection of reading difficulties* (3rd ed.). Portsmouth, NH: Heinemann.

Coddington, C. S., & Guthrie, J. T. (2009). Teacher and student perceptions of boys' and girls' reading motivation. *Reading Psychology, 30,* 225–249. doi:10.1080/02702710802275371

Cooper, E. (2010). *Beaver is lost.* New York, NY: Random House Children's Books.

Copple, C., & Bredekamp, S. (Eds.). (2009). *Developmentally appropriate practice in early childhood programs serving children from birth through age 8* (3rd ed.). Washington, DC: National Association for the Education of Young Children.

Council of Chief State School Officers (CCSSO). (2012). *Our responsibility, our promise: Transforming educator preparation and entry into the profession.* A report by the CCSSO Task Force on Educator Preparation and Entry into the Profession. Washington, DC: Author.

Council of Chief State School Officers (CCSSO). (2018). *Preparing "learner-ready" teachers: Guidance from NTEP states for ensuring a culturally responsive workforce.* Washington, DC: Author. Available from http://www.ccsso.org/sites/default/files/2018-02/Preparing%20Learner-Ready%20Teachers.pdf

Crenshaw, K. (1989). Demarginalizing the intersection of race and sex: A black feminist critique of antidiscrimination doctrine, feminist theory and antiracist politics. University of Chicago Legal Forum. Retrieved from https://chicagounbound.uchicago.edu/uclf/vol1989/iss1/8

Cronin, D. (2003). *Diary of a worm.* New York, NY: HarperCollins.

Cunningham, P. M. (2017). *Phonics they use: Words for reading and writing* (7th ed.). New York, NY: Pearson.

Currie, B. M. (2015). *All hands on deck: Tools for connecting educators, parents, and communities.* Thousand Oaks, CA: Corwin.

Dana, J. C. (n.d.). Retrieved from https://www.bartleby.com/73/1799.html

Delpit, L. (2006). *Other people's children: Cultural conflict in the classroom.* New York, NY: Norton and Company.

Delpit, L. D. (1988). The silenced dialogue: Power and pedagogy in educating other people's children. *Harvard Educational Review, 58,* 280–298. https://doi.org/10.17763/haer.58.3.c43481778r528qw4

Dewey, J. (1933). *How we think.* New York, NY: D. C. Heath.

Dewey, J. (1938). *Experience and education.* New York, NY: Macmillan.

Dewitz, P., & Jones, J. (2013). Using basal readers: From dutiful fidelity to intelligent decision making. *The Reading Teacher, 66,* 391–400. doi:10.1002/TRTR.01134

Domínguez, M., & Gutiérrez, K. D. (2019). Best practices for teaching dual language learners: Leveraging everyday literacies. In L. M. Morrow & L. B. Gambrell (Eds.), *Best practices in literacy instruction* (6th ed., pp. 127–149). New York, NY: Guilford Press.

Donovan, C. (2001). Children's development and control of written story and information genres: Insights from one elementary school. *Research in the Teaching of English, 35,* 394–447. https://www.jstor.org/stable/40171493

Doyle, A. (2019). *How to use the STAR interview response technique.* Retrieved from https://www.thebalancecareers.com/what-is-the-star-interview-response-technique-2061629

Dresser, R. (2012). The impact of scripted literacy instruction on teachers and students. *Issues in Teacher Education, 21,* 71–87. https://eric.ed.gov/?id=EJ986817

Duckworth, A. (2016). *Grit: The power of passion and perseverance.* New York, NY: Scribner.

Duffy, G. G. (2005). Developing metacognitive teachers: Visioning and the expert's changing role in teacher education and professional development. In S. E. Israel, C. C. Block, K. L. Bauserman, & K. Kinnucan-Welsch (Eds.), *Metacognition in literacy learning: Theory, assessment, instruction, and professional development* (pp. 299–314). Mahwah, NJ: Lawrence Erlbaum.

Duffy, G. G., & Hoffman, J. V. (1999). In pursuit of an illusion: The flawed search for the perfect method. *The Reading Teacher, 53,* 10–16. https://www.jstor.org/stable/20204735

DuFour, R., DuFour, R., Eaker, R., Many, T. W., & Mattos, M. (2016). *Learning by doing: A handbook for Professional Learning Communities at Work™.* Bloomington, IN: Solution Tree Press.

Duke, N. K. (2000). 3.6 minutes per day: The scarcity of informational texts in first grade. *Reading Research Quarterly, 35,* 202–224. https://www.jstor.org/stable/748074

Dweck, C. S. (2006). *Mindset: The new psychology of success.* New York, NY: Ballantine Books.

Dyson, A. H. (2001). Writing and children's symbolic repertoires: Development unhinged. In S. B. Neuman & D. K. Dickinson (Eds.), *Handbook of early literacy research* (pp. 126–141). New York, NY: Guilford Press.

Elbow, P. (1981). *Writing with power.* New York, NY: Oxford Publishing.

Elish-Piper, L. (2008). Open houses, family literacy events, and family special events: Strategies to make them more family-focused. *Illinois Reading Council Journal, 36*(4), 51–55.

Elish-Piper, L. (2014/2015). Moving from parent involvement toward family engagement. *Illinois Reading Council Journal, 43*(1), 54–58.

Elish-Piper, L. (2015). The ABCs of reaching ALL families. *Illinois Reading Council Journal, 43*(2), 38–42.

Elish-Piper, L. (2018/2019). Flipping parent-teacher conferences. *Illinois Reading Council Journal, 41*(1), 42–45.

Elish-Piper, L., & L'Allier, S. K. (2014). *The Common Core coaching book: Strategies to help teachers address the K–5 ELA standards*. New York, NY: Guilford Press.

Elkonin, D. B. (1973). USSR. In J. Downing (Ed.), *Comparative reading: Cross-national studies of behaviors and processes in reading and writing* (pp. 551–579). New York, NY: Macmillan.

Ericson, L., & Juliebo, M. F. (1998). *The phonological awareness handbook for kindergarten and primary teachers*. Newark, DE: International Reading Association.

Fairbanks, C. M., Duffy, G. G., Faircloth, B. S., He, Y., Levin, B., Rohr, J., & Stein, C. (2010). Beyond knowledge: Exploring why some teachers are more thoughtfully adaptive than others. *Journal of Teacher Education, 61*, 161–171. doi:10.1177/0022487109347874

Family Educational Rights and Privacy Act. (1974). Retrieved from https://www2.ed.gov/policy/gen/guid/fpco/ferpa/index.html

Ferlazzo, L. (2011). Involvement or engagement? *Educational Leadership, 68*(8), 10–14.

Ferlazzo, L., & Hammond, L. (2009). *Building parent engagement in schools*. Santa Barbara, CA: Linworth.

Fisher, D., Frey, N., & Quaglia, R. J. (2018). *Engagement by design: Creating learning environments where students thrive*. Thousand Oaks, CA: Corwin.

Fives, H., & Buehl, M. M. (2012). Spring cleaning for the messy construct of teachers' beliefs: What are they? Which have been examined? What can they tell us? In K. R. Harris, S. Graham, & T. Urdan (Eds.), *APA educational psychology handbook* (Vol. 2, pp. 471–499). Washington DC: APA.

Fosnot, C. T. (1996). Constructivism: A psychological theory of learning. In C. T. Fosnot (Ed.), *Constructivism: Theory, perspectives, and practice* (pp. 8–33). New York, NY: Teachers College Press.

Fountas, I. C., & Pinnell, G. S. (2012). Guided reading: The romance and the reality. *The Reading Teacher, 66*, 268–284. doi:10.1002/TRTR.01123

Fowler, G. (2019). *Gene Fowler quotes*. Retrieved from https://www.successories.com/iquote/author/29/gene-fowler-quotes/1

Fox, B. J. (2014). *Phonics and word study for the teacher of reading: Programmed for self-instruction* (11th ed.). Upper Saddle River, NJ: Pearson.

Frayer, D., Frederick, W. C., & Klausmeier, H. J. (1969). *A schema for testing the level of cognitive mastery*. Madison, WI: Wisconsin Center for Education Research.

Fredericks, J. A., Blumenfeld, P. C., & Paris, A. H. (2004). School engagement: Potential of the concept, state of the evidence. *Review of Educational Research, 74*, 59–109. https://doi.org/10.3102/00346543074001059

Fulkerson, R. (1996). *Teaching argument in writing*. Urbana, IL: National Council of Teachers of English.

Fulmer, S. M., D'Mello, S. K., Strain, A., & Graesser, A. C. (2015). Interest-based text preference moderates the effect of text difficulty on engagement and learning. *Contemporary Educational Psychology, 41*, 98–110. doi:http://dx.doi.org/10.1016/j.cedpsych.2014.12.005

Fulwiler, T. (1987). *The journal book*. Portsmouth, NH: Heinemann.

Gambrell, L. B. (2011). Seven rules of engagement: What's important to know about motivation to read. *The Reading Teacher, 65*, 172–178.

Gambrell, L. B., & Dromsky, K. (2000). Fostering reading comprehension. In D. S. Strickland & L. M. Morrow (Eds.), *Beginning reading and writing* (pp. 143–153). New York, NY: Teachers College Press.

Gay, G. (2000). *Culturally responsive teaching: Theory, research, and practice*. New York, NY: Teachers College Press.

Gay, G. (2010). Foreward. In T. C. Howard (Ed.), *Why race and culture matter in schools: Closing the achievement gap in America's classrooms* (pp. xvii–xxii). New York, NY: Teachers College Press.

Gay, G. (2013). Teaching to and through cultural diversity. *Curriculum Inquiry, 43*, 48–70.

Gentry, J. R. (1982). An analysis of developmental spelling in GNYS at WRK. *The Reading Teacher, 36*, 192–200. https://www.jstor.org/stable/20198182

Gibson, C. (2016). Bridging English Language Learner achievement gaps through effective vocabulary development strategies. *English Language Teaching, 9*, 134–138. https://eric.ed.gov/?id=EJ1110015

Giorgis, C. (2002). Jack Gantos—Journal keeper extraordinaire. *Language Arts, 79*, 272–276.

Giovanni, N. (1988). "Knoxville, Tennessee." *Sing a song of popcorn: Every child's book of poems*. New York, NY: Scholastic.

González, N., Moll, L. C., & Amanti, C. (2005). *Funds of knowledge: Theorizing practices in households, communities, and classrooms*. Mahwah, NJ: Lawrence Erlbaum.

Goodman, K. S. (1965). A linguistic study of cues and miscues in reading. *Elementary English, 42*, 639–643. https://www.jstor.org/stable/41387554

Goodman, K. S. (1967). Reading: A psycholinguistic guessing game. *Journal of the Reading Specialist, 6*, 126–135. http://dx.doi.org/10.1080/19388076709556976

Goodman, Y. (1985). Kid watching: Observing children in the classroom. In A. Jaggar & M. T. Smith-Burke (Eds.), *Observing the language learner* (pp. 9–18). Newark, DE and Urbana, IL: International Reading Association and the National Council of Teachers of English.

Graves, D. H. (1983). *Writing: Teachers and children at work*. Portsmouth, NH: Heinemann.

Graves, D. H. (1994). *A fresh look at writing*. Portsmouth, NH: Heinemann.

Graves, D. H. (2001). *The energy to teach*. Portsmouth, NH: Heinemann.

Graves, M. F. (2016). *The vocabulary book: Learning and instruction* (2nd ed.). New York, NY: Teachers College Press.

Greene, F. (1979). Radio reading. In C. Pennock (Ed.), *Reading comprehension at four linguistic levels* (pp. 104–107). Newark, DE: International Reading Association.

Griffith, R., & Lacina, J. (2018). Teacher as decision maker: A framework to guide teaching decisions in reading. *The Reading Teacher, 71*, 501–507. doi:10.1002/trtr.1662

Guernsey, L., & Levine, M. H. (2015). *Tap, click, read: Growing readers in a world of screens*. San Francisco, CA: Jossey-Bass.

Gullo, G. L., Capatosto, K., & Staats, C. (2019). *Implicit bias in schools: A practitioner's guide*. New York, NY: Routledge.

Guthrie, J. T., & Barber, A. T. (2019). Best practices for motivating students to read. In L. M. Morrow & L. B. Gambrell (Eds.), *Best practices in literacy instruction* (6th ed., pp. 52–72). New York, NY: Guilford Press.

Gwynne, F. (1988). *A chocolate moose for dinner*. New York, NY: Aladdin Paperbacks.

Hague, K. (1984). *Alphabears*. New York, NY: Holt.

Hall, A. H., Simpson, A., Guo, Y., & Wang, S. (2015). Examining the effects of preschool writing instruction on emergent literacy skills: A systematic review of the literature. *Literacy Research and Instruction, 54*, 115–134. https://eric.ed.gov/?id=EJ1053472

Hansen, J. (2001). *When writers read* (2nd ed.). Portsmouth, NH: Heinemann.

Hart, B., & Risley, T. R. (1995). *Meaningful differences in the everyday experience of young American children*. Baltimore, MD: Paul H. Brookes Publishing.

Hartman, D. (1992). Eight readers reading: The intertextual links of able readers using multiple passages. *Reading Research Quarterly, 27*, 122–123.

Harvey, S., & Ward, A. (2017). *From striving to thriving: How to grow confident, capable readers*. New York, NY: Scholastic.

Hasbrouck, J., & Tindal, G. (2017). *An update to compiled ORF norms*. Eugene, OR: Behavioral Research and Teaching, University of Oregon.

Hattie, J., & Timperley, H. (2007). The power of feedback. *Review of Educational Research, 77*, 81–112. doi:10.3102/003465430298487

Haussamen, B. (with Benjamin, A., Kolln, M., & Wheeler, R. S.). (2003). *Grammar alive! A guide for teachers*. Urbana, IL: National Council of Teachers of English.

Helman, L., Rogers, C., Frederick, A., & Struck, M. (2016). *Inclusive literacy teaching: Differentiating approaches in multilingual elementary classrooms*. New York, NY: Teachers College Press.

Henderson, A. T., & Mapp, K. (2002). *A new wave of evidence: The impact of school, family and community connections on student achievement*. Austin, TX: National Center for Family and Community Connections with Schools.

Herman, J. L., Osmundson, E., & Dietel, R. (2010). *Benchmark assessments for improved learning* (AACC Policy Brief). Los Angeles, CA: University of California. Available: https://files.eric.ed.gov/fulltext/ED524108.pdf

Herrera, S. G. (2016). *Biography-driven culturally responsive teaching* (2nd ed.). New York, NY: Teachers College Press.

Heyck-Merlin, M. (2012). *The together teacher: Plan ahead, get organized, and save time!* San Francisco, CA: Jossey-Bass.

Hildreth, G. (1936). Early writing as an aid to reading. *Elementary English, 40*(1), 15–20.

Hill, R. T. G. (1997). Methodological approaches to Native American narrative and the role of performance. *American Indian Quarterly, 21*, 111–147. doi:10.2307/1185590

Hollie, S. (2001). Acknowledging the language of African American students: Instructional strategies. *The English Journal, 90*, 59. doi:10.2307/821903

Howard, T. C. (2010). Why race and culture matter in schools: Closing the achievement gap in America's classrooms. New York, NY: Teachers College Press.

Hoyt, L. (2002). *Make it real: Strategies for success with informational text*. Portsmouth, NH: Heinemann.

Iaquinta, A. (2006). Guided Reading: A research-based response to the challenges of early reading instruction. *Early Childhood Education Journal, 33*, 413–418. doi:10.1007/s10643-006-0074-2

International Literacy Association. (2018). Explaining phonics instruction: An educator's guide. [Literacy leadership brief]. Newark, DE: Author.

Invernizzi, M., & Buckrop, J. (2018). Reconceptualizing alphabet learning and instruction. In C. M. Cassano & S. M. Dougherty (Eds.), *Pivotal research in early literacy: Foundational studies and current practices* (pp. 85–110). New York, NY: Guilford Press.

Invernizzi, M., Juel, C., Swank, L., & Meier, J. (2015). *Phonological awareness literacy screening—kindergarten*. Charlottesville, VA: University of Virginia Printing Services.

Iwasaki, B., Rasinski, T., Yildirin, K., & Zimmerman, B. S. (2013). Let's bring back the magic of song for teaching reading. *The Reading Teacher, 67*, 137–141. doi:10.1002/TRTR.1203

Jeynes, W. (2012). A meta-analysis of the efficacy of different types of parental involvement programs for urban students. *Urban Education, 47*, 706–762.

Johns, J. L., & Lenski, S. D. (2019). *Improving reading: Strategies, resources, and Common Core connections* (7th ed.). Dubuque, IA: Kendall Hunt Publishing Company.

Johns, J. L., Elish-Piper, L., & Johns, B. (2017). *Basic reading inventory: Kindergarten through grade twelve and early literacy assessments* (12th ed.). Dubuque, IA: Kendall Hunt Publishing Company.

Johnston, F. P. (2001). The utility of phonic generalizations: Let's take another look at Clymer's conclusions. *The Reading Teacher, 55*, 132–143. https://eric.ed.gov/?id=EJ632367

Jones, C. D., & Reutzel, D. R. (2012). Enhanced alphabet knowledge instruction: Exploring a change of frequency, focus, and distributed cycles of review. *Educational Psychology, 33*, 448–464. doi:10.1080/02702711.2010.545260

Joubert, D., & Joubert, B. (2001). *The Africa diaries*. Washington, DC: National Geographic.

Juel, C. (1994). *Learning to read and write in one elementary school*. New York, NY: Springer-Verlag.

Kaplan, R. B. (1996). Cultural thought patterns in inter-cultural education. *Language Learning, 16*, 1–20. doi:10.1111/j.1467-1770.1966.tb00804.x

Kaye, E. L., & Lose, M. K. (2019). As easy as ABC? Teaching and learning about letters in early literacy. *The Reading Teacher, 72*, 599–610. https://doi.org/10.1002/trtr.1768

Kendi, I. X. (2019). *How to be an antiracist*. New York, NY: One World.

Kirsch, I., DeJong, J., Lafontaine, D., McQueen, J., Mendelovits, J., & Monseur, C. (2003). *Reading for change: Performance and engagement across countries: Results of PISA 2000*. Paris, France: OECD.

Kissel, B. (2017). *When writers drive the workshop: Honoring young voices and bold choices*. Portland, ME: Stenhouse Publishers.

Kissel, B. T., & Miller, E. T. (2015). Reclaiming power in the writers' workshop: Defending curricula, countering narratives, and changing identities in prekindergarten classrooms. *The Reading Teacher, 69*, 77–86. https://eric.ed.gov/?id=EJ1065920

Krakauer, J. (1996). *Into the wild*. New York, NY: Anchor Books.

Kremer-Sadlik, T., & Paugh, A. A. (2007). Everyday moments: Finding "quality time" in American working families. *Time and Society, 16*, 287–308.

Kuhn, M., Rasinski, T., & Young, C. (2018). Best practices in reading fluency instruction. In L. M. Morrow & L. B. Gambrell (Eds.), *Best practices in literacy instruction* (6th ed., pp. 271–288). New York, NY: Guilford Press.

LaBerge, D., & Samuels, S. J. (1974). Toward a theory of automatic information processing in reading. *Cognitive Psychology, 6*, 293–323. http://dx.doi.org/10.1016/0010-0285(74)90015-2

Ladson-Billings, G. (2006). "Yes, but how do we do it?" Practicing culturally relevant pedagogy. In J. G. Landsman & C. W. Lewis (Eds.), *White teachers in diverse classrooms: Creating inclusive schools, building on students' diversity, and providing true educational equity* (pp. 33–46). Sterling, VA: Stylus.

Ladson-Billings, G. (2014). Culturally relevant pedagogy 2.0: a.k.a. the remix. *Harvard Educational Review, 84*, 74–84. https://doi.org/10.17763/haer.84.1.p2rj131485484751

Lane, H. B., & Pullen, P. C. (2004). *Phonological assessment and instruction: A sound beginning*. Boston, MA: Allyn and Bacon.

Lapp, D., Flood, J., & Goss, K. (2000). Desks don't move—students do: In effective classroom environments. *The Reading Teacher, 54*, 31–36. http://www.jstor.org/stable/20204875

Lawrence, D. (2017). The explicit teaching of vocabulary. *Educating Young Children: Learning and Teaching in the Early Childhood Years, 23*, 33–36.

Lenski, S. D., & Johns, J. L. (2004). *Improving writing K–8* (2nd ed.). Dubuque, IA: Kendall Hunt Publishing Company.

Levin, B., & He, Y. (2008). Investigating the content and sources of teacher candidates' personal practical theories (PPTs). *Journal of Teacher Education, 59*, 55–68. doi:10.1177/0022487107310749

Lortie, D. (1975). *Schoolteacher: A sociological study*. Chicago, IL: University Press.

MacLachlan, P. (1985). *Sarah, plain and tall*. New York, NY: Harper and Row.

Madda, C. L., Griffo, V. B., Pearson, P. D., & Raphael, T. E. (2019). Current issues and best practices in literacy instruction. In L. M. Morrow & L. B. Gambrell (Eds.), *Best practices in literacy instruction* (6th ed., pp. 27–51). New York, NY: Guilford Press.

Malloy, J. A., Marinak, B. A., & Gambrell, L. B. (2019). Evidence-based best practices for developing literate communities. In L. M. Morrow & L. B. Gambrell (Eds.), *Best practices in literacy instruction* (6th ed., pp. 3–26). New York, NY: Guilford Press.

Martinez, M., Koss, M. D., & Johnson, N. J. (2016). Meeting characters in Caldecotts: What does this mean for today's readers? *The Reading Teacher, 70*, 19–28. doi:10.1002/trtr.1464

Martinez, M., Roser, N. L., & Strecker, S. (1998/1999). "I never thought I could be a star." A Readers Theater ticket to fluency. *The Reading Teacher, 52*, 326–334. https://www.jstor.org/stable/20202073

Marzano, R. J. (2012). *Becoming a reflective teacher*. Bloomington, IN: Marzano Research Laboratory.

Maulana, R., Helms-Lorenz, M., & van de Grift, W. (2015). A longitudinal study of the acceleration of growth in teaching quality of beginning teachers through the eyes of their students. *Teaching and Teacher Education, 51*, 225–245.

McCarrier, A., Fountas, I., & Pinnell, G. S. (2018). *Interactive writing: How language & literacy come together, K–2*. Portsmouth, NH: Heinemann.

McClure, E. L., & Fullerton, S. K. (2017). Instructional interactions: Supporting students' reading development through interactive read-alouds of informational texts. *The Reading Teacher, 71*, 51–59. doi:10.1002/trtr.1576

McDonald, J. (2018). *Hello world: Dinosaurs*. New York, NY: Random House Children's Books.

McKenna, M. C., Kear, D. J., & Ellsworth, R. A. (1995). Children's attitudes toward reading: A national survey. *Reading Research Quarterly, 30*, 934–956. doi:10.2307/748205

McKeown, M. G., Deane, P. D., Scott, J. A., Krovetz, R., & Lawless, R. R. (2017). *Vocabulary assessment to support instruction: Building rich word-learning experiences*. New York, NY: Guilford Press.

McTigue, E. M., Washburn, E. K., & Liew, J. (2009). Academic resilience and reading: Building successful readers. *The Reading Teacher, 62*, 422–432. doi:10.1598/RT.62.5.5

Mikita, C., Rodgers, E., Berenbon, R., & Winkler, C. (2019). Targeting prompts when scaffolding word solving during guided reading. *The Reading Teacher, 72*, 745–749. doi:10.1002/trtr.1778

Milner IV, H. R. (2015). *Start where you are, but don't stay there*. Cambridge, MA: Harvard Education Press.

Milner IV, H. R., Cunningham, H. B., Delale-O'Connor, L., & Kestenberg, E K. (2019). *"These kids are out of control." Why we must reimagine classroom management for equity*. Thousand Oaks, CA: Corwin.

Moll, L. C., Amanti, C., Neff, D., & González, N. E. (1992). Funds of knowledge for teaching: Using a qualitative approach to connect homes and classrooms. *Theory Into Practice, 31*, 132–141. https://eric.ed.gov/?id=EJ452272

Moll, L. C., Amanti, C., Neff, D., & González, N. E. (2005). Funds of knowledge for teaching: Using a qualitative approach to connect homes and classrooms. In N. E. González, L. C. Moll, & C. Amanti (Eds.), *Funds of knowledge: Theorizing practices in households, communities, and classrooms* (pp. 71–88). New York, NY: Routledge.

Monobe, G., Bintz, W. P., & McTeer, J. (2017). Developing English learners' reading confidence with whole class repeated reading. *The Reading Teacher, 71*, 347–350. https://doi.org/10.1002/trtr.1642

Mora, O. (2018). *Thank you, Omu!* New York, NY: Little, Brown and Company.

Morrow, L. M. (2015). *Early development in the early years: Helping children read and write* (8th ed.). Boston, MA: Pearson.

Morrow, L. M., & Gambrell, L. B. (Eds.). (2019). *Best practices in literacy instruction* (6th ed.). New York, NY: Guilford Press.

Morrow, L. M., Dougherty, S. M., & Tracey, D. H. (2019). Best practices in early literacy: Preschool, kindergarten, and first grade. In L. M. Morrow & L. B. Gambrell (Eds.), *Best practices in literacy instruction* (6th ed., pp. 75–103). New York, NY: Guilford.

National Association for the Education of Young Children (NAEYC). Position statement on developmentally appropriate practice and the Head Start Early Learning Outcomes Framework. https://www.naeyc.org/sites/default/files/globally-shared/downloads/PDFs/resources/position-statements/2009%20Professional%20Prep%20stdsRevised%204_12.pdf

National Governors Association for Best Practice & Council of Chief School Officers (NGA Center & CCSSO). (2010). *Common Core State Standards for English language arts*. Washington, DC: Author. Retrieved from http://www.corestandards.org/ELA-Literacy/

National Reading Panel. (2000). *Report of the National Reading Panel. Teaching children to read: An evidence-based assessment of the scientific research literature on reading and its implications for reading instruction*. Washington, DC: National Institute of Child Health and Human Development.

Ness, M. (2016). "Is that how I really sound?" Using iPads for fluency practice. *The Reading Teacher, 70*, 611–615. https://doi.org/10.1002/trtr.1554

Neuman, S. B., & Celano, D. (2001). Access to print in low-income and middle-income communities: An ecological study of four neighborhoods. *Reading Research Quarterly, 34*, 286–312. https://eric.ed.gov/?id=EJ619536

Neuman, S. B., & Celano, D. (2018). Enhancing children's access to print. In C. M. Cassano & S. M. Dougherty (Eds.), *Pivotal research in early literacy: Foundational studies and current practices* (pp. 279–295). New York, NY: Guilford Press.

Nichols, W. D., Rasinski, T. V., Rupley, W. H., Kellogg, R. A., Paige, D. D. (2018). Why poetry for reading instruction? Because it works! *The Reading Teacher, 72*, 389–397. doi:10.1002/trtr.1734

No Child Left Behind (NCLB) Act of 2001, Pub. L. No. 107-110, § 115, Stat. 1425 (2002). Retrieved from https://www2.ed.gov/admins/lead/account/nclbreference/reference.pdf

Numeroff, L. (2010). *If you give a mouse a cookie*. New York, NY: Harper Collins.

Ogle, D. M. (1986). K-W-L: A teaching model that develops active reading of expository text. *The Reading Teacher, 39*, 564–570. http://dx.doi.org/10.1598/RT.39.6.11

Opitz, M. F., & Rasinski, T. V. (2008). *Good-bye round robin: 25 effective oral reading strategies* (updated edition). Portsmouth, NH: Heinemann.

Orloff, K. K., & Catrow, D. (2004). *I wanna iguana*. New York, NY: G. P. Putnam's Sons Books for Young Readers.

Ourkids.net. (n.d.). Montessori, Waldorf, and Reggio Emilia: A comparison of philosophies. Retrieved from https://www.ourkids.net/school/montessori-vs-waldorf-reggio-emilia.

Pajares, M. (1992). Teachers' beliefs and educational research: Cleaning up a messy construct. *Review of Educational Research, 62*, 307–332. doi:10.2307/1170741

Paris, D. (2012). Culturally sustaining pedagogy: A needed change in stance, terminology, and practice. *Educational Researcher, 41*, 93–97. http://dx.doi.org/10.3102/0013189X12441244

Parish, P., & Siebel, F. (2013). *Amelia Bedelia* (50th anniversary ed.). New York, NY: Greenwillow Books.

Parsons, S. A. (2012). Adaptive teaching in literacy instruction: Case studies of two teachers. *Journal of Literacy Research, 44*, 149–170. doi:10.1177/1086296X12440261

Parsons, S. A., Dodman, S. L., & Burrowbridge, S. C. (2013). Broadening the view of differentiated instruction. *Phi Delta Kappan, 95*, 38–42. doi:10.1177/003172171309500107

Parsons, S. A., Malloy, J. A., Parsons, A. W., & Burrowbridge, S. C. (2015). Students' engagement in literacy tasks. *The Reading Teacher, 69*, 223–231. doi:10.1002/trtr.1378

Pavlov, I. P. (1928). Lectures on conditioned reflexes. London, England: Allen and Unwin.

Penford, A., & Kaufman, S. (2018). *All are welcome*. New York, NY: Alfred A. Knopf.

Piaget, J. (1977). *The origins of intelligence in children*. New York, NY: International University Press.

Piasta, S. B., Petscher, Y., & Justice, L. M. (2012). How many letters should preschoolers in public programs know?: The diagnostic efficiency of various preschool letter-naming benchmarks for predicting first-grade literacy achievement. *Journal of Educational Psychology, 104*, 945–958. http://dx.doi.org/10.1037/a0027757

Piasta, S. B., Purpura, D. J., & Wagner, R. K. (2010). Fostering alphabet knowledge development: A comparison of two instructional approaches. *Reading and Writing, 23*, 607–626. doi:10.1007/s11145-009-9174-x

Pikulski, J. J., & Chard, D. J. (2005). Fluency: Bridge between decoding and comprehension. *The Reading Teacher, 58*, 510–519. doi:10.1598/RT.58.6.2

Poe, V. L. (1986). Using multipaired simultaneous oral reading. *The Reading Teacher, 40*, 239–240. https://www.jstor.org/stable/20199359

Popham, W. J. (1997). What's wrong—and what's right—with rubrics. *Educational Leadership, 55*, 72–75. https://eric.ed.gov/?id=EJ552014

Pressley, M. (2000). What should comprehension instruction be the instruction of? In M. L. Kamil, P. B. Mosenthal, P. D. Pearson, & R. Barr (Eds.), *Handbook of reading research* (Vol. 3, pp. 545–561). Mahwah, NJ: Erlbaum.

Pressley, M., & Allington, R. L. (2015). *Reading instruction that works: The case for balanced teaching* (4th ed.). New York, NY: Guilford Press.

Protacio, M. S. (2012). Reading motivation: A focus on English learners. *The Reading Teacher, 66*, 69–77. doi:10.1002/TRTR.01092

Purkey, W. W., & Novak, J. M. (1996). *Inviting school success: A self-concept approach to teaching, learning, and democratic process* (3rd ed.). Belmont, CA: Wadsworth.

Quinn, J. M., Spencer, M., & Wagner, R. K. (2016). Individual differences in phonological awareness and their role in learning to read. In P. Afflerbach (Ed.), *Handbook of individual differences in reading: Reader, text, and context* (pp. 80–92). New York, NY: Routledge.

Rasinski, T., & Nageldinger, J. K. (2016). *The fluency factor: Authentic instruction and assessment for reading success in the Common Core classroom*. New York, NY: Teachers College Press.

Rasinski, T., Paige, D., Rains, C., Stewart, F., Julovich, B., Prenkert, D., Rupley, W. H., & Nichols, W. D. (2017). Effects of intensive fluency instruction on the reading proficiency of third-grade struggling readers. *Reading & Writing Quarterly, 33*, 519–532. doi:10.1080/10573569.2016.1250144

Read, C. C. (1986). *Children's creative spelling*. London, England: Routledge & Kegan Paul Publishers.

Renninger, K. A., & Bachrach, J. E. (2015). Studying triggers for interest and engagement using observational methods. *Educational Psychologist, 50*, 58–69. doi:10.1080/00461520.2014.999920

Reutzel, D. R. (2015). Early literacy research: Findings primary-grade teachers will want to know. *The Reading Teacher, 69*, 14–24. doi:10.1002/trtr.1387

Reutzel, D. R., Child, A., Jones, C. D., & Clark, S. K. (2014). Explicit instruction in core reading programs. *The Elementary School Journal, 114*, 406–430. doi:10.1086/674420

Richgels, D. J. (2001). Invented spelling, phonemic awareness, and reading and writing instruction. In S. B. Neuman & D. K. Dickinson (Eds.), *Handbook of early literacy research* (Vol. 1, pp. 142–155). New York, NY: Guilford Press.

Rosenblatt, L. M. (1938). *Literature as exploration*. New York, NY: D. Appleton-Century Company.

Rosenblatt, L. M. (1978). *The reader, the text, the poem: The transactional theory of literary work*. Carbondale, IL: Southern Illinois University Press.

Routman, R. (2000). *Conversations*. Portsmouth, NH: Heinemann.

Rumelhart, D. E. (1980). Schemata: The building blocks of cognition. In R. J. Spiro, B. C. Bruce, & W. F. Brewer (Eds.), *Theoretical issues in reading comprehension* (pp. 35–58). Hillsdale, NJ: Erlbaum.

Samuels, S. J. (1979). The method of repeated readings. *The Reading Teacher, 32*, 403–408.

Samuels, S. J., & Farstrup, A. E. (Eds.). (2006). *What research has to say about fluency instruction*. Newark, DE: International Reading Association.

Schickedanz, J. A. (2018). Writing in the early years: Understanding the past, confronting the present, imagining the future. In C. M. Cassano & S. M. Dougherty (Eds.), *Pivotal research in early literacy: Foundational studies and current practices* (pp. 55–84). New York, NY: Guilford Press.

Schön, D. (1983). *The reflective practitioner: How professionals think in action*. New York, NY: Basic Books.

Schraw, G., Flowerday, T., & Lehman, S. (2001). Increasing situational interest in the classroom. *Educational Psychology Review, 13,* 211–224. doi:10.1023/A:101661970518

Scott, J. A., Miller, T. F., & Flinspach, S. L. (2012). Developing word consciousness: Lessons from highly diverse fourth-grade classrooms. In J. Baumann & E. Kame'enui (Eds.), *Vocabulary instruction: From research to practice* (2nd ed., pp. 169–188). New York, NY: Guilford Press.

Sendak, M. (1963). *Where the wild things are.* New York, NY: HarperCollins.

Seuss. (1974). *There's a wocket in my pocket!* New York, NY: Beginner Books.

Shepard, L. A. (2000). The role of assessment in a learning culture. *Educational Researcher, 29,* 4–14. https://doi.org/10.3102/0013189X029007004

Skinner, B. F. (1953). *Science and human behavior.* New York, NY: Free Press.

Skott, J. (2015). The promises, problems, and prospects of research on teachers' beliefs. In H. Fives & M. G. Gill (Eds.), *International handbook of research on teachers' beliefs* (pp. 13–30). New York, NY: Routledge.

Sleeter, C. E. (2012). Confronting the marginalization of culturally responsive pedagogy. *Urban Education, 47,* 562–584. https://doi.org/10.1177/0042085911431472

Spivey, N. N. (1997). *The constructivist metaphor: Reading, writing, and the making of meaning.* San Diego, CA: Academic Press.

Springer, S. E., Harris, S., & Dole, J. A. (2017). From surviving to thriving: Four research-based principles to build students' reading interest. *The Reading Teacher, 71,* 43–50. doi:10.1002/trtr.1581

Stahl, K. A. D. (2016). A new priority: Comprehension intervention in the primary grades. *The Reading Teacher, 69,* 627–631. doi:10.1002/trtr.1454

Stanovich, K. E. (1989). Mathew effects in reading: Some consequences of individual differences in the acquisition of literacy. *Reading Research Quarterly, 21,* 360–407. http://dx.doi.org/10.1598/RRQ.21.4.1

Stanovich, K. E. (1993). Romance and reality. *The Reading Teacher, 47,* 280–291. https://eric.ed.gov/?id=EJ477302

Stauffer, R. G. (1969). *Directing reading maturity as a cognitive process.* New York, NY: Harper & Row.

Stein, N. L., & Glenn, C. G. (1979). An analysis of story comprehension in elementary school children. In R. O. Freedle (Ed.), *New directions in discourse processing* (pp. 53–120). Norwood, NJ: Ablex.

Stiggins. R. (2005). *Student-involved assessment for learning* (4th ed.). Upper Saddle River, NJ: Pearson, Merrill, Prentice Hall.

Teale, W. H., & Sulzby, E. (Eds.). (1986). *Emergent literacy: Writing and reading.* Norwood, NJ: Ablex.

Teale, W. H., Hoffman, E. B., Whittingham, C. E., & Paciga, K. A. (2018). Starting them young: How the shift from reading readiness to emergent literacy has influenced preschool literacy education. In C. M. Cassano & S. M. Dougherty (Eds.), *Pivotal research in early literacy: Foundational studies and current practices* (pp. 181–200). New York, NY: Guilford Press.

Therrien, W. J. (2004). Fluency and comprehension gains as a result of repeated reading: A meta-analysis. *Remedial and Special Education, 25,* 252–261. doi:10.1177/07419325040250040801

Thomas, J. (2009). *Rhyming dust bunnies.* San Diego, CA: Beach Lane Books.

Thompson, L. (2019, January 20). Importance of self-care as a teacher. *NEA Today.* Retrieved from http://neatoday.org/new-educators/importance-of-self-care-as-a-teacher/

Thomson, S. L. (2006). *Amazing whales!* New York, NY: HarperCollins.

Thorndike, E. L. (1913). *Educational psychology: The psychology of learning.* New York, NY: Teachers College Press.

Toppel, K. (2015). Enhancing core reading programs with culturally responsive practices. *The Reading Teacher, 68,* 552–559. doi:10.1002/trtr.1348

Treiman, R. (2018). Teaching and learning spelling. *Child Development Perspectives, 12,* 235–239. doi:10.1111/cdep.12292

Trousdale, A., & Harris, V. (1993). Interactive storytelling: Scaffolding children's early narratives. *Language Arts, 67,* 164–173. https://www.jstor.org/stable/41961718

Turner, B. (2019, March 26). Teaching first-graders about microaggressions: The small moments add up. *Teaching Tolerance.* Retrieved from https://www.tolerance.org/magazine/teaching-firstgraders-about-microaggressions-the-small-moments-add-up

U.S. Census. (2016). Retrieved from https://www.census.gov/

Van Allsburg, C. (1986). *The stranger*. Boston, MA: Houghton Mifflin Company.

Van Allsburg, C. (1991). *The wretched stone*. Boston, MA: Houghton Mifflin Company.

van den Brook, P., Kendeou, P., Lousberg, S., & Visser, G. (2017). Preparing for reading comprehension: Fostering text comprehension skills in preschool and early elementary school children. *International Electronic Journal of Elementary Education, 4*, REtr259–268. Retrieved from https://www.iejee.com/index.php/IEJEE/article/view/223

Veenman, M. (2016). Metacognition. In P. Afflerbach (Ed.). *Handbook of individual differences in reading: Reader, text, and context* (pp. 26–40). New York, NY: Routledge.

Vespa, J., Lewis, J., & Kreider, R. M. (2013). America's families and living arrangements: 2012. *Population characteristics*. Washington, DC: U.S. Census Bureau.

Vygotsky, L. S. (1962). *Language and thought*. Cambridge, MA: Massachusetts Institute of Technology Press.

Vygotsky, L. S. (1978). *Mind in society: The development of higher psychological processes*. Cambridge, MA: Harvard University Press.

Waldon, H. (2016). *What's your teaching identity*? Brighton, England: Academic Study Kit.

Welner, K. G., & Carter, P. L. (2013). Achievement gaps arise from opportunity gaps. In P. L. Carter & K. G. Welner (Eds.), *Closing the opportunity gap: What America must do to give every child an even chance* (pp. 1–10). New York, NY: Oxford University Press.

Wiggins, G., & McTighe, J. (2005). *Understanding by design* (2nd ed.). Alexandria, VA: Association for Supervision and Curriculum Development.

Wilkinson, P. (1998). *Spacebusters: The race to the moon*. New York, NY: DK Books.

Williams, S. (1989). *I went walking*. New York, NY: Trumpet.

Wilson, M. (2017). *Reimagining writing assessment: From scales to stories*. Portsmouth, NH: Heinemann.

Wlodkowski, R. J. (1983). *Motivational opportunities for successful teaching* [Leader's Guide]. Phoenix, AZ: Universal Dimensions.

Wolgast, A., & Fisher, N. (2017). You are not alone: Colleague support and goal-oriented cooperation as resources to reduce teachers' stress. *Social Psychology of Education, 20*, 97–114.

Wolsey, T. D., Lenski, S. D., & Grisham, D. L. (2020). *Assessment literacy: An educator's guide to understanding assessment, K–12*. New York, NY: Guilford Press.

Woolman-Bonilla, J. (2000). *Family message journals: Teaching writing through family involvement*. Urbana, IL: National Council of Teachers of English.

Wright, T. S., & Cervetti, G. N. (2017). A systematic review of the research on vocabulary instruction that impacts text comprehension. *Reading Research Quarterly, 52*, 203–226. doi:10.1002/rrq163

Wright, T. S., & Neuman, S. B. (2013). Vocabulary instruction in commonly used kindergarten core reading curricula. *The Elementary School Journal, 113*, 386–408. doi:10.1086/668766

Wright, W. E. (2019). *Foundations for teaching English language learners: Research, theory, policy, and practice* (3rd ed.). Philadelphia, PA: Caslon Publishers.

Wylie, R., & Durrell, D. D. (1970). Teaching vowels through phonograms. *Elementary English, 47*, 787–791. https://www.jstor.org/stable/41387692

Yosso, T. J. (2005). Whose culture has capital? A critical race theory discussion of community cultural wealth. *Race Ethnicity and Education, 8*, 69–91. doi:10.1080/1361332052000341006

Zembylas, M., & Chubbuck, S. M. (2015). The intersection of identity, beliefs, and politics in conceptualizing "teacher identity." In H. Fives & M. G. Gill (Eds.), *International handbook of research on teachers' beliefs* (pp. 173–190). New York, NY: Routledge.

Zygouris-Coe, V., Wiggins, M. B., & Smith, L. H. (2004). Engaging students with texts; The 3-2-1 strategy. *The Reading Teacher, 58*, 381–384.

Index

C

CAFÉ, 359–360
CCSS. *See* Common Core State Standards
central message, 271
characters, 275–278
chunking, 153
classical conditioning, 26
classification context clues, 176
classroom environment, 64–65
classroom organization, 340–369
close reading, 271
closed syllables, 170
coaches, working with, 389
cognates of English, 244–245
cognitive development, 99–100
cognitive engagement, 61
cognitive theories, 27
cognitive theorists, 27
collaboration, 382–390
Common Core State Standards (CCSS), 14
communicating with families, 372–374
community resources, 381–382
comparisons/contrasts context clues, 176
complications in career, 5–6
composing process, 300
compound word, 251
comprehension, 263–298
    authentic language, 279
    bilingual children's books, 267
    central message, 271
    characters, 275–278
    close reading, 271
    connecting ideas
        informational text, 275–278
    controlled vocabulary, 279
    craft, 278–283
    cultural wealth, 267–270
    defined, 264
    Developmental Reading Assessment, 288
    developmentally appropriate lessons, 287
    diversity of texts, providing, 266–267
    expository text structures, 265
    ideas, integration of, 283–287
    illustrations, combining with print, 287
    Informal Graded Passage Reading, 288–290
    informational texts, 265–266

    kinds of texts
        informational texts, 264
        literary texts, 264
        narrative texts, 264–265
    main idea
        informational texts, 271–274
    meaning of words/phrases, 278–279
    moral of story, 278
    plot outline diagram, 269
    poetry, 266
    point of view, 283
    reader response theory, 283
    reading levels, 287–295
    rhyming poetry, 266
    story structure, 279
    text complexity, 287–295
    theme, 271
conferences, 377–378
connecting ideas
    informational text, 275–278
connecting with families, 208–209
    for fluency, 224–225
constructivism, 27
constructivist theories, 27–29
content words, 234
context clues, 176
    read-alouds, 177
    teaching, 177
    visual cues, 177
contractions, 104–106
controlled vocabulary, 279
core reading programs
    adapting, 357–358
    materials, 357
craft, 278–283
criterion-referenced tests, 53
    state tests, 53
CRT. *See* Culturally relevant teaching
cueing systems, 35, 156
cultural awareness, 120–122
    world's alphabets/languages, 124
cultural background, 89
cultural competence, 398–400
cultural identity, 397–398
culturally relevant teaching, 17
curiosity, replacing judgment with, 399
curriculum nights, 378–379

D

Daily 5, 359–360
daily literacy schedule, 344–345
decoding skills, 155
deficit perspective, avoiding, 55–56

developmental characterisitcs
    activity level, 99
    cognitive development, 99–100
    physical characteristics, 99
    social-emotional characteristics, 100
    stages of development, Piaget, 99–100
developmental continuum, 12–13
Developmental Reading Assessment, 288
developmentally appropriate lessons, 287
dialect, 170
dialect differences, 235
digraphs, 158
directionality, 107–110
diverse families, working with, 374–376
diversity
    funds of knowledge, 16
    individuals, students as, 16
    linguistic differences, 17
DRA. *See* Developmental Reading Assessment

E

editing, 330–333
ELA standards. *See* English Language Arts standards
elementary reading attitude survey, 76–84
    interpretation, 82
emergent literacy theory, 11–14
emotional engagement, 62
engagement, 60–95
    academic resilience, 75–82
    background knowledge, 89–92
    behavioral engagement, 61
    biography-driven instruction, 91–92
    classroom environment, 64–65
    cognitive engagement, 61
    cultural background, 89
    defined, 61–62
    elementary reading attitude survey, 76–84
        norms for, 82
        scoring, 82
    emotional engagement, 62
    importance of, 62
    motivation, 63–64, 85–88
        extrinsic *vs.* intrinsic, 86
        growth mindset, 86
    research, 63
    students' interests
        learning, 67–74
        research, 71–72
    trust, 64